COUNTRY OF ORIGIN

COUNTRY OF ORIGIN

E. DU PERRON

PERIPLUS

Paperback edition published in 1999 by Periplus Editions (HK) Ltd.
ALL RIGHTS RESERVED

ISBN 962-593-510-X
Printed in Singapore

Publisher: Eric Oey

Distributors

Asia Pacific

Berkeley Books Pte. Ltd.
5 Little Road, #08-01
Singapore 536983
Tel: (65) 280-1330
Fax: (65) 280-6290

Indonesia

PT Wira Mandala Pustaka,
(Java Books – Indonesia)
Jl. Kelapa Gading Kirana
Blok A14 No.17, Jakarta 14240
Tel: (62-21) 451-5351
Fax: (62-21) 453-4987

Japan

Tuttle Publishing
RK Building 2nd Floor
2-13-10 Shimo Meguro, Meguro-Ku
Tokyo 153 0064, Japan
Tel: (03) 5437-0171
Fax: (03) 5437-0755

United States

Tuttle Publishing
Distribution Center
Airport Industrial Park
364 Innovation Drive
North Clarendon, VT 05759-9436
Tel: (802) 773-8930, (800) 526-2778

Preparation and publication of this work were supported by the Translation
and Publication Programs of the National Endowment for the Humanities, the
Foundation for the Promotion of the Translation of Dutch Literary Works, the
Prince Bernhard Fund, and the Dutch Ministry of Welfare, Health, and Culture
(Ministerie van Welzijn, Volksgezondheid en Cultuur), Department for
International Affairs, The Netherlands, to whom acknowledgment is grateful-
ly made.

Contents

Preface to the Series

This volume is one of a series of literary works written by the Dutch about their lives in the former colony of the Dutch East Indies, now the Republic of Indonesia. This realm of more than three thousand islands is roughly one quarter the size of the continental United States. It consists of the four Greater Sunda Islands—Sumatra, larger than California; Java, about the size of New York State; Borneo, about the size of France (presently called Kalimantan); and Celebes, about the size of North Dakota (now called Sulawesi). East from Java is a string of smaller islands called the Lesser Sunda Islands, which includes Bali, Lombok, Sumba, Sumbawa, Flores, and Timor. Further east from the Lesser Sunda Islands lies New Guinea, now called Irian Barat, which is the second largest island in the world. Between New Guinea and Celebes there is a host of smaller islands, often known as the Moluccas, that includes a group once celebrated as the Spice Islands.

One of the most volcanic regions in the world, the Malay archipelago is tropical in climate and has a diverse population. Some 250 languages are spoken in Indonesia, and it is remarkable that a population of such widely differing cultural and ethnic backgrounds adopted the Malay language as its *lingua franca* from about the fifteenth century, although that language was spoken at first only in parts of Sumatra and the Malay peninsula (now Malaysia).

Though the smallest of the Greater Sunda Islands, Java has always been the most densely populated, with about two-thirds of all Indonesians living there. In many ways a history of Indonesia is, first and foremost, the history of Java.

But in some ways Java's prominence is misleading, because it belies the great diversity of this island realm. For instance, the destination of the first Europeans who sailed to Southeast Asia was not Java but the Moluccas. It was that "odiferous pistil" (as Motley called the clove), as well as nutmeg and mace, that drew the Portuguese to a group of small islands in the Ceram and Banda Seas in the early part of the sixteenth century. Pepper was another profitable commodity, and attempts to obtain it brought the Portuguese into conflict with Atjeh, an Islamic sultanate in northern Sumatra, and with Javanese traders who, along with merchants from India, had been the traditional middlemen of the spice trade. The precedent of European intervention had been set and was to continue for nearly four centuries.

Although subsequent history is complicated in its causes and effects, one may propose certain generalities. The Malay realm was essentially a littoral one. Even in Java, the interior was sparsely populated and virtually unknown to the foreign intruders coming from China, India, and Europe. Whoever ruled the seas controlled the archipelago, and for the next three centuries the key needed to unlock the riches of Indonesia was mastery of the Indian Ocean. The nations who thus succeeded were, in turn, Portugal, Holland, and England, and one can trace the shifting of power in the prominence and decline of their major cities in the Orient. Goa, Portugal's stronghold in India, gave way to Batavia in the Dutch East Indies, while Batavia was overshadowed by Singapore by the end of the nineteenth century. Although all three were relatively small nations, they were maritime giants. Their success was partly due to the internecine warfare between the countless city-states, principalities, and native autocrats. The Dutch were masters at playing one against the other.

Religion was a major factor in the fortunes of Indonesia. The Portuguese expansion was in part a result of Portugal's crusade against Islam, which was quite as ferocious and intransigent as the holy war of the Mohammedans. Islam may be considered a unifying force in the archipelago; it cut across all levels of society and provided a rallying point for resistance to foreign intrusion. Just as the Malay language had done linguistically, Islam proved to be a syncretizing force when there was no united front. One of the causes of Portugal's demise was its inflexible antagonism to Islam, and later the Dutch found resistance to their rule fueled by religious fervor as well as political dissatisfaction.

Holland ventured to reach the tropical antipodes not only because their nemesis, Philip II of Spain, annexed Portugal and forbade the Dutch entry to Lisbon. The United Netherlands was a nation of merchants, a brokerage house for northern Europe, and it wanted to get to the source of tropical wealth itself. Dutch navigators and traders knew the location of the fabled Indies; they were well acquainted with Portuguese achievements at sea and counted among their members individuals who had worked for the Portuguese. Philip II simply accelerated a process that was inevitable.

At first, various individual enterprises outfitted ships and sent them to the Far East in a far from lucrative display of free enterprise. Nor was the first arrival of the Dutch in the archipelago auspicious, though it may have been symbolic of subsequent developments. In June 1596 a Dutch fleet of four ships anchored off the coast of Java. Senseless violence and a total disregard for local customs made the Dutch unwelcome on those shores.

During the seventeenth century the Dutch extended their influence in the archipelago by means of superior naval strength, use of armed intervention which was often ruthless, by shrewd politicking, and exploitation of local differences. Their cause was helped by the lack of a cohesive force to withstand them. Yet the seventeenth century also saw a number of men who were eager to know the new realm, who investigated the language and the mores of the people they encountered, and who studied the flora and fauna. These were men who not only put the Indies on the map of trade routes, but who also charted riches of other than commercial value.

It soon became apparent to the Dutch that these separate ventures did little to promote welfare. In 1602 Johan van Oldenbarneveldt, the Advocate of the United Provinces, managed to negotiate a contract which in effect merged all these individual enterprises into one United East India Company, better known under its Dutch acronym as the VOC. The merger ensured a monopoly at home, and the Company set out to obtain a similar insurance in the Indies. This desire for exclusive rights to the production and marketing of spices and other commodities proved to be a double-edged sword.

The VOC succeeded because of its unrelenting naval vigilance in discouraging European competition and because the Indies were a politically unstable region. And even though the Company was only interested in its balance sheet, it soon found itself burdened with an expanding empire and an indolent bureaucracy which, in the eighteenth century, became not only unwieldy but tolerant of graft and extortion. Furthermore, even though its profits were far below what they were rumored to be, the Company kept its dividends artificially high and was soon forced to borrow money to pay the interest on previous loans. When Holland's naval supremacy was seriously challenged by the British in 1780, a blockade kept the Company's ships from reaching Holland, and the discrepancy between capital and expenditures increased dramatically until the Company's deficit was so large it had to request state aid. In 1798, after nearly two centuries, the Company ceased to exist. Its debt of 140 million guilders was assumed by the state, and the commercial enterprise became a colonial empire.

At the beginning of the nineteenth century, Dutch influence was still determined by the littoral character of the region. Dutch presence in the archipelago can be said to have lasted three and a half centuries, but if one defines colonialism as the subjugation of an *entire* area and dates it from the time when the last independent domain was conquered—in this case Atjeh in northern Sumatra—then the Dutch colonial empire lasted less than half a century. Effective government could only be claimed for the Moluccas, certain portions of Java (by no means the entire island), a southern portion of Celebes, and some coastal regions of Sumatra and Borneo. Yet it is also true that precisely because Indonesia was an insular realm, Holland never needed to muster a substantial army such as the one the British had to maintain in the large subcontinent of India. The extensive interiors of islands such as Sumatra, Borneo, or Celebes were not penetrated, because, for the seaborne empire of commercial interests, exploration of such regions was unprofitable, hence not desirable.

The nature of Holland's involvement changed with the tenure of Herman Willem Daendels as governor-general, just after the French revolution. Holland declared itself a democratic nation in 1795, allied itself with France—which meant a direct confrontation with England—and was practically a vassal state of France until 1810. Though reform, liberal programs, and the mandate of human rights were loudly proclaimed in Europe, they did not seem to apply to the Asian branch of the family of man. Daendels exemplified this double standard. He evinced reforms, either in fact or on paper, but did so in an imperious manner and with total disregard for native customs and law (known as *adat*). Stamford Raffles, who was the chief administrator of the British interim government from 1811 to 1816, expanded Daendels's innovations, which included tax reform and the introduction of the land-rent system, which was based on the assumption that all the land belonged to the colonial administration. By the time Holland regained its colonies in 1816, any resemblance to the erstwhile Company had vanished. In its place was a firmly established, paternalistic colonial government which ruled by edict and regulation, supported a huge bureaucracy, and sought to make the colonies turn a profit, as well as to legislate its inhabitants' manner of living.

It is not surprising that for the remainder of the nineteenth century, a centralized authority instituted changes from above that were often in direct conflict with Javanese life and welfare. One such change, which was supposed to increase revenues and improve the life of the Javanese peasant, was the infamous "Cultivation System" *(Cultuurstelsel)*. This system required the Javanese to grow cash crops, such as sugar cane or indigo, which, although profitable on the world market, were of little practical use to the Javanese. In effect it meant compulsory labor and the exploitation of the entire island as if it were a feudal estate. The system proved profitable for the Dutch, and because it introduced varied crops such as tea and tobacco to local agriculture, it indirectly improved the living standard of some of the people. It also fostered distrust of colonial authority, caused uprisings, and provided the impetus for liberal reform on the part of Dutch politicians in the Netherlands.

Along with the increased demand in the latter half of the nineteenth century for liberal reform came an expansion of direct control over other areas of the archipelago. One of the reasons for this was an unprecedented influx of private citizens from Holland. Expansion of trade required expansion of territory that was under direct control of Batavia to insure stability. Colonial policy improved education, agriculture, and public hygiene and expanded the transportation network. In Java a paternalistic policy was not offensive, because its ruling class (the *prijaji*) had governed that way for centuries; but progressive politicians in The Hague demanded that the Indies be administered on a moral basis which favored the interests of the Indonesians rather than those of the Dutch government in Europe. This "ethical policy" became doctrine from about the turn of this century and followed on the heels of a renascence of scientific study of the Indies quite as enthusiastic as the one in the seventeenth century.

The first three decades of the present century were probably the most stable and prosperous in colonial history. This period was also the beginning of an emerging Indonesian national consciousness. Various nationalistic parties were formed, and the Indonesians demanded a far more representative role in the administration of their country. The example of Japan indicated to the Indonesians that European rulers were not invincible. The rapidity with which the Japanese conquered Southeast Asia during the Second World War only accelerated the process of decolonization. In 1945 Indonesia declared its independence, naming Sukarno the republic's first president. The Dutch did not accept this declaration, and between 1945 and 1949 they conducted several unsuccessful military campaigns to re-establish control. In 1950, with a new constitution, Indonesia became a sovereign state.

I offer here only a cursory outline. The historical reality is far more complex and infinitely richer, but this sketch must suffice as a backdrop for the particular type of literature that is presented in this series.

This is a literature written by or about European colonialists in Southeast Asia prior to the Second World War. Though the literary techniques may be Western, the subject matter is unique. This genre is also a self-contained unit that cannot develop further, because there are no new voices and because what was voiced no longer exists. Yet it is a literature that can still instruct, because it delineates the historical and psychological confrontation of East and West, it depicts the uneasy alliance of these antithetical forces, and it shows by prior example the demise of Western imperialism.

These are political issues, but there is another aspect of this kind of literature that is of equal importance. It is a literature of lost causes, of a past irrevocably gone, of an era that today seems so utterly alien that it is novel once again.

Tempo dulu it was once called—time past. But now, after two world wars and several Asian wars, after the passage of nearly half a century, this phrase presents more than a wistful longing for the prerogatives of imperialism; it gives as well a poignant realization that an epoch is past that will never return. At its worst the documentation of this perception is sentimental indulgence, but at its best it is the poetry of a vanished era, of the fall of an empire, of the passing of an age when issues moral and political were firmer and clearer, and when the drama of the East was still palpable and not yet reduced to a topic for sociologists.

In many ways, this literature of Asian colonialism reminds one of the literature of the American South—of Faulkner, O'Connor, John

Crowe Ransom, and Robert Penn Warren. For that too was a "colonial" literature that was quite as much aware of its own demise and yet, not defiantly but wistfully, determined to record its own passing. One finds in both the peculiar hybrid of antithetical cultures, the inevitable defeat of the more recent masters, a faith in more traditional virtues, and that peculiar offbeat detail often called "gothic" or "grotesque." In both literatures loneliness is a central theme. There were very few who knew how to turn their mordant isolation into a dispassionate awareness that all things must pass and fail.

E. M. Beekman

Introduction

Charles Edgar du Perron was born in Java in 1899, the only son of wealthy parents of French descent, whose families had been well integrated into the colonial aristocracy of the Dutch East Indies for generations. His background was not unlike that of a plantation owner's son in the Old South; he was given all the advantages money could afford and was subject to all the racial prejudices of a ruling class dependent on virtual slave labor. For long periods of time he lived in a remote part of the island and had no contacts with Dutch friends his age, so his only contemporaries were native children. In *Country of Origin*, Arthur Ducroo, the narrator who meticulously records a childhood in the Indies, is an alter ego of Du Perron. Gifted (or cursed) with a prodigious fantasy, he suffered like Du Perron from the heavy demands of his mother's affection. His vivid imagination, combined with a lack of self-discipline, made him see reality in an unusual light. Once back in Batavia, the capital of the colony, Ducroo was a failure in school. This didn't seem important, for it was unlikely that he would ever have to earn a living; the wealth of his parents guaranteed him a comfortable existence.

At an early age Du Perron discovered his talents, which included an excellent memory and an ability to write. He made conscious and fairly successful attempts at overcoming a neurasthenic condition, and was thus transformed from a mother's son into a modern D'Artagnan (he even took boxing and fencing lessons). He combined his new image as a man of action with his talent as a writer by joining a newspaper in Batavia. The experiment did not last long, for at about this time his parents sold most of their vast land holdings and decided to go to Europe, and they took their son along. They settled in Brussels and also acquired a castle at Gistoux in the Belgian countryside. Fleeing the company of his parents, Du Perron sought refuge in Montmartre, in an attempt to get a taste of the artists' Bohemia. He stayed there most of 1922, and made a number of contacts, the most fruitful of which was with Pascal Pia, an aspiring French writer usually in dire financial straits.

Du Perron was introduced to Pia's artist friends and he felt at home in their company. In a short time the wealthy young man from the Indies had accomplished an almost total metamorphosis: he had become a bohemian of the Place du Tertre. He even began to write, and he published a small volume of satires in French, but after this questionable debut he returned to Dutch. Around 1926, within this bohemian circle, Du Perron met André Malraux, who had just returned from Indochina and was still unknown as a writer. In 1934 Malraux was to dedicate his novel *La Condition humaine* (*Man's Fate*) to Eddy du Perron, to the surprise of the French critics. Thirty-five years later, in his *Anti-Memoirs*, Malraux simply stated, "He was my best friend."

Upon his return to Belgium, Du Perron entered into great literary activity. Between 1924 and 1928 he provided at least part of the financial support for a number of avant-garde magazines. Short-lived as they were, these magazines today document the lively and creative modernism of Flanders in the twenties. Du Perron's most notable companion in these adventures was Paul van Ostaijen, the incomparable poet who died in 1928 at a young age. "Alpenjagerslied" ("Song of the Alpine Hunters"), one of the last poems Van Ostaijen wrote in the sanatorium where he had gone to cure his tuberculosis, is dedicated to E. du Perron.

In the Netherlands Du Perron was still virtually unknown at the time. He was discovered by a Dutch newspaper correspondent in Brussels, Jan Greshoff. His real breakthrough, however, came in 1930 when he met the brilliant young critic Menno ter Braak. In what was perhaps the most fruitful collaboration in the history of modern Dutch literature, they founded the magazine *Forum*, which lasted for only four years but which to this day exerts its influence as the most important literary voice of the century.

When fascism came to power in Germany, Ter Braak and Du Perron felt forced to speak out politically. With their constant pleading for an enlightened, liberal individualism, they attempted to create a barrier against totalitarian thinking. *Country of Origin*, though not without a peculiar admiration for brute force, in the end comes out clearly in favor of individualism and tolerance.

In the early thirties several important events changed Du Perron's existence. He had fathered a child with one of his mother's maids, whom he had later married, in 1928. It was in 1932 that he divorced this woman in order to marry Elisabeth de Roos three months later. The couple moved to Paris, where they started free-lancing for Dutch newspapers and periodicals. Shortly after the wedding, Du Perron's mother died, and her death liberated him from the immediate dominion of the complex love-hate relationship he had had with her. His financial illusions ended then too, because Du Perron discovered that every penny of the immense family fortune had been squandered.

After *Country of Origin* was published (1935), Du Perron continued his precarious existence as a free-lance journalist for some time in Paris, but in the fall of 1936, attracted by vague promises of a job, he decided to return to the Indies. The Depression hit the European community in the Indies probably harder than any other group of people, and Du Perron found it impossible to find work. Nonetheless, his literary career flourished in this state of continued unemployment, and his productivity was at its greatest during his second stay in Java. His uncommon openness, which had brought him easily into contact with so many people in Europe, now made him friends with a few Western-oriented Indonesian nationalists. Their distrust of the Dutch went very deep, but with Du Perron, who spoke their language like a native and who had become some sort of an antiestablishment individualist, they cast away their suspicion. Politically, Du Perron had come full circle. The son of autocratic landowners became the nationalists' friend, supporting their political views and cultural interests.

Du Perron returned to Europe in 1939 in ill health, just in time for the beginning of the Second World War. On May 14, 1940, the day the Dutch army surrendered to the German invaders, he died of a heart attack, in the same hour that his friend Menno ter Braak committed suicide out of fear of reprisals for his opposition to the Nazis. The tragic death of these two men became a strong symbol of cultural resistance during the war, with the result that for the first fifteen years after the war their work influenced much of literary and cultural life in the Netherlands.

Country of Origin is a balanced combination of reflections on a childhood in the Indies and contemporary reporting on Western Europe in the period between the two world wars. Most readers, however, recall it as an exciting panorama of colonial life in West Java at the turn of the century. The narrator, Arthur Ducroo, a keen observer of the people around him, portrays the arrogant colonial elite with a mixture of irony and sarcasm and the Indonesian community with sympathy and compassion, but also with an unexpected directness. He is not satisfied with simple explanations and does not spend too much time on descriptions of exotic decors. He is convinced that people all over the world, whether Dutch or Indonesian and regardless of race or skin color, share one essential quality: they all play a role. He does not exclude himself from this role playing, for at times he unmasks himself as ruthlessly as he does others. The result is a critical, often trenchant tale of a childhood in *tempo dulu*, the not-so-good old days of colonial rule in the Dutch East Indies.

Perhaps because of its title, Du Perron's *Country of Origin* has usually been considered merely as colonial literature. Ducroo's need to unmask Javanese and Europeans alike shows, however, that he is in search of universal values. He does not restrict himself to painting only the colonial situation, with its victims and its dominant race. For him, every character in this tale is a human being; Ducroo probes the human condition.

It must be admitted in favor of those who see *Country of Origin* as a colonial novel that the Javanese fragments are narrated with an intriguing directness, which is often sorely lacking in the chapters about European life. The closer Ducroo gets to the source of his existence it seems, the more easily his narrative flows. But what is precisely this country of origin? Is it, as the text suggests a few times, the island of Java, where he was born? Or is it Europe, more specifically France, where the Ducroo family came from? The emphasis placed on genealogy in the first chapters lends support to the latter supposition. The title is at best ambiguous. However, its significance is not just geographical: what Ducroo sets out to explore is not a distant country, but the origin of his Self, his feelings and emotions, his view of humanity and his view of himself.

There is much more besides the Javanese episodes. At irregular intervals Ducroo inserts fragments portraying his financial distress. Recently remarried and living with his wife in a cheap rented room in a Paris suburb, his problems are more than economic. He is also obsessed by what he perceives as the possible collapse of Western civilization. In the account of his present hardship and in the addition of complicated, sometimes rather awkward discussions with his Parisian friends, as well as in the recounting of his amorous search for his ideal woman, Ducroo gradually relegates his childhood narrative to the background, until finally the furtive present dominates the foreground and narrator and narrative together drown in the flood of the trivial minute-to-minute events of the day. After this excursion into society and its fleeting concerns has demonstrated to Ducroo that for him—in contrast to Héverlé (the novel's "shadow" of Malraux)—collectivity is not the answer to the problems created by the disintegration of the self, *Country of Origin* comfortably returns to the creed of individualism.

For those readers who like colonial literature for its variety of exotic people and scenery, or maybe only for its nostalgia, the European chapters appear as just so many interruptions, so many obstacles to reading pleasure. But for others, the labyrinthine discussions between Ducroo and his friends, Guraev, Héverlé, Viala, and Wijdenes, are enjoyable as the rendering of the intellectual climate of Paris in the thirties.

Country of Origin is also a *roman à clef,* a genre that was always welcome in the gossip-ridden colonial establishment of the Dutch East Indies. Ducroo's confidences about his family and about his own failures certainly appeal to the voyeur in the reader. But when he speaks about his European friends this *chronique scandaleuse* aspect becomes even more important. Malraux is shown in his early period of left-wing activism. In *Country of Origin,* Héverlé joins the Communist party at the end (which Malraux probably never did), but one can see why the later paragon of Gaullist policies did not lift a finger to get *Country of Origin* published in French. At least one translation remained dormant in the archives of a Paris publishing house, but it wasn't until 1980 that Philippe Noble's excellent, completely new translation came out. There may have been political reasons for preventing the publication in France, but there were certainly also personal ones. In one of the long discussions between Ducroo and Héverlé, a veiled allusion is made to a scene in *Man's Fate*: it is the scene between Kyo and May, in which he rejects her offer to accompany him on a dangerous mission because she has been unfaithful to him by comforting a comrade who was almost sure to die in an act of terrorism. Kyo and May portray aspects of a marital conflict that had been going on between André and Clara Malraux since their first trip to Indochina. Ducroo's response to that scene certainly reflects Du Perron's notion of absolute faithfulness, and *Country of Origin* could be read as one gigantic trope of this particular Malrovian problem.

Other friends are easily recognizable, certainly to a French literary audience. Viala is a "shadow" of Pascal Pia, Du Perron's friend from the days in Montmartre, who at the time *Country of Origin* was written had not yet risen to fame as the friend and mentor of Albert Camus during Pia's tenure as editor of the newspaper *Alger Républicain*. Together they would later edit the resistance newspaper *Combat*. And Guraev, the Russian émigré of the first chapter, is the "shadow" of the famous graphic artist and experimental filmmaker Alexandr Alexeiev, who never was a very good friend of Du Perron.

Among the Dutchmen portrayed in *Country of Origin* is Wijdenes, a caricature of Menno ter Braak. Graaflant is Jan Greshoff, the Brussels newspaper correspondent who first discovered Du Perron and who became a close friend. Rijckloff, finally, is the poet A. Roland Holst, here shown in his more personal pursuits, but in reality one of the most refined poets in the Dutch language.

Is it important to know that Lieutenant Arthur Hille was in reality Edy Batten, a friend from the Indies, or that the colonial portrait gallery is based on real personalities, or even that the real-life model for the Englishwoman Ducroo visited in Oxford later had two sons, one named Charles, and the other Edgar? It seems that all these vignettes, unreliable to the point of caricature, have the principal function of highlighting particular aspects of Ducroo's character. Wijdenes, for example, serves as a contrast to Arthur Hille, but both also set in relief what Ducroo perceives in himself. Guraev's lack of self-confidence, because he remained so much a Russian, underlines Ducroo's feelings about provincial inadequacy. The main question remains: How can a person, who has friends as divergent as the ones portrayed and a past as divergent from his present as Ducroo does—how can such a person identify himself as an integrated entity?

The theme of the disintegration of self has a long history. When the traditional religious beliefs gradually lost their grip on Western society, the interest in eternity gave way to an ever greater involvement in the temporary world surrounding mankind. The soul, until that time the one solid, unshakable component of the human personality, was felt to be vulnerable. But when the soul became adumbrated, a new ally came to the rescue of human personality: the mind, with its auxiliary, memory. Together they could help mold the separate, disjointed events of a fragmented existence into a meaningful whole. Hegel, Nietzsche, and Freud (to name just a few) attempted, each in his chosen field of philosophy or psychology, to satisfy the sudden demand for memory and history as memory. In literature, the struggle against the fragmentation of the human identity was most impressively fought in Marcel Proust's *Remembrance of Things Past*. At the end of its last volume, the narrator takes it upon himself to rescue the past, no matter how deeply it has withdrawn into the human mind. Total retrieval is necessary to preserve the narrator's sense of identity, even if conscious memory can no longer accomplish the task.

Just as in Proust's *Remembrance*, the theme of *Country of Origin* is the victory of memory over destructive, disintegrating time. Although on the whole Du Perron did not try to imitate or emulate Marcel Proust (whose works he knew well), there are a few scenes in *Country of Origin* that are strongly reminiscent of Proust's technique of involuntary memory, for example, when Ducroo at the beginning of his concentration on the past closes his eyes, and "suddenly the decor of our villa in Tjitjurug appeared, clearly and vividly present." He tries to hold on to his return to the past: "And before I realized it, I was sobbing uncontrollably. The metamorphosis slowly melted away. I lay there looking at myself, watching my body 'inexplicably' shaking with sobs" (p. 18). *Country of Origin*, innovative and profoundly probing of the human mind, should perhaps not be compared to Proust's masterpiece. But the grand design of both texts is undoubtedly the same.

Ducroo's sense of disintegration of the self finds perhaps its most important counterweight in his idea of faithfulness. First of all it means faithfulness to one's self, to the person one once was—even if that person turns out to be nothing but a spoiled child. It also means loyalty to the friends one once had—even if these friendships have lost their validity. Ducroo feels no longer close to the colonial officer Arthur Hille, but he does not repudiate him, for that would mean denying an aspect of himself that he may have outgrown but that still needs preservation. Ducroo also reproaches his wife Jane and Wijdenes for being willing to give up their friendship once it is no longer meaningful. Ducroo refuses to let his life be fragmented by such passing phenomena as taste or fashion. He goes as far as to proclaim an eternal faithfulness, dating backwards as well as forwards, and he demands it from the woman he just married. He wants to show the origins of his feelings and he wants to show that he never really was unfaithful to her, even when he didn't know her yet, even when he was still married to his first wife, even when he went through the turbulence of a sometimes sordid love life. He was always faithful to her, he insists. The problem is that he expects her, and everybody else, to nurture the same sense of loyalty. His friends, the Héverlés, argue that modern life requires more flexibility, but Ducroo is adamant.

Ducroo's other obsession, closely related to his insistence on faithfulness, is his quest for authenticity. When he first came to Europe, he tried to shed his colonial past and become a "young European." He went through a period of role playing, but now has reached the stage in which he energetically searches his own truths. The locus of these truths is the mystical country of origin, the tropical paradise of the mind.

One clarification needs to be made: for Ducroo, creating one's own personage is different from merely playing a role in life. He admires Héverlé for working constantly on the personage he wants to be without playing a role. It may seem that there is not much difference between play-acting and creating one's own personage—and observers of Malrovian posturing would certainly agree on this—but Ducroo in all probability anticipates here the existentialist demand of creating one's own existence by continuously choosing what one wants to be. A role is something objectionable, because it is forced upon a person by society. A personage chooses his own way. Ducroo hates the conformists, and there is an endless row of objectionable characters in *Country of Origin*—teachers, cowards, attorneys, "notaries." His real heroes are the outsiders, the eccentric government officials, the mad planters, the anarchists. They are the creators of their own destiny.

For all the resemblance between the lives of Du Perron and his narrator Arthur Ducroo, we should keep in mind that Ducroo never focuses on what was Du Perron's main activity: literature. Although Ducroo is intensely conscious of his function as the writer of a book, he does not mention any experience he may have had in the past as a writer of fiction. Given his close relationship with Du Perron, knowledgeable readers could expect Du Perron's early literary activity to be reflected in *Country of Origin*, but such is not the case. As a result, a friend like Paul van Ostaijen, unquestionably of great influence on Du Perron's life as a writer, does not appear in some barely disguised form. He is completely filtered out of the picture.

Whoever wants to do justice to *Country of Origin* should not solely explore the real people behind the novel characters. The reader must not concentrate on just one of the narrative components either, but try to take into consideration the intricate relationships between them. Ducroo's Javanese past must be considered in light of his Parisian present, and vice versa. The integration of various narrative levels and of the numerous incongruous compositional elements (letters, dialogues, and diary fragments) presents a challenge to the reader; the consciously created textual chaos demands to be reconstituted by the reader into a meaningful whole. As such, it parallels the main thrust of the novel, namely the search for reintegration of the fragmented individual self, disintegrated by the destructive force of Time.

Although *Country of Origin* is written for Jane (Shelley's "It keeps its highest, holiest tone for our beloved Jane alone" is its secret motto), she hardly ever appears in it, but she is the silent listener. Ducroo's notion of authenticity ultimately originates, not in himself, but in his companion. She is the reason for all the soul-searching. Why not once more trespass the borderline between fiction and the real world and say that Du Perron, like Nabokov in exile from himself, asked his memory to speak and created a monument to Elisabeth de Roos?

F. Bulhof

To retain the colonial flavor of the original text, we have resisted modernization. The Indonesians in this book are still "natives," offensive as it may sound to us today. Also, the term "Indonesia" is avoided, because it was not a common designation of the Dutch East Indies at the time *Country of Origin* was written. Batavia has become Jakarta; Meester-Cornelis, on the outskirts of Batavia, is now Jatinegara; Buitenzorg is now Bogor. The archaic Dutch spelling of Indonesian words has been preserved, with the exception of *oe*, which was replaced by *u*. This was done for the sole purpose of preserving some of the characteristics of the colonial period; it does not imply any disagreement with the rationalization of Indonesian spelling in recent years.

Country of Origin

For Elisabeth de Roos

One must look inside oneself for something other than
oneself, if one is to look for a long time.

André Malraux

1 An Evening with Guraev

February 1933. Since Jane and I moved to Meudon, on the outskirts of Paris, the inner city has come to resemble a busy square where the streetcars and buses seem to take care not to run us over, now that we're no longer strangers. The ugly Montparnasse Station has gradually become a familiar home for us, with its flat façade and its shops below. It has two entrances, to the left and right of the double staircase that leads to the trains, and there's an unbelievably spacious elevator run by a disabled veteran. For us the station is like a vestibule where we leave the city behind, and the fifteen minutes in the train back to Meudon don't amount to anything anymore. Particularly after my last trip to Brussels, I suddenly felt, like a child, that this unexpected fortress would protect me from a fate that was pursuing me.

Last night, I sat in the café cross the street from the station, reading the newspaper and looking through the revolving doors every now and then for the man I was supposed to meet. Night had fallen early but I could see the station's well-lit façade. It was too cold to sit outside but I had found a table close to the entrance. As usual, the newspaper irritated me, but only left me with a slight, cooled-off annoyance, something much more superficial than the deep-seated fear the bourgeois must feel these days. I looked at the picture of a certain Corneliu Codreanu,[1] the leader of the Rumanian nationalist Iron Guard, one of those power puppets these times cough up as heroes, perhaps even a little bit more primitive than those in Germany. There he was in his Rinaldo Rinaldini outfit, which made me think of my friend Arthur Hille, that model of strength and courage when I was young. Hille later became an officer in Achin,[2] where he was called "Lieutenant Tiger" by his native fusiliers. The idea came to me that someone should put Arthur Hille and Mr. Codreanu in a pit together, unarmed except for their strength and their nails, and their grimly opposed preconceived ideas. . . .

Behind the revolving door an improbably elegant character suddenly appears, all dressed in gray except for a red scarf. He looks inside with the searching eyes of a conqueror, and then materializes from behind the spinning glass door and with one step he's standing next to my little table: Guraev in person. He doesn't give me a chance to exclaim about the way he's dressed. He puts his index finger on the picture and asks me to explain it. So I paraphrase the caption for him: "He used to be nothing but an intellectual, an unsure and pale student, until somebody told him that 'Rumania' is the generic name for 'kleptomania.' Perhaps this pun is equally offensive in Rumanian. At any rate, it turned Codreanu into the fearsome character we see here. Maybe you didn't know it could be this easy. What do you really think about the political forces of these times, Guraev?"

"Pretty much what you do, probably; I get my information from the newspapers too. Ask me what I think of Paris. The world is just as unreal here as anywhere else. Do you have any idea, Ducroo, how the neon signs affect us, how, for instance, they prevent us from being sensitive to the moon? Have you ever figured out what you feel exactly about the new neon signs of the Eiffel Tower, that yellow circle around a clock, with the one hand green and the other yellow? Now why yellow? Why not red, blue, or purple? That would have been more honest and just as easy to do. Do you think I say this just to show you how imaginative I am? Not at all, this is just one of many things I don't understand and that bother me. I'm disturbed because—how shall I put it—because I'd like to know who was in charge of putting those neon signs up there. But there are also things I don't understand and which don't bother me, among which are the political forces of these times."

By my silence I let him know that he should go on. And he does.

"Do you know what I think nowadays? That it's just a French mystery. Even though I may live in Paris until I'm an old man, I'll never understand the French. A Russian would have given that hand its own color. You mustn't doubt me on this point."

He has gotten on his old hobby horse again which I have watched him ride each of the three times I've been with him. What have the French done to him? Or, what is the basis for this need to be Russian vis-à-vis the French?

"I don't doubt it for a second."

"That's what you say, but you think you're a Frenchman next to me. Don't believe Héverlé when he tells you that you're almost French. It isn't true, you're no more French than I am. Tell me, seriously, what do you see in this country that's real?"

"The better you know something, the less real it can turn out to be. When I had just arrived from the Indies, I thought that Marseilles was a very normal town. I thought I was finally in the country where I belonged. And not only that, I felt I recognized the houses and the completely different street scenes. I knew all of it from the movies I had seen. And in a short time everything became almost too real. It annoyed me that the people in Europe looked so bourgeois, not only the people I talked with, but those in the streets too, in the sidewalk cafés, the crowds, and even the faces in the bad sections. I thought they probably even killed in a bourgeois fashion. Adventure—the people from books and movies—for years I wasn't able to identify them. And now.... It's eerie how I can spend hours trying to figure out the monster behind even the stupidest face. If I'd go and look around the Arab quarter I would find fewer monsters than on that sidewalk. Take a look. Is that typically French? Isn't this the American world of Faulkner, a world of drunken sex-murderers, hebephrenes, and impotent men? Perhaps I still harbor colonial ideas about the real people of Paris...."

"I don't think so. What you're doing is giving in to your romanticism in another way. Of course you're very romantic, and so am I, but maybe... maybe it's only a result of these times. And so we are both, in our own way, busily loathing these great times."

"That would prove that you are not a real Russian."

"Where did you get that communist jargon? I, who am a white Russian only by accident, have always had just as much or just as little sympathy for the Reds as for the Whites. I would even agree that, in principle, the Reds have right on their side—as if that were important! —but I also know that I'd rather live in exile in Paris, in an obsolete and corrupt democracy, than in my own country under the dictators of a new fanaticism. I don't have the slightest faith in the fanatic zealots. And, sad to say, these revolutionaries have nothing but their new creed to live for. I'm not saying I'd immediately commit suicide rather than think and feel like the herd. I feel guilty sometimes... out of some fraternal sense, when I see those films where suffering is justified in the last scene by either a group of gymnasts who form a pattern of the letters LENIN or by two strong proletarian faces that smile seraphically at each other over a piece of working machinery."

"So much of what you say I might think myself, but we're wrong. Besides, are you absolutely sure you're not homesick?"

"Of course I am... sometimes. But you must learn to distrust your feelings. I don't think of myself as an emigrant, I am an exile by nature. But I sometimes recall landscapes from back there, God knows why, and they are the only ones which—it's hard to say—which I might enjoy in my old age, while I'm sure it will be impossible for me to grow old here. Then I think that I'd be able to illustrate childrens' books back there and that the children and I would be equally happy with my drawings. And then I realize that these children must be systematically alienated from everything that I could possibly come up with, and that they are brought forth as the real revolutionaries; they are not contaminated by anything bourgeois. So, those 'Soviet men'—listen carefully, Ducroo! —they represent the worst neo-bourgeois for me, the one-hundred-percent neo-Soviet bourgeoisie, although this must sound absurd to the little pseudo-Marxists who have read Marx just as badly as I did. And if it's a military and not a bourgeois society—a term such as 'shock brigadier' says enough! —it would make me even more of an idiot. But you're not dabbling in politics, I hope?"

"No. That is to say, as little as we can still afford not to."

His neck muscles tighten as he looks at me from the side, searching. He has put his hand on my knee and he shakes his head before he asks:

"In general, do you feel yourself to be a man, or a boy?"

"I don't believe I have ever thought of myself as a man. What does that mean, exactly?"

"Ducroo!" (I'm afraid he's going to embrace me.) "You are worthy of being my friend. No decent person knows what that means. Only die-hard capitalists and die-hard Communists know it. And when there's nothing left of the child in them, either physically or morally, then they are proud, because that is the finishing touch! They are proud that they never had a childhood, or an abominable childhood, or no past whatsoever, so they can forget what is not the most immediate Now. I don't talk to capitalists very often, only when I must defend my interests, but if I meet a Marxist, I'm always inclined to treat him to a ghost story."

He throws his head way back and chuckles silently. If all this were not a posture, if this somewhat overdone fantasy—which I noticed the very first moment I met him—had a serious foundation, I would almost envy him. So I disregard his mannerism. "All this," I say, "only proves that we have no empathy for the proletariat."

His head snaps back.

"I do, or at least.... When I was still a sailor, I felt that I could identify completely with a number of proletarians! But you're fooling yourself if you think that a generic term is proof of excellence. Beyond a certain point I believe just as little in the proletariat as I do in humanity. The symbolic proletarian! I've had enough of that concrete Apollo with his rolled up sleeves, his courageous face of a cow, and his fists that are twice as big as normal—all those stupid symbols. If that is the only Russian left, I will fall in love with the French proletariat. The best proletariat. Did you read about that wonderful murder in Le Mans last week?[3] What those two servant girls did impressed me more than the latest bulletins from Moscow. They had been exploited from childhood on—orphans to begin with, or something like that—and at a given moment they attacked their mistresses. After some remark from her employer, the older girl smashed the skull of the employer with a pewter pot, while the other, a docile creature with a timid little face, stopped the other woman on the stairs. Then they proceeded to slaughter the two bourgeois women, with their nails. Twenty years of loyal services preceded all this. And in no way were these employers more loathsome than any others. They only happened to symbolize at that moment the full twenty years of service. So they were beaten to a pulp with the pewter pot. Their eyes were ripped out and hurled across the landing. Imagine the girls's heavenly exhaustion when they went to bed afterwards, in the same house, just as they had done every other evening. And they never slept so blissfully. And now that they are standing trial, they maintain their roles so well that the bourgeois press has no recourse but to proclaim them insane. Nobody understands anything about it in Le Mans: why precisely those two sweet and respectable women? And that poor husband! He is a magistrate, who had been waiting all evening for his wife and daughter at another magistrate's house. The older sister answers every question with 'We got 'em good.' The younger one cries when she hears the fatherly voice of the judge but doesn't for a moment lose her trust in the older sister, who has a face like a flatiron and who only shows her eyelids. I would like to make a picture of them and distribute it as a supplement to L'Humanité. Not because that newspaper deserves it, but to give truly revolutionary minds something else besides the symbols of Soviet religion. But you're a journalist, you would know more about it than I do. Didn't you have to report about it for your newspaper?"

"Jane and I have been hired to report on the cultural aspects of

Paris. A minimum of murders, therefore, and in the case of a cause célèbre, only what the Parisians think of it. If Jane writes the article, usually I'm that Parisian. Criticism is allowed, but only under the motto of
'Paris will never change.' In Paris Dutchmen accept a lot more than
you might think; the main thing is that the paths of sin follow a traditional course. We can even write, though delicately, about the latest
brothel that has a dance hall downstairs with women naked as jay-
birds, but where drinks cost only five francs and the audience is made
up of petty bourgeois carrying umbrellas and accompanied by their
lawful, completely devoted wives.... Now don't look so disgusted,
Guraev. When I was growing up I was never able to get excited about
twelve girls kicking up their legs. And now I sit with my wife in the audience. Besides, you have to make some sort of living, when the Depression has hit you as hard as it did me."

He looks at me with tired eyes and smiles, revealing teeth that are a
bit too long. There are magnificent wrinkles in his forehead and his
narrow face shows some sort of benign old age, which contrasts with
his long, thick, strawberry-blond hair, like that of a romantic student.

"Héverlé told me that you were almost ruined by an inheritance."
Cheerfully he adds: "Now don't worry about that, you will always have
enough money, Ducroo. I'm telling you, I can feel it. You'll never lack
money."

Perhaps he felt that right at this moment I lack quite a bit of it, but he
reverts quickly to fantasy: "When Héverlé used to buy my engravings
for you, he called you the 'rich Javanese.' I had a peculiar mental image
about the two names Ducroo and Grouhy. The rich Javanese Ducroo
from the Belgian village of Grouhy. I thought you had a castle there,
maybe in the form of a tulip, very round yet also high, with gigantic
steps in front, and that every morning you would come out for a minute, just to look at your castle from the lowest step. You would never go
beyond that last step, I thought. That was as far as you would go into
the outside world."

"So when you met me at the Héverlés, you couldn't believe your
eyes? Well, neither could I. Less because of my new poverty though,
which somewhere deep inside me I always knew would come, than
because of other things.... If you begin life with a woman on a material
basis which you take for granted, it's strange to notice that because of
the material collapse *her* life becomes totally different, aside from the
personal changes. Despite all the platitudes about suffering bringing

people closer together and the unexpected chance of being able to prove how much you love each other, I sudenly felt, physically, that Marx was always right: you feel so hurt by an economic change that before you know it you are a different person. And if after a certain time this is true for both people, you wind up with two new people. In itself this can yield a successful combination, but it still is some sort of... treason, with respect to the personalities you started out with. Maybe you don't understand."

To the contrary, he looks at me as if he understands this much more profoundly than anything I could ever say. Platitude or not, I must take into account the Russian soul of my new friend, Guraev. And I in turn change the subject.

"Tell me something about your childhood in Constantinople. How old were you when you left? Do you remember anything about the Bosporus and the Golden Horn and the minarets?"

"The Bosporus, yes, but not the rest. I was four years old when I left. My father was a military attaché in Constantinople and we had a house with a lot of marble and broad stairs that went all the way to the water. That was the Bosporus. Behind the house there was a steep slope and I was not allowed to climb it. It seemed like a mountain. Should I give you my oriental impressions?... There was a Greek gardener named Christo. I still remember him because of that name. And we had a black dog, Arapka. My brother, who was two years older than I, used to pester Arapka by tying a scorpion to a string and dangling it in front of his nose. That happened in the garden by the green bench in the shape of a horseshoe. We also had a little boat which was moored in a tunnel, and when we wanted to go for a ride in it, it drifted out of that tunnel all by itself and came up along the steps. But I remember nothing about the trips, except when we left for good, because Arapka jumped into the water and swam after us and after long discussions we decided he had to be taken back. There were crayfish in the tunnel, and I could not tell them apart from the scorpions. I was told to watch out for them, but my brother would catch them very easily with a short piece of string. When one of these creatures was dangling from a piece of string, I didn't know whether it was black or pink. And I also got many toys, the most marvelous steamboats and sailboats, from spies who wanted to be friends with my father. And furthermore... I remember the marble most of all. They told me later on that it was necessary there because the rats ate wood. The house also

had a large marble staircase with a magnificent curve that led to the
ballroom. The only clear picture I have of my father is connected with
that staircase. I must have been three years old and they had dressed
me up as Cupid, completely nude, with a silver bow—charming, isn't
it? My father carried me on his shoulders up the staircase and I held
on to his hair as tightly as I could. When he died we had to leave immediately 'and the extent to which I must have been affected by the
oriental atmosphere became obvious from the aversion I had for Saint
Petersburg. But maybe it was just the poverty."

"Both of us will always associate the notion of a carefree youth with
marble staircases. When you told me this, I suddenly realized that I
still look for them in Meudon. I imagine that some houses there look
like Javanese estates. What a wonderful feeling for a child to sit on such
a staircase, which is cool when it's hot, high against your back like
an easy chair, and so wide that it's like a couch when you stretch out
on it."

"Is there no Indonesian blood in you, Ducroo?"

He likes that idea, it's not the first time he has asked me this question. I have to disappoint him again. *His* name, he says, suggests a
strange ancestry, Tartar maybe, or more likely Persian. Suddenly he
gets up and says that he made a killing on the stock market this week,
and wants to take me out to dinner, on the condition that I will guide
him through a Javanese *rijsttafel*, because he heard some time ago you
could get such a thing in Paris, but so far he hasn't dared to try one. He
is a little overly tactful, but he doesn't know how little it matters to me
to have someone buy my dinner. All things considered, my new circumstances haven't lasted long enough yet to give me "the pride of the
poor." And while he lets me pay here—a small compensation—he
goes outside to call a taxi. Suddenly I feel that a taxi belongs to the forbidden things: another treat. Guraev stands beside the open car door
and makes a grand gesture with his head thrown back. His gray hat,
made of alluring felt, has no ribbon around it, but instead a subtle little
edge. It's somewhere between that of a dandy and a hunter. It's striking how carefully he matched the gray of the overcoat to the gray of
that felt and how his fuzzy orange-red scarf contrasts perfectly with
the right shade. He has a cane in his hand, which is not only strange in
winter but also looks completely out of style. I'm shorter than he is,
and in my Belgian winter coat, which doesn't have much form anymore and which was never very elegant, I suddenly feel I must com-

pliment him. It's a joy to be sincere in spite of the usual irony, because clothes were never important to me: "You're as handsome as Onegin, Guraev."

He smiles, happily. In the taxi he explains where he bought the hat. If it hadn't been abroad, he would like to buy one for me exactly like it, and offer it to me because it would suit me perfectly. The light from the neon signs he talked about just a while ago splashes against our car windows. He holds his cane between his knees and looks as if he has forgotten forever how they could torment a person.

First we have to look for the Indonesian restaurant in the north of the city. It has a cheerless dining room with one booth that offers a little privacy, to the right of the door. Fortunately there are few people here. Is that also the result of the Depression? The *rijsttafel* is bland, and incomplete besides: there are three or four specialties that supplement a badly improvised main dish. The *sambalans* that must overcome the bland taste are also uninspiring. Guraev only enjoys the *krupuk*, which, after he has heard my explanation, he prefers to call shrimp cookies.

"I thought this food would be much spicier," he says. "We have spices that are much more dangerous than this."

I feel obliged to respond in kind. "Don't denigrate Indonesian spices," I tell him. "Remember that they turned hordes of Calvinists into determined bandits. It's unbelievable what those shopkeepers did in their search for new wares. They became seafarers and then found out that they could also change into robber barons, with their fortified warehouses. They politely asked permission from their dark-skinned brothers to open a grocery store in their territory, almost as if asking for their protection. Afterwards it turned out to be a fortress, which allowed them to plunder the surroundings quite easily. Running these predatory expeditions provided the education for our first great governors. With his Calvinistic hand in the cookie jar the greatest of them wrote to the home office that they could easily continue to rely on the God of robbery: 'Don't *despair*, there's really enough for everyone here.' Did you even hear of Amboina? That was the richest Spice Island. They were so crazy about its spices that they didn't bother to learn magic there, although the most famous magicians of the islands lived there. And what's more, they converted the magicians, not because they were interested in what kind of strange magic mishmash that would make, but because they had brought their own magic formulas with them: their own Bible, which proved quite clearly that they were completely justified in attacking their fellow human beings who had never even heard of it.

"But the history of the British interim government is even more fantastic. Ours were no match for these new robbers. In two weeks' time they had lost the booty of centuries. And what do you think happened then? The biggest robbers apparently couldn't count too well. They thought that they had been given the short end of the stick, that they had made a bad bargain, and so they gave the whole thing back except for a few trifles, all the while spouting the most noble and humanitarian slogans."

"But if that's the way you feel about it, Ducroo, you should never eat these spices again. Or go back to that country you consider your own. Don't you ever want to go back? How long have you been living here now?"

"Twelve years, but if I went back it would be with a feeling of resignation, as if there were no other choice. It's like the place Gide describes so perfectly in just one undulating sentence: 'Là, plus inutile et plus voluptueuse est la vie, et moins difficile la mort.'"[4]

"If you took up a real cause, you'd lose this desire for death, and even stop thinking about it. I know from experience what it is. During the revolution I never thought about death, not even a moment, which was probably nothing else than the instinct to protect myself: if you see so many people getting killed all around you, you're no longer certain that you have the right to live yourself. But you also have no time to have a 'death wish.' You can be an individualist as much as you like, but at that time you learn to say we and to think and to feel we. I'll tell you more about it some day, but not now. Don't think I actually like that kind of situation. There are enough Russians who could tell you much more. It was bad from every point of view, but still, I sometimes think that compared to them, I'm beginning to become quite bourgeois."

"Be careful not to fall into the facile habit of calling things 'bourgeois' when they are only human."

This I say to myself. Guraev lives together with his wife and daughter, his girl friend and his wife's lover, in two studios, but they do a lot together. This relationship works out well, because it's Russian. Other-

wise it would be contemptible, of course. "Because it's Russian...."
I laugh when I think about it, and yet, for some reason, it's not so ridiculous. Besides, I'm worried about something completely different: when you first love somebody you're not really part of his or her life. To live close to him, to live beside him seems enough of a miracle to you. And later when you've become part of that life, the slightest detail of the other one's life matters to you. It would be madness to think otherwise. You're angry at any secret territory the other could still share with somebody else. This isn't being possessive, rather the desire for the absolute. What is bourgeois is the indifference, the attempt to keep everything calm and rational....

I'm only aware of the conversation again when Guraev starts to formulate a tentative critique of Héverlé: "In many respects he's still much more of a Frenchman than he thinks. There's something strange about him. He needs to prove himself all the time, or rather, to feel his worth."

I'm tempted to tell him he can spare himself such subtleties: *he* needs to take a critical look at Héverlé, in order to overcome the great influence Héverlé must have had on him. With almost flattering eagerness he told me that I knew more about literature than Héverlé did. That was as early as our second meeting. I had to insist that I probably don't possess even half of Héverlé's intelligence and certainly not a sixth of his erudition. He smiled, nodding his head at my modesty. Why does he need to use me as a counterbalance to Héverlé? Perhaps this explains his urge to contrast the Russians and the French; a disillusion, the feeling that Héverlé on his part does not give enough, that he is unwilling to share his feelings. Guraev feels no bond with him, because he has come to see that they will never lean on each other in a communion of human weakness. He thinks he will have more luck with me; unfortunately, this may well be true.

"It's easy enough to criticize Héverlé," I say, "but every criticism I've heard has only put him a little higher in my estimation. Does it bother you that he doesn't indulge in intimate confessions? Does it give you the feeling that he is short-changing your friendship? Héverlé's confessions take place on an impersonal level, a kind of plateau where everything is carried on the wings of cultural history and philosophy. But in this he is genuine, because he is one of those very few people who on the surface appear to be acting, but who in essence are continuously trying—and they are very intense about it—to create their own personality. For us there is no casual Héverlé, because he denies the existence of such a person himself. When anybody criticizes him, I'm always curious about what he himself has to offer as a... personality."

We are outside again. With his most serious voice Guraev says: "Don't misunderstand me, I'm not criticizing him. For me, he is the most worthwhile of all my friends. But still, there's something wrong when you realize that you'd like to tell him all sorts of things and you find it increasingly hard to do so. If he's my friend, why don't I feel at ease in his presence, as I am with you, for instance? Friendship is something very beautiful, but I distrust somebody who is only willing to sacrifice everything to his *conception* of friendship! I'd rather have him feel I am a friend in spite of all conceptions, otherwise I feel that I happened along by accident when he needed a friend for his conceptions...."

"If you want to dig that deeply, this 'accident' explains nothing at all."

But he quickly continues. I said something about personalities. No, one should never be a personality in the eyes of a friend. Although real confessions are still impossible, except when you're drunk, perhaps. Only when you're drunk like a Russian, can you make confessions without being hindered by your personality anymore. He suggests we go to Poccardi's bar, where he orders *passito vecchio*. With those sweet wines I'm sure I at least won't forget myself in a bout of Russian drunkenness. He talks to me about his little daughter and then asks about Guy. How old he is—seven. Don't I have any fatherly feelings for him? Once again, I do not really know what that means. Where is he now? With his mother in Brussels. What does he look like? A rather round, strong boy with a funny, sensitive face, who is surprisingly blond for a son of mine.

Maybe he has too many fatherly feelings himself, Guraev suggests. Maybe the only reason he didn't divorce his wife was because she is the mother of the child. And everything is still simple. He loves his girl friend just as much as he loved his wife ten years ago. Ten years ago she was the reason for his existence. Why? Because at that time nobody else cared about him.

His wife is Russian, his girl friend Swedish, though she looks Mediterranean—except for her eyes, which are a deep green—with a brown complexion, full lips, and dark curly hair. "And you love Harriet just as much as you used to love Shura?" This time he evades me by propounding a general theory, but it's so radical it frightens me for a moment: you can't love a woman more than ten years, whoever she is. *Therefore*, ten years from now, he will not love Harriet anymore. *Therefore*, ten years from now, I will notice the same thing with my feelings for Jane. He is on the verge of telling me precisely what I must have noticed with my "first wife." I have to interrupt him abruptly and even then he looks at me suspiciously (maybe he suspects me of French manners) when I tell him I never thought of Suzanne as my "first wife." For me she was always the woman I had not chosen. He makes objections such as, "and yet, you never can tell." I again avoid any confidences and wonder how many times in this conversation we have approached and evaded one another, and why people like us always get involved in it again and again. "Héverlé has been with his wife for more than ten years," he says, "and maybe you'll say that they clearly belong to each other or that they are happy. I believe (without criticizing though!) that Héverlé has been the least courageous of the three of us, or the least honest with himself in this respect." Again, Guraev, you should leave me out of this comparison.

He looks me deep in the eyes again and then begins a conversation in which we toss about generalities until we retreat shyly into a newly filled glass. Heroism, mysticism, cynicism, individualism, and again his lack of political interest. Mysticism amuses me most of all, because it may explain something about him. He says at one moment: "You and I both need mysticism," and at another moment: "As a Russian I know what to think about mysticism. All Russians become fools as soon as they start talking about it."

Just before the last train I could take, he wanted me to tell him about my life in the Indies, insisting that I present my father as a character out of a Conrad novel.

"He couldn't have been a common bourgeois, otherwise he would never have gone there."

"He was born there, and he was certainly nothing more than a bourgeois. I am really a señorito pure and simple, a bourgeois' son."

At the foot of the staircase in the Montparnasse Station I shake his hand.

"But a bourgeois like my father *is* courageous, most of all when he has to defend his possessions. And the money I have lost now was stolen in the tradition of the great governors. I can't deny that."

I was going up the stairs and he was waving, his head tilted backwards, when suddenly he ran after me and while one step below grabbed my sleeve with his fingers.

"You really must be careful not to sob when you're confessing, Ducroo. You should not sob when you confess something, even when you're drunk. See you soon."

He ran back down the stairs.

And in the train, as soon as I was alone again, there was that stubborn melody I'm learning to distinguish better and better, which is never completely drowned by conversation, never silenced by somebody else's agreement or disagreement: the chorus of all the feelings of helplessness in me—as they harmonize in every area, since the collapse of the one stronghold I had never seriously worried about.

2   All Roads . . .

I wrote till two in the morning, a time when my mind becomes tired enough to let itself be overcome by the sleepiness of the body. I can still do this: force the body to continue with the conscious task, instead of being dominated by its disordered resistance, while only a witness to its half-conscious anxieties and protests, and its lust for control in the dark. With the new day nothing remains, except for the aftertaste of fruitless fatigue. Later on, when circumstances will have forced me to take an eight-to-five job, writing at night will be an exceptional luxury. After my report on Guraev I fell almost immediately into a dream-filled sleep and awoke the next morning with this dream clear in my mind:

I brought a young Russian to meet Guraev. He received us in his studio. Later I went back alone to the studio when he was there with Harriet and asked him his impressions of the young Russian. He sat in his easy chair, looking concerned, and was very critical. At this point I realized that the Russian was none other than Guraev himself at an earlier age, an amazing phenomenon since he would have talked no differently if I could have actually introduced him to himself. But suddenly he said, "Oh yes, he also has many fine qualities. I must even confess I was afraid he would impress Shura too much. Ask Harriet."

And Harriet, with her drawl and Swedish accent precisely as it would have been in reality, said, "Yes, we had already said to each other that gentle Shura would be the victim again." They had let her leave apparently. I noticed only then that Harriet had been the only one in the studio the first time too.

I must tell Guraev this dream. Maybe with his imagination he can evaluate its deeper sense. He'll certainly pretend to do so. This is really a unique dream for me. Usually my dreams consist of bizarre encounters with acquaintances or total strangers, which are senseless but sometimes unspeakably sad. There is for example the image of a Javanese woman who suddenly and unexpectedly meets her dead child playing in a garden: "What are you doing here?..." What makes such dreams so extraordinarily and completely sad is that the melancholy you feel when you recall them is already present in the encounter; that the latter takes place and at the same time is irrevocably gone, leaving the taste of the first and the last time. Yet the *essential* character of the encounter remains, because it takes place in a realm which has filtered out all by-products of reality.

Thus sadness hurts and heals at the same time, but without tears, even without the need for tears. It's as if everything ordered and explained itself, just as music sometimes does.

Why this expert last remark of Guraev about sobbing? I still remember Wijdenes's remarks on this subject, as well as those of others: my father loathed the "sobbing" that poets could do so easily in verse. He thought this was the main reason why he didn't like poetry. Wijdenes, who has read much more, abhorred the kind of sobbing you find in German novels: "All kinds of bullies, who resolve innumerable problems all day, come home to lie down next to a woman and pass the night crying inconsolably. You can't say it's not true to life, and sometimes it even has an effect, but it remains completely objectionable." Problem: where and how often can a man allow himself to cry in a book. What book? Rousseau, who initiated a certain kind of literature, was unusually liberal with his tears. Still, it's easier to be unchaste in erotic than in sentimental matters: a rooster always keeps some dignity.

I should remember that I have sobbed several times myself. I should be unchaste enough to confess this, although I run the risk that all my acquaintances—those marvelously interested readers!—will respond immediately, "Well, you certainly look the part," or, "I hadn't expected that of you," all depending on how they feel about me.

The first time it happened almost without cause, as in a dream, unannounced. I was in bed at the normal time, with my back to the woman I hadn't chosen. It was in one of those middle-class apartments we shared, in the Rue Lesbroussart, above the shirt store. In the evenings we sat together although there was no reason to. The cold bothered me; the winter was damp and it got dark early, which I've never become accustomed to. We went to bed early most of the time. Maybe this is how I developed my premature insomnia. That night, with my back to her and, as always, reading, I felt a drowsiness coming over me, but not sleep. Our ceiling light was off, but the one in the adjoining room was shining right on me. I closed my book and asked her not to turn off the light, because the dark would make me start to think, quite lucidly, about a thousand meaningless things. (Even then: the way experience forms you cannot go against your own nature.)

I closed my eyes and tried to enjoy the drowsiness. Now it seems to me that there was no transition at all, although I may be wrong about this, of course: suddenly the decor of our villa in Tjitjurug appeared, clearly and vividly present, although I haven't been back there since I was five. The dome-shaped porch of the house had a view of the sky which was almost completely filled by a classically shaped, perfectly triangular, blue mountain: Mount Salak. Below it were the rice fields and the train that went to Batavia. Our terraced garden passed gradually into the rice fields. At the beginning of the path that led to the gazebo where we had tea sometimes were two small statues, black and disfigured, as if pockmarked: the *artjas*. I saw all this in my mind, even when I opened my eyes. Stranger still, my body had shrunk to that of a boy. I knew that I had to be thirty, that Suzanne was lying beside me, and that I lived in a miserable apartment above a shirt store in Brussels, but I *felt* that I was four or five, that I was lying on the leather sofa on the dome-shaped porch in Tjitjurug, just as I lay then, looking at Mount Salak. I felt the short, wrinkled, cylindrical brown leather cushion under my head; it was hard against my neck. I also felt the flat leather buttons under my hands. Through the fields where the little train ran I had seen my mother a short while ago, plump as she was then, in a gray dress with balloonlike sleeves which was fashionable at that time, waving from the door of the train. I waved back from the garden. My cross-eyed Miss stood next to me; she was to be fired because she was so cross-eyed that she broke all our plates. It was one of the first times, maybe the very first time, that my mother left me; she had promised to bring back something for me from Batavia. All these details I was aware of, because I had remembered them often, and also the picture book she brought me, but at *this* moment I also recalled the name of the book: *Wilde Bles*.[1] I saw it very clearly: the flat shiny cardboard cover, with a galloping brown horse below in the right corner and curly red or dark brown letters intertwining above it. I must have held my breath so I wouldn't betray anything to Suzanne, and also to hold on to this metamorphosis as long as possible. At the same time I was still my earlier self, yet I knew that it would disappear almost im-

mediately again, knew how it would be irrevocably gone. And before I
realized it, I was sobbing uncontrollably. The metamorphosis slowly
melted away. I lay there looking at myself, watching my body "inexplicably" shaking with sobs. Behind me, Suzanne showed no more concern than was necessary. She had always been easily moved to tears;
perhaps she wondered why it had taken me this long.

How long ago is that now? It wouldn't be hard to figure it out, but for
that very reason, let's not bother. How much further back is the world
I really want to reach, the country of origin, the homeland? Should I
string together my memories of it, write ordered memoirs, at this time
already, before I'm even thirty-five? It's almost unbecoming, given a
tradition that says memoirs should be written when you're between
sixty and seventy. Should I put to use the freshness of my memory,
now, and only for this period? It's removed enough from me now, at
least, and it's part of a wholly different world that lies far behind me.
What ties remained intact except the deep and vague ones of memory?
A moonlit night in Grouhy was sometimes the most immediate message that came from back home: "This moon was sent over here, especially for you. The voyage didn't do it any good: it's less shiny and, although just as round as ever, it shines with only half the strength and
intimacy. But acknowledge it, its meaning is still the same."
Not even letters arrived to keep up the tie, or if one did come, it was
disguised, spoiled by traditional European epistolary formulas. Someone who went back a short while ago wrote, "Don't come back. The Indies aren't what they used to be. You wouldn't like it," and things like
that. All I should use are my memories, nothing else, memories from a
time when I experienced this particular beauty and paid no attention
to it, and without ever trying to restrict myself to it. I was always distracted because Europe was on the horizon and I thought that it was
my real home. But now, how can I draw from myself what the Indies
gave me, and be loyal to the moments when it emerges? Or should I lie
and turn my memories into something like a novel, the favorite reading matter of the public?
I can tell such nice stories about it, make that land come alive for my
European friends—especially if they know Dutch. There are people
who suggest that I write about it just the way I talk about it. That isn't
so easy. My colonial accent can't be reproduced on paper, at least the

means to do so are in such bad taste, even if they are effective. And I must also be careful not to lapse into that disgusting European exoticism, that false romanticism that is fashioned from a few strangely resonant names, some brown skins and velvet eyes. For some people this never fails to have the desired effect, this and some mention of the docile oriental soul.

In Grouhy I longed for the Indies like nowhere else. The moonlight there, the light that fell between the blue firs (so unlike the Indies) on the grass; the ridiculous brown star that my mother designed in the middle of the lawn, a somber spot when the shrubs were not in bloom; the gate, and behind it, dogs barking (that was almost like the Indies) but their barking wasn't stubborn enough nor was it exasperating enough—in the final analysis these details only stirred my memory.

At night, when we walked through the tall iron gate, down the stony village path to the cemetery, the Indies were slowly replaced by a romantic Europe: the three oaks standing together in the cemetery, two of which were later disfigured when they were struck by lightning; the long, high wall around Grégoire's neglected farm, which we called the ghost farm or *Wuthering Heights*; further on, the hedge with holes in it, through which we looked to see if there was something to be seen, sometimes apparitions of horses in the meadow, plump European horses, the shining circle of the moon which hid behind the hedge.... These were no longer the mystical nights of the Indies, but the nights of European romanticism, of Musset and of Byron: "So we'll go no more a-roving, so late into the night...."[2]

The illusion was stronger inside, behind the window, when the light was shining outside on the grass and the trees lost their own character. It was strongest from the window of my mother's room, when the room itself was dark. But while I write this, I feel it's wrong to evoke this room, that I'm deceiving myself with no more than a memory from a falsified past. Any tender thought about Grouhy, any endearing memory of that place, no matter how justified it seems, is a lie for me. The simple historical truth is that it was an arena, a small and isolated space where endless collisions took place between the "incompatible" personalities who were living there at the time, where resentment was held in check at all times, though it always remained just beneath the surface, and the fighting could flare up at any time. It was a madhouse, before it became a hospital.

One day I fled all this. It was a flight I had announced long in advance. Then the happiness: first a long and complicated waiting mixed with the fear that this could not be possible for even one moment. Three weeks passed. Sometimes you succeed in forgetting almost everything else during such a long time. And then, just as before, a telegram arrived.

It was almost as if all the monsters had been exorcised by my happiness or, at least, had receded in a respectful half-circle. Everything seemed provisional—my happiness too, just like every other happiness. It appeared as if the monsters wanted to respond to my forgetting by forgetting me in return. I knew though that one, my mother's sickness, would make itself known soon enough. How much self-control had it exerted, how much renunciation had it exercised, trying to conform to the general truce? And when its scream finally reached us, how busy we were in the room with suitcases, exactly like the previous times. It was as if even there Jane had nothing else to do but to share my fate.

Did I look long enough at those words, "happiness" and, soon enough, "poverty"? What is happiness, you bourgeois, and how dare you mention poverty unless you've slept on the subway stairs or have rolled up in front of a closed door which, moreover, you hope will remain closed? Where is the empty stomach, the hard floor, the vermin of this poverty? Or when can you promise us it will come to that?

During those three weeks our happiness, especially for Jane, depended on the weather. There were rainy days when walks were impossible and we were forced to take cover under the arcades. I still remember the terrace at Cassarate, the small patches of clear blue sky above me, as I lay in a lawn chair, staring endlessly at the wisteria, my open notebook on my knee—I had announced days before that I wanted "to work"—and the lines I lazily wrote down: all of this took on the form of happiness....

We had just decided to apply ourselves more seriously to walking, when the telegram arrived, destroying everything. It wasn't even the last telegram but the next to the last one. The last one came *here*. That was Lugano, this is Meudon. My mother's death came between the two, like a definitive change of weather. Our poverty is approaching. While I try to go back further into the past, and while I submit to the present, the misery of the future forces itself upon me. I have to brace myself, to be fatalistic about it. This apartment, where we thought we would continue our happiness for at least two years, is ours only when we manage to think away the threat. We are really too poor to still live here, only our lease keeps us here, and the hope for a somewhat normal sale of the unsalable Grouhy.

"*Rumah sial*," my mother would have said, "House of Misfortune." My father's suicide was connected with it. The family hate that soured the last years of my mother's life came to full expression for the first time there. But the garden was always delightful, it was so private and, to my mother's mind, it suited a country gentleman from the Indies so well....

Three weeks in which we began to feel our own warmth as a lasting summer. At first I said, "I would give anything for ten days like this; I only ask for ten such days." When the telegram came I felt that it was an injustice, of course. Every visit I've made to Lugano was broken off by a telegram about my mother's illness. And that last time I said, "I will not go back to Lugano as long as such telegrams are possible." Half a year later the possibility was gone; *it* was gone.

It doesn't matter where I start now, because even this very moment seems to be arbitrary. Today, yesterday, tomorrow, or any other moment, doesn't make any difference. Along with the forced awareness of a new beginning comes the real awareness that everything is irretrievably lost. I have never been able to keep a regular diary; I write mostly to forget the future. As long as the lease keeps us here and the other decisions have not been made yet, as long as practical matters force us to play this chess game—although we hardly know the moves—we can still be served by memory or poetry. And poetry is always a little naïve. My feelings for Jane: poetry, opium, and naïveté. Just like poetry, love must be based on naïveté, naïve self-deceit. Some people don't believe this, but such self-deceit is equally naïve and even more damaging.

Jane. Essentially, it all comes down to her or, rather, as far as my past is concerned—from the time I had become *me*, destined to find her just as I did—all roads of memory lead to her, to the one focus, the one essential change in my life. I would like to write just about her, if it were possible. Maybe, in the future, I will give in and leave just one thing behind, a portrait of Jane. However, the deceit in these words is shameless. It's all too clearly poetry again and can be refuted with few words: the portrait of Jane would always be different from Jane herself.

3 Family Album

It may be madness to want to put down what is living in us now, but I can still try to write down for Jane what I was like before she came along. The difference between the authenticity of letters and the unavoidable falsification of a diary lies in the sincerity of the motivation. Because of the library work I'm now doing with Viala, I feel attracted to going back in history. It has to begin with something like that, with a justification from the past, a shuttle between Europe and over there. How much would remain unexplained, even between us, if "there" were not the country of origin—in spite of everything, in spite of Europe's rights that go back further. My curious search for the Indies in Grouhy was really going against the grain, after my father bought that castle almost to prove to himself that he had feudal ancestors in Europe. He had put a suit of armor in the hall as a symbol. His own French name and that of the village completed the illusion. He only noticed later that he had made an unusually bad choice, and on other than geographical or genealogical grounds. The Walloon population probably made him feel doubly French. The Belgian count, who had every appearance of being an untrustworthy village notary, probably made him feel—who knows?—like a Burgundian nobleman. Bearing a striking resemblance to Guy de Maupassant, my father looked much more French than I did. I never had any delusions in this respect, since the Parisians always thought I was Rumanian or Brazilian. And yet, I would have felt a "young man from the Indies" through and through, a colonial deep down, if heredity had not implanted some of the French country gentleman in me.

My father never knew the work, *Origin and Establishment of Indo-European Families in the Netherlands East Indies*, by W. H. van der Bie Vuegen, state archivist in Batavia. There it was, in black and white: Ducroo, from Du Crault. The first one of this family known in the Indies was a Jean-Roch, born around 1765, an artillery cadet who fought against the British in Ceylon, was taken prisoner of war in 1795, then left for Java. On May 4, 1807, he made his will while a captain in the

Corps of Engineers in Batavia and named as sole heirs his adopted sons, Nicholas, 20, and Louis, 14, both cadets in the same Corps. His three brothers were then living in France."

How painful it would have been for my father if he had known that those were *adopted* sons! When he finally came back to Europe from the Indies, he was almost certain he was a count. I made him unhappy when I said that I preferred the title of viscount or even of chevalier. Passing through Dijon on his way to Marseilles to Paris, he stayed at the Grand Hôtel and immediately began his investigations. The doorman of the hotel was a disabled war veteran who had lost his legs but had a red, round face and rows of medals on his chest. He certainly knew about the noble families in the area. My father was sure we were of Burgundian lineage—even though the spelling of our name seemed to indicate a southern French origin—because our coat of arms supposedly appeared in the *Armorial de Bourgogne*. He looked it up in the Bibliothèque Nationale in Paris and found that what his father had told him was correct. There it was: "Du Crault—d'azur au chevron d'argent accompagné de trois tours d'argent."[1] He also wanted to uncover possible ancestors, but he only found Du Craults who had added other names and with much different coats of arms, with eagles and harps on a background of gules.

For the fun of it I helped him and accidentally found something that excited him very much. In the *Archives de la noblesse de France* the name we were looking for unexpectedly caught my eye, in the margin of a completely different family tree. A Gaudechart married the daughter of a Messire Louis du Crault in Rouen in 1488; it brought us almost all the way back to the Crusades! Unfortunately his title wasn't mentioned; his coat of arms, however, matched completely except that the little turrets were in gold. Still, this was only a slight disappointment to us, because we could comfort ourselves with the idea that it was perhaps an older branch.

Another finding touched me much more personally. I came upon a certificate given to a certain Antoine du Crault who had served satisfactorily with the musketeers for a couple of months. It was signed by D'Artaignan, the greatest hero of my youth. No coat of arms here, but seeing our name connected with d'Artagnan—even if only in this way —didn't surprise me at all, strangely enough. It rather filled me with a satisfaction I had expected. I had known that I would experience such things in Europe.

In a library in The Hague my father came in contact with somebody who specialized in this kind of investigation. The man started his work, had to travel quite a bit and needed a large expense account. Time and time again he required "funds." Finally he discovered that our Jean-Roch was born in Bulon, which could be Brûlon, and indeed wasn't too far from Burgundy. It sounded scholarly and even probable. However, it didn't satisfy my father because a letter the investigator sent to Brûlon was never answered. The expedition was stranded on this Brûlon, which was at best only probable, and thus the gap which separated us from the French Du Craults was not bridged. We had to restrict ourselves to the Dutch Ducroos who, starting with my great-grandfather, spelled their name differently. "If only we had the damned birthplace of that Shan-Rock!" my father said when he had decided not to send the investigator any more funds, and just do without a count's coronet.

It would have upset him, however, if he had read that his own grandfather, Colonel Louis, was only the adopted son of Shan-Rock. Mr. Van der Bie Vuegen's disclosure came in my hands only later through Graaflant who, given his old sympathies for the Action Française,[2] was also interested in my family. I actually was frightened for a moment by the unexpected perspective. Where did our *own* ancestors come from then? But after all, my father didn't have his characteristic French complexion for nothing; he was short and sanguine, with quick movements. And Colonel Louis didn't look any less French, with the broad chest of the Ducroos and his friendly bulldog face sticking out of the absurd high military collar of that time. If we were bastards, we were still French. I wrote Mr. Van der Bie Vuegen for information. He answered that he didn't know anything more about the adopted children, but he was able to tell me that Jean-Roch lived on the outskirts of Batavia, that he willed twenty-five guilders to the reformed churches there, and that the guardians of his adopted sons were Dominique Chevereux, Lieutenant Colonel of the Infantry, and Charles Legrévisse, Captain of the Artillery. From the memoirs of Dirk van Hogendorp[3] I later learned what had happened to Jean-Roch in Ceylon, where he was serving in a French-Swiss regiment under the command of a Colonel De Meuron. The colonel himself was in Europe where he sold his regiment to England. Officers and soldiers refused to go along with this arrangement and remained loyal to the Dutch governor of Ceylon. He, however, thought they had to obey the colonel and he literally forced them to go over to the British. So that was the "captivity" poor Jean-Roch had to endure! Later he apparently went further east, which was the fate of many French officers who, though in the service of the Batavian Republic[4] and allies of the Dutch, were ready to fight them at the drop of a hat. I can't imagine his looking any different from my father and great-grandfather, although he must have worn a powdered wig. He must have felt rather strange on the outskirts of Batavia with his comrades, those other two *didongs*[5] in uniform. It may also have been fairly pleasant. He probably lived there till he died. The Hague investigator found some trace of his first adopted son, Nicholas: "He served with the Cavalry and was killed in action." The second, Louis, made more of a name for himself. If he wasn't the son of Jean-Roch, at least he was born in Ceylon in 1793. He was also— barely eighteen years old—taken prisoner of war by the British and sent to England, but this was in 1811, when Java was easily conquered by them in spite of the renowned courage of our General Janssens. Nicholas, who was six years older, must have been killed in the same campaign, maybe in the famous battle of Meester-Cornelis.

Released as a prisoner of war a year later, Louis came to Holland (probably for the first time) and fought against the French during the last years of Napoleon. Then he was sent back to Java as a captain and distinguished himself in the war against Dipo Negoro.[6] In 1825 he was the commander of Magelang, which was threatened by the "bandits," as we mindlessly called the troops of the Javanese ruler. The resident commissioner was absent and the garrison was only fifty men and *djajèng sekars* strong; nevertheless, my great-grandfather remained unshaken. The attackers burned the bridges to the south of the city and occupied a *desa* close to Tidan Hill. They repulsed a reconnaissance patrol and when my great-grandfather himself arrived, "the bandits were undaunted and attacked us with such fury that Ducroo decided to retreat, firing." A local chief, who apparently recognized Dutch rule as irrevocable, came to the rescue with a troop of lancers. In the meantime Ducroo had regrouped, mounted a new offensive against the bandits, and this time "he had the good fortune to disperse them, inflicting significant losses." Then he set fire to the reed fields where they were hiding and they emerged from the smoke, "right in front of our soldiers," who defeated them and chased them away once more. Upon his return, my great-grandfather was complimented by the resident commissioner, mentioned in a dispatch, and awarded the Military Order of William.[7] He became a major and then a colonel. I would like to know what he thought when his superior, Baron de Kock, violated his word of honor. History is also silent about the fact that he failed the general's exam because he completely fouled up a big parade in Waterloo Square in Batavia. My Aunt Tina, who used to sit on his lap as a child, thought he was "unbelievably good-natured." He was discharged as a colonel and allowed to continue wearing the uniform.

He married an Amsterdam girl of good standing, Lucretia Wilhelmina de Ronde. My father preferred to pronounce this name in the French manner, to keep the race pure, but there's every reason to think she came from a solid Dutch background. Their son, Willem Hendrik Ducroo, who was my grandfather, had a great career as a judge and married a rich woman who, once again, had a French name: Lami. She was the daughter of another colonel, who didn't look at all like Colonel Louis, and he never chased bandits out of reed fields. All that is known about his military prowess is that he took part in Napoleon's Russian campaign as a conscript. He is also said to have had certain talents as a strategist. A portrait of him shows a big belly protruding from under a white vest, and a small round face with an apoplectic but cunning expression. He made his two daughters immensely wealthy by managing his second wife's fortune masterfully. This was not the mother of the daughters, but a childless widow who trustingly gave up her last lonely years in order to share His Honor's honored existence. It was the stepmother's fortune which was finally divided between the two daughters, and about half of it rained upon all later Ducroos.

Both of the daughters were strange, which is to say that later on both went off their rockers. The one who was my grandmother was well known in the family and among friends for her satirical wit, even as a young girl. She lived in Meester-Cornelis in the house where I was born and which was named Gedong Lami after her family. In her old age she was surrounded by adopted native children who had to taste her food and drink because of her unshakable fear of being poisoned. She had a round face with keen eyes and a rather tense mouth. She looked like her father. I'm told I look a little like her which, though I don't believe it, doesn't bother me, because she has one of the most intelligent faces in our family album. She lived unhappily and was constantly at odds with her husband, even though she had five children by him, thanks to all the reconciliations. He left her finally in her huge house in Meester-Cornelis and went to live on Koningsplein in Batavia. Later, after he had retired, he went to Brussels, where he took a mistress. As a young man my father met this woman in Brussels, when he came to visit them unexpectedly one evening. He had no opinion about her beauty or her charm, which disappointed me when he told me the story.

My grandmother's sister—the other half of the fortune—married a young officer who later became the famous General Marees. There were two Marees brothers in the army: one of them, a lieutenant, cut his superior in half in a duel and, in so doing, his own career. The other one, after a more prudent beginning, managed to distinguish himself mostly in expeditions in Borneo and Sumatra, and later on even more so as a favorite of King William III, who simply could not give him enough medals and honors. But his wife, who had devoted the greater part of her life to his military career and who was much loved by the soldiers, was rarely seen toward the end. People said my grandmother was a little odd, but this sister was completely insane. No doubt about it, we come from a strange family. My father's sister Tina had at least inherited her mother's satirical spirit, yet, despite her insights about people and her pessimism, she lost all judgment as soon as mention was made of theosophy. When my father was young, he was energetic, quick-tempered, autocratic yet cheerful, and had an eye for women. Later on he tried to communicate with the spirit world, but he ended up a neurasthenic and, finally, when he was completely world-weary, he committed suicide.

But now I've come too close to the present. What is important in the context of this family is that my father also married a woman with a French name, one of those hyphenated names of the so-called colonial nobility, when a Mr. Bonnet gradually becomes Mr. Bonnet de la Colline, and a Mr. Perrichon turns into Mr. Perrichon de la Plaine. My mother's family came from Réunion. I owe my first name, Arthur, which does not occur in the Ducroo family, to an uncle whose last name in the old days of the Indies was synonymous with the wines he sold, in particular with his Cantenac. According to my mother's description he must have been the père noble type. He would ride with his big white beard in an open carriage at the hour when everybody came outside, and on his wine bottles he had put the motto: *Fais bien, laisse dire.*[8] My mother spoke solemnly about this phenomenon from her youth, a man who sometimes took her with him on his daily ride.

On the table at which I'm writing all this there is a picture of my mother that clearly shows her Réunion origin. She looks plump and like a Creole in a dark dress with bows at the shoulders: curly hair, sultry eyes, twenty-eight years old, and yet, as an elegant landlady of mine put it once, "In those days, when you were twenty-eight, you were forty."

4 Death of My Mother

For Graaflant, my mother's death was a fact with only practical significance. For a long time he had classified her as an egoist, an old
woman who could not restrain herself, not even materially, and who
had no idea of the mental anguish she caused me. In his opinion I was
a model son, in spite of my short temper. What bothered him was the
fact that I was not consulted in financial matters, that until I was past
thirty I was satisfied with my small monthly allowance and even docile
about it, while my mother denied herself nothing, even though she
thought she made the greatest sacrifices. And when he said, "I don't
like your mother," it resounded with great conviction. Sometimes I
had the feeling that I had been unfair in talking to him about my mother as I did. I would defend her then and point out the mental anguish
and the terrible loneliness which caused her to pine away. He thought
it was sad but not out of the ordinary; he mentioned some other lonely
old women, among them his own mother, and only felt confirmed in
his conviction that I was much too sensitive a son. The inevitable telegram that called me back time and time again, right when I was finally
gaining some freedom, got on his nerves. He must have breathed a
deep sigh of relief when he heard that this time she had died. He offered me his condolences casually that evening. "Now at least you
know where you stand," he said.

I knew it the next afternoon, to my great distress, and a week later I
knew it even better after I had been at the bank in Amsterdam.

In Holland, Wijdenes tried in his own clumsy way to express his
emotions or at least his ideas about emotion. He knew, he said, how
much my mother meant to me in spite of everything. I had talked with
him one time about the world that would disappear for me when she
died. Even when we had nothing to say to each other, or when we were
quarreling, which happened whenever we expressed our own views
to each other, the past was almost always present. It was there in her
room, it was in the smallest space she lived in, how ever shortly, when
she imbued it with a feeling of home. Her way of sitting in a kimono, on

the bed or on the couch, said everything. She should have gone back to the Indies. There, in the evenings, she would have talked with her trusted *babu*, who would massage her after helping her prepare various special dishes all day. My mother's loneliness wasn't at all surprising, but when illness kept her from leaving the house it became disastrous because she had no other recourse. She may have read Lamartine or Musset as a young woman, but later on she read nothing. I have known few people who were so indifferent to reading as she was; all she would look at was a newspaper, a cookbook, or a medical guide for the family. When I pointed out to her how important reading could be in her present situation, she assured me she used to read a lot during her first marriage. She still knew three titles: *Les femmes qui tombent, La Bouche de Mme X,* and *La Maîtresse masquée.* All three books were fascinating, she said, and the first one also had a deeper meaning. It was the story of a pretty young widow who, although she could not get over the death of her husband, finally succumbed to a rich suitor in order to save her sick child; but on the same night that she gave in to him, she came home to find her child dead.

I explained to Wijdenes how little time I had for emotion, how everything had been suppressed by the actions of the legal officials. I talked to him barely a week after her death. Now, two months later, it's still the same. There is no lack of time anymore, but I live in a constant state of emergency which is overtaking everything else. In order to think back to my mother with emotion (I've succeeded in this once), I have to look for her in my childhood. I'm certain this feeling won't go on indefinitely. I know that one day I'll feel in my heart what I now only know rationally, how sad the last year of her life must have been, especially after I left with Jane. The last telegram came from Aunt Tina: "Come back both. Mother dying." When we arrived she was dead. She was already dead when the telegram was sent, the chauffeur told us on the way home from the station. We found Aunt Tina sitting downstairs with the new housekeeper, a nurse, and the masseuse. "She called me last night and I brought the nurse with me. At eleven o'clock the doctor came and he saw no immediate danger. At three o'clock she became really sick and at three-thirty it was all over, my child, but only after she first experienced a radiant vision. Oh God, I don't know what she saw, but it must have been wonderful!" The end was quick and easy. Her small weakened body had hardly any resistance left. She was angry because the priest didn't come. "But then I told her, 'Go, go in peace, you have been a good person. Don't you want to go to heaven?'"

Jane and I went into the room where I had said goodbye to her barely a week before going back to Meudon. She was lying in the big bed which came from Grouhy, in that room where I had seen too little of her to feel her presence now, where she may have felt the loneliest of all. And indeed there was nothing left of her, just a moist plaster mummy, more gray than yellow, with a handkerchief around her head.

"She's so small," said Jane. The nurse came in and stood behind us. Suddenly she bent forward and wiped some foam from her mouth. The lips didn't close very well. She had died with her mouth open and, because the lower jaw kept falling down, someone had tied that handkerchief around her head.

I turned aside and went into the adjoining room that had been prepared for us. I had to fight back a short but violent surge of tears. What she had always feared had happened: I hadn't been there. I had comforted her by saying, "It's only four hours from here," but this had turned out to be the comfort you sometimes give to children just to quiet them. And yet I had hurried home more than ten times whenever I received a telegram—sometimes I was more than thirty hours away—and it had never been necessary. I had been at her deathbed in various stages, in the same sinister Brussels neighborhood: middle class, cheap, horrible in winter, and avoided by everybody because of its dreariness. The doctors had given her up, one because of her heart, the other because of cancer of the liver that he thought he had discovered, a diagnosis that was later reversed. I used to sit with her during the night until I would fall on my own bed, dizzy, my heart seeming to stop again and again along with hers. This time there was only that mummy in which I couldn't recognize her.

The same afternoon the first notary showed up, the one with the round pig's head and the well-intentioned informality, who spat through his teeth when he talked, who had not been able to keep her away from a worthless will, who smacked his lips and responded "yes" to everything you said to him when he didn't repeat your sentence. He did his best to be paternal, interfered in the discussions with the funeral director, and promised to be back the next day with money for the funeral. There were also negotiations with the priest for a Mass, there were letters and telegrams to the Indies, and there were the nervous fumblings of people who didn't live here and had not received their monthly salary and had left on the train with their last money.

The next day we had the second visit of the notary, accompanied this time by an elegant younger colleague who came to take care of the case in his stead. He had a neat part in the middle of his pasted-down hair, a short mustache, and the piercing eyes of a thief. He would be perfect in the role of a gangster in the movies which are currently so popular, if only he hadn't looked so impossibly Belgian, if he weren't so boorish as only someone from Brussels can be. "Un charmant garcon," thought the attorney from Namur, who had become something of my mother's chargé d'affaires and who, therefore, had also been called. Vulgar, ill mannered, with a fat balding head, he was loud, but on the whole he was still more human than the other two combined. He seemed to be irritated when he heard the will declared invalid. Since my half-brother had died in the Indies, his children who were not of age yet had to have part of the inheritance. Otto had signed a waiver renouncing any claim to my mother's estate because he knew that this money came from my father. The waiver had to be confirmed now, but he had died four months before. So I couldn't touch anything. The estate had to be sealed immediately. According to the law the stock was held at the Amsterdam bank and everything, with the exception of Grouhy which fortunately had been put in my name, had to be divided. The notaries could give me some money while we were waiting for the estate to be probated, but because of those relatives in the Indies it would take a lot of time. They would give me the money with Grouhy as security, and not the inheritance. They gave me very little and even then did so grudgingly, because they remembered that Grouhy had already been mortgaged. "And what am I supposed to live on while we're waiting for Grouhy to be sold or the estate to be probated?"

"Well...," and they waved their arms and shrugged their shoulders.

"Do you realize that I live in France with my wife and that I must support my first wife and little boy here in Brussels? With the money you give me I'll just be able to pay for the funeral and give the servants their severance pay."

"That's very unpleasant, but the law...."

And the attorney started to shout as if he were personally offended by the matter: "I knew this would happen. I know my great friend, Mr.

Ducroo here! He's fed up with what's happening. He's quite upset because this possibility never occurred to him."

I had indeed never thought that the notary with the pig's head who spat out his yes's so readily and who was so well informed about Otto's minor children might have purposely neglected to tell my mother that her will was no good, because it provided such a marvelously complicated case, that two colleagues were hardly enough. And the attorney who had written Otto's waiver could have figured out before that it would be worthless.... The days succeeded one another like a nightmare of practical steps. The funeral, with a Mass I had to attend, the recommendations for the servants who had to be dismissed, a trip to Namur and back in a third-class compartment among identical creatures talking about identical things: the Depression. There were discussions with the attorney that centered mostly on the desirability of accepting the inheritance without prejudice. Our fears were later confirmed in Holland. There was a huge debt at the bank for monies advanced, while the shares that served as collateral had dropped so low they were worth little more than the drafts. If the world economy improves, the shares will go up again and the inheritance won't be so bad, but if it continues to go down, the bank will give us nothing and then the furniture, which is now under seal, will have to cover the bills. And then there's the mortgage on the house that has to be paid, even if the law demands it being sealed, which does no one any good, particularly the joint heirs in whose interest that measure seemed so necessary. "There is a hold on everything. The shares will drop more, the mortgage accumulates. We blame the Depression when everything has become worthless, but our honesty requires us to do our job well, at your expense. We know business and legal procedures."

I've never before felt so vulnerable at the hands of such inferior human beings. This type knows how to fight procedural rules, and the fact that I still had to learn even the most elementary ones gave me the feeling that I was present as a child who wasn't allowed to speak.

Having the furniture sealed was a show in itself: the senile county judge with his goatee seemed to have stepped out of a vaudeville act. There was a registrar and a notary clerk whose vulture's instinct was at odds with the formality of his attire. Five men in all. With the two notaries in front, they were suddenly let loose in the now-empty room where she had died, and they began to open cabinets and drawers with a set of keys. They carried away fur coats and then began to study the jewelry box and the safe until a locksmith (who had quickly been summoned) broke them open too. The senile county judge told a story about a family of cats that had forced them to reseal a house three times, to placate the SPCA.... They required an oath from Jane and me and the remaining personnel that nothing had been stolen from the estate.

It's possible that I'm unfair to these people, that the disgust I felt as I hurried to the train was exaggerated, certainly the disgust I felt when I allowed them to take custody of the jewelry. My correspondence with both notaries lasted a short time, to our mutual displeasure, I hope. Then I left everything to the attorney. Since I signed a release declaring the inventory without prejudice, he has answered my letters—which I admit are not written in legalese—in an abrupt tone, as if he wants to get rid of the whole thing. I continue to believe he's a decent man; at times he helped us quite a bit in Grouhy. But my distrust and the awareness of my bad judgment of men have been aroused to an extreme. Deep down I sympathize with the unhappy people who no longer see the law, only its representatives, and who will shoot the man serving a summons because they really can't take it anymore.

One of the last conversations with my mother—during Christmas when I was at her home for the last time—led to the veiled reproach she always made since Jane had been with me: "I understand that you can't come very often. You're living with someone you love very much. I won't be in your way much longer. Mark my words, next year you will bury your mother. Only then will life begin for you, when you get the money I now still need for myself. I pray to God that I will still be able to arrange everything for you and also for poor little Guy."

I summoned all the calm I possessed (we'd had a scene the day before): "Let me tell you once more that I never include your death in my plans for the future. Besides, I almost count on the fact that there will be nothing left." There would certainly have been nothing left if she had lived a few more years. Now our predictions were coming true all too quickly. She died indeed the next year, the night of January third, and the notaries are fulfilling my prophecy.

Suzanne, with whom she quarreled to the very last, laid her in the coffin. She even attended the funeral, although Jane and I followed the coffin together. I didn't see her at the Mass, but at the cemetery she came forward as the coffin was being shoved into the vault.

"What karma binds her to your mother, my child?" asked Aunt Tina, bobbing her head. "Isn't it strange that this creature had to lay her in her coffin?"

Suzanne had ridden to the cemetery between the masseuse and the chauffeur—a strange attitude, karma or not. For a short while I went to see her every evening in the two cheap rooms she had stuffed with furniture from Grouhy. I felt miserable there, perhaps because a picture of me looked at me from every corner of the room. I talked with Guy about his grandmother. She had died two houses away in the same sinister neighborhood where she had lived in order to see him daily. When she died he was more attached to her than to his mother. But suddenly he didn't want to hear any more about it. He looked unhappy and started crying, saying that he was afraid of me. I explained to him quietly that his grandmother was dead and that as a result he would never see her again. He nodded, pried himself loose from me, and asked his mother to come and listen to the radio. "You must not do that, Guy," Suzanne said the next day. "You must not forget your grandma." They stood at the door ready to leave when she said this. He went quickly outside and hurried down the street, refusing to look at the door of the house where she had died. "Yes, yes," he said. "Don't talk about it, I know." He seemed to shy away from death instinctively. A month later when I saw him again and asked if he still remembered his grandmother, he said very calmly, "Oh sure."

Now I want to write down the scene that took place on Christmas Day, not for the quiet feelings of remorse but rather as an explanation of why part of my being flared up when something reminded me of the poisonous atmosphere with which Grouhy was impregnated. I reacted so quickly and so violently only later, when I had withdrawn from it, perhaps because of the contrast. I was sitting on the bed next to my mother, listening to her talk about the Austrian companion she had just fired. For the hundredth time she called someone a snake, the cause of all evil, incredibly vicious; she wouldn't talk about her anymore, but what a relief that she was gone, and so on. To be followed, of course, by some examples of her viciousness. They were so disgustingly stupid, so completely devoid of any understanding, so unreasonably egotistical, that I thought of the dismissed Frieda as she was, as I had known her for years: totally devoted, doing without sleep for nights, her nerves worn out. I couldn't help pointing out her good qualities, and my enthusiasm carried me along as I implored my mother, in her own interest, not to see human beings first as angels only to revile them later as vipers. She suddenly nodded her head sadly, asked for water in a broken voice, and when I brought it, scared, she spit out most of it. I felt she was just acting, and suddenly I threw the glass on the floor. "On Christmas," she said immediately, and I said, "Yes, on Christmas, I want you dead and so I came especially on Christmas to murder you." I was beside myself with anger and shouted, "Stupidity, damned stupidity. Always the same damned stupidity."

Her attack was over in a couple of seconds. Later, when I sat down next to her, she took my hand: "I want you to know that I never hold it against you, even when you treat me like this."

I felt no remorse. I said, "You know better than anybody else that I was slowly brought to this point." But I stroked her hand and a little later drew her head to me. The morning I left our farewell was spoiled, however, because the chauffeur was a few minutes late. She was in a bad mood and intended to scold him at length. I embraced her quickly and called the man to come with me down the stairs.

5   The History of My Parents

March. No news from Brussels from the attorney or even from Graaflant. It's as if it were completely normal that part of my fate is to be decided over there, without my knowing anything about it. But I've come
to terms with it, and I'm "writing away the threat of the future."

I'd like to tell about my parents now, at least a few things of their
lives before I came along. I'm afraid, though, that some falsification will
be inevitable. Who could do otherwise? You always know too much
and too little about your own father and mother. Even if you try to see
them objectively, as if they weren't related, you end up judging them
either too harshly or too gently. The latter of these attitudes is called
normal, while the former is either a conscious or an unconscious reaction to this normal attitude, though from the point of view of historical
fact, it is merely one falsification pitted against another.

I can't say I never heard them talk about themselves, but they were
like so many other people who, even though they talk about themselves happily, never reveal anything essential, not out of reticence but
because they don't see what is essential. Only after my father's death
did I talk to my mother about him in a more confidential tone. She
thought he was a man, a real man, with his thick hair, his mustache,
and his mole. He was small but so strong, and at the same time kind to
women, and a gentleman. She could never have loved anyone, she
said, no matter how nice, who was the least bit common.

My father was an excellent dancer and horseman. Although he was
very short, he was indeed very quick and strong. As a boy he could
swing double giants on the horizontal bar and was a master of all
weapons. Later he won many gentleman's races in the Buitenzorg
area. When he was twenty-five he had a European mistress, which was
not very common in the Indies in those days. She was striking, had
short hair, and rode horses with him on the highway to Batavia. But although at that time he had already received the Villa Merah estate
from his mother, his older friends thought he was much too young to
keep a European woman. His brother-in-law was going to lecture him

about it but was stopped short when my father asked how much money he had borrowed from him. That kind of argument is enough for such people.

The word "mistress" must have had a mysterious sound in the Indies in those days, even if the mistress was in reality a healthy young woman with bright insolent eyes and a large pouting mouth. In almost all the pictures my father had, she wore riding clothes, and in some of them she must have been with a previous admirer. At least there's a picture of a front porch of a colonial country house, with three gentlemen on horseback on one side and her on the other side, standing next to her horse, a crop in one hand. In another picture she's sitting with one of the three gentlemen in a buggy, while the other two are sitting on the steps, their different relationship underscored by a bottle and glasses. My father must have conquered her with his horses, just as in certain circles a man now conquers a woman with an automobile.

However, she must have been more or less abandoned too, because it turned out she was not able to pay for the jewelry she had bought from an Arab. He was young and insolent, and one evening he sat down in a rocking chair on her front porch, saying that he would not go away until she had paid him one way or another. My father was seeing her already at that time, and he had come up to the house through the backyard to find her both frightened and indignant. So, surprising the Arab, he took the role of the angry white man—"You miserable Arab, get the hell out of here"—and had the pleasure of seeing the creditor vanish from the rocking chair into the night in no time at all. He met the same man later as a captain of the Arab quarter in Batavia and a Knight of the Order of Orange-Nassau. "Everyone knew he was a dirty rat," he said. As a matter of fact, the Arab ended by being implicated in a city hall scandal and was written up in all the newspapers.

As for the lady, after rescuing her so chivalrously, he took her home to live with him. She often went horseback riding with him and was seen everywhere, much to the irritation of respectably married women. She dared do even more: one day she went with my father to have her picture taken, nude, at the famous photographer's studio of Charls and Van Es. The young photographer who took the picture must have blushed terribly, I'm sure, but the picture didn't show any such embarrassment. It was very clear, and later I looked at it with some emotion, although it had been torn off at the level of her breasts.

After a quarrel with my father one day, she said something deroga-
tory about him to a servant, calling him "*itu blanda*," which is like "that
Dutchman over there." So my father beat her up mercilessly in front of
the same servant. But when he later saw the bruises on her wrists and
shoulders, he cried with remorse, according to my mother, and never
again raised his hand to a woman.

Those who knew my father said he was a sensitive man, even sentimental and melancholic. The end of his life proved it. But he didn't let
it show; he only revealed his bad side, that of the short-tempered autocrat or, hardly any better, that of a "hell of a guy." When I was still a
child I often heard him classify his friends as being either "great guys"
or not, and for a long time I thought this must be the highest virtue for
a man. Be that as it may, the little "Duke" was greeted with great fanfare when he appeared at parties in the club at Batavia as well as in the
Buitenzorg manors and in Priangan. In a large photograph of a garden
party with more than a hundred planters and their wives—the nineteenth-century conquerors of the Indies at their best—one can see
him in the first row with a drum between his knees. Because he was
fond of music, though he didn't play an instrument, he had been part
of the performance of *Unter dem Doppeladler* as a drummer. Undoubtedly, however short and frenchified he might have been, in Batavia and Buitenzorg he was very much a gentleman. Once he had a
professional jockey removed from a race exclusively for gentlemen,
saying, "If he's a gentleman, I am not." He loved good clothes, even
later when he was an old man in Brussels. When he died he left seventeen pairs of shoes that were too small for me. There's a picture of him
in his heyday in the tropics, with a glengarry, a short black jacket, well-
fitting white trousers, boots, and a whip he held folded double in his
hand. Jane's comment was: "There's really not a bit of a human being
left in him."

He was not born in my grandmother's big house where I was born,
but in his father's on Koningsplein. Perhaps one of those reconciliations between his father and mother had just taken place, times when
their children were conceived. His father, the judge—or was it his
mother?—had a stable of race horses. When he was about seven years
old, my father went there and a heavy board fell on his foot, chopping
off two toes. They were just dangling from his foot, and the only thing
he said was: "Will they grow back soon?" And after they told him they

would, he wasn't the least bit concerned about it—just as I would have expected of him, because he was tough throughout his life. Later he used this injury to be exempted from the militia.

Even in his youth he was always around horses, and as soon as he returned from Europe he bought a race horse that was relatively cheap because it was mean. One afternoon he ran the horse around a tree at the end of a rope until it finally was pressed up against the trunk, and then he whipped it until it stood "trembling like a puppy." He then fell on his back in the grass from exhaustion and lay there out of breath for almost half an hour. Afterwards the horse and he were "good friends."

When he was ten he was sent to Holland to school, and he lived in the house of his uncle, General Marees. He was proud of the fact that he had been brought up in the family of his uncle, who was so decorated that William III almost had to invent new medals for him. There's a huge collection of cousins in the family album, all children of the general, and a couple of pictures of the general himself. They show little more than a face—rather noble in its kind, I must say—above an abundance of stars of various sizes.

One military exploit impressed my father very much. During an expedition in Borneo or Sumatra, the natives kept poisoning the wells his soldiers had to drink from. So the general stuffed his cannons with a number of prominent natives from the area and shot the pieces all over the village, and that, my father said, without waiting for permission from Batavia.

I found a letter he wrote on the occasion of my father's marriage, containing some remarkable phrases. "With all the most important milestones of your life, you come to my mind as you were when you were taken into my house as my son.... I hope that the wife you have chosen will bring you everything you expect from her: happiness, pleasure, and most of all, contentment.... Your aunt is reasonably well; it's true that she's still a little disturbed, which keeps her away from our common roof, but in front of acquaintances and strangers she knows how to control herself and doesn't show anything.... The children are all well and successful."

Of my father's school days I only know that he undertook a long skating trip from one Dutch town to another. Later he studied in Paris at the École Nationale Agronomique. He had many tintypes of himself and his friends from that period. He was about the only one without a beard. Although his fellow students were all under twenty-five, almost all of them had full beards and looked as if they were well over thirty. He had a Dutch friend with a bear who was called the barboteur[1] because his name was Morbotter. I remember such a detail because I probably thought it was a "funny" French joke, most of all because my father always added that the barboteur got very mad when you called him that. Neither he nor my father studied very hard in Paris. After two years my grandfather came from Brussels to visit him; he took my father out of the École Agronomique and put him in a factory in Lille as an apprentice, because, after all, without European training he couldn't run a plantation in the Indies.

In Lille my father had a girl friend by the name of Mathilde—he always pronounced it with a clear French *i*—who actually may have been the prettiest woman in Lille. One afternoon, while he was sitting with her in a café, a man insulted her. At the instigation of a jealous girl, he asked for Mathilde's "card" as he passed her. My father was one step behind Mathilde and answered for her with a downward blow (a "thump," he called it), so that the man "was up to his nose in his hat." After he pulled his hat off, he ran after my father, who grabbed him by the collar outside the café. He pushed the man against the wall with one hand and with the other worked him over until they were pulled apart. The two women were getting ready to join the fight with their umbrellas but disappeared when the police arrived. The man with the hat was also able to escape, but my father was grabbed by two policemen and escorted to the station. Maybe he spoke very bad French in his excitement or his accent became more noticeable; at any rate the crowd shouted, "Assommez-le, c'est un Prussien."[2] (It was around 1880, not so long after the Franco-Prussian War.) At the police station it turned out that he was not a Prussian but had a rather familiar French name, and when he gave his birthplace as Java, the police chief showed a great interest in geography and let him go, apologizing for the roughness of his officers (this was at a time when French politeness was not just a legend). My father went immediately to Mathilde, of course, and spent a great night with her, because, as he said, "Such a woman appreciates your standing up for her." A few days later, when a regiment of soldiers passed her in the street, Mathilde recognized a second lieutenant as the man who had insulted her. He still had an enormous black eye.

I never saw Mathilde's picture among those tintypes, but there were two other girl friends whose names were Blanche and Valentine. I didn't think they were pretty, just as I didn't think the pictures of the actresses my father covered our walls with were pretty. They came out of *Paris la nuit*, dating from the time when a woman still had to be one hundred percent female, complete with bust, hips, and hair and wearing brocade, buttons, bows, and lace. Perhaps in spite of myself I still think this type of woman is the most feminine, and I still prefer it to the boyish beauty that's in fashion now. But the specimens of beauty on our walls at home didn't do much for me; there were gigantic colored plates of Lina Cavalieri and La Belle Otéro, of Gilda Darthy and Cléo de Mérode. I assumed that these famous women were beauties just as I accepted that the romantic engravings of Goupil, which also filled our house, were rich, artistic, and beautiful. Those were our "paintings," as they said in the Indies; I still remember how later on I thought that people were rich and impressive when I saw a real painting in their house. I barely believed it was real and the only one in the whole world.

When my father went back to the Indies at twenty-two, it seemed he wanted to bring Paris with him and, to everybody's amusement and in spite of the broiling heat, he paid his first visits in morning coat and top hat, which, to make matters worse, were considered the privilege of the members of the Council of the Indies.[3] For a short time thereafter he worked at a sugar plantation in East Java, but his independent nature soon got him into trouble, so his mother, with whom he always quarreled though he remained her favorite, let him come back to Batavia and gave him the Villa Merah estate in the Buitenzorg area. Here he kept that European mistress, and he'd take his buggy or ride his horse all the way to Batavia so he could dance at the club.

Among his friends were many officers. Once, when his mistress was ill, he sent her to one of these men, an army doctor who had the Order of William. The doctor propositioned her, and in due course she told my father about it. When he was sitting on the terrace of the club with some other officers as well as the doctor, he told the story as if it had happened to one of his friends. He emphasized particularly the trust his friend had had in the doctor with the Order of William and then asked what they would think of such a person. The doctor was silent, but the other officers unanimously exploded with "the bastard," and similar remarks.

The doctor was pale and silent when he left and afterwards would not say hello to my father. One of the officers later complained about being put in such an embarrassing position with respect to the doctor. When my father asked whether he didn't think the man had been a bastard, the officer didn't deny it, but as a friend of the doctor he was annoyed to have said what he did to his face, so to speak.

Another friend of my father's was a well-known cavalry captain, Veersema, whose murder was one of the greatest scandals of Batavia and even served as the source of inspiration for dime-store novels such as *Hot Blooded* or *A Drama in the Tropics*. According to my Aunt Tina, the hot blood in this case was that of a rather sultry, lisping nymphomaniac from Koningsplein who was married to a Norwegian she had been cheating on long before the captain came along. After he left his club, the captain used to go to her house late at night—she didn't sleep in the same room as her husband but in a separate pavilion— and was received with chilled champagne. But he failed to tip the servants enough who stayed up for these rendez-vous, or perhaps the woman had forgotten herself once with the houseboy (an unbelievable shame for a European woman who lives on Koningsplein), which had brought his feelings into play. One evening when the Norwegian husband was drunk as usual and had fallen into his bed, he was awakened by a loud knock on the door, and there was the houseboy, who whispered in his ear, "Sir, get up, there's a thief in my lady's pavilion." The gardener and the houseboy, both armed with machetes, and the still half-drunk husband went to the pavilion. The captain jumped out of the window and ran to the square, pursued by the two servants. Since he was unarmed, they hit him with their machetes until he fell down, severely injured. The drunken husband tottered forward, lit a match, and only then recognized the thief as his friend from the club. "Is that you, Veersema?" he said sleepily. "For God's sake, finish me off, don't let me lie here like this," said the captain, who was lying in his blood with only his shirt on. But the husband retreated, and other people had to take the captain to the hospital. My father came over from Villa Merah to see his friend, but he had died that morning and the army doctor suggested that he shouldn't spoil his memory by looking at the disfigured corpse. The captain had been a cheerful, friendly man, thin and blond, with a pleasant smile. He was so loved by his men that the afternoon after his death a number of European soldiers and non-commissioned officers went to the house on Koningsplein. For half an hour they shouted in the street, "Where is that woman, where is that whore?" They insisted that the husband come out, then forced their way in but found the house empty. So they broke all the vases and the mirrors. What they really were looking for was "that woman," but my father had taken her away to Villa Merah in an *ebro* (an ordinary rented four-wheel carriage which goes slower and more solemnly than the more common two-wheeled *sado*), and the trip had taken several hours. He thoroughly disliked the woman, he said. During the trip she barely talked; what she did say was just as detached and cold as usual, though this was not because she had her emotions under control but simply because she was annoyed by the incident and was beginning to worry about her reputation. She stayed at his house for a week because she didn't dare go back to Koningsplein, and left for Europe as soon as possible. Her picture was in our album, but I could never learn enough about her to satisfy my curiosity. She was a blonde with rather thick lips and dark eyes. I continued to see something romantic in her despite my father's antipathy until my Aunt Tina dispelled the illusion by telling me about her lisping; in addition, she said she was very, very stupid.

My father was a great success with the women who lived on Koningsplein and elsewhere. My mother was convinced of that, and in Grouhy we sometimes talked about it, though on the other hand she couldn't understand what a woman could possibly see in me. She herself had enjoyed a great reputation for charm and amorous successes as a young woman and even later, so I killed two birds with one stone by saying it was impossible for me to understand this—that as a man I would never have been in love with my mother, and as a woman I would never have been in love with my father. We had this conversation one beautiful morning sitting in the shade of a tree in the garden, not because we wanted to hurt each other but from a need to confide in one another.

My mother's maiden name was Ramier de la Brulie. Her father was the youngest and most gifted of the family. He started new business ventures repeatedly, and repeatedly they failed. In Réunion he married a sickly woman who went everywhere with him and who bore him four children although she was only twenty-eight when she died. My mother was born in Malaya shortly before her parents went to Java, where other relatives on her father's side had preceded them. Her father died when she was two years old, and she was brought up in the home of a paternal aunt who had married a Dutchman. She had known her French grandfather, as well as her uncle with the white beard, who sometimes took her for a ride when she was a child. The grandfather made her and her cousins line up, put a finger on his tobacco box, and sing, "J'ai du bon tabac dans ma tabatière." My mother used to sing another song she had learned from him—"J'irai revoir ma Normandie"—and the last syllables had to be held very long, so that I associated it with bathing and cool bathrooms, because of the Dutch-Malay word *mandiën*.[4]

Later she was sent to a convent school, which at that time was the best education a girl could get in the Indies. She was never overly religious but she remained a Catholic, although her Catholicism was mixed with the most bizarre local superstitions. She learned to cook from a Chinese woman in a way and with a feeling I have never observed in any other European woman. In her youth she was also poetic, which means that she liked moonlight, flowers, music, and dancing. She also read French poetry, perhaps Lamartine, and she knew by heart the verse a young man had written in her poetry album. She sometimes recited them with pride and pleasure:

> Ne crains pas que le temps efface
> L'amitié que je ressens pour toi.[5]

It really was "l'amour," she said, but he didn't dare write that. It ended with the lament that one day everything would be erased—"tout, excepté le souvenir."[6]

She met her first husband at a ball in Priangan, I think. He was half Spanish, a gentleman just like my father and as good a dancer, but he had a bigger mustache. Even after she had been married to my father for some time, she kept his picture barely hidden in her closet. I sometimes got to see it: she is standing next to her first husband and has a Spanish comb in her hair, and you could see how big his mustache really was. For some reason or other—probably because he didn't make much money at the time, working as an assistant on a plantation —she was not allowed to marry him and was "exiled" to central Java, to her guardian, who was a resident commissioner there. This guardian was another swaggering male, and yet also a gentleman. He too had a French name: Barnabé. He was tall and heavy and had a mustache and a goatee of the kind Viala calls "la grande connerie française"[7] in the style of the Duke of Aumale. He also had proved his manliness several times by putting His Royal Highness the Susuhunan of Solo in his place.[8] He achieved this by subtle touches, by placing the *pajung*[9] of the resident commissioner higher than the sultan's or by ignoring the salutations of the other, who, according to protocol, was supposed to initiate them. My mother had at least as much admiration for her guardian Barnabé as my father had for his Uncle Marees, and life in his house must have appealed to her need for respectability.

Barnabé was married to a much older cousin of my mother's, also a Ramier, and because her parents had objected to her marriage too, they had eloped, although it was all above board, and they were always chaperoned. This had happened more than ten years before, but it wasn't enough to make him the right person to convince my mother of the foolishness of her love. I knew his wife, my Aunt Luce, very well. She was the "little marchioness" of the family, very fragile and delicate with a marvelous complexion and jet black hair and eyes. When she talked about her deceased husband she always said, "that poor *grosmari* of mine."[10] In Bandung, when I was about fifteen, I would read to her for nights on end, serial novels mostly, like those of Dumas Père. She was an old woman then and had to have one stomach operation after another. She lived with a younger sister, who was overly religious and went to church constantly and checked to see if I went too. She was never as pretty as Aunt Luce, but the prettiest of them all was yet another sister who had died young. She had been even more beautiful than a sister-in-law who was called the Yellow Rose of Surabaya because she had native blood, something the older members of the family had never forgiven her. Those Frenchmen in Java, even if they came from Réunion, had a stubborn desire to keep their race pure, which of course turned out to be impossible. Aunt Luce's mother allowed all her grandchildren to embrace her except for the little son of the Yellow Rose, who was only allowed to kiss her hand. The aunt in whose house my mother was brought up had married a Dutchman and she shared the same prejudices about skin color herself, but she paid for them dearly. When she was sixty she said to her unmarried youngest daughter, "Well, my child, now I've been through almost everything. Your brother married a Negress; your sister married a Eurasian; now if you go and marry a Chinese, the collection will be complete."

When it was clear that my mother's "exile" hadn't done any good, she was allowed to return to West Java and marry the man of her choice. She was then nineteen years old. First they lived the life of a married assistant on a plantation, which meant seeing the manager socially from time to time, occasionally going to a party in Sukabumi, and taking many walks on the plantation. But her husband's career rose quickly. He became a manager himself and later on was one of the richest of West Java. In the years when he was first a manager, my mother went through the most delicate romance of her life. Two young Frenchmen who were on a research trip through the Dutch colonies arrived on her husband's tea plantation, where they were received with great joy. One of these young men, although a little effeminate and overweight, was an authentic marquis by the name of Daniel de Méré. Once he had arrived at the tea plantation he didn't leave. His traveling companion had to tour the rest of the islands by himself. "Tout ce que j'aurai vu aux Indes," he said later, "ce sont les yeux de Madeline."[11] My mother's name was Madeline, not Madeleine, she would emphasize, and Daniel de Méré had a particularly lovable manner not only of appreciating this name but also of pronouncing it almost as "Mèdeline." He admired my mother from afar as well as up close when she walked in the garden wearing a *sarong* and *kabaya* with her hair down. He said openly that he was madly in love with her but remained so respectful that even her mustached husband was very attached to him and allowed him to stay there for months. Finally he left for France without a single confrontation occurring. He wrote long letters from Paris to both of them, and his mother, who had heard so many wonderful things about Madeline, wrote her also. The mother too acted as if there was absolutely nothing to hide and later, when Daniel had stopped writing, she continued to do so just to inform them how he was doing. For years he wouldn't hear of any other woman, but he finally married, mostly to make his mother happy. His wife was an American heiress who provided for him in the style he seemed to be born for. Years later his mother wrote, "Daniel *commence* seulment à aimer un peu sa femme."[12] I'm trying here to give the same accent to this sentence that my mother did whenever she would say this. About then the correspondence stopped for good.

What I would have given to read the letters of the Marquise de Méré! But even more, perhaps, the letters my mother wrote to her. They must have been generously sprinkled with what my mother called "poetry." The possibility of her being unfaithful to her husband, even with such a nice man who was an authentic marquis, didn't occur to my mother. She was very happy with her husband, particularly in that early period when he was still far from rich. She bore him a son, Otto, my half-brother, older than me by twelve years, and everything went well until her husband's half-Spanish temperament started to play tricks on him and he began to cheat on her.

At that time there were quite a few parties in Sukabumi and horse races in Buitenzorg. My mother would go to them, wearing an orange and black dress "nobody else would dare wear." She also played the role of Cleopatra in a tableau vivant taken right out of Couperus's novel *Eline Vere*,[13] which everybody was excited about, although some men whispered, "Cleopatra is a little too short." As for my father, he excelled at the races. He raced a horse for the Kühne family from Buitenzorg, Thistle, considered too old, against Lonely, a marvelous sorrel belonging to the Halls, a British family; and after he had been behind for about one and a half laps, he beat that wonderful sorrel so soundly that Mrs. Hall sobbed in her box. My father was almost killed by the people who wanted to carry him around in triumph. They all thought that the older horse wouldn't have had a chance if the little "Duc" had ridden the sorrel. Then he met my mother. He had met her before but had found her pretentious and a bit fat. Now she had slimmed down a little and fitted his conception of the ideal woman perfectly. He courted her and, since she couldn't tolerate being cheated on, he took her away from her husband and she became his wife. To do so, he had to break a secret engagement with an extremely wealthy girl of mixed blood he had wanted to marry because of her money. It was because of her he had sent his European mistress, the horsewoman, away. The mistress had cried in despair and his tears had flowed too, because in a way he did love her. But this time he had found real love. He had said that he wouldn't marry before he was thirty-five and he had kept his word, but his intentions of marrying a rich woman, which he had energetically pursued and almost succeeded in, were now hopelessly lost. It was his fiancée's turn to cry now. She made the trip to his isolated villa in the middle of the night to compromise either herself or him. She crawled on her knees around the room, but he remained firm and didn't even cry this time. Life copied a bad novel in almost every detail.

My parents married for love, although my mother was also past thirty. During the eleven years she was married to her first husband, all his friends knew that they could flirt with her but that was it. Here fate and my father's charms worked together, and even the strongest argument, my half-brother Otto, was not enough. His father sent Otto to Holland to be educated. I was born in Gedong Lami, which my father had inherited in the meantime. Were my father and mother lovers before they married? I never asked her and I don't know if she would have answered truthfully, but I remember the wisdom *he* proffered in my presence about not being jealous: whatever happened before you came along shouldn't concern you, and so on. It is with curious self-assurance that the tolerant bourgeois puts himself up as a criterion: the past is *dead*, from then on *I* was there. I would be inclined to consider this attitude characteristic of a strong personality, if I weren't sure these victories over the past are actually very easy for those who have blissfully little imagination.

In a short time my father became known as a landowner in Meester-Cornelis also. On the road to Buitenzorg, at Villa Merah, he repeatedly made his presence felt. I don't know whether forced labor—the cause of so many "Russian conditions"—had been abolished by then, but the landowners who lived in isolated places or who had enough character to stand up to the "ethically" oriented government officials still lived like kings. Multatuli's influence was only beginning to be felt.[14] My father was a landowner who spoke with contempt about "the ethical mess." He divided government officials into two groups: capable and incapable. The former were those who saw the necessity of the independent and arbitrary action on the part of the private owners, while the others were arrogant bureaucrats who thought they were superior to the private-*sadja*[15] because they had a gold braid around their cap. It was hard for the landowner to maintain his authority, since the police couldn't always get there before he was robbed or murdered. At the time groups of bandits regularly attacked the private estates between Buitenzorg and Meester-Cornelis.

My father had to deal with rebellion at Villa Merah right from the start. The people on his estate refused to pay the rent for their small stores. He booted them out and shut the stores down—"shacks," he called them. The same afternoon he was warned by his *djuragan* that the people were opening them up again. My father sent somebody to inform the closest *demang* but knew that he wouldn't get there for a few hours. He took the *djuragan* with him to meet the restless natives. They arrived at the shacks at about the same time, my father and his overseer from one side, the natives from the other. The leaders started to shout. My father took a pistol out of his pocket, stood in the middle of the road in front of the shacks, and made it clear that he would shoot the first person who made a move forward. The crowd murmured, hesitated, mulled around, and finally withdrew. When the *demang* finally arrived, it was almost night and he could content himself with just lecturing them.

It was maybe twenty years later when I was walking with my father in Bandung that we were hailed by a *warung* keeper—or rather, since his store was so nice, a *toko* keeper. He nearly threw himself at my father's feet and asked if he were not *Tuan Dikruk*. This name, which came from his earlier landowner days, pleased my father. He accepted the man's invitation to visit his store and drink his bock beer. His name was Sarib. He used to be a tenant at Villa Merah but now, after working hard, he had become a wealthy man. This brought up the episode of the shacks, which I had never heard before. Sarib had been one of the malcontents. I stopped by his store a couple of times when I had to wait for the train to Tjitjalengka at a nearby station. He always talked to me about my father with respect but also with some of the old fear, a fear he seemed to have overcome now. I remember one sentence: "Kalu tuan Dikruk sudah plintis kumis, kita semua gemeter" ("If Mr. Ducroo just twirled his mustache, we all trembled").

In between Villa Merah and Gedong Lami my father managed an estate that belonged to a Chinese. He had sold Villa Merah and rented this estate, though it was known to be unsafe. His predecessor, the Chinese, closed all doors and windows at six o'clock in the evening and let nobody in after that, no matter who knocked on the door. My father was warned that one of the *djuragans* had connections with the bandits. He lined up the tenants of the Chinese for a roll call to get to know them better. He came to the name of Ali Biman, a stocky Malay, who got up from his crouching position, walked over, and stood very close to my father, who was still sitting with the roll at his desk. The man stretched, looked down at him, and said with the contemptuous voice of a Javanese who feels he has the advantage, emphasizing each word, "I am Ali Biman." My father realized this was the *djuragan* he had heard about and jumped up immediately. Standing only an inch away from him, he almost spat in the man's face as he told him, "And I am *Tuan Dikruk* and we must get to know one another very well, Ali Biman, because I know you and you don't know me yet. So look at me closely and remember that I can crush you like a louse whenever I want to." Speaking Malay, in which the metaphor sounds less dramatic than in translation, he had found the right tone. Ali Biman began to blink, lowered his head, went to his place, and crouched again.

Later, it turned out that he really was involved in robberies. My father told him in advance that he would hold him responsible for every robbery that occurred on his estate. "I'm not a policeman and I have nothing to do with other estates, but if something happens here I know where to find you, Ali Biman." Nothing happened, but one day Ali Biman himself disappeared. My father asked around and learned that somebody had tried to tunnel into an Arab's house. The Arab woke up and saw a hand sticking through the bamboo wall. He drove his spear through the hand, but the intruder was able to pull his hand back through the wall, tearing it between two fingers. A few months later Ali Biman came back to my father with his right hand bandaged. He had been called away, he said, because of a death in his family, and had decided to stay there to help with the rice harvest.

"And what happened to your hand?"

"I cut it with my pruning knife when I was weeding."

"And since when do you hold your pruning knife in your left hand?"

Ali Biman smiled. My father told him once more that he was not a policeman but that he expected him to see to it there were no robberies on the estate.

As soon as my father had arrived, he left the doors and windows open at night and sat down on the front porch to read. They warned him not to do this because of "bad people." "Well, people I'm not afraid of, only tigers and snakes." Sometimes he saw shadows in the garden and would fire a warning shot with his pistol. He also bought a couple of dogs that roamed the estate and sometimes ate the tenants' chickens because they were not fed very well. Once in a while a dog was poisoned, so my father announced that for every poisoned dog he would buy two in its place. These were mongrels and very cheap. When at last he had twenty-four dogs, the poisoning stopped.

Another incident occurred with a rebellious *hadji* called Miing. That was in Gedong Lami shortly after my birth. *Hadji* Miing didn't want to work or pay his rent. My father, who had to choose between the two, finally insisted that the man go to work for *his own* pleasure. The other natives made fun of *Hadji* Miing for this. When my father came to take a look at his work and made some critical comments—and my father certainly must have taunted him—*Hadji* Miing looked at him angrily and suddenly attacked him with his pruning knife. Being unarmed,

my father rushed into the house, and *Hadji* Miing thought for a moment that he had tamed him. But my father came back with a sword
stick and yelled at him from a distance, "I believe this thing is longer
than your pruning knife, but you can try again." *Hadji* Miing fled to the
mosque, where he was safe, but finally he got hungry and had to go
back to work. For days my father enjoyed watching him toil in the sun,
sweat running down his face below his turban and his hands rubbed
raw.

I'm not entirely sure that in writing this down my tone doesn't belie
some sort of hero worship, which as a child, of course, I must have had
for my father. The only excuse my father had was that he had chosen
sides once and for all; he was irrevocably one of the landowners. He
was born in the Indies and had always known the Javanese as subser-
vient beings. He was convinced he was right and that his method was
the only way of getting along with them, "Or else they will laugh at you,
and if you give them a chance they will spit in your face." From a purely practical point of view he was probably right. The people from
around Batavia and Buitenzorg, in any case, feared him, but they also
respected him because he paid them fairly and they were impressed
by bravado, even from a European. But this method didn't work at all
when he went to the Sunda region. The Sundanese did not resist one
bit; they hated him and simply ran away. He must have been powerless, because he got nothing done. It infuriated him, and it was up to
my mother—who spoke fluent Sundanese because she had lived in
Priangan for a long time with her first husband—to patch up whatever
trouble he had caused. In the Sunda region my mother took control
and my father was reduced to a brutal and useless figure.

I want to tell one more story, because it also typifies the struggle between the landowners and the government officials at the time. After
my mother divorced her first husband and was "engaged" to my father, she lived with a sister of hers whose husband was the assistant
commissioner of Meester-Cornelis and as such was supposed to restrain my father. Although they were soon going to be brothers-in-law
and my father came to dinner three times a week, they couldn't stand
each other. The assistant commissioner, Fredius, was at least as much
of an autocrat as my father and protected a *demang* who, according to
my father's informants, was in collusion with the bandits and got a big
share of their loot. One night they had a terrible fight before they had

gotten past the first course of the dinner. The assistant commissioner said emphatically, "Not one of those landowners has any manners."

"Thanks a lot," my father said, "but among the government officials there are some who are just as rude—you, for example, since you insult a guest at your own table."

The assistant commissioner threw his napkin down, left his soup, and stormed out of the room. His wife ran after him to calm him down. My father stayed at the table with my mother and didn't get up until the dinner was finished.

It turned out he was right. The *demang* was caught and sent to prison for setting up robberies and fencing stolen goods. My father wrote a few articles about this and about some other disputes, which were used as editorials in the *Bataviaasch Nieuwsblad*.[16] By that time he had married my mother and didn't set foot in the house of his brother-in-law, who was transferred not long after. The newspaper reported that Assistant Commissioner Fredius of Meester-Cornelis was leaving because he was promoted to commissioner of Besuki and wanted to thank everyone for their congratulations. My father went to his friend at the newspaper and had the following words printed underneath the announcement: "Oh poor Besuki now besought." Such puns were highly prized in clubs in the Indies.

My father's wit—supposedly he was very witty—was based entirely on word plays like this, which would now fall flat but were the rage in Paris when he was a student. He was popular with the officers and landowners, who knew him superficially, but from my earliest recollections he was only cheerful when we had company or were visiting other people. Personally, I was so afraid of him that I only began to talk to him when I was seventeen.

Maybe this is not completely true. As a child I used to sit on his lap every evening and play with his watch chain. But it's still the feeling I have when I think of those days; there was a time when I'd run away whenever I heard his voice. That was roughly between my eighth and tenth year, after he had beaten me several times in a fit of anger though I was probably no more than a scapegoat. My relationship with my mother would probably have been completely different if there hadn't been that persistent fear of my father. I can still feel my helplessness in his presence when I think of the intensity with which, after having been scolded, I whispered all the profanities I knew: bastard, pig, crook, scoundrel, bum, wretch, idiot, bully, skunk, fool, swine. I learned all these words from him, except "fool," which stood out like a rose. Sometimes my mother heard me and, while shaking her head, would say, "You shouldn't call your father that." But she knew just as well as I did how pitiful this hatred was.

6 Mostly Viala

April. Now that I have finished my work in the library and Viala has no use for me, I'm slowly forgetting Paris, and Meudon is taking over. Jane's love for the barren snow-covered trees can no longer be satisfied. It's as if spring suddenly snuck up on us. Right after the last snow there were two hot, clear days. Jane is working with the doors and windows open. I now enjoy making my daily trip to the post office, and I walk slowly.

The day before yesterday, in the afternoon, we went looking for things that in the fall had reminded me of the Indies: white free-standing buildings, a certain perspective of an overgrown fence, a wall with a small, old door in it, the whole building itself. But looking from the end of a street, around, or through the trees, it's hard for me to explain to her what it is in some landscapes, houses, or roads that makes me stop and say, "The Indies." It probably depends a lot on the light. Curiously enough, the houses that in autumn reminded me of estates in the Indies have lost all resemblance in this bright light; it took this light for the difference to show up. I no longer saw the building standing by itself in a garden but noted the character of its architecture, which was stark and real, compared to what it was for me just a while ago. A little down the road a small old-fashioned hotel, however, would fit the illusion, just like a Swiss pension near Cassarate or some houses in Hilversum where you can see the wicker chairs from the street. There are wicker chairs here too on a narrow veranda with two ugly columns in the center that are unnecessary and therefore "like the Indies." We had coffee there, the first in the area that was drinkable. There was a terrace and a huge garden hidden behind it, without any leaves yet but which must be delightful in summer. And it had a wonderful name: La Feuilleraie.

Yesterday was another beautiful day. I went to the post office by way of the very narow alley that comes out on the main street right next to the post office and is called "Sentier des Balysis." This reminds me of the Indies as much as anything—a back alley, one of the small alleys where the poorer Eurasians live with an occasional Javanese among them. On the left there is a wall, on the right hedges—*paggers*—above them roofs with ivy hanging down along the columns. There are old-fashioned windows with venetian blinds, just like back in the Indies, a Moorish lantern even, with copper points and colored glass like the one my father brought home once from an auction. When I stretched out both arms, my hands were only inches from the wall and the hedge. I stood still a couple of seconds in the alley and looked at my shadow stretching out directly in front of me. It was one of those moments when you are aware of your own presence, when you pull yourself free from your inner self and try to make the individual, the person, fit in the setting. A couple of times in Brussels, when I was walking across a square that had nothing to do with me, I found myself thinking, "Why am I walking here, in Brussels instead of Bandung?" But it was different yesterday. A slow, more growing awareness, a little bit more intentional also, just like when you're frightened and you don't pant but force yourself to take long deep breaths, fighting the rhythm of your frightened heart.

I walked back slowly from the post office. At the square and near the church, everything that reminded me of the Indies was gone. There was nothing left but the quiet of a French village. I had *Henri Brulard*[1] with me, and I reread the beginning, this time focusing not on the similarities but on the differences between Brulard and me. Anyone who likes Brulard—and you don't read him very long if you don't—identifies with him. I imagined his walking in the sunlight and looking at his shadow just as I did when I went back home, past the little church, with my rather tall felt hat and my unbuttoned overcoat, and I imagined that the exaggerated proportions which are assumed by such a compressed or elongated shape could have made my shadow look like his. But the differences are even greater: his dandyism, his love for the "world," his desire, even in his early days, to live with an actress, his craving for a medal, which he never completely overcame. And I could not write like that, so delightfully unconcerned, so indifferent to repetition, apologizing for his use of the first person but in reality not worrying for a moment about what might be important to anyone else (I can't think of a more arrogant word than "important" in certain circumstances), so bemused by his own record keeping, sometimes half in code.

I came home with the intention of immediately writing down the history of my own life, but in vain. Suddenly I was overcome by exhaustion and was powerless to see anything but the present. The vexation was aggravated by a report I had to do for the newspaper. Four times I had to force myself back to my desk to finish it, no matter what.

Viala does his best to hide from us the fact that he doesn't really need us for the book we are doing together. It is an anthology of poetry by doctors and pharmacists for a limited clientele. At the moment he is working all by himself on the short scholarly biographies that are necessary, and he is working hard because he knows how much we need the money. I used to be able to help him at times when I was what they call rich and he made a living just as he does now. His last publication was a success. He expects less from this one but still enough to live on for a couple of months, and for our minimal work he wants to give us half the profit.

With the exception of Wijdenes, who bought some of my books, Viala is the only one of my friends who has helped me in my present predicament with more than just encouragement and advice. Graaflant's is the most generous friendship one could ask for. I'm always welcome in his house and his concern is sincere. We have become so close over the years that he acts immediately on his intentions whenever I am concerned. I wouldn't feel there was any difference between his support and that of Viala if I didn't have to take into account the practical results—the practical point of view which I still have to *learn* to accept is one of the base qualities my new existence has forced on me. Graaflant looks tired and sick. His blood pressure is too high, and when I don't hear from him for a while I worry that he might be seriously ill —another characteristic of my present situation—while it might be nothing more than his finally deciding to follow through on the idea he has expressed ten times over, that is, to save a little money on stamps.

Now that two or three others have left, Viala is my oldest friend in Europe—a strange realization. For years he was much more than a friend to me: he was a person whose integrity served repeatedly as a point of reference, a guide. But I'm a little uncomfortable when I visit him these days, for him as well as for myself, and I wonder if he takes into account how I feel about his contribution to my life, or about our present relationship.

But there are other areas where I seem to be playing a role too. I'm more of a settled bourgeois, much less cynical or even rebellious than I appear when I talk to him. It's an old game we've been playing for ten years. I talk the way I think he wants me to talk to him, to the Viala I once knew. But during these ten years, life has demonstrated over and over again that he couldn't possibly be that person. Perhaps it's partly due to my admiration for the old Viala that he devotes such energy and optimism to our interests. He took charge, became the leader of this enterprise, which could fail just as easily as anything else these days. The loss from such a failure would be too much for him to handle too. He's doing it not because he has to (he could have waited for a more opportune time), or because he feels that he has to pay me back, but because he, like me perhaps, is not completely free of the roles we used to act out for each other. I was a nice, wealthy young man then, while he was someone thrown into life too early. He was disillusioned in advance, but that didn't keep him from energetically searching out loopholes in all the laws society inflicts on the average citizen. No doubt, he was a sincere anarchist then, and one I idealized completely.

There is a positive pride in Viala's saying "no" to life, however disillusioned or passive he may appear. His revolt is somewhat masochistic when, for instance, he makes himself sick on purpose by taking on a number of disagreeable tasks which he really could avoid. If anyone suffers from conflicting emotions, it's Viala; he wants neither to be bitter nor to show his extreme sensitivity. His violent, embittered outbursts against society don't mesh with the resignation he assumes at other times, and everything he does is done with sensitivity, no matter who is involved. Perhaps the reason he talks so little about himself is that in this manner he can avoid explaining these conflicts or even having to recognize them. For a couple of years he has purposely avoided everything intellectual. Why go over the fact, again and again, almost with relish, that life is a mess? It has been obvious to him for a long time. "No matter what you accomplish," says Héverlé, "Viala will still think it is senseless. For you intelligence is a necessity; for him it isn't anymore."

While Viala emotionally still ranks Héverlé as one of the greatest human beings he has ever known, he has withdrawn somewhat from him, probably because of Héverlé's fundamental intellectualism.

I avoid topics with Viala that appear intellectual as much as possible or, rather, I disguise them, talk casually about them, as if I don't really take them seriously. The few times he responds I realize that his mind is just as sharp as ever. He must really be tired of the game, that's all—I can sometimes clearly imagine the moment when I myself will be tired of it. More and more he judges people exclusively for their human value, for moral qualities that are ignored as such only by those who have retained a childish fear of the word morality.

I admitted to Guraev the first time we met at the Héverlés that I was making moral judgments again, based on a certain dignity, because all relationships with friends are based on dignity. I was thinking particularly of Viala. Then Guraev quoted some philosopher who used to say, "the dignity of my ass."

"That's a powerful argument for ladies who go to church on Sunday," said Héverlé, "but for us you'll probably have to find something stronger. Ducroo is right, although he probably doesn't know what that dignity is either. But we all are well aware of what the opposite is, what is unworthy, what is cowardly, and what is base."

Guraev nodded his head in agreement but didn't stop smiling. When a little while ago I wrote down the word "noble" in connection with Viala, I was actually quoting Héverlé again: "Viala est essentielle-ment noble,"[2] which he likes to say in the casual tone with which one states the obvious.

When we spend an evening with Viala in a restaurant and then in a café, our group is split in two: he and I on one side, Jane and Manou on the other. He appears convinced that you always talk on a lower intellectual level with a woman. Maybe he places all women on the same level as Manou. Or maybe he doesn't want to leave himself open to the control her instinctive intelligence might have over him: "You always say this . . . but tonight you did that."

At first I though that there would be a better rapport between him and Jane. Now I'm resigned to the fact that this will never happen. Jane is the last person to draw somebody out by anything more than her ability to listen or an occasional gentle suggestion. Viala sticks to his conviction or his ideas. I'm sure, though, that he likes Jane, that he counts her almost completely among the friends to whom he is devoted, even though she is a woman and he hasn't known her very long.

Everybody thinks that Viala has changed since he got married. He didn't hesitate for a moment in assuming the extra burden of supporting a wife, although he barely had enough for himself. If it's true that such circumstances can change a person, then no other explanation is necessary. A stroke of luck sometimes allows them to go on a short trip; at other times they can't even find the money to pay the rent. "But all these problems will ultimately take care of themselves," he comforts me.

There's nothing more lovable than Manou's radiant yet fragile face, her slightly pouting mouth, and her downcast eyes below the soft curl on her forehead, when she concentrates with great seriousness in the library, trying to keep up with us in copying. She forms her small letters slowly and carefullly, working sometimes for months on end, for example, during the period that Viala's only source of income was the editing of some seventeenth-century text. He must love her both as a devoted comrade-in-arms and as a playmate. Besides being a woman, she must fulfill all the childish instincts which remain alive in him. Consequently, even when things are at their worst, he can sometimes laugh heartily and be truly cheerful for hours.

All this seems painfully incomplete to me. But it would be still more painful if I tried to fill the holes artificially, to give the well-rounded picture I would like. It's as if I would have to write things about Viala— things I would have discovered through analysis—which I have as little right to do as to repeat someone's secrets after I had encouraged him to confide in me.

I would rather try to examine the basis of the feeling of complete brotherhood I have with Viala, a feeling that is stronger than with almost anyone else, no matter how much or how little of real importance is said. This is due not only to how long we have been friends. There is something which has remained real in spite of the role I sometimes think I'm playing. I could never tell Viala that I am bourgeois. He would refuse to believe me and insist that I have much more of the anarchist in me. His thinking I'm an anarchist is as far-fetched as his belief that Héverlé is an adventurer, a revolutionary, a politician if need be—anything but a writer. But what he is right about is essential. When all posturing is set aside, even "self-criticism," then Viala's denial of what he likes best about his friends is equally false.

"Why," I say, using a diversionary tactic, "are there people who want to impose the image of an adventurer upon Héverlé, people who almost resent him for not being six feet tall and having the face of an animal and hairy hands? It's as if being a talented writer were really humiliating. As a writer he probably does more for the revolution than he would as a man of action, which would turn him into something disgusting like a professional politician. Do you realize that in reality a politician is a whole lot worse than a writer? And nowadays adventurers and homosexuals are considered fashionable by people who are connected with art in any way at all."

"The last straw for me," says Viala, "is that talent emasculates you before you realize it. If your books are so great that the enemy admires them or awards them prizes, then it's over: then you have become part of respectable literature and you contribute only to the higher glory of national art. I have no more respect for politics than you do, but human dignity requires resistance on various levels which also come under the heading of 'politics,' if you like. I have never been a member of any party, because I hate all the leaders in this country, including the Communists. But if you're honest you'll concede that those poor devils are also doomed if they can only think in terms of their organization, when they become officials of the government. Try as they will, they can only give what they have! Circumstances are to blame that after a couple of years of politics they turn into this, and you can't even say they're waiting for circumstances to change before they'll change themselves. But this doesn't bother me, really. I have never had any illusions about leaders and I have as little taste for reading about the dignity, the task, the essence, or whatever, of the proletariat. My response to whatever I'm told about it, no matter how well put, is that nothing is as valuable as my own feeling of being a proletarian, of always having been one, with all the squalor that was attached to it, since I was a child. The only proletarians for whom I have any real feeling are the people who pay with their whole rotten existence without ever being able to understand why. The kind of people who will never be able to produce art and who take damn little comfort in the art of somebody else who shows how well he understands their fate. Nobody will ever give me back even the slightest bit of my youth which was so completely wrecked."

"It's a disease without a cure, because if you look at it carefully," Héverlé explains, "it's all based on a misunderstanding between Viala and God."

7 The Child Ducroo

The story of my childhood begins with some facts I've learned from older people. The first document is a yellowed copy of the *Bataviaasch Nieuwsblad* with the announcement of my birth. On the front page there's an article on the war: "The Boers calmly continue their siege of Ladysmith, encircling it more and more closely."

I came into the world on All Souls' Day, 1899, on a Thursday, at quarter to two in the afternoon. My mother had had a difficult delivery with my half-brother Otto, twelve years before. She was now much older and, concerned about her health, the doctor had "kept me small," which means that he had put my mother on a special diet to carefully check the growth of the bones in my unborn body. I don't think this method is used much anymore, but in my case the desired result was apparently achieved. I weighed about six pounds when I arrived. It should be considered a miracle that I grew taller than either of my parents. My nose, however, was unusually big, probably because it had more flesh than bones. It scared my father, who asked the doctor if it would go away, and wondered where it came from.

I was born in the *kamar pandjang* in Gedong Lami, in the main pavilion on the river side. My mother had a difficult delivery and had to recuperate for a long time. She believed that the only way she had kept herself alive was by drinking red wine with ice. The doctor was a "sweet" man; his name was Wittenrood, which the nurse always pronounced as *wit en rood* ("white and red"). My mother had no milk for me, and neither canned milk, fresh milk, nor cream of wheat agreed with me. After two days they thought I was going to die. My father sent messengers all over his estate to look for a woman to be my wet nurse, but nobody came forward. Perhaps they were afraid of him and his house, or maybe they wanted to get even with him. Two or three young mothers were forced to appear, but they looked so dirty and unwilling that my parents thought it in my best interest not to insist. Finally, when I was very pale and emaciated and my parents were looking mournfully at me, Niah appeared, a woman from the village of Kebon

Dalem, with my suckling sister Tjemplo at her breast. She was, according to my mother, "a giggling woman with wonderful milk." My memory of her comes from later experiences and from a picture. She had a good-natured but bovine face with sleepy eyes and a protruding mouth. My suckling sister was the spitting image of her mother. When I saw her later—she was about eight—she was fawningly polite to me. When I was four months old my faithful Alima arrived.

When I was eighteen months old, my parents were in Sukabumi with me, and I almost died there from a sudden and violent fever. This was during the eruption of Mount Kelud. All day long ash rained down on the city. My parents stayed at the house of the *patih*, whose wife was a good friend of my mother. They saw that I was about to die and thought there was nothing to be done. According to the doctor, it was meningitis. When they thought I was lost, my mother and the *patih*'s wife gave me an enema. In a few hours the fever was gone, and when the doctor came back that same evening I laughed cheerfully at him. He insisted on the silly explanation that a miracle had taken place. There's something about my narrative here which somehow rings false. It's false as a recollection, for what my mother told me about it is connected to another disease story. When we were in Sukabumi, a doctor with a blond goatee, by the name of De Haan ("Rooster")—the name alone impressed me—made me drink a laxative which tasted good but had an awful aftertaste. I threw it up before it had time to take effect. I had a splitting headache, many Sundanese women bustled in and out, and this time my mother disagreed completely with the doctor and confronted him when he returned. But that was four years later, in 1905, when we were about to go to Sand Bay.

If I can say "I" at this point, I couldn't do so earlier, because I could not have known that consciously. If an adult says "I" about himself as a child, it always sounds somewhat false, and if for technical reasons it didn't come down to another falsification, I would prefer to continue for a couple of chapters—until my sixteenth year, for instance—to talk about little Ducroo in the third person. That would take away from the personal character of my memories, but it would certainly not be incorrect for the relationship between my present self and the child that has long disappeared. Early autobiographical writing in the first person, however pure in tone (at least, pure to adults), is always faulty. Therefore it is better to use the simplest form.

What were my first impressions, or what did I register later on as

such? The open door of a dark room leading to the *kamar pandjang*.
Light was visible on the other side, and I was carried back and forth in
the dark of that connecting room, past the open door with the light.
Alima carried me. She was small and slim, and I felt the contrast with
the fuller figure of my mother, who apparently had carried me just before. While I tried to sleep against her breast in a *slendang*, she sang
"Dung-indung, Si Toetoet bobo . . . ," a slight variation in words and
tune of the famous "Nina bobo." "Little Toetoet is asleep," that apparently was my nickname already. And she was Ma Lima, the last "a"
pronounced as a soft "e" as they do in Batavia, drawing it out almost
impertinently. Ma Lima also occurred in another song:

> Burung Kakatua
> Mèntjlok di djendéla
> Ma Lima sudah tua
> Giginja tinggal dua.
>
> The bird Kakatu
> sits down on the window sill.
> Ma Lima is old,
> she has only two teeth left.

And then another one, which we sang mostly in Tjitjurug and which
was even sadder:

> Ular kili, ular kumbang
> Kumbangnja djamur
> Ma Lima gedé utang
> Ditagih, mabur.
>
> Two types of snakes,
> The spots of one are like a fungus.
> Ma Lima has big debts
> When they come to collect them, she'll leave.

I wouldn't want to leave out these two songs. They're the most touching ones of my childhood. The fact that Ma Lima figured in both of
them, and in such a funny role, didn't make me laugh at all. In reality
these songs were sad and melancholy, like songs you sing when you
leave someone.

A couple of times in Tjitjurug, when I was about four, there was the
threat that Alima might leave. Her husband came to see her from Ba-

tavia and insisted she go back with him. His name was Djimbar, and he had a serious face and a gray mustache. He was not an ordinary native, like a houseboy, but something like like an overseer. He carried a stick when he walked, and my mother always treated him with respect. He always brought me some present, so I liked to see him and I respected him, yet I didn't trust him, because there was always the possibility that he would take my Ma Lima away.

One evening in Tjitjurug it came to a head. Alima was in tears, and Djimbar left angry. She had decided once and for all in my favor. My mother supposedly said to her, "You're not going to leave little Toe-toet, now are you, Alima?" to which the maid, who was already old then, answered, "No ma'am, don't worry." That same evening she cried, but she sent away her dignified husband. Years later, when she got word of his death, she cried again. Her daughter Djasima came to ask for some money for the funeral. Alima gave it to her and talked to her with a kind of reverence which I had never heard from her before, but she didn't go to the funeral.

I have a picture of Alima and me together, maybe a year before her death, and I'm already a little taller than she is. Later on my mother had a picture of her enlarged from a time before I consciously knew her. The enlargement was bad, but according to my mother it was nevertheless a true likeness of her, when she had just started to work for us. "You must never throw this picture away. This poor woman left her husband and her family for you."

If I think back now it seems to me that this notion of "leaving" is somewhat simplistically stated. If I recall correctly, Djimbar took a young woman for a second wife. Be that as it may, this picture was never able to replace the image my memory preserved, although I might be seeing her as she was when I was about thirteen years old.

Sometimes memory itself throws off the chronology by putting things further back in time. For instance, I may have moved two of my toys back to that "earliest period." One was a little mechanical toy with dogs in brightly colored coats that climbed a green pole; the other was a harlequin that I found next to my bed one morning, right after I had learned about the nightly visits of Saint Nicholas. It would squeak when Alima pressed its belly. But certainly these two details belong to Gedong Lami.

A picture of myself and a swan may go back even further than that. I'm standing in my pajamas with my bare feet firmly planted wide apart, with big, black eyes and a serious little mouth, not at all afraid of the swan—it wasn't a real swan, anyway—and I look like a sweet but also sturdy little fellow, very much the son of "Tuan Dikruk," whom I resemble more in this picture than in any other.

What a spoiled child I must have been by that time! Whenever I started crying even a little bit, my mother would come running as if a disaster had happened. Throughout my youth I heard my mother scold the servants, especially the cook Sipa, in her kitchen. When she was angry her voice became high and shrill, which would make my father say, "That falsetto, I hear that falsetto again." But whether or not it annoyed him, he came to the rescue of his *njonja* whenever necessary, and as soon as he arrived on the scene the last bit of resistance of the poor servants was squashed.

But one day when my parents were sitting together and I was whining for my mother, he came to my bed instead (I have no conscious recollection of this, but I assume it marks the beginning of my fear of him) and gave me a couple of slaps which were much too hard for a baby. Moreover, he might have smothered both me and my crying with a pillow, if my mother hadn't stopped him. Alima was terribly upset. This treatment surprised me so much that later on I remembered it as a rough game in which I was used as the ball. I vaguely remember that afterwards, mostly to impress my father, my mother and Alima made a big fuss treating the red splotches he had caused, with a cooling mixture of *bedak* and *genever*.

On other occasions, when Alima and I quarreled, for instance, my mother would come and blame one of us almost in turn, as if to keep a necessary balance or good relationship. I didn't understand it when it was my turn to be blamed. Several times I had to apologize to Alima, but I always knew she would be scolded later. It still seems highly improbable that my mother would ever think a servant could possibly be right.

Old Alima was my indispensable guardian angel, yet my position as a gentleman's son seemed to require that I also have a European nurse, who was called "Miss." I had seven of them before my ninth birthday. Only one, Bertha Hessing, the sixth in the series, was completely European. The others were Eurasian, some a little more white, some almost completely "dark." The first one, Minet Badon Gijben, I only know from what I've been told. She didn't stay with us for very long, because she committed suicide as a result of an unhappy love affair. "She drank carbolic acid," Alima told me, "after her fiancé left her. Fortunately, she didn't die in our house, but in the hospital, *kasian*." She was a sweet person, my mother always said—which in itself would indicate a short stay in our house. She had a friendly, rather dark face.

The second was a white *nona* named Jeanne Ende; this was the cross-eyed Miss that broke so many plates. All I know about her is that she lived with us in Tjitjurug and that I used to take walks there with her and Titih, the daughter of *koki* Sipa, a girl of about sixteen at the time and very pretty for a native girl: slender, and yellow instead of brown, as if she were Chinese. The house in Tjitjurug was only a cottage, much smaller than Gedong Lami. There's an atmosphere of vacation happiness connected with it. Maybe it was there that I began to live consciously. The house had a melodious name—Tinggalsari— and was located high above the road. To get to the highway (Daendels's famous Post Road),[1] you had to go down a winding staircase with huge stone steps.

One morning, when we left the house, I fell on the steps and hurt my hand. It was the first time I had even seen my own blood, and I was so scared I forgot to cry. The cross-eyed Miss kneeled before me begging me to be quiet. Titih took some dew from a grassy slope and quickly washed away the blood; only a little spot remained. They pulled me along quickly. A little further down the road old Mr. Kaffer, wearing his cap, would always be standing in front of his factory. By the time I passed him and greeted him I had forgotten my cut. I was amazed that Miss was able to hide it from my mother. Shortly thereafter she was sent away, but that would have happened anyway.

The house had two small pavilions where we would sometimes drink tea, and there was a gazebo in the garden by the rice fields. The view there of Mount Salak, described in the vision I had of it, marks the real beginning of these memories. The house itself seemed to me full of folding doors. As I recall, Isnan the houseboy could open and shut whole walls, just as I could set up a fence out of my books.

One day a fat German took my picture: there I was in a European suit I never wore at any other time, with a tartan tie. I look sad and sullen, sitting on the edge of a chair with my little legs dangling, looking at the world very suspiciously, as only a child can, intensely and maybe with some premonition of what's to come. This is the picture I like best from my childhood. I was so small then, and not yet the gentleman's

sweet son they turned me into for other pictures, with his neatly
brushed hair and a well-fitting sailor suit.

In Tjitjurug a family came to stay with us (in Gedong Lami, or maybe
later) who was always described as undesirable. It consisted of the immensely fat Mrs. Mollerbeek and her two sons. The older son, Bernard,
was too big to play with me, but the younger one, Tjalie, organized all
our games. While his mother competed with mine in making Javanese
cookies, he and Titih turned a whole room inside out. He put one
couch on end to make a sort of stage and sang songs from *bangsawan*, a
Malay opera, until his mother came to yell at him to be quiet. He knew
all those Malay songs with European barrel organ motifs, and he
belted them out. And the rest of us sang the refrain, "Ajun-ajun in die
hoge kapperboom,"[2] and so on.

What struck me most was something from the play *Njai Djasima*,
one of the tropical dramas based on a real murder case. Njai Djasima,
kept by "*Tuan W.*," arouses the lust of a Javanese, Samiun, who sells
her jewels or is in business with her without her *tuan*'s knowledge. He
finally murders her. The first lines of the song that Tjalie always began
in a loud voice went:

> Hé Samiun, berani sekali
> Bunuh Djasima perkara peniti!
>
> Hey Samiun, how did you dare
> murder Djasima for a diamond clip!

While we were eating the cookies our mothers had made, a vendor
would come by with all sorts of knickknacks, including cheap German
oleographs, which were sold in quantity to the Javanese: Boer generals, the German kaiser's family, other crowned heads, and religious objects. The young Mollerbeeks came rushing in and covered the floor
with pictures. Their mother bought many pictures for them: the German emperor with his unforgettable mustache, with or without his
family, and a Turkish potentate with a beard and a red fez. Because the
Mollerbeeks had left nothing else, my mother bought me a picture of a
pierced and flaming heart and one of Jesus smiling seraphically, his
face surrounded by wavy curls. She also bought a picture that showed
the profile of a marvelously beautiful child with the same long curly
hair, praying to a woman in a blue veil. Maybe the child was also supposed to be Jesus and the woman Mary, maybe it was Mary as a young

woman praying under the direction of her alleged mother Anna; I never knew exactly, although I kept this picture for a long time.

Another time I showed Tjalie a drawing in an illustrated magazine that I had picked up, depicting an old man with a little skull cap, with wavy hair and beard, his mouth open and teeth clenched. He stood in the stirrups, riding a horse galloping between two rows of trees. I asked Tjalie if he knew what this was. "Of course," he said immediately, "a *sètan*." I had heard the servants use this word, but when it was used in connection with that little picture it scared me. I decided that all *sètans* must look like this and ride around the Indies in this way too. At night when the wind blew, I thought I heard that old man on the highway between the two rows of trees.

I used to speak Malay with Tjalie, just as with all other Europeans. They tried to teach me my first Dutch, but I refused contemptuously. "Now you must learn to say '*tafel*.'" "Ah! Bukan. Ah! Medja!"[3] Despite their attempts, my Malay continued to improve. The same train I once saw my mother go away on carried tiny people walking or squatting on open coal cars. When I asked Isnan the houseboy what kind of people these were, he said, "*Binatang* (animals)." I didn't know any better, and thought they were called that officially. One day an old *hadji* woman was at our house; she gave me a raspberry drink and said that this was water from the spring Zam-Zam in Mecca. At that moment the train passed by and I shouted cheerfully, "Look, the *binatang*."

"*Binatang?*" she asked in surprise. "Where?" And when I pointed at the little people she was shocked by the arrogance of this little European.

"How dare you say that," she said in a tone of serious reproach. "Those are not *binatang*, those are *manusia*."

"*Manusia?*" I asked hesitantly, because in her seriousness she had used a bookish word for "man," which I knew by the much more common word, "*orang*." "Of course, *manusia*," she repeated. As a result I assumed that this was the profession of the little people who walked on coal cars.

Another childhood friend, Munta, a son of the houseboy Isnan, was unsurpassed as a tinkerer and as an inventor of new games, but I don't remember him from this period. Later he married Titih, who then disappeared into the servants' quarters and didn't play with me anymore. The day before her marriage her teeth were filed according to native custom. I didn't know anything about it and was walking past an open room of the servants' quarters when I suddenly saw it taking place: Titih was lying on the floor, her head in the lap of an old woman who had come specially for the occasion, a cloth over her eyes, moaning and seemingly unconscious. The old woman with instruments in her hand smiled at me invitingly. I was terribly frightened and rushed to my mother to make quite a fuss about it. I think I already resented Munta at that time for marrying my girl friends. He was very much a lady-killer in his own way and later married another playmate of mine, the pretty Itjah, after my mother caught him with her in a room. She was the daughter of our gardener and just as yellow-white as Titih. Yellow seemed to be attractive to Munta. When later Munta had "sent her away," Itjah married a chief *mandur*, an older man. Both times I experienced feelings of resentment and loneliness and asked myself why I hated these marriages, although I was sure all along that I wasn't the least bit in love with these girls. I was only five when Titih got married, and nine at the most when Itjah did. At least with Itjah I was able to tease her for pouring water from a kettle on her husband's big toe. I asked her if she wanted to boil his toes. Since of course she didn't understand the ritual, or couldn't explain it, she pretended to be insulted. This is the way we compensate for being hurt, even later on in life.

A rich Chinese in Tjitjurug invited my parents to a showing of the first movies to come to the Indies. All the planters of the area were present with their wives. I can't remember the lights being turned off when the film began; in my memory the lights stayed on. I watched all these Europeans, nothing but Europeans, even in the streets. I was amazed to see the huge faces in the foreground and looked closely at all the gentlemen with beards. But suddenly I developed a chastity complex, as they would say now. In the film was a scene in which a woman undressed in a bath house and was about to go in the water in a bathing suit, when in the distance a gentleman wearing a cap came rowing closer. This scene turned out to be more than I could bear. I thought the woman would take off all her clothes before going into the water.

"Oh, now Toet doesn't want to look anymore. Toet wants to go home now," I said, pulling on Alima's hand. Nothing could be done about it. Alima had to take me home, while the planters and their wives choked with laughter.

I was, in my own way, equally chaste in other matters. I wouldn't allow anybody to enter the room when Alima undressed me. Later, back in Gedong Lami, I hated it when the bigger girls would sweep down on me, while we were walking—assault me, pick me up, and kiss me. I particularly disliked a fat brown girl who always embraced me noisily. Alima and I called her *Nona Gembrot* (Miss Tubby). It was she, though, who restored my self-image as a boy, when my parents thought it was cute to send me outside dressed as a girl. She rushed toward me, shouting, *"Noni! Noni!"* so that, when I came home again, I said to my mother bitterly that I was a *sinjo* and that never again would I go outside dressed as a *noni*.

By that time Koba Verhaar, my third Miss, was already living with us. She used to tell me wonderful stories and take me to the carriage house, where sometimes we would sit in a stuffy carriage all day long, until my mother got worried because she hadn't seen us. The carriages, which were rarely used, were covered with an inch of dust. They were parked so closely together that we had to climb across one to get to another. Our goal was a small musty carriage with a thickly padded, yellow-gold interior. I could identify these carriages better than later I could identify cars: a coach, a tilbury, an américaine, a landau, a bendy, and a milor'.

Koba Verhaar was snatched away from us, my mother told me later, by a handsome Catholic priest who often came to talk to her. She imagined that she had religious inclinations, "while in reality," my mother added, "she was, I believe, just in love with that priest." His name was Van der Kuil and, although my mother was herself a Catholic, she refused to let him in the house, or rather, she had my father refuse him. I was baptized by a Father Schets, whose name my mother always mentioned with great respect. The name Van der Kuil, on the other hand, was the first sign that there were also bad priests. He had given my Miss a Bible storybook with illustrations, which she sometimes read to me, but when she left she took the book with her. I asked my mother to buy me another one, which must have seemed to her proof that there was a pious streak in me. But any Bible storybook she found or showed to me had different pictures in it and didn't satisfy me. I kept the silent conviction that Miss Koba had left with the real Bible stories.

There was never much of a religious strain in me. I said my prayers faithfully because my mother had said that God saw everything and would be angry otherwise, but my favorite stories in the little book were David and Goliath, Jonah and the whale, Samson and the lion, and Samson bringing down the temple. The story of Jesus I liked as a dramatic fairy tale. From the moment I was told he was the son of God and almost as powerful as God himself, and had heard of his miracles and believed that he could have killed all the Romans on the spot if only he had wanted to, I felt instinctively that he got what he wanted, and that was that.

"What are your feelings when you read how they hit him?" my father asked one evening, and I didn't understand what he meant (I was eight or nine then).

"When I was your age," he continued, "I wanted to help him, I wanted to fight for him!"

I found that strange, although I didn't even dare think that my father could be wrong. "Maybe he would have been able to save him," I must have thought, or something like that. "But why? If the miracle man had wanted to be saved, couldn't he simply have come down from that cross?" The notion of killing all the Romans with one word and getting off the cross without being hurt fit into the world of oriental magic, which all my friends believed in, but I didn't really admire or even like it. According to them, any *Said* (an Arab, supposedly a descendant of Mohammed) could kill an ordinary person by cursing him just once, and these *Saids* didn't appeal to me in the least.

Koba Verhaar was replaced by the darkest of all my Misses; she was almost "black" and had kinky hair. She was the one I came to like the most quickly and intimately. Her name was Lotje Kroone and she won everybody over with her great simplicity and warmth. But she didn't stay long, because she was about to be married when she came to our house. When she left without saying goodbye and I discovered I had been deceived, I experienced heart-rending grief for the first time. My parents said that she had left for just a little while and would be back in the evening. What a common stupid hope of adults, to think that children will forget everything within a couple of hours. I was inconsolable. I wouldn't see Alima and rolled on the ground like a native child until my father appeared. That marriage had always seemed like a threat to me, and I didn't understand why Miss Lotje didn't stay with me as Alima had done.

This happened in Sukabumi in a rented house, Turpijn's house, which had large colorful decals on all the windows; aside from these it was gray and unpainted but those unknown colors made it wonderful to me. In the house there was a French book with dark, old-fashioned woodcuts of ancient tortures and executions. I was allowed to look at it so that I would be comforted. In one picture was yet another bearded man. He was handcuffed and up to his waist in water; his teeth were clenched and there was some sort of torture device on his head. Immediately I recognized him as a *sètan*. Identifying him with the man who made me suffer by taking Miss Lotje away, I went crying angrily to my mother, and said, "All right, she doesn't have to come back, but if that *sètan* ever comes here, papa must kill him." And I wasn't comforted until my mother promised me, on my father's behalf, that he would see to it.

There were griffins on the decals in Turpijn's house: golden brown on a blue background. My father pronounced their wonderful name for me. He also said that fortunately they didn't exist, not even in Europe. I treasured these decals which could make any ordinary window beautiful. Later in Gedong Lami they were glued on all the windows of the big house and there were all kinds of images: red and white lilies, violet and gold tulips—the tulips were prettier because they were less stylized, and they were the first tulips I ever saw, even in pictures— and stained glass, but no griffins. I include this because, despite all logic, these griffins are just as important as events. My grief for Miss Lotje was surrounded by them.

It was at this time that I became sick and the doctor with the goatee came. My father was in Sukabumi to inquire at the civil-service office about some remote land on the south coast of Priangan. If a Royal Packet Company ship would come every now and then to pick up a cargo, he could make a killing. My father was the landowner of Kampung Melaju and he was rich enough, but maybe he was bored. He got more and more excited about the idea. Even though my mother had been isolated long enough when she was still married to her first husband, in circumstances like these she was fearless. She encouraged him and said she would go with him if he really thought the enterprise would be worthwhile.

So we went to Sand Bay. I wasn't even six years old. We went by boat: the *Speelman* (named after the governor-general, but I identified it with a character from *Prikkebeen*).[4] We had planned to go directly from Sukabumi, but transporting the gang of workers my father wanted to take along without losing anybody turned out to be the biggest problem. In Sukabumi three people suddenly ran away—Charles Mesters, Munta, and his wife, Titih. Munta's father, our houseboy Isnan, went after them and caught them when they were about to get on the train. I still remember the commotion it caused and Charles Mesters's unhappy face when he was brought back like a thief. He supposedly talked Munta in deserting, because he was in love with Titih. He was a good-for-nothing, the neglected half-brother of someone we knew who had rented a pavilion in Gedong Lami. Before being hired as an overseer by my father he had been baptized a Catholic in our house, which in itself seemed mysterious and a little scary to me. He and I had spent whole afternoons sitting together on the grass, and so we were on intimate terms. A silent young man with a narrow face and protruding eyes, he looked like somebody out of a house of correction. Perhaps he was some sort of poet or artist. He had come up with a fantastic plan to become rich with Munta and Titih, instead of going to Sand Bay with us. My parents were definitely insensitive to this fantasy. While Munta was quickly chased out of the room by his father Isnan, my father and mother unleashed all their anger on Charles Mesters. The mildest reproach was that he was a thankless dog. I listened trembling. I knew how quickly my father would beat up a native and I fervently hoped that he would not hit Charles, because he was a European and because he used to sit on the grass with me all afternoon. But Charles was merely chased away; he walked through the garden and all alone got into the cart which had brought all four of them back half an hour earlier. I never heard anything more specific about him, except that he was a "worthless character."

The *Speelman* brought us from Tandjung Priuk to Sand Bay. Most of the trip took place at night. I learned about seasickness for the first time. My new Miss was in the same cabin, unable to help me because she was just as sick. My parents had hired her at the last moment because, after all, I had to have a Miss. We got to know each other more intimately because of the seasickness. It was so strange to me in that odd decor of a little swaying room with a porthole, two narrow bunk beds, and the sound of splashing water, and the night outside closing in on us. My mother was seasick too and didn't appear. Isnan told me later that during the night, while the workers slept on deck, he and my father stayed up to stand guard, my father with a pistol in his pocket and Isnan with a loaded rifle, because all my father's money was there on the deck, stashed away in some oil cans. They must have needed a couple of thousand guilders in silver to pay the coolies in such an isolated spot. Still, the story seems a little fantastic, but that's Isnan's fault.

8 Gedong Lami

Before I describe Sand Bay, I have to write in praise of Gedong Lami. It was the largest house in Kampong Melaju, one of the few that really deserved the name *Gedong* (manor). It was perhaps a hundred years old when I was born there, and my grandmother Lami had grown up in it. This I identified with a hundred years' existence, a time span too long to alter lightheartedly here. The lane that ran up to the house was an extension of the driveway on the other side of the wide entrance which we called the gate, and it was still named after my grandmother's family. Just as in Tjitjurug old Mr. Kaffer had provided a sort of marker on my walks, here was another old man I had to greet who was always standing at the fence in *Gang* Lami. His name was Langkau and he never wore a hat; he had white hair, a round face, and a white mustache. He always smoked a cigar, as Alima pointed out to me, and wore sandals, pajama bottoms, and a *kabaya*. He always nodded in a friendly way, sort of grinning. Only later, when I was in school and still said hello to Mr. Langkau, did it occur to me that I didn't really know him.

Nonetheless, for me he was the counterpart of the old woman who came to our house every day. She was the grandmother of my friend Flora, six years older than I and the only European child (even though she was dark) I was allowed to play with. The old woman was called *Tjang* (Grandma) Panel. She was tall, still stood quite straight, and had a wrinkled, ivory-colored face. She always wore slippers and Javanese clothes, and she smoked the same long black cigars I used to see old Mr. Langkau with. She bought those cigars just as eagerly as Flora and I bought our candy, in a Chinese store at the corner of *Gang* Lami, right across from one of the two big columns of our "gate." It was a typical Chinese *warung* where you could buy everything: candy, matches, canned goods, candles, cigars, macaroni, and spices—all this piled up and mixed together to form towers of boxes and jars. The store was almost completely open, but dark and dirty everywhere. An open door in the back wall led directly into the living room, where you could see a Chinese picture and the family altar, and smell the Chinese incense, the same we burned at home to ward off mosquitoes. How easily children are upset by change. This store is a good example: it belonged to an old woman, *Njonja* Anji, who was helped by her son, a gawky teenager whose head had already been shaved except for the pigtail. He had friendly Chinese eyes and protruding teeth. Long after the woman had died and had a typical burial with a lot of fanfare, Flora and I continued to say "at *Njonja* Anji's," even when the son, Po Sen, the new lord and master, was the one to count out candy for us.

Next to this store, on a front porch, an old European used to lie all day on a long chair. He had a small head, completely expressionless glassy eyes, and almost no facial features. He was none less than the father of old Mr. Langkau, and he was a hundred and one years old. "Imagine, a hundred years and then still one more on top of that," Flora said. And she meant more or less that every day he was dying on that front porch. One day he did die, but we didn't notice. There was no fanfare, no people in white dresses (as in the case of *Njonja* Anji) to carry him away. Suddenly he was gone, as if he had evaporated through the roof at night.

The house sat far back in the yard—if you went through our "gate" you ended up standing at the side of the house. Then you could do one of two things—either go to the right and walk along the fence to what was called the front pavilion and which seemed to grow out of the side wall, or you could go straight ahead until you came to a sort of dome, which in reality was the front entrance of the main building. To get into this wide open dome, where only a short parapet and some potted palms prevented people from looking in, you had to climb three broad white steps. Two huge marble busts had been placed on the lowest step: a man with a helmet and beard (Ajax or Menelaus) and a woman or boy, at least somebody with long hair and a sadly distorted face (maybe it was the dying Patroclus). As a child I used to sit on the shoulders of these statues; the female statue would wiggle a little bit under me. Of course I assumed she was the man's wife and was never worried by her painful expression. "Women cry a lot," I probably thought.

Through the dome you entered the wide, long hall of the house. Its floor was completely marble. Before you entered the real hall, you stood in a large room, which seemed to be made up of two rooms because of the walkway, or rather the red runner spread across the whole length of it. Moreover, the two sections were furnished differently. On the left there were chairs and couches almost always under dust covers; on the right a gigantic window coming down almost to the floor looked out onto the fence and the street. We used to sit there often. There was more light and the furniture was less formal. I think it was mahogany "Viennese furniture"; at least, it didn't have velvet like the furniture on the other side. Above the actual beginning of the hallway, and therefore between the two sections of this front hall, there was an arch, its central portion decorated with a symbol of luck: a green, stylized four-leaf clover.

Spread along the front hall were four bronze sculptures on stands; they were dark brownish green and always greasy—four knights, I thought, whose names I was only later able to decipher: Columbus, Vasco da Gama, Camões, and Ariosto. This transition from navigation to poetry, however, held nothing symbolic for our family. There were also etchings by Goupil: *Le Puits qui parle*, *La Fête de la Châtelaine*, and so on. As far as I can tell they were chosen with more taste than the monstrous objects my father bought in Brussels, a few of which he took to Grouhy. The curtains here were made of thick velvet with sumptuous folds, in keeping with the grandiose windows they were meant to decorate rather than cover. In reality the rooms were the "parlors" of the house, but I only realized this later, when we had guests more often.

The walls of the hall were covered with all kinds of objets d'art. On the left there was a wallful of plates in various sizes and from different places, delft blue next to large, richly illustrated Chinese plates and delicately painted smaller Japanese plates with flying birds and other animal motifs. On the right an enormous etching depicted a gentleman with a pointed mustache helping a turn-of-the-century lady either put on or take off her coat while they looked at each other and laughed. The gentleman looked very much like my "uncle," John Panel, the oldest son of *Tjang* Panel and the father of Flora—he had the very same sharp chin and mustache. Near it, again on stands, were colorful statuettes—a Moor with a curly beard and a Savoyard with a green hat, both with their female counterparts.

At the far end of the hall, where the floor was still marble, there was another large room which was really a continuation but seemed to be separate. The red runner continued here too. On the right was a light square room, with the piano my mother used to play in the evenings. On the walls were a couple of pictures of cats staring at birds and also formal photographs of La Belle Otéro and Cavalieri, in color. In the evening the gas light was lit and it was very cosy here. I used to sit on the floor almost under my mother's piano stool while she played all the romantic music from around 1900—Crémieux's and Berger's waltzes, "Nuages roses," "Amoureuse," "Réponse à Amoureuse," "Quand l'Amour meurt," "Quand l'amour refleurit," "Pourquoi ne pas m'aimer," "Loin du Bal," "Loin du Pays." One touches me the most when I think about it: "Sourire d'Avril"; and a piece from a waltz by Weber or Chopin (which one, no one was ever sure) which, if I whistle it, summons up Gedong Lami as strongly as the incomparable cradle song, "Nina bobo." I can't imagine that the lullaby "Slaap kindje slaap"[1] could be just as moving to Jane as was that strange exotic song an old dark maid used to sing for me. It may actually be a corruption of the Dutch lullaby, but the Malay adaptation was altered by the melancholy native rhythm, by the sultriness and shadows of the tropics.

My mother used to play her romances and waltzes with feeling and almost without mistakes, although her hands were so small she could never reach a whole octave. Her hand made a little jump at the last moment to catch the elusive note. While she was playing from sheet music or from memory, I would page through the bound music books she had but almost never placed on the piano. Some etchings in them attracted me: a man with a red skullcap and a drooping mustache standing next to a huge yellow suitcase, or a batlike devil against a flaming background. But whenever I asked my mother to play the music that went along with these etchings, I was disappointed.

On the left was the dining room, dark and cool, with dark curved chairs. On the wall, in keeping with typical bourgeois taste, were nothing but still lifes, of course, a number of dead birds in colored haut-reliefs on wooden shields. At night this room glittered from the many crystals in the chandeliers, but during the day even these seemed dark and dull. When I was about twelve it was here that my father first began to complain about my table manners. He usually started with a question directed to my mother: "I don't understand it; where did this boy get such awful manners? He can't have learned them in our house. Look how he holds his fork!" (I always kept a bent finger pressed on top of it, just as I did with my fountain pen.) Eventually he would turn to me and scold me directly. I'd look at the label of the wine bottle and automatically refuse when Isnan brought in another dish. Later on, when I was twenty and came home from the museum at about two-thirty in the afternoon, I would eat there alone, and the cool darkness of the room felt doubly good. Behind the dining room was the pantry (*dispens*, *sepèn*), where blue-and-yellow tiles replaced the marble floors. It was here that my mother saw Isnan spit in Alima's food, when she was sick and he was ordered to serve her.

At the end of the red runner you went down one step to the long back porch. Here too tiles replaced the marble floor—yellow and black ones. The back porch was open but separated from the back garden by a low wall, whose top surface consisted again of tiles, supported by a rather grotesque row of miniature pillars whitewashed a light yellow and standing just high enough for me to look through them when I was about five. They were so close together that I couldn't squeeze my head through the narrowest spots. The furniture on the back porch wasn't as good, but we sat here often, especially in the evenings, because of the breeze. I'd do my homework here, at a long table. I heard the gas hum in the tubes of the lamps, louder here than anywhere else, and this was the first place I was allowed to light the lamp. It sputtered at first, which caused the wick to glow and temporarily endangered the crown, which was placed more or less loosely on the glass. Never again did I stare at or was I so fascinated by a globe as those that hung around the wick like a second piece of clothing, a sort of coat. They were light cream-colored balloons with milky figures, angels, guirlands, fairytalelike, and wonderful, as was everything else in our house. Two palms in vulgar wooden flowerpots stood at the end of this porch, softening the bareness.

Back through the hall on the street side was my father's study (the office, they said). Later on I ventured only rarely into this lion's den, but as a small child I must have torn up the magnificent Doré Bibles that were given to me to look at, and I must have drawn mustaches and beards on pictures of my father's friends, even if they were already well equipped. There was a huge gun cabinet with eight, later eleven, guns against a wall. Above the cabinet were two tigers' heads, one large and one small, which came from my mother's first marriage and might have been shot by her ex-husband. In addition there were trophies of bulls that looked lifeless because they were not stuffed like the tigers but just whitewashed skulls with more or less thick, curved horns. Here again on the wall were all the turn-of-the-century photographs and etchings you could want—women on horses, ballerinas, actresses, and other beauties. Not only on the side tables but also on the desk in the middle were a number of family pictures. The women seemed to compete with the commercial photographs, with their loose hair, pushed-up breasts, and wasp waists. Everything on the desk seemed to be dominated by a bronze horse rearing high above the ink pots. A small porcelain Napoleon next to that horse was beautiful, I thought, until my father said it was all right because it was really a cigarette lighter but that, as far as its face was concerned, it looked more like a Punch and Judy character than Napoleon. My strongest memory of this room is that I was punished there one night when it was very dark and still, with nothing to relieve my fear but the ticking of a clock. My father had put me in a corner below a horrendous red Japanese mask, with protruding eyes, which even he said must have been a murderer's face. I stood there motionless as if I were part of the wall, although at night I was always so frightened that I would hurry past this room.

On the other side of the hall was a dark room, called my mother's dressing room, though sometimes my parents would put their bed in it. They had an old-fashioned wooden bed, from Grandma Lami, with very ornate bars and panels; it had wooden balls at the headboard, with copper rings through them. It usually stood in the *kamar pandjang*. Here the beauties on the walls wore less clothing and almost all had their hair down. Even Cléo de Mérode had surrendered her barrettes and bandeaux. Hair was one of my father's fetishes. When he was well into his fifties he would cut out pictures of women with abundant hair from the magazines we shared with others, and go to work on them with colored pencils. The thicker the plaits or the loose curls, the warmer the red-brown he colored them. When I was in high school I collected "Westminster pictures" for him—pictures of girls that came with cigarettes. I brought a couple of them home and paid no attention to them, but my father gave me no peace until I had the entire series of one hundred.

The atmosphere was oppressive in all these dark rooms, even if they were pleasantly cool. This was where my father lay ill at the time when the family doctor, a former military surgeon, said in an authoritative voice that he thought an operation would be necessary. I heard my father say, "That will never happen to me, Godammit, as long as I'm conscious." And to my mother he said, "And if that's not the case, it's up to you to see that those butchers keep their knives away from me. I want to die a natural death."

My mother had to take the doctor hurriedly into the hall so as not to excite my father anymore, and within a few days he was better without an operation. But there was also a time when my father languished on a chaise lounge, because every night, at exactly two o'clock, he would wake up frightened, as if he had been called. He thought he would go insane; nothing could interest him. In short, he seemed to be going through an early stage of the later neurasthenia which baffled all his European doctors and which they couldn't even diagnose. At the time a village chief in Tjitjurug sent my mother a *hadji* woman who was famous for her powers against black magic. She prayed over a bowl of water in which seven kinds of flowers were floating, and she walked through the garden looking for the evil. Under the *bungur* tree she found a little doll buried, rusty pins stuck through its head—everything in keeping with the black magic they used to practice at the Italian and French Renaissance courts. The source appeared to be the following: a couple of Chinese who had not obtained a parcel of land my father also wanted saw to it that he was "called" every night at two o'clock sharp. This explained his sudden waking. The voodoo doll was used to drive him mad. Perhaps it was the power of counter-suggestion, but the *hadji* woman achieved her goal. After he had seen the little doll unearthed, my father slept quietly again and the neurasthenia disappeared. This was one reason he became interested in the occult and started his spiritualist library. It was not the first time he had this kind of trouble from the Chinese, he decided. Years ago, even before his marriage, he had been in a lawsuit with the heirs of an old Chinese, about a house that was on his estate. The evening before this lawsuit was to be decided—and he was certain to win—he was lying in bed thinking about it, when all of a sudden the bed was shaken so fiercely that the iron frame rattled. Thinking that one of his dogs was the cause, my father jumped up to look under the bed. He struck several matches but couldn't see anything. "Even then I thought," he said, "that it might well have been that old bastard trying to get back at me in this way."

Between the alternating bedrooms of my parents, this dark one and the light *kamar pandjang*, was the narrow middle room where I slept as a child, with Alima. It was also where another old maid, Bogèl, who was born as one of my grandmother's slaves, used to tell me fairy tales before I went to bed. My mother had ordered her never to frighten me with the *momok*, but her fairy tales were full of *djins, sètans*, and cruel men and women, and sometimes the two of us would look around warily while she told the story at the foot of my bed.

There was one cruelly touching story of a poor princess, the step-child of a queen who gave golden bracelets to her own daughters but when it was the little princess's turn, said, "Here you are," and cut the child's wrists so that she got red bracelets. In the same manner the little princess got jewelry around her ankles, knees, elbows, a belt, and a necklace. The story went on and on like this, but it never occurred to me that the girl should have been dead for quite some time. Bogèl's fairy tales were the most wonderful ones I had ever heard, and Alima simply couldn't equal her. Bogèl was a tall woman with almost white hair but a smooth, unwrinkled face.

For my fifth birthday, I believe, my parents invited a number of European children from the neighborhood and hired a barrel organ. When they heard the music, the children immediately started to dance— even Flora, who was one of the older children. Wide-eyed, I watched a small girl with thick curly hair, whose name was Nicky and whom I had sometimes seen in the street. Suddenly my father took me by the hand, led me up to her, and said that I had to dance. I rudely refused. The idea that I would have to jump around among all those unknown children and, moreover, with this girl, was too much to bear. My father's anger, however, was even worse. He was furious, grabbed me by the scruff of the neck (as he used to say), dragged me through the house, away from the party which continued without me, and put me in a corner of the *kamar pandjang*. Bogèl was there, closing the windows. (In those days we still had sash windows which had to be handled patiently and with care.) In his anger my father didn't even notice her. He hurried back to the party and Bogèl stayed with me; and since she thought that it would be too absurd to punish me on my birthday, she told me a fairy tale. I forgot the whole party, the lemonade, and the barrel organ, and only started to worry again when Flora came to get me, because I still had to apologize to my father for having spoiled my birthday.

The *kamar pandjang* was on the *kali* side. There was only a small strip of garden next to it, just the width of the back pavilion which was built almost out over the river. Far below flowed the Tji Liwung. You had to go down a sort of ravine to reach the water, which seemed impossible since the slope was densely covered with thorny bushes and because garbage was thrown down there—cans, glass, and so on. On the edge above the ravine stood our *angsana* tree, which had medicinal properties. If you made a fairly deep cut in its bark, sticky blood-red drops appeared which were horribly bitter but marvelous for canker sores and sore throats. That is how the tree had earned the poetic name of "tree of the world's suffering."

On the other side of the river was supposedly a *kampong*, but you couldn't see it because of the high trees where Javanese children sometimes yelled down at us. The current was at times very strong, when there was a *bandjir*, and at times gentle, but there was always a host of little whirlpools. Most of the time the water was a light ochre color, but during a *bandjir* the dirt that was washed along made it muddy and reddish-brown. From our garden you could see the bend in the river. It was exciting to watch the praos appear and disappear around the bend, manned by Javanese who almost never used oars but a long pole instead. Only later did I venture into the water, in the afternoons, when my parents were taking a nap, but even then I would go quite a distance from the house, down a path made by the servants for their own bathing.

As a child I had a vague fear that bandits might come up from the river, in spite of the ravine. The *tongtong* (a hollowed-out tree trunk which was hit to sound an alarm) rang out almost every evening. There was the *tongtong amok* (manslaughter alarm) and the fire *tongtong*. The servants immediately heard the difference; I didn't. To me it all had to do with bandits. They were particularly active in the direction of Buitenzorg. The assistant commissioner of Meester-Cornelis, Hartelust, was a man advanced in years who, according to the newspapers, always arrived just after the bandits had left. The sheriff's name was Calmer and the controller's Shilling; and the newspapers made this word play—so typical for the Indies—that the bandits murdered and stole "*naar hartelust*" (to their heart's delight), the sheriff became ever calmer, and the controller wasn't worth a shilling. I often crawled into my bed when the *tongtong* could be heard, sometimes as early as eight or nine o'clock. Only my father's presence, feared by everybody, kept my fears in check—twice over. (Several years later, when I was about eight, Gedong Lami was rented to an assistant commissioner, an old friend of my father, who put an end to those disturbances.) We slept in the pavilion on the *kali* side, which could be very frightening, particularly at night. We sometimes heard an owl hooting all night long in the tall trees on the other side, over and over again—a short, high-pitched sound that was incredibly sad. It was even more frightening than the *tongtong*. There was also the shrill sound of a nocturnal bird which, according to the natives, was a *kuntianak*, a pregnant woman who was killed by a piece of fruit that fell out of a tree, and because she went mad her ghost laughed into the night.

At that time we were about to go back to Sand Bay and the assistant commissioner had just moved into the main building. I thought it was wonderful, because there were native policemen all over the yard. Although they were treated like servants, their uniforms made me think that even the least of them was more impressive than our dignified Isnan. A short time before, a whole Chinese family had been murdered on their estate. I heard the most horrible stories about it—how they had saved a baby that was playing in the blood from the mutilated body of its mother. Late that night we woke up from a knock on the door. It was the assistant commissioner, who was getting ready to go out and had come to borrow a revolver from my father. "This is a job for a man," I thought, and I regretted that my father didn't go along. He offered, of course, but my mother's concern kept him from going.

The front yard seemed endless to me. There were few fruit trees except on the *kali* side, where there was a *pala* grove—small, gnarled, black nutmeg trees which produced a lot of windfalls and where people always feared there might be snakes. I was not allowed to go there very often, how ever much Flora and I liked to pick up the fallen fruit. What I remember best about this yard is that once I lay there in the grass with Flora and a girl friend of hers. I thought that the girl, who was perhaps seventeen, was very pretty and a mature woman, despite the fact that she wore her hair down. I lay between the girls in their *bébés* (loose house dresses), and it seemed to me as if Flora didn't exist anymore, because I was attracted, as if by magic, by the *bébé* of the other girl. I imagined she had come to see me and not Flora, and they both played along with that illusion.

The real yard turned into a grassy field. A little more toward the street was the *bungur* tree, where the voodoo doll with the pins in it had been found. It scattered little purplish-pink flowers on the grass. It was a majestic tree—tall, full, with a rich, light green foliage. The servants sometimes saw the ghost of an Arab under it—a tall man with a beard, in full regalia—while in the *pala* grove the most they saw was the ghost of a small *hadji* woman wandering around.

The servant who saw the most ghosts was Yung, an old man who, when my parents were out late at night, would sit faithfully on the steps, next to the bust of Ajax, nodding off to sleep. The houseboy Isnan, a Sundanese, had come with my mother from her first marriage, but Yung was an old servant from my father's bachelor days. Even then he waited up at night, when my father had gone to the club, and he seemed to be unsurpassed in cooking a steak. When I knew him, he had bags under his eyes and though his beardless face sagged, it had no wrinkles. The way he sat on the steps gave him a sort of European dignity: he could have been a former civil servant or, without his headcloth, a retired commissioner. He walked with difficulty because he had elephantiasis in a place that all the children pointed at, laughing to each other; even his own children said shamelessly, "Pa Yung *kondor!*" The disease made him incontinent, and sometimes he spread an unpleasant smell all over the house. My father was always very nice about it. He had no intention of firing him and would simply say, "Come on, Yung, why don't you change your clothes."

Yung was especially bothered by the ghosts when he had to close the windows. One evening when he was standing next to one of the windows that looked out on the *pala* grove, he said that a face suddenly appeared right in front of him. He couldn't tell precisely what it looked like, but he did know that his own head had become twice as large.

In my grandmother's time the front pavilion had been some sort of *gudang* with one story. Over the years bats moved into the top floor, probably because of the fruit that was stored there, so that the whole wing was called Bats Hall. Its windows were narrow and black and fitted with bars. From the street it might have looked as if a madman was confined there. Shortly after I was born, my parents transformed it into an ordinary pavilion so typical of the Indies, with only a ground floor and an open front porch. After that Yung saw fewer ghosts there, but he still avoided this part of the house which he considered the most dangerous. A handsome young Eurasian lived there at a later date. He had a small turned-up mustache, spoke fluent English (he worked for a British firm), and even had an English name—Mr. Frank Robertson. He was the half-brother of young Charles Mesters, who had been baptized as a Catholic in our house but behaved so badly later. Mr. Robertson played the violin and sometimes came to play music with my mother, and we all liked him very much. But even though he was much younger than my mother, the harmony of their music

seemed to resonate too much in his soul, and my mother finally decided it was better to put an end to the musical evenings. He was engaged to a Eurasian girl from the neighborhood who became terribly
jealous of the musical evenings at our house. One night when we were
sitting on the dark front porch of Mr. Robertson's pavilion, a *sado* entered the yard and a frightened *Tjang* Panel came up to tell Mr. Robertson that his future mother-in-law wanted to talk to him. He ran inside
and asked *Tjang* Panel to tell her that he wasn't home. He was even going to hide in a big laundry basket. Everyone was laughing, and then it
turned out that *Tjang* Panel had agreed to take part in a joke my mother had concocted. We were all amused by Mr. Robertson's ashen face
and his hurried retreat—me too, even though I didn't understand the
deeper meaning of the joke. He suddenly broke his engagement and
married the nurse who had assisted at my birth. She was a little older
than he but was a pure European with jet black hair and white skin.
She came to live with him in the pavilion and had her first child there,
while we were living in Sand Bay. After leaving his British firm, he went
into business for himself, hiring coolies for the outer islands. He became a rich man and left for Europe, but then he went broke, as if there
had been a curse on his money, and was forced to return to the Indies.

The mood of the house is inextricable from these anecdotes. Together they form the world I grew up in. *Tjang* Panel was no less a part
of Gedong Lami than the *bungur* tree or the *kamar pandjang*. She was a
means of communication with the outer world. She visited everybody
until she quarreled with them. Her only indulgence was a cigar, and in
return she peddled her stories to all the houses in the neighborhood.
Since my mother never read and was easily bored when she wasn't
running the household, she enjoyed *Tjang* Panel's company more
than she liked to admit. *Tjang* Panel brought a friend with her every
now and then and was frightened away only by the fierceness of my father, who always let her know that she came to the house only to see
his wife. She also had her enemies. "Imagine, this morning when I
went to the *pasar* I met Mrs. Cohen. She was in a *sado* too and then she
looked at me, but I threw away my face."[2] *Tjang* Panel played a role in a
dramatic interlude that took place when I had the measles and my father had gone to Sand Bay for the first time, to survey the property. He
had left with Umar, a half-Arab whom my father liked because by just
mumbling an incantation over ordinary peanuts, Umar could turn

them into a potent laxative, as he had once demonstrated on all of our servants.

At that time we had a maid who was a real European but was married to a Javanese. Her name was Lies and, according to *Tjang* Panel, she had a *mulut busuk* (bad mouth), because she always spoke evil. One evening Lies came to beg my mother to have the Master come home, because she had heard, with her own ears, how Umar had arranged with *Tjang* Panel's second son, *Sinjo* Dirk (our overseer), to murder my father. Umar was supposed to stab him to death in the prao and throw him into the ocean. My mother became very upset and immediately sent a telegram to my father, telling him to come back. He received the telegram in Pelabuhan Ratu, when he was just about to begin the last part of the voyage by prao. Dirk Panel was summoned by my mother; even in my sick room I could hear her shouting, "If you ever try such a thing, Dirk, promise me that at least you'll spare my child." Dirk was embarrassed and fidgety. My father returned, confused and upset. The whole thing finally blew over, but we never knew what actually went on. The last round was fought by *Tjang* Panel and Lies. Nobody ever thought that it might have been a joke which Lies had taken seriously. All the participants in the conspiracy fell into disgrace. Shortly thereafter Lies started to have fits of hysteria and would run through the house stark naked. One day, when I had just come back from a walk, I saw her forcibly restrained by the gardeners, who picked her up and carried her back to her room. She left the house after that, and my mother didn't doubt for a second that this was the result of Umar's powers. But when we left for Sand Bay, Dirk was again appointed overseer, and *Tjang* Panel, who had declared Lies her mortal enemy, remained undiminished in my mother's favor. When later *Tjang* Panel too fell into disgrace, my mother didn't fail to notice that her arm was misshapen by rheumatism, which led my mother to compare the woman to Kumbajana—a schemer and Polonius-like minister from a Javanese shadow play (*wajang*).

Usually when there was a quarrel, Alima quickly pulled me away. She herself couldn't stand harsh words and tried her best to avoid being scolded; when it did happen, she never said anything, to get it over more quickly. "She has a delicate soul," my father used to say emphatically, probably without realizing that she was indeed far more delicate than anyone else in the house. Alima let me cut out pictures, and she knew how to make me eat if I didn't want to—by giving names to the bites: "This is *nona* Dientje; you know, that pretty girl who goes to school in the morning. If you make her stay on your plate, she'll cry."

One day the Chinese district master, Bek Yam Seng, sent us a little horse. I was given a uniform, a bearskin cap, and a tin sword, and was led around on the horse by the stable boy. I was bursting with pride and saluted all the soldiers I encountered, who of course saluted me back. The illusion was no less real for Alima. She imagined, no doubt, that I'd be a general one day, and she ran after the horse, looking as if she were about to either laugh or cry. Unfortunately the horse was soon taken back. It had only been borrowed, and my father already owned too many horses to buy another.

Bek Yam Seng was later murdered by a poor old Chinese man who owed him money and whom Bek Yam Seng had persecuted mercilessly. I had known Bek Yam Seng very well. A stocky man, he was a slippery character who always gave us presents; he had given me a box full of figures made out of soap. The two men were in a *sado* together, when the old Chinese cut Bek Yam Seng's throat and threw him out in the street. He landed right in front of a tent where a traveling movie theater was giving a show. In less than a minute the theater had emptied, and everybody could tell the story of how the district master had been lying in his own blood. The *tongtong* was sounded. In our house they immediately said, "Bek Yam Seng has been murdered!" Isnan said, "That's why there was a ring around the moon yesterday." My father was not at home, and my mother, *Tjang* Panel, Flora, all the female servants, and I hurriedly locked the house and hid in one room, huddled close together. It didn't matter that the murderer had already turned himself in at the police station. We sat there trying to convince each other that the old Chinese was really a poor, nice man, whom we had often seen in the street. This murder obsessed me more than any other, and I couldn't sleep that night because of the vision of the bleeding district master who had once sent me a horse.

The outbuildings had been built perpendicular to the back porch and formed a single unit. There was a two-story storage barn next to them; it was full of building materials—lime, planks, and tiles on the first floor and furniture on the second; the wooden floor was covered with a layer of coal dust. You had to climb a long staircase to get there, and it was always a big event for me, when somebody went up with the requisite heavy keys. I wandered around in the dark "coal attic," careful but full of curiosity. You could find all sorts of things there—old pictures, fans, books, even my father's school books that he had never unpacked. The servants' rooms were dirty, stuffy, and uninhabited, but marvelous for playing hide-and-seek. Later, when we played "musketeers," the staircase to the attic was a wonderful place to defend and attack with bamboo swords.

The back yard extended to the stables. At first my father had a lot of horses, but when we came back from Sand Bay their number dwindled steadily. I remember the time when Yung went to live in what had once been the stables, with his dirty wife Djahara and their children. In front of the stables stood a *karèt* tree (a dwarf rubber tree? My knowledge of botany is lacking); it had a short thick trunk and thick irregular branches with snakelike twigs. It was the easiest tree to climb, so I probably practiced on it. Sitting on the thick branches you could read happily with no fear of falling. On the ground there were seeds you could blow up and then the transparent film would burst.

From the *karèt* tree back to the street wasn't very far. If you had come in through the dome, you would have completely circled the house. Retracing your steps through the yard, back to the back porch with the little yellow pillars, you first came to the well, then to the lilacs. In the evenings the whole yard was fragrant from them. The moonlit nights we spent on the domed front porch between the palms were the most beautiful ones. The light reflected off the rainwater collected in two large shells, which Flora called the dolphins. The smell of the lilacs in the back yard was another aspect of the tropical night. Whenever I smell that fragrance now, I think of that part of our yard in Gedong Lami where I looked at the little pillars from between the bushes. You could hear *krontjong* music sometimes, played by the older brothers of children I wasn't allowed to play with. These were the older *buajas* (rowdies, tramps, literally: crocodiles) of the Eurasian families (like the Mollerbeeks and the Leerkerks), whom I was warned not to go near, though my mother liked their music. We talked about them condescendingly: "Tonight they're going to howl again at the Sersansis." The families themselves joked about it too: "Where are the kids? They're probably out howling again."

Krontjong music has a Portuguese origin, and the names of those families also had a southern European ring, with a charm I won't deny, nor can I laugh at their music, which experts put down as a cheap imitation. If I had been born elsewhere or felt more European, I'd be less sensitive to the sultry, seductive atmosphere of that nightly guitar-playing and singing, and I don't know which I like more—the names of Rosario and Quartero that were connected with the most famous *buajas* or those of their Ambonese rivals such as Latuperissa, Tuanakotta, and Tehupeiori. Here is a song I find just as touching as "Sourire d'Avril" on the piano:

> Terang bulan, terang bulan dikali—
> buaja timbul, disangka mati.
> Djangan pertjaja mulut lelaki—
> Berani sumpah, tapi takut mati.

> Moonlight on the river—
> a crocodile is floating, looking
> dead. Never believe the mouth of
> a man. He dares to swear but is afraid to die.

What things outside of Gedong Lami can I compare to this? Perhaps Chinese New Year when I was still a very small child. The whole neighborhood exploded with fireworks, and we also fired rockets from our yard. Before dark, large crowds came running by with ordinary dragons and fire-spitting ones too, *barong-saïs* and *liongs*. As a small boy I was also awestruck by the *djenggés*—huge floats with swaying little girls, disguised by paint and costumes which to me seemed regal, lit from below in a bizarre way by torches. But gradually I felt that I lost interest in the Chinese noise, and the princesses on the floats became children again, smaller than I was. The death of this illusion happened perhaps at a *tjokèk* performance, where the noise, which went on for hours, was so shrill, unmelodious, vulgar, and monotonous, that my interest waned because of the absurdity. "The natives are right," I must have thought, "in despising those Chinese." As for me, as a true child of the Indies, I prefer one evening of derivative *krontjong* music to a whole series of select Chinese performances. "Non mi tocca, il mio cuor non ci si trova."[3] What I remember best are the Malay lines of the man with the blue glasses who introduced such a group or a friend of his, dressed as a bear, dancing at the end of a chain. But those were actually local take-offs of the Chinese celebration.

The shrill sounds of the native *ronggèngs*, which for European sensibilities are bad enough, are not as deafening and certainly not as frantic as what the Chinese soul was capable of producing. In the Indies all women, including those who took part in a *krontjong* band, sang with a shrill nasal sound. Only a single *nona*, led by her European instinct, avoided this nasal singing, but Batavian singers did so very deliberately, as if they were competing with the Chinese.

But I'm still in the back yard with the lilacs, the porch with the little pillars in front of me, the long warehouse to my right. Me? The little Ducroo I placed there. At night only one light was on near the kitchen, a flickering gas flame without a mantle. I see Isnan squatted next to it on the floor, turning the ice-cream machine, because on Sunday evenings we always had vanilla ice cream. Later, when I was in school, Saturday evenings made me happy because I could look forward to Sunday. Sunday afternoon, when the sun was going down, the thought of school the next day would make me sad, but there was one bright spot, one last pleasure: the ice cream shortly before going to bed. Isnan, squatted next to the kitchen door, with the ice-cream machine between his knees. Between him and me there was a huge round *tempajan*. I had to hoist myself up in order to look down in it. In the rainwater swam mosquitoes in their early stage as small wriggling pins— at least, I never doubted that those creatures later emerged from the water on wings to bite us in bed. I have never looked it up in a book.

One day my father stood by that *tempajan* shooting sparrows with a small rifle, to make sure he hadn't forgotten how to shoot. "Pick them up," he said abruptly, and I went with a heavy heart, fighting back my pity and revulsion, to pick up the dead bodies. My father thought he could harden me this way, as if children don't become cruel all on their own, when they have their own gun. My mother finally called me, and I clung to her and burst into tears: "Why must Daddy shoot these poor little birds?" When I later got a BB gun I went around the house shooting the *tjitjaks* off the walls with the excuse that the blackcock we kept in a cage had to eat them. They fell at almost every shot and lay on their backs, small and slippery. I left it to somebody else to pick them up. When I became bored with it I only shot off their tails, because these would grow back anyway. There was something comical about the tail, pinned to the wall with a BB, wiggling up and down, while the *tjitjak* ran away. I thought of course that I was as good a shot as the Marksman or Old Surehand.[4]

I can describe the surroundings of Gedong Lami better after I've returned from Sand Bay. All of this is only above the house. To somebody else it must seem like an inventory, only a floor plan. Aesthetically it would have to be arranged differently, because this seems as if I'd been writing with the sign "Don't forget anything" above my desk. That is really the disadvantage of remembering the past too well. I have not mentioned a hundred details I could have easily recalled. The way I've done it is for me the most natural, and all things considered, I can't find a better argument.

9   Bella on the Couch

End of April. I answered a letter from a real-estate agent in Brussels who wants to try to sell Grouhy and who said that he had been in touch with my mother. The persecution of the Jews in Germany gives this man hope that some refugee financier will want a "deluxe object" like this. I've decided to get rid of the attorney in Namur if he remains so indifferent. At first he seemed anxious to go to the bank in Amsterdam with me, when he still thought the inheritance would be significant.

With a sense of feverish but genuine relief, I went to Paris and had dinner with Jane at the Héverlés. Bella's pregnancy is so far along that she is sure she looks awful and has to be contradicted strongly; for a small woman the disfiguration is really quite attractive. She lies on the couch and pulls the corners of her robe around her waist. For a moment she talks seriously about the child, but about herself and her friends she talks with her normal levity and with the slurred pronunciation which Jane sometimes doesn't understand. Viala and Manou had visited her the week before. They hadn't seen her in ages and were astonished when they saw her in this condition. Héverlé had run into Viala a few days before and, when Viala asked about Bella, had answered casually, "Oh well, she's fat at the moment, but that'll soon be over with." Viala interpreted this to mean that there had been a small accident and that they were taking care of it. Manou had gone through something like that not long before. They seemed to have difficulty believing that Héverlé would be a father and that the intelligent Bella could long for a child. "I never saw a woman get so pale when she heard that somebody was having a baby," Bella said. It makes one wonder what kind of desire is suppressed here. Will Bella's example provide a justification for Manou to insist upon becoming a mother after the next accident? Bella has wanted a child for years. Manou might have adopted Viala's desperate attitude toward life in this respect, or it may be a result of nothing more than a fear of pain. Taking care of the accident must have been painful too, no matter how early it was done. In order to avoid that kind of pain again it's quite possible that she might prefer the birth of a child next time. Something like that is completely within the realm of human emotions.

It's the maternal instinct, the irrefutable right to motherhood, even now, and it also includes intellectual women who in theory are against war, against life, even against the human condition. "To exercise the right to procreate at someone else's expense is absurd," says Héverlé. It's an idea a woman can agree with until the mysterious instinct begins to speak for itself. Viala's resistance is more emotional, less intellectual than in Héverlé's case. Besides, you have to have a very deceptive feeling of security in order to consciously father a child in these times. The only children who are born now, he thinks, are those that are the result of foolishness, no matter if conceived by accident. But Bella has enjoyed her pregnancy without worrying about any ideology, blissfully defenseless to the dominance of the body ("as if somebody else were living her life"), with a dreamy interest in its independent rights.

Bella has laughingly switched to a completely different story, this time about a virgin. I know her thoughts on this subject. There is something in the way she talks about virgins that reminds me of my past zeal to be first and foremost "a European and nobody's fool." She would like to give the impression that virginity has not the slightest importance but rather is something inferior, that essentially an intelligent woman is never a virgin, at least not from the moment she has perceived certain things. She believes it is simply a physiological necessity that there be a first time. She chose Luc and he chose her, but given their youth they must have been bothered by their lack of experience. Although Bella's lilting laugh can be explained as coming from a real sense of humor, it sometimes strikes me as fake. It's not just the Parisian attitude of seeing the farce in everything and fearing naïveté more than anything else, but it also has to do with a certain need for drama here. It can be felt in the atmosphere at the Héverlés—a need for drama that she seems to try to defuse in this manner. He betrays it in the way in which he frequently uses the word as part of a general truth, while she betrays it with her laughter which, though it relaxes her face, leaves a tension under her eyes and around her mouth— something strained and weary. "How Jewish," she would say about herself. She insists on her Jewishness all the time as if it were self-evident, while I have trouble remembering it in spite of her obviously Jewish features, because for me she is first and foremost a Parisian.

"Every night when the sun goes down I close the windows and curl up like a ball to forget the hour and I'm sad and lost, and feel abandoned until it is completely dark." She says this with the same laughter, especially when Héverlé is there. His sensitivity for the humanity in everybody does not prevent the fact that Bella laughs much more frequently when he's around. It is like the excuse of somebody who, though intelligent, feels inferior under the scrutiny of a more powerful intelligence, as if her woman's intuition were not enough in itself to justify her right to speak.

"Tell us something about when you were a virgin yourself," I say.

"Oh, Arthur, I was engaged first as one's supposed to be. I had a fiancé, as every respectable girl should, who had the complete approval of my family though I couldn't stand him myself. It was a classic case. I thought at once that he was insufferable and said so. He responded by holding forth for a long time about himself, and then asked me if I was still mad at him. When I had said no, he asked me to marry him. I said I hadn't thought about that yet. "Is there somebody else?" he asked, and when I responded negatively again, the matter was settled for him: I was no longer mad at him and there was nobody else, so everything was in order. I didn't quite see it that way but I couldn't fight the logic, and the next day he started to bring me flowers and candy. So we were engaged and I suffered a great deal, because, for example, he never learned to kiss properly. He tried hard but never quite got the hang of it. It seemed to be unbelievably difficult for him. When I finally decided to break the engagement, I wrote him a letter in verse, which I still must have around somewhere because I realized in time that he wouldn't understand a word of it and rewrote the whole thing in prose. That's what I was like as a virgin! And when it was all over, I was still unhappy about it, not so much because of him but because of all those silly flowers and candy."

"And then came Luc"—it still gives me some trouble to call Héverlé "Luc," even when I'm talking to Bella about him.

"Yes, but not right away. There was another man, but that wasn't a real engagement, because my family had no part in it. That man was very intelligent, but also very sadistic and I was no match for him, so he hurt me as much as possible. He made me feel that I was only an ordinary, vain little woman with a shallow appreciation of anything worthwhile, that I didn't know myself, that I needed him much more than he needed me, and so on. And he was a bit younger than I was. You'll appreciate this, Arthur; even when I was still so young and a virgin, I never longed for older men! And when I had again suffered a lot, Luc came along and, surprisingly enough, turned out to be even more intelligent and not the least bit cruel. I didn't trust him at all. I had just learned that intelligent men were always horribly cruel! The more intelligent Luc was, the more I thought he must be hiding something. When he is sure of me and doesn't have to hide anything anymore, he'll turn out to be a cruel monster, I thought. When we took a trip together, I was amazed every day that nothing had changed in our relationship. And he wasn't older than me, either. Discovering him was probably the smartest thing I ever did."

"No doubt," it seems to me and not only smart, either.

She concludes: "Still, at the time, he wasn't nearly as nice as he is now. When you're around twenty and you're intelligent, you're hardly nice at all."

Was I nice? I was incapable of giving in, if it was a question of remaining true to the character I had decided to play in life, but I dearly needed to devote myself to something or somebody, even to somebody as shallow as Teresa. I was still wet behind the ears when I arrived from the Indies at twenty-two and in many respects barely eighteen, according to European standards. I chose Teresa because I took seriously her artistic pretenses and her clever play-acting to gain attention in fashionable society, because she represented *the* European woman I had only dreamed about thus far, and because of her noble profile, her heavy eyelids, and her vaguely Italian grace. Teresa was not a bad choice in terms of a physical specimen; but as far as her human qualities were concerned, she was deplorable. But I had no point of comparison, nothing but my stubbornness, which eventually resisted everything she stood for and all the overbearing things that went along with her. It was exactly the opposite of my feeling for Jane, if you can analyze things like that. If being ten years older made me any "nicer," it's only because now I do have a point of comparison, and with Jane I could choose with much greater certainty the opposite of the type of woman I had encountered before her.

I didn't think of this, sitting next to Bella's couch; it's only now that it occurs to me. Then I thought it was a pity to find the right person when you're so young and might have to make up for the lack of experience later, when you're unsatisfied with life anyway until it offers something interesting. The victory over what is interesting!—but you always have to pay a price for it, and when you've paid it, are you satisfied? Do you at least have the feeling that the past doesn't concern you anymore? Among the things that my relationship with Jane has taught me—the real things, not the romantic ones we all know so well—this stands out: there is no such thing as a temporal sequence of events; you pay for the past, if not for the future. You can only avoid paying for interesting experiences by rejecting them in advance. Such a victory is never easy. The Héverlés couldn't reject them in advance, because of Luc's knowledge of the human soul, which he needed as a writer, and because of their shared desire for drama. And yet Héverlé says: "I am not French in this respect: I've always believed more in l'amour-passion and I was never very sensitive to l'amour-goût."[1] But this terminology itself is obsolete; the twentieth century accepts the possibility of purely sexual infidelity. You can negotiate, but arguments are quickly countered. If I asked Bella, who is so much a part of this age, "Why do you have to cheat on each other?" her answer would be prepared well in advance: "It's not cheating if you tell each other everything," and it goes without saying that a wife's liberty—so newly acquired, after all—is a whole lot more important than her husband's, the old tyrant. She is capable of saying, "A woman is sometimes unfaithful for her husband's sake, to make him feel he too is *really* free."

I would like to tell her that cheating really has nothing to do with him, only with her. But I might be insensitive, for what do I really know about her? Is she the kind of woman I would want her to be, the only kind of woman I want to recognize as being real? I want very much to put myself in a woman's place, without taking into account either morality or my own possessive instincts; my source of information here is my feeling and it never fails. When I was in love with Teresa, I was obsessed by the woman she was. Her way of being charming made it impossible for me to recognize any other type of charm. I went through the same thing with Jane, but only with Jane, in the ten years after Teresa; and the absence of this obsession is enough, it seems to me now, to demonstrate the imperfection of amour-passion.

"What would you do if Jane were unfaithful to you?"

Although I don't doubt for a moment Bella's good intentions toward me—an old friend—when she asks me that, laughing in her characteristic way, I recognize behind it her attitude toward life: something like that might not be so bad, to teach us more about what we really are. And I answer to that: "Do you believe it's necessary, for either one of us?" The laughter disappears for a moment, "Necessary . . . no," but then it comes back: "But things like that happen...."

"Maybe," I say, "it wouldn't last long after I found out about it."

"And what would you do then?"

"Good God, Bella, you're going to force me to reveal that as a husband I'm not in the least a man of the world. My friend Wijdenes would say, 'Why do you have to talk about such things before you've encountered them?'"

"That's irrelevant. What would *you* do?" She furrows her brow so seriously that I try to answer seriously, as if it weren't just an amusing parlor game.

"What if Jane were unfaithful? Of course it would matter who it was. If he were a fool or an infamous playboy, I would determine the physical strength of the man in question and choose accordingly a revolver or a whip. There are those wonderful flexible whips, which I once saw a wronged husband use in an American movie. If he were a black or a masseur I would probably want to shoot him, but more likely I'd just walk away and imagine that my love for her had evaporated out of disgust, even if that weren't true right away. I think I would act out this fantasy although it would still wreck my life. If he were a truly superior person, I'd have to leave, of course, for a variety of reasons...."

"The only right you have is to leave," declares Bella. "Jane never loses the right to play the game she chooses."

Jane says nothing and looks from one to the other, somewhat bemused but probably feeling that she'd really prefer to decide her own fate. She's sitting next to Bella on the couch, the long lines of her body even more pulled together than at other times. When she's not really at ease, like now, the sharp, yet soft features of her narrow face take on a harsh, almost dramatic duality. But when Héverlé looks at her, she suddenly smiles and I think of Vigny's verse which could have been written for her: ". . . ton pur sourire amoureux et souffrant."[2]

"I think all those hypotheses are ridiculous; besides, you can't determine what your reaction's going to be beforehand," specifies Héverlé. "If Jane would suddenly develop a great desire for blacks, Ducroo would probably start coddling her like a sick child. Bella's argument is stupid and should be declared null and void. Ducroo will always keep the right to play *his* game the way he wants to, so if he feels that he must respond by pulling out his gun.... One thing is certain: the desire to kill in such cases is real."

I don't really understand it, maybe because deep down I'm still mulling over Bella's indifference toward virginity. So I must consider myself lucky that Jane didn't long for interesting experiences she might have missed. This in itself shows that I'll never agree with modern woman's insistence on the triviality of sexual experiments. Unfortunately for me, I have to go along with those who maintain that a woman who behaves in this fashion commits a "sin." In spite of everything, it comes down to the Christian heritage, whose hypocrisy is the basis for bourgeois morality. Be that as it may, I remember the guilty aftertaste of my own first carnal knowledge so well that in the case of a virgin the absence of such guilt seems monstrous. I can, if necessary, forget the clinical aspects of the first time, whether it was brutal or masterful, butcherlike or painless as with a good dentist—but not this. I would like to ask Bella to explain herself, explain her resentment or whatever it is. There are women who can't forgive either their partner or themselves for being physically inferior that first time.

But the conversation is past that point; we're still only concerned with someone's right to be unfaithful and everything that goes along with it. I interrupt: "It's one's own insufficiency that you would expect to be reflected in the other. At least, that's all that would matter to me."

Bella looks away, reflectively.

"She's completely confused," Héverlé teases, "hearing the only one of our friends who dares say out loud that his wife's life might be in danger if she goes to bed with somebody else."

"So, once you've fallen in love with one woman, Arthur, you couldn't go to bed with another?"

"I guess not. Or if I could, it would be unpleasant because the other one would still be there."

Afterwards I think what a great answer that would be to give to a woman who might be interested. For Bella, the thought of that invisible one in bed must have been most amusing, as if there weren't enough women who might actually find it appealing. Bella used to tell me interesting stories about her friends, who always seemed to be named Alice. There was someone named Alice, who wanted to go to bed with everyone right away, and when she would meet these partial strangers later on in the street, she would remind them of their performance in bed. I absolutely had to meet this woman, although I never did. There was another Alice, who had become frightfully fat and had lost her teeth. She lived with a Polish baron, who had served in the Foreign Legion but who was frightened of her when they quarreled, because she had shot her first husband three times during a fight. This one I met and remember, but she didn't want to talk about the shooting while I was there. There was a third Alice, who spent one afternoon a week talking to the man who had been the love of her life, and still was, but who no longer returned her love. So as not to lose him completely she became interested in his current exploits and enjoyed herself as much as she could on the one afternoon he reserved for her. With this Alice I once must have spent half an hour waiting, that is, if it wasn't still another one, since I can't remember whether she was blond or brunette, pretty or ugly. "Did you flirt with her while you were waiting?" Bella asked. "No? You're chaste, Arthur, but you're not polite...."

And finally there was a poor and starving Gina, who always went cheerfully to see her fabulously wealthy lover and never asked him for money, which he could have given her so easily. And it wasn't out of shame or pride that she didn't ask, but simply that they had once agreed never to talk about material things. For years I imagined this Gina—who was from Rome—as a woman with an old-fashioned romantic appearance: slender, pale, and with thick dark hair. Some time ago, when Jane and I were leaving Bella's place, we met Gina at the door—a thin woman with a sharp profile and mahogany-red hair, a mahogany-red tending toward crimson, with an accent and manner that were anything but Italian; she could have been from Poland, Yugoslavia, Hungary, Czechoslovakia, or any place like that. Why did Bella hang onto those friends? She can dismiss in two terse sentences a woman who annoys her, if she thinks that Héverlé is interested in her for the wrong reason. He talks condescendingly about her friends, as if they were a collection of harmless fools, and I'm almost positive that Bella has the same opinion of them. Would she say, "My Jewish loyalty," if I asked her about it? If it's loyalty that, moreover, can indulge in a "funny" story every now and then, I would value it almost more than anything else. This is a big point between Jane and me—this unwarranted loyalty to past friendships, the last-ditch effort against decay. A person who I once accepted totally and who has only changed, not diminished, or only diminished with regard to me, to my needs, or to me when I take myself seriously—what reason could I have to abandon him as long as he doesn't abandon me? It sounds almost too noble and it's probably false; it's probably that loyalty again that we have to the person we once were.

"I don't like my earlier selves," says Jane. I think I would have loved them as much as her present self. The only thing I can't love is the past that turned her into the Jane she was when I met her. Against all logic I refuse to believe that if it had been different, she would have been different for *me*. It's the only point of her past I would like to see her betray, for the sake of the present.

Jane finds an ally in Héverlé, who also claims to abjure his whole past. "I don't think about the past," he says, in a tone which makes me wonder, like some second-rate Freudian, what kind of painful childhood he tries to flee in the increasingly tense character he now assumes.

"I love my childhood," Bella declares. "I was really myself then. After that, my life merged with Luc's."

"They're crazy about themselves," says Héverlé to Jane, "and we're not."

"They're so crazy about themselves now," I say to Bella, "that they can't bear to think they were ever lesser creatures."

We laugh, but while I recall my childhood in the Indies, I am suddenly amazed that writing about it really can distract me from my present worries.

"The image we have of ourselves now is inaccurate, but our image of what we once were is no doubt pure fantasy," says Héverlé, looking as cynical as possible for Bella's sake. And Bella says, as if speaking for me, "That's irrelevant, for I can applaud myself or be hard on myself for something I did years ago just as easily as for something that happened only yesterday."

The south coast of Priangan: a bay and a kind of island. Coming from the sea, you would first see a narrow, gray-white beach, coconut trees, some thatched huts, and a row of outrigger praos in the middle of the gray strip of sand. I will have to use points in the compass, for what do left and right mean here? Having surveyed all of the sandy beach, from which the bay took its name in European geography, you would see, after a few steps, how much more colorful the local name was: Balekambang—floating *balé* (bamboo bed).

Perhaps two hundred steps from the sea and across the island there was another body of water, a small river, the Tjikantèh. It ran parallel to the beach and more than anything else made the island appear to be floating. The names sounded different from those around Batavia: less bold, more drawn out, and with vowels that dropped pleasantly at the end. On the left, when you stood with your back to the sea, this river ran into another one. It was a crystal-clear, lively mountain stream which came directly from a high waterfall in the forest: the Tjimarindjung, a sharp, clear name, just like its water. This was the northeast corner of the bay and the eastern end of the island. There were large rocks in the water here, just before the Tjimarindjung ran delicately out into the sea, in the shadow of the forest and the high dark rock wall against which the waterfall contrasted a radiant white.

The rock wall ran north and formed a mountain range which extended far into the sea. If you went around the edge of the range in a prao, the bay was no longer visible, and with the wooded mountain wall on the right and nothing but the open sea on the left, you were on your way to another harbor, Wijnkoops Bay. Later on when we had our own boats we made this trip often.

The other, western end of the island was also washed by the mouth of a river, the Tjiletuh, whose water merged with that of the Tjikantèh. The Tjiletuh was a powerful river: somber, though with splendid vegetation on both sides, still, deep, and wide. Standing there later on, at the very edge of Balekambang, buried up to my ankles in the wet sand

and looking around to see if someone might be calling me back, I said to myself: "This is really a tongue of land, a tongue of sand that sticks into the water, and I am standing on the very tip of that tongue."

The Tjiletuh flowed silently though impressively into the blue water of the sea. Its own water was a grayish yellow, neither clear nor really murky, and full of crocodiles. It came from deep within the interior. The Tjimarindjung didn't have any crocodiles and was a delight to bathe in, as my parents did for a while until they contracted malaria and blamed it on the river.

Crocodiles from the Tjiletuh swam often enough into the Tjikantèh, the stream between the two larger rivers. The Tjikantèh was less than half as wide and for the most part shallow, except for an occasional hole in the bottom, where a crocodile could feel quite at home for days on end. The natives called this a *kidung buaja*, which means something like "crocodile bed." When our ducks and chickens ventured close to the water, they would sometimes disappear by the dozen if a crocodile had installed itself in the Tjikantèh. One day my mother was arguing about this with the woman in charge of the chicken coop. She had just suggested that there might be a two-legged crocodile—a normal suspicion, under the circumstances—when she saw a duck being dragged away from the dam with a sound that went right through her. After that Isnan stood guard with his gun, and even if he did not kill the robber, he managed at least to chase him away.

The village was located more or less in the middle of the floating *balé*. It seemed quite large to me at the time, but in reality it must have consisted of perhaps forty bamboo houses of varying sizes. The houses of the village chiefs and other notables (including the *warung* keepers) were rather large, while most of those belonging to poor fishermen were small, musty, and dirty. Most of the houses were built on stilts which were usually so dirty that they were sticky. The space underneath the houses was called the *kolong* and was used to store firewood, tools, and garbage. Native children, even babies sometimes, played there and were on quite intimate terms with all sorts of vermin. You climbed very crude steps to reach the porch, which usually represented the only open sitting area in these houses. The rest was made up of one or more rooms that were dark because they had no windows, since the natives felt that enough air came in through the cracks in the wattled bamboo walls. We slept in such a house in the beginning. It belonged to the *lurah* (village chief) who was called Pa Djuwi. I remember that under his headcloth this man had his hair in a bun like a woman—something I had never seen before—yet he also sported a black mustache.

Two events took place when we lived there, while waiting for our own house to be built. In addition to my Miss, Alima, Isnan, and a couple of other servants, we had a family of fox terriers living with us: Lulu, the male, who later became famous in the area, Lili, his bitch, who died after a little while, and their brood of six fat waddling puppies. One of them, Spotty, was bitten to death by a village dog. He was our favorite, of course—a pup with a funny face and a spot next to his nose. I saw Isnan bring him in, hanging limp but not dead yet. I heard the cries of pity from my mother and Alima. Everyone ran back and forth with water and bandages. My father went outside with a rifle and had the culprit pointed out to him. It was around six in the evening. The dog ran into the sea and stopped in the surf with his head facing my father and the light of the setting sun behind him. A shot rang out but there was no sound from the dog. "He died instantly," Isnan said, "he fell over on his side and the sea carried him away." Little Spotty lived through part of the next day—a moist ball smelling of smoke, moist because the lukewarm bandages were changed regularly. When I think of it now, there were dark pink spots, not red, on the white bandages or on the skin.

The other event happened one evening when I went to say good night to my parents, who were sitting outside by the beach. Jumping off the crude steps I fell, and when I got up I felt a terrible pain in my left arm. I had not broken my wrist, but I had sprained it so badly that a *dokter Jawa* (Javanese doctor) had to come from Wijnkoops Bay in a prao. It was at least a week before he came. In the meantime I walked around with my arm in a sling and comforted myself with the thought that I now looked like a wounded Transvaal Boer. My mother had promised me something if I were good while my arm was being treated, and I had asked for a book about all the Boer generals (which I didn't get, probably because it didn't exist). I still remember that in my fever I dreamed about General Cronjé, but how in the world did I come across that name?

It is strange: from that time I can clearly see the new Miss beside me, but not Alima, the one who always slept next to me. I can recall Alima only once in all of the Balekambang period: when my parents had left me alone in her charge, but that was probably about five years later. So close was she, so naturally my guardian angel, and so silently she went about her work.

Our own house was built next to the village, toward the Tjimarin-djung. It was a bamboo house just like the others but without a *kolong*, built from more solid materials and containing three living rooms and three bedrooms, with windows and rattan blinds for thunderstorms and trade winds. After we moved in our life became more comfortable again, and I readily accepted the more pleasant aspects of life here. The only thing that annoyed me was the language of the natives, who were friendly but whom I couldn't understand. We were the first Europeans to live here and were followed and surrounded everywhere, particularly my mother, who was the first white woman in this area. They had seen some European controllers, but no women.

My mother did her shopping in fluent Sundanese and she soon became popular with the villagers. Later, when they feared my father as much as they hated him, they still came from all over to see her. They let her take care of their sores, which sometimes were large festering wounds, infected by dirt and sea water, right to the bone. My mother treated them with the devotion of an amateur doctor. She obtained great results in little time with iodoform and cajeput oil (even this was unknown to the natives). She even cured a woman, Djasilem, who was a celebrity in the village because she had been pulled into the water by a crocodile. While she was being dragged through the water she remembered the jackknife in her belt, and had the presence of mind to open it and stab the crocodile in the eye. He let her go. She came back on land with four large holes in her leg, and those holes had remained open sores ever since.

I remember her particularly from this time, and also another one, Lindeung, who had a *warung* at the entrance to the village and was therefore, in a sense, our neighbor. Her merchandise was mostly balls of yarn and glass jars which were only half filled. She looked like an Indian squaw and had the reputation of being a great lover and card player, and she always lay lazily on her side behind the glass jars.

Between the first few houses of the village, which included hers and ours, were two hedges of *djarak:* a fast-growing plant with light green leaves which, if you broke off a branch, secreted a sticky, bitter, and milky liquid. I was quickly told that this plant was poisonous. The first hedge ran along our own house; the second, a double hedge, formed the actual entrance to the village.

There were other poisonous plants. In our own backyard, for example, there was a *bintaro* tree that dropped hard, oval-shaped fruit with a spongy center, the size of a mango but with an even more attractive green skin. Less than a month after our arrival, the children of Dèn Sukma,[1] one of the overseers we had brought along, ate some of the fruit and died, with their mouths, it was said, horribly distorted. They were buried not far from the house. They were such beautiful children, my mother said—a boy and a girl four and five years old. Their grave was a sort of poetic spot, until their father also died and everyone forgot them. Sukma had been everywhere, even in America, where he had been an extra or something in Buffalo Bill's circus. He spoke a little English and was unusually humorous for a Sundanese.

After our house and the servants' quarters were finished, work was begun on the rice warehouse and the mill, both next to the Tjimarindjung, whose current was to drive the turbine. Sukma was put in charge of building the canal that was to lead the water to the turbine, and to do so he had to blow up the rock. At first the other natives refused to do this, not only because they were afraid of the explosive itself and the terrible blasts, but also because they feared they would disturb the forest spirits. Sukma's American past made him rise above this fear. After his children died and later Sukma as well, the natives said that he had brought it on himself.

Sukma also liked to explore the area. Once he went into a cave half filled with water, followed by a young villager carrying a torch. Standing in the water up to their waists, they heard a noise above them and saw an enormous snake looking at them. The young man was so scared that he dropped his torch in the water, Sukma lost his gun, and, panic stricken, they splashed around in the dark, terrified when they came into contact with each other, thinking it was the snake, until quite by accident they happened to find their way out. When Sukma told this story and imitated the cries of the young man, my mother laughed over and over again until she had tears in her eyes, particularly when he said: "Allah, madam, there was this mouth above our heads, about this big, and it said 'kok-kok-kok.'"

Sukma died years later. He had been gone a long time but suddenly returned, though he was never able to work again. He squatted, or crawled around a dark room in the servants' quarters, and I never saw anyone with him. Only once in a while did my parents visit, but I often sat with him. He couldn't see very well anymore but he still liked to tell stories. He spoke a little Dutch to me but reverted to Malay when he'd start to talk about Captain Nemo from *Twenty Thousand Leagues under the Sea*, whose adventures he had read in that language. When he died, in incredible filth, there was nobody with him. Even then my mother went to have a look but told me not to go. Only later did I learn that he was riddled with syphilis. He was a man with a lean face, lively eyes, a somewhat protruding mouth, and a large strawberry mark on one cheek. He was a son of the *rangga* of Tjimenteng, who was not only of very old nobility but also lived in the odor of sanctity.

The furniture in our bamboo house came mostly from my parents' villa in Tjitjurug, which they had sold before they went to Sand Bay. One of the pieces was a symphonium on which I learned my first European songs—a sort of organ in which you put big metal discs; as they turned, a cog system, like in a music box or player piano, produced a jingling sound, which you could make louder or softer. When we unpacked this organ, stood it upright, and played its program,— "Torgauermarsch," "Bimmel Bolle," "Lina-Walzer," "Transvaal National Anthem," and so on—everyone in the village rushed in and craned their necks to see whether somebody was in or behind the instrument. And with characteristic folk poetry, one of the young fisherman said, after some reflection, "The singing princess." The symphonium lost its prestige, however, when a Chinese peddler penetrated as far as Balekambang and brought a gramophone, on which he would play a record for two and a half cents. Although it was impossibly scratched, you could make out human voices. He also came to our house and I had him play "The Battle of Sedan" at least four times; in it you could hear commands shouted. The one who liked him best was Lindeung; she first hired him, perhaps as an attraction for her *warung*, but she then became so addicted to his music that she almost went broke.

Slowly our colony filled out. Our backyard with the *bintaro* tree, under which I later bowled, turned into a sort of courtyard once the servants' lodgings with their *kolongs* were completed in the back. The kitchen was there, too, connected to our house by a covered walk. My parents' bedroom was more or less in the middle, with a dressing room on the seaside. My Miss, Alima, and I slept in the third room, which was separated from the bedroom by a hall. At night there was *gamelan* music in the pavilions. All our male servants played those instruments; Isnan was a virtuoso at it, and his son Munta made so much progress that he was able to run the *wajang* and became the self-appointed *dalang* (storyteller/speaker), although he had not been properly ordained. The audience from the fishing village listened to Munta with admiration. The dedication of house and plant provided the opportunity for *sedekahs* and *wajang* performances, and Munta did an excellent job. Not only did he know many stories, he also knew how to make the puppets enter the stage with the appropriate dance. Moreover, he changed his voice for men and women, using a contemptuous intonation for the evil characters and a solemn voice for the confident heroes. He also knew how to draw out a story with the most ornate speeches, for a hurried *wajang* performance would never satisfy the natives. No wonder he was so successful with women. From my earliest childhood I would sit right behind him during his performances. I handed him the puppets that he didn't hang on a banana tree and had to come out of a box. For nights on end the clatter of the steel plates, which he operated with his one foot to accompany the heroes' entrance, resounded in my head. Not only did I know all the puppets, I had my favorites, which as far as I was concerned did not appear often enough. One of these was Abimandju, the son of Ardjuna, whom I preferred by the name of Ankawidjaja. I also had my favorite play, which had an endless series of fights and dealt with the heyday of an illegitimate son of Ardjuna named Gandawerdaja. Everybody, Munta told me, had his period of glory when even Ardjuna himself could not defeat him. But Ardjuna's never waned. I longed to see the very last battle, the *Perang Djaja*, when all the slain heroes don't revive as in the other plays, and when the Hastina and Pandawa empires destroy each other. But Munta was not ready to take on that twilight of the gods. The ritual of this play required seven evenings to complete; moreover, the *dalang* had to fast beforehand to protect him from misfortune. After all, he was not a real *dalang*. He told me the story in great detail, but I never saw it performed.

My parents listened to the *gamelan* music from their back porch, which was lit by a kerosene lamp. Beyond this the courtyard was completely dark, and even the outbuildings were scarcely lit. The melancholy music and the tropical night blended perfectly; the only discord was the white man, who considered himself superior, even here. There were other evenings which my parents spent by the ocean, that is, in the front yard, on a tile patio they had had made in the sand. When the weather was nice, they had their rattan chairs placed there. I was sometimes allowed to sit with them if it wasn't too late. My father's presence kept me from feeling at ease most of the time. Our chairs were set very close to the fence; the beach was right in front of us, and past that, the sea, which was deep blue at sundown and black at night, with an occasional light glowing from a fisherman's prao. The bay opened up abruptly in front of us. To the left there was a short peninsula—in reality, several huge rocks with an island at the end, close to the mouth of the Tjiletuh; to the right, the mountain range, whose darkness stood out against the evening sky. From around that range came the praos that brought us our mail. The sunsets were sometimes breathtaking. At night the silence gave the impression of complete rest, detachment, eternity. My parents sometimes commented to each other on how beautiful it was, but did I as a child appreciate, even instinctively, the full value of those hours? I don't believe so; I think I only made up the memory later. But one thing I'm sure of: there was a song that touched me even more deeply than the *gamelan*, and that was the *ngagóndang* (a rice-threshing song), which really seemed to conjure up the soft fragrance of night flowers. Four ugly women, dressed worse than poorly, would hum while they rhythmically pounded the paddy in a wooden block. They didn't really sing and therefore didn't make those shrill nasal sounds. One hummed a little louder, the others with their mouths almost closed, and the rhythmic pounding of the large pestles made up part of the music. It was something unique; it was sad and yet so disarmingly sweet that only the sweetness remained. The voices came from the night, and since you barely saw the singers, you could easily blot them out.

This memory certainly dates back to that first period, although I may have heard them again later. But how often did we go back and forth to Meester-Cornelis, to Sukabumi, via Wijnkoops Bay, directly from the harbor of Batavia? It all blends into one big panorama, held together by the landscape, but separated by the stages of my childhood. Yet I can't distinguish clearly and I wonder how much of what I felt more consciously later, when I was ten or eleven, was not already present in this first period, when I was six. As far as the decor is concerned, I have no doubts. A child in his environment is not distinct from that environment; only occasionally is his individual character revealed by an individual preference. All things considered, I often sat with my parents on the square, tile patio, close to the ocean. And yet it occurs to me that when the problems started—when the water ducts to the plant continually collapsed so that the plant had to be shut down, and when the workers became more and more dissatisfied and ran away—my parents could only rarely take pleasure in the night and the *gamelan* music anymore. My father preferred to retreat by going to bed or by reading. He didn't have any literary standards but he read avidly and sometimes for evenings on end: Walter Scott, Marie Corelli, Justus van Maurik,[2] or from his special collection on spiritualism. No doubt his mind needed some distraction. He gradually felt defeated, while my mother was never really out of her element in the Sunda lands. Later on he would say, "My neurasthenia started in Sand Bay." She was very sentimental, very sensitive too, but not susceptible to neurasthenia, as he was. She could have continued to enjoy the environment while everything went wrong at the plant, and she would never have given up the struggle against misfortune. She sometimes sent my father home and stayed by herself with the workers, who would work much harder for her than for him. I remember seeing her sit day after day in the rice barn with a cloth over her head to protect her from the irritating rice hulls which filled the air. In the evening she would have a native woman massage her, or she would keep my father company. She was always cheerful as long as she wasn't quarreling with one of the servants.

She was not only sentimental but had a good heart. Whenever it was touched, she was ready to help, even if it took all her time. However, she always ruined things because of her feeling that others had the right to be helped, but no other rights. Moreover, she never realized how great her own demands were; she didn't have the vaguest notion of somebody else's viewpoint, and as soon as there was any difference of opinion she only took into consideration her own point of view, and she was simply right. I asked her once, since she was so religious, if she might be able to admit to God that she was wrong, if they had a disagreement. She was completely convinced that she led an exemplary life with nothing but very small sins. "Oh, don't you say such things," she answered.

This kind of goodness is quite common among ladies in the Indies; in part their hospitality is based on it. But you would be wrong to think that it's only a matter of tradition. There is a genuine need to do good, combined with a crass shortsightedness as to the results. Within two days these women can become friends, only to deplore their mistake ten days later—a result of their abundant good will. But in their devotion to their husbands and children they are often admirable.

Whatever my mother meant to my father, particularly in Sand Bay, she meant even more to me as a child; she was the one who removed all problems. This is the case with all children, they say. What children consider to be great problems can be resolved by mothers. My mother's role was amplified by contrast to my father. In the battle against outside forces threatening our family, my mother also displayed an extraordinary élan and energy. She fought against disease—not only my father's or mine, but anybody's. She would take sick people into Gedong Lami and nurse them, sometimes for months. She also had what was called in the Indies "a cool hand"—intuition or luck in these things. Even my toothaches seemed to go away when she just touched them. Since there were no dentists in Sand Bay, she treated me with home remedies, but what did the most good was being able to lie down next to her. At that time the bond between us was probably stronger than ever. I was happiest when my father was not around and I could have her all to myself.

You could get off the island by crossing the Tjikantèh on a creaking, rocking, but actually quite safe, bamboo bridge. Right across the bridge we had a cow pen which my mother managed on her own. She had a great preference for a Bengal cow, Sajati, which she had helped deliver and which later threw me into the mud of the Tjikantèh with one butt of its head. Fortunately, its horns were dull. Kitty-corner from the cow pen was a flower garden mostly filled with *melati* (jasmine). When I accompanied my mother to see the cows and then the flowers, I was always so happy I would sing all the songs I could think of. She thought that very sweet of me, but the most obvious pleasure I gave her was when I said she looked pretty. I thought she was at her most beautiful in a dark brown *kabaya* with white flowers on it that looked just like *melati*. She looked younger in it, and not so plump as in lighter *kabayas*. She remained young for her age. When she was well in her fifties, everybody thought she was not even forty. When Gerard Rijckloff first met her in Grouhy, he thought she was about fifty and she was actually sixty-four. My mother's youthfulness was a source of real pride for me, although I never felt that she was really pretty.

On the tile patio by the sea we developed a sentimental game, which she liked so much that it almost became a ritual for us. I remember that it never failed, even in my father's presence. She would begin, "Later, Toet, when Mama is dead...," and I would respond immediately

with, "Oh, no, don't say that!" and she would continue, "Later, when
Mama is dead, you must remember once in a while that she used to
sing 'Bintang Surabaja' for you" (or something else), and then she'd begin to laugh loudly because the tears would be streaming down my
cheeks. No doubt her laughing was a way to keep from crying. "And
later, when Mama is old...," but that didn't work; I couldn't imagine
how she would be, later, when she was old. "Then Mama might be all
shriveled up, and bent over, with a small *kondé* (bun) of gray hair just
like Ma Umi." But I couldn't believe it. I couldn't imagine, either, that
she would die—only what her death would do to me, when she
couldn't be found anywhere in the whole wide world.

Every evening when I said good night to my parents, I added very
softly to my mother, "Will you come in a minute, Mama?" because she
always came to tuck me in. I believe this irritated my father. He sometimes said, "No, none of that," and then my mother came to the rescue:
"Oh now, don't tease the child." I was amazed when some time later
she said, "You don't ask me anymore, 'Will you come in a minute.'"

One evening when I had been naughty, she involved my father in a
small drama. He called me from the front porch where he was sitting
by himself, and said in a low voice, "Look, you see that light out there
on the sea? That is Mama. She's leaving, because she doesn't want to
live here anymore, since you are so naughty."

This made a deep impression on me, but more because of my father's resigned attitude than because I really believed the story. Instinctively I rejected the notion that my mother, who was so afraid of
being seasick, would cross the sea all by herself, at night, in a little fishing boat. The idea of remaining alone with my father, on the other
hand, was enough to make me cry. And with surprising speed my
mother appeared on the dark front porch. Because of her cape, she
looked really as if she had come in from the sea, but the light continued to glow in the distance. "It's another boat," they said, once I
promised to be good, and the family was united again.

I was familiar with these threats of desertion from when I was still
very young. My parents had a happy marriage and remained in love
with each other up to the very end, I believe, but they needed occasional violent outbursts and dramatic reconciliations to renew their
love. After such a quarrel my mother would decide to leave, and often
she would take me with her. In Gedong Lami she simply withdrew to

one of the guest rooms and waited in the dark, or even to a pavilion if it wasn't rented out. In Sukabumi she took me in a *sado* to Wa Gedah, the *hadji* woman who had explained to me the difference between *binatang* and *manusia*, and sometimes we stayed there overnight. The next morning, at the very latest, we would see my father appear, wearing a straw hat and carrying a cane, as he stepped out of a *sado*. My mother would hurry inside, but my father would enter the yard resolutely. All my life I watched this melodramatic reconciliation. It had two acts: "We can't live together anymore" and "Living apart would be even worse." My father said to me later, "Your mother is still as romantic as ever, but we're really getting a bit too old for it." My mother didn't agree with this at all. Once reconciled, they sat close together, not actually embracing, but looking as if nothing in the whole world could come between them. I was both happy and disillusioned by this: each time it was the same old thing. When there was a new conflict and Alima and I had to go along again, Alima would calm my fears by saying quietly: "*Ah, biar* (don't worry), they're a little crazy again, but things will be all right again." The worst scare occurred later, when my mother took the train from Bandung to Garut and stayed there for two days in my brother Otto's cottage, and my father didn't follow right away. Suppose he had refused to come after her this time! I think my mother was about to send a telegram asking for a divorce when at last he turned up.

She treated me the same way later. She really loved me, according to Jane, who knew her only briefly, but this love too was purely egocentric. She was the one who stood in the center of her love; she always had the best role. She knew all too well how beautiful and unique mother love was. She used to talk to me about it when I was maybe eight years old, and even then it irritated me. Some time later she brought me one of those vulgar pictures, a reproduction of Whistler's mother with a verse under it about "Mother o' mine," written in a horrible ornamental script. I didn't fail to respond in the most unpleasant manner. I said that I was sorry but I couldn't stand to have an ugly thing like that on my wall. Her adopted native child, Sylvia, seized the opportunity to score a point by saying she would like to hang it above her bed.

My mother could only live instinctively; any rational adjustment was alien to her. She piled her kindness on me; she did everything she needed to do and gave everything she could give, to prove to herself, if not to me, that it was really my fault if, after all this, there might be something else I wanted.

"Go away if you want to," she said, "I won't hold you back," and she acted as if she were amazed (and maybe she really was) that I didn't take her literally. Not long before her death she called me back from Lugano to discuss "business." We came to a complete disagreement, and in front of the notary with the pig's head she virtually called me a fool: "Don't pay any attention to him, he's just as neurasthenic as his father." Then, in all simplicity, she tried to placate me by offering me money.

"No, really, I have enough now; why don't you take this?"

She was upset, however, when I said good-bye and left the room, leaving the money by her pillow. "Why won't you take it? You're not mad at me, are you? You're my darling, aren't you?..."

Was she really jealous of Jane? I once told my mother that I began to think so, and she swore it wasn't true. If it were, she wouldn't have known. She was so far removed from the "Oedipus complex"! Her naïve egocentricity, her childlike way of dominating people without realizing how tyrannical she was, those stupid creatures she brought home time and again, out of compassion as well as loneliness—all this could fill a book, a chronicle I would only write with resentment. But in spite of everything, if there ever was anybody who could start all over again, in all honesty, and whom you couldn't really hold responsible, it was my mother. Her end, her last years, were so sad that I cannot see my own point of view when I think of it. She should have died earlier, shortly after my father. She only died early enough to escape poverty.

I couldn't imagine how she would look when she would be old, and it happened in a few months. She really shrank, her back was bent, her hair thinned out, hinting at gray. Only her teeth remained so strong and white that some people thought she wore dentures. It made her laugh with pride. But although being thinner became her in certain respects and made her seem more delicate and reflective, she was weakened physically, so much so that Gerard Rijckloff told me the last time he saw her that he was worried. She liked him very much and was happy when he wrote her a letter. Of all my friends, he was the only one who seemed to like her for herself, not because of me. "It's clear," she said, "if I'd been younger, we would certainly have gotten along very well. I was a charmer and so is he" (not at all like you, was the implication). Gerard did indeed treat her as if she were a charmer, and sometimes she said, without believing it for a moment, that he was only kidding her; but up to the very last she appreciated this kind of homage to her femininity.

What weighed heavily upon her in the last years, even more than old age, was her loneliness. After Guy had to go live with Suzanne, she lay alone in her big room in Grouhy at the end of the wing that looked out on the garden on both sides, with the spruce trees right under her windows. She had made an altar out of the mantelpiece and had pictures and statues of saints placed all around her. On account of her weak heart, she said, and the stuffiness in the room with the windows closed, she left the hall door open. In reality I think it was to ward off loneliness. The Austrian companion slept in the next room. In the Indies she would have asked one or two *babus* to sleep in her room. In Grouhy, the forester, Télès, with his good-natured face and his drooping mustache, sometimes slept for weeks in a room across the hall from the Austrian lady, with a gun in the corner in case of thieves—a reincarnation of Isnan. In the Indies, when my father was gone, one of the male servants always slept in the house like that, and I slept in her room. Before she went to sleep, a masseuse came in to massage her and would tell endless stories of the old days, about native rulers or the eruption of the Krakatau, if the masseuse happened to be old enough to have experienced that as a child. How do you overcome such an upbringing? No Soviet indoctrination would have had any effect whatsoever!

She turned fifty-eight on the day she first set foot on European soil. She would have certainly been much less lonely in the Indies, and yet, when I urged her to go back and even said that I would come along, she didn't want to go, saying that my father's grave was in Europe. She had Guy sleep in her room, also because of her loneliness; yet here too her egoism showed up. Even when she was sick and coughing, the child was not allowed to sleep anywhere else. She didn't accept the possibility that she might infect anybody anymore than she would accept being wrong, and as it turned out, she usually was right—except in business matters. And with some sort of holdover of my trust as a child, deep down I thought that even there *she* might be able to save the day. Lonely, she would lie in her room in Grouhy and say, "You don't know how I lie all by myself, sometimes crying half the night about Papa."

She had copied a stanza from the poems I read to her at times, and which she kept on a piece of paper in her glasses' case:

> Memory will fade like someone sighing,
> on my grave are waving grasses,
> And nobody, nobody who passes
> will guess this life was merely dying.[3]

"Yes, that's what my life is like since Papa's death." No doubt she did sob half the night, but what could I do or say? I sat next to her on her bed and tried to distract her with stories about my friends, with what was still really alive. And in the end, how pathetic was her moving from one house to another. Only in her room did she create her own atmosphere, indulging her need for luxury; she didn't seem to notice the neighborhood. She was sick, pathetic, and increasingly lonely. I write this down quite consciously, and yet it may be true that nobody will every really know the vulnerability of his parents, who were for such a long time invulnerable grown-ups to him.

I let myself digress from Balekambang to think of my mother, who brought me to my present worries. Her death is not something separate, something I can feel the same way I do about the last scene of her life. After her death worse problems cropped up, in the form of a humiliating financial distress I had never known before. "My death will mean the beginning of your life." The money I borrowed from the notaries for her funeral still has to be repaid. Her crypt, No. 3337 in the Laeken cemetery, awaits a simple name plate. I asked the funeral director to send the bill for that plate to the notary. That was six months ago. Suzanne went to my mother's grave, and she writes me that the plate is still not there. A simpler funeral car, saving 375 francs; a name plate still missing after six months, perhaps because they think it won't be paid—all this is nothing compared to the problems of death and eternity, but I feel a suppressed anger at my inability to take care of these things easily and without any obstacles, like any bourgeois family could.

11 Conversation with Héverlé

May. I see Viala only occasionally, in the Bibliothèque Nationale. When I insist on helping him, to keep me quiet he tells me white lies, which usually take the form of some superfluous little chore. I saw Guraev again yesterday, and left him hurriedly because he wanted me to go with him to meet some businessmen he's currently dealing with. This way he'd have someone to trade sly remarks with, as if to convince himself that they are worthwhile too, and to show off his wit.

"I don't want to play the fool," I said. "It's bad enough to realize that I'll always be a fool in their eyes."

"Oh, fool, nonsense," shouted Guraev, with the intonation he assumes whenever he thinks you're talking like a Frenchman. "Are you so afraid of looking foolish, Ducroo? I'd just love to be able to be a real fool again."

An hour later I tried to write a letter for the newspaper "by turning off my mind," according to Graaflant's prescription—another white lie. Too much of ourselves is always lost, even in the most inane writing, even in an almost random collection of sentences where you maintain the exact opposite of what you really believe. What remains is "to be true to yourself" but at the same "put water in your wine." The result is something as pale and slippery as dishwater.

The word "fool" was still ringing in my ears when I entered Héverlé's house. He was out, said the maid, but he'd be back soon. So I waited more than twenty minutes in the study, looking at magazines full of political surveys, sometimes looking at the Greco-Buddhist head with a profile that reminds me so much of Héverlé's, and then again thumbing through all sorts of reading material. Finally I asked the maid where Mrs. Héverlé was.

"What? Don't you know? In the hospital!"

Mrs. Héverlé had given birth to a baby girl and both were doing fine, the maid said proudly. She thought I must know, because by now the child was four days old. At that moment Héverlé entered, pale and nervous (but he's always that way), elegant and slightly bent over, and he took me to the other room. "Let's see if we can get something to eat, because I'm here all by myself. Oh, yes, that.... After we have eaten we can go and look at the 'object.'"

It would be fruitless to congratulate him. Such domestic affairs seem insignificant to him. I throw out the word "fool." He strokes a long dark blond curl behind his ear, thinks about it a moment, and says:

"Yes, you don't want to be fooled by a collectivity, I believe, but in the name of what? Of individualism? There's something that will fool you very easily. There's no reason whatsoever to assume that a thousand years from now the belief in the individual will not appear just as ridiculous as a fire-worshiper's belief is to us now. The Buddhists already think so...."

He's talking about something entirely different from what I want to talk about. We're back to cultural history again, but I haven't gotten there yet.

"Nonetheless, the 'I' will always have some importance. It's based on a feeling we never lose. The events that happened to *us*, that are recorded by *our* feelings: how do we explain them, if we deny the 'I'?"

"What nonsense! That way of feeling is culturally determined. Your 'I' cannot escape being part of an environment, dependent on country, race, education, historical moment...."

I let him continue. I know what he's going to say, but it bores me, because there's never a hole in his logic. It must be awful not to have a single feeling without knowing that only a northern European, in the year such-and-such A.D., influenced by the Judaeo-Christian tradition, can have such a feeling. There are two things about Héverlé that discourage me: one is the scope of his culture. It makes me wonder how long I would have to study, how many philosophical systems and historical surveys I would have to master, just to be his equal. That is the irrational aspect. The other one, the one that's real, is the difference between his need for activity and what I call my mental masturbation, my situation of being a mere paper-scribbler. This is why he has always been the most life-giving of my friends, why he has sometimes disconcerted me when I approached him openly and he responded just as openly: "I think I'll leave again soon. Did I ever tell you about an adventurer by the name of Davidson who crossed the desert by himself, through rebel country all the way from X to Y? He thinks that we should try something together. The treasures he hopes to find seem suspect to me, but staying behind would be more than I could bear." And I'm sure he'll leave, just as he did when he went to Persia, to Tibet, and to China. Before Jane came along, it was my dream to go with him. My mother held me back then; there was no way to send me telegrams in such places.

"Héverlé," I said, "next to you, I feel that I'll never be more than half a man."

"That's because you have formed illusions about me that are completely ridiculous," he answered. "Once you find a woman who loves you, she'll take care of that."

"It'll be hard for her to change my cowardly characteristics."

"I have a couple of those myself, only in a different area."

From the other side of the table his voice reaches me again: "… And don't worry, intelligence can never be destroyed by any one civilization. Your principles have always existed after all, even in the time of Saint Paul, and Saint Paul was a greater danger than Lenin."

I look at him again. When he speaks it's as if his thought is concentrated in his eyes, and yet most of the time he looks to the side or above the person he's talking to, as if even eye contact would interfere with the transmission of thoughts instead of furthering them.

But Saint Paul doesn't interest me; I bring the conversation to the latest excerpt of his novel which has just appeared in a magazine: the scene between the Communist and his wife, who wants to share his fate, knowing he's heading for almost certain death. He refuses, as if he wanted revenge for her going to bed with a comrade shortly before.[1] Héverlé thinks the scene is all right in itself (after all, something like that is rather realistic, he says), but he relies on everything being transposed, or at least dominated by the particular world of the author.

"No doubt such a world exists," I say, "but inside or outside of it: why do these two people have the problem of absolute freedom with regard to each other? In the name of what? Of an intellectual-communist ideal?"

"No, or at least not only for that reason. If her husband wants to recognize her freedom—the freedom she wants—even if it conflicts with his own feeling, it is because he needs such an attitude, to support his idea of being noble. Every being—superior being, I mean—strives to attain his greatest degree of nobility. And precisely because it would be so easy for this man to prove to his wife, with the help of thousands of philosophers and thousands of years of civilization, that in reality she is not free, all this offends him and he looks for a counterargument to his own belief."

"And so he ruins their love for both of them. Or did their love need to be spiced up this way? If they really loved each other, how could they be fooled—to use that word again—by this sort of freedom?"

"Again, in order not to be fooled by something else—egoism, for example. The character in my novel does not think like this because he is a Communist; he would never have become a Communist if it weren't in his nature to think this way. He needs to efface himself, in this case in favor of the freedom of the woman who entrusted her existence to him."

"And so he insults their love, her idea as well as his, if she loves him, that is.... That's the basis for the false arguments you have them use against each other, when the conflict finally arises. That's why she says, 'But didn't you say yourself that I was free?' and then he can only say, 'But you knew better than to believe me.' If they were open and honest, they would understand that some forms of freedom cannot exist in love, because they undermine the essence of love itself. I am not a true friend if I go around slandering you to my heart's content just because I'm ready at any time to follow you into danger."

"That's a bad example. If you were my friend you couldn't slander me."

"While a woman can love this man and yet go to bed with another? I don't accept that, but maybe what you just said clarifies everything. If all the man needs is to sacrifice himself, then the woman would just be a means—his supreme self-humiliation, perhaps. And then everything is all right. Then all we have to do is to conclude that he failed when he got angry."

"One element you overlook: death—the importance of death in all this. You forget that this takes place, and maybe only can take place, in the face of death."

"Yes, but to a certain extent this is begging the question. If sex is no longer binding enough, then there still is death. This woman gains the right to betray her husband sexually, because she is willing to die with him. She even insists on it. What would have happened if this willingness had not existed? I understand that you shifted the emphasis from sexual faithfulness to faithfulness in death, that the latter must appear more definitive and greater, since the man apparently doesn't have the right to demand both. And if the purpose of the scene is to show the value of a death shared, it is certainly successful. But then the love of the characters hardly concerns us."

"Yes, it does, because the course of this love is determined by death. Not only this last scene, but its whole existence, and they all run the risk of being killed—the woman too, and also the comrade she went to bed with. I think a woman does something like that more easily, if the comrade who asks her is threatened himself."

"If the man she loves is equally threatened, then it doesn't hold true. That comrade's rather vulgar desire doesn't compare with the risk she runs of poisoning her husband's final moments. Even in the face of death she hurts feelings in him that are worth more than the short-lived comfort she gives the other man. Or ... in that case maybe she should not tell him. If she believes her act is justifiable, she would do better to be silent for the sake of his last moments."

"In my opinion, that lie would be the worst of all. How would you feel if you didn't even know where you stood with the other, with the person you lived with.... How can you say that—you who don't ever want to play the fool?"

"Well, if she told me that, I'd be an even greater fool, wouldn't I? I'm not saying that I wouldn't want her to tell me anything; I'm saying that that's what she should want. Because I would be fooled by my feelings, I would take it ten times harder than she had meant it; therefore, if it were up to me...."

"Isn't this view still a form of egoism? You tie her to you because you've given up your freedom. Because you've given up your freedom too, haven't you?"

"I would have to do that. I wouldn't know what to do with that freedom. I'm no longer interested in that game. I used to think you had to try everything once. And without believing.... No, without ever really feeling that something like that tainted me. It was always something that you could easily wash off, as soon as you were alone again. But now, well, now I would feel tainted. I had a friend who called such a conception of love the final childhood disease: 'If you go about it like that, good Lord, then disaster will really strike.' All right, part of that conception is, first of all, the destruction of any illusion concerning that freedom, which is the central issue between your characters. That illusion is based on a lie too. You can't be really united and still separate. In the charming relationship between the two, both independent and yet living happily together, this freedom is entirely justified. In the other relationship, if both lives flow together, the life of the one becomes that of the other. If a woman has wasted ten years of her life before she meets the man who will really love her, she can be sure that he will pay for those ten years which she may easily forget. Before, I would have said: 'Nonsense. Our intelligence allows us to distinguish between something so simple as what came before me and what came after me!' But that's not true, and the so-called jealousy of the past is less trivial than an intelligent man would think, because the truth is that there is no such thing as time sequence in these matters. Fidelity or infidelity has nothing to do with time, and jealousy of the past therefore can be logical, because it's not really jealousy with regard to oneself, but to the 'whole,' the 'absolute.' "

"All theories pertaining to love—or death—before you have experienced it are based on nothing. You always see it differently when you're faced with it. Real intelligence only takes experience into account. It's possible that experience sometimes teaches a person that he is jealous, even though he never would have pictured himself in this way. The main thing you have to struggle against in jealousy is the possessive instinct. But everyone's weakness is different, and you can only know where yours is when experience has revealed it to you."

"Yes, you learn that things are different than you had imagined so well in advance. Experience has disabused me of the notion of 'ecstasy,' 'losing your senses,' 'fusing your souls,' and so on. I used to be well versed in that. And what I have learned is ten times simpler and more real; all that happens is that the emphasis is constantly shifting. I've learned that it's impossible to feel two things at the same time with equal intensity: the senses and . . . the soul. I've learned that you always feel one and then the other, with a strong emphasis on the soul, as long as.... No, maybe I shouldn't say this, because I don't know enough about it yet."

"You're forgetting one thing: your whole argument rests on the value of the woman. Whereas you should remember that among a whole platoon of men no more than three would be capable of loving anyone; the rest would almost all equate the word 'woman' with a body. The greatest obsession with a body is also a part of this: Don José's love for Carmen comes down to mere negation of the soul."

"While this endless quest for the soul.... Every victory over the body is but another defeat for him who is searching for the soul. It's the only reason why the routine in certain loves... is postponed forever."

"The problem is that people like us almost always love someone. Still, we shouldn't cease to respect those for whom this love does not exist, those who respond to other laws. If you happen to be one of us, it's difficult to understand those others, but...."

"Why? Why wouldn't I understand them and respect them? I will— as long as they don't interfere with my love."

"I know this kind of respect which really consists of pushing aside the others contemptuously! Contempt is one of the greatest mysteries of our moral make-up. I can feel the greatest contempt for a hundred believers and then, as soon as I think of Pascal, it all dissolves."

"And then again, if you think of Nietzsche, you realize that maybe you shouldn't be so proud of your respect for Pascal."

"But I accept him completely. Now think of a womanizer, a man who breaks all your laws and yet is great in his own way...."

"Again, I'll gladly accept him; all I ask is that he restrict himself to his own laws and keep away from my love."

"No, it's never so simple. It's a good thing even, because carnal love would be almost impossible for anybody in search of a soul. You'll have to respect the womanizer and accept him too, even if his motives aren't as simple as I have just pictured them."

"Let's say then that we will respect him and accept him... until he adds our sister to his many conquests. Then no doubt we will feel the urge to smash his face in."

"And we'll be terribly wrong. But that's perhaps the best part: to smash his face in when you know that you're wrong."

"But afterwards, after hitting him, then you blame yourself for every mistake and every stupidity, don't you? And you're even ready to respect the womanizer again.... Well, maybe not that particular one, especially if his face is completely ruined, but his type."

"That reminds me of a wonderful story I heard recently. It's about a husband who is not exactly like ours, because he cheated on his wife all the time. One night he goes out to dinner with her and her lover, who of course is a friend of his as well. They have dinner. The lover and the husband profess their friendship a hundred times over, the meal is expensive and delicious, the atmosphere perfect. After twenty minutes the husband suddenly becomes somber, picks up a carafe, and shatters it in the face of the lover. He gets up, leaving the half-butchered man with his wife."

"We have a sort of artists' club in Amsterdam, called The Pit.[2] I can perhaps describe it best by saying they all have read Dostoyevsky and they imagine that his world makes their petty dishonesties meaningful and justifiable. I had two friends who were members. You would never think they really belonged, because everybody puts down the other members and bad-mouths the club in general. The wife of one of them was neglected by her husband. He thought she was becoming something of a burden and too possessive. The other friend lived in their house and fell in love with the woman. Out of... well, Dostoyevskyism, he talked about her to his friend all the time, in the hope that he would notice what was going on. But the husband simply didn't notice a thing, maybe because he trusted his friend, and even more likely because his wife really didn't interest him anymore. One day he took a trip to Germany, and at long last the other man had his way with the woman. When the husband came home she insisted they not say anything. 'I love him and not you; I want to win him back, and if you stand in my way, you're taking unfair advantage of the situation.' The poor lover then recognized the appeal to the gentleman in him—to the gentleman and the superior mind in these matters of bed and heart. He kept silent and, living under the same roof, he had to witness the outcome of the reconciliation efforts. I believe that this time they made up and the husband didn't notice anything. The lover's role became very Dostoyevskian.... Not long afterwards I spent a few nights there: the woman had just left; the break-up was final this time. The lover still lived there, although he would also leave soon. The husband talked to me about the matter: he was somewhat suspicious because of the lover's imminent departure. In the evening I was alone with the lover for a moment. He was dying to talk about it; he was unhappy with the way he had been forced to treat his friend. Besides, he probably thought that he had earned the right to let the other know how long he had been the winner. The problem of 'who won: you or me' was tremendously important to him. As he himself admitted, he was rather Teutonic in this matter. That night it so happened that the three of us were together; suddenly the lover declared that my presence as an impartial observer made it easier to talk, and he began to describe the affair in detail. He spoke with obvious pleasure. He was sitting in an armchair, somewhat nervous because he still felt guilty and also exalted because now it really was Dostoyevskian and because, in that context, he was the more evil and therefore the superior one. Fidgeting all the time, he spoke in long, slow sentences and looked furtively from me to the husband and back again. In the meantime I watched the husband. Slender and pale, he was normally cynical and had a dry wit, particularly when talking about deeper feelings. Now he was even more pale and his lips were pressed tightly together. When he answered he sounded rather tense, and he played nervously with an ashtray. I kept waiting for him to throw the ashtray in the other one's face, but he never did. I still think he came close to doing it; maybe the only reason he didn't was that the other man appeared to be stronger."

The telephone rings. Still smiling, Héverlé walks into the study and talks a long time. When he comes back, it's time to go to the hospital.

Bella is in bed, pink, with a chin that has become pointed and eyes sparkling with happiness. The child lies close to her in a small cradle covered by netting; it's no longer red but deep orange. "There she is," says Bella, "the Tangerine Princess. You probably think she's only a tangerine, but she's also a princess."

I compliment her on her splendid, rejuvenated appearance. "Gosh, Arthur, at my age.... I was beginning to fear that the so-called pregnancy mask would never go away."

"She feels young now," Héverlé says, "because she has the right to laugh so innocently." The nurse comes in to say there's a woman downstairs, and Héverlé goes down to meet her. I do my best to talk to Bella about the child, and I say she'll be a horrible mother; I tell her she'll have to curb her instincts completely, to put the child before motherly love when the time for conflict arrives. Bella looks up at me with one eye: "The worst of this is that you're kidding and I'm afraid it really will be like that. I already can't bear the thought that the child will have more use for Luc than for me. Oh well, we'll see how far intelligence gets us. At the moment, motherhood looks rosier than I ever imagined. Arthur, let me tell you a wonderful story. When I was about ten I was in a museum with my mother, and we saw a painting that depicted the Earth as a mother lying down and nursing more than a dozen children, with a breast for each child. I didn't dare ask my mother anything. Or maybe I was too proud to; I thought I understood it all by myself. You started with two breasts, I thought, and then with each additional child you got another one. And I became so sure of this that later on when I saw women who I knew had five or six children I stared at them, wide-eyed. 'Where,' I wondered, 'did they hide all of them?'"

She laughs, then suddenly becomes serious again: "The last months of pregnancy closely resemble old age. Nature undermines your resistance to the point that you long desperately for release, just as you do for the release of death when you're old, I think. Unless...."

The lady who now enters chases me away. I'm writing this in Meudon. Jane's presence, in the other room, fills the house; it's as if she had taken part in my conversation with Héverlé. How much did he and I confess to each other? What emotions did we work off? And for anyone who might read these pages ten years from now, they probably will be nothing more than the minutes of a conversation between intellectuals that took place in Paris around 1930.

12 The Precocious Child of the Indies

The factory on the Tjimarindjung was not finished fast enough. My father decided to go back to Batavia to contact the shipping service, so that ships that stopped at Wijnkoops Bay would also stop at Sand Bay and he could load his rice there. I can date this by thinking of my Misses, the only thing I have to go by for the chronology of my story. The same Miss who was seasick on the *Speelman* went back with us to the "civilized world" and gave me my first writing lessons in Gedong Lami, which made her impatient and hysterical. Over my sloppy "A's" she scratched her perfect "A's" so deeply that she ruined the slate. She rapped me on the knuckles to teach me how to hold my slate pencil, and that's probably why I still hold my pen so oddly. I started to hate her intensely during these first lessons, but in the afternoon she was my playmate again, with the same enthusiasm she showed when she taught me how to write. I didn't trust her anymore. Although her name was Kitty Wahl, for me she was *Nona Dobléh*, the Miss with the big lip. She had kinky hair and small black eyes and was full of spunk. She preferred to play wild games with us, that is to say, with Flora, me, and the native children of our compound. She would fall down exhausted and we had to pull at her or step over her until she revived. With her heavy Javanese accent she added a lot of explosive "h's" when she spoke Dutch. It sounded like somebody hitting a gong, one of us said.

Her mother was Javanese and sometimes came to see her. Out of consideration for her mother, who felt so shy in our house, Kitty Wahl asked permission to meet her twice a week in Po Sen's *warung*. Faced with such a delicate form of a child's love, my mother could not refuse. It seems that in the little *warung*, it wasn't her shy Javanese mother she went to see, but a European sergeant. I knew about him because my Miss had proudly shown me his picture. With my admiration for the military, I was the obvious confidant. When the servants reported the metamorphosis to my mother, however, Kitty Wahl too was suddenly sent away.

I never understood why my mother insisted so strongly on the sexual abstinence of my Misses. The only explanation she ever gave was that it was to protect us from *sial.* Just before Kitty Wahl left I became aware of something peculiar going on inside me. I imagined, or perhaps I dreamed at first, that she would fall down as when we played, but that she would send all the native children away and then ask Flora and me to massage her while she was completely nude.

There is no doubt about my sexual precociousness. Much earlier I had made friends with an Ambonese woman who was married to a European and therefore was addressed as Mrs. So-and-so. Each time I came to visit, she gave me engravings of princes and Boer generals that hung in her house. But this wasn't the principal attraction. She was no longer young and was dark as an African, but underneath her white *kabaya*, which always sloppily hung open, were a pair of enormous black breasts. One day she herself brought me back to my mother, saying, "It's strange, yes, ma'am, you wouldn't believe it, but this child looks at nothing else but my *tètèk.*" The grown-ups laughed with secretive superiority at this kind of innocence.

A year later perhaps, a real European lady stayed in our house—a statuesque white woman, who read a great deal and took walks with me in the yard. I made up fantastic stories for her about all sorts of things—among others, that I always swam across the river. She seemed to listen attentively to these stories and never let on to my parents that I fantasized so much. She called herself my friend, which no other adult had ever done before. It made me very proud.

One day she was going shopping with my mother; the milor' came round and my mother sent me to her room to tell her. She wasn't dressed and, probably to keep me from telling my mother and also because she wanted company, she called me in and had me sit down. As a "cavalier servant" I watched her final stages of dressing. She sat down in front of the mirror and quickly stripped to the waist. When she bent forward I had two views of her, more of her front in the mirror and more of her side from where I sat. I had seen my mother undressed often enough, but this time I held my breath, didn't say a word, and took in the sight, which I have not forgotten to this day. She was fair with a pink complexion, perhaps thirty-five years old—her black hair piled high, her white body, particularly her breasts, and the perfect ease with which she dressed in my presence—how little such a woman knows of what she gives a seven or eight-year-old boy for the rest of his life. I thought of her naked body even when she was sitting next to my mother in the carriage, wearing a very prim dress. That same day she bought me a book and wrote in it in big letters: "For Arthur Ducroo from his great friend Mrs. O."

I never saw her again, not up close, at least. When I was around eighteen she drove by in a car, while I was standing on the front porch of a house of an acquaintance. There were two ladies in the convertible, and both waved; she was one of them. What I caught of her face as she sped by didn't correspond with my memory, but I felt as though she waved only to me. I forgot the people around me. If she had stepped out of the car and shaken my hand I would no doubt have tried to relive the secret I shared with my great friend. I really had all that it takes to be initiated by one of my mother's friends, but it didn't happen that way. I was meant to have my first sexual experience, just to prove myself in my friends' eyes, with a native whore who had a face like a shoe turned inside out. That's what I later told my French friends, to their great amusement.

If it's true that our sexual attitudes are determined by our first impressions, then maybe I was fooled by the older women who were always around me when I was a child. A woman with small, high breasts always seemed unreal to me and even ridiculous, whereas, when I was still a child, I was sexually aroused by the story of the *kèlong wèwè*, a large-breasted female spirit who steals children who are later often found sleeping in or underneath a tree. During all the time they were gone, she used her breasts as if they were wings—to cuddle and hide them. In my mind this spirit was in no way repulsive. Later, when I saw a picture of Catherine the Great in a history book, I thought she was more desirable than any young woman. I never did anything about these fantasies, but maybe more out of shyness than a healthy attitude. Even now an older woman with a little bit of charm seems fundamentally more attractive and more exciting to me than a young one. The problem is that past a certain age very few of them still retain the necessary charm.

Nonetheless, when I was very young I fell in love with young women, too. In Sukabumi, at the house of Wa Gedah, I once met a girl of about sixteen, named *Dèn Buah*.[1] I have forgotten her completely, but old Wa Gedah teased me because I was so unmistakably in love with her. I moved around her, didn't dare to look if she looked at me, and when they once pushed me toward her, I supposedly said quite coyly, "No, I don't talk to anyone whose name is fruit." Clear signs of love, indeed.

But at the same time I was mostly a quiet and serious child. My parents took me along to visit my uncle, the general. He was a big man with a deep voice, bags under his eyes, and a gray mustache. He was an old grumbler but I thought him impressive in his uniform. One day he rolled up his *batik* trousers and showed me a large, puffy, star-shaped scar below his knee. "That was an Achinese bullet that hit uncle!" His wife, my father's sister, was the image of the lovable old lady. She gave me lots of lemonade, while she quarreled with my parents about teaching me the Lord's Prayer at that age. Their twenty-three-year-old daughter was called a beauty. She let me sit on her lap while she played the piano. My aunt said, "I simply don't like talking to that child. He looks at me with his big black eyes and that ironic smile, I'm telling you."

"And what will you be when you grow up?" she asked.

"A naval officer," I said.

"And what will you do then?"

"Then I will sink Uncle Jan."

They told him this, and he shouted with his thundering voice, "And then you will sink me?"

And I hid behind a chair, scared to death, and had to be drawn out and comforted again with lemonade.

One afternoon the daughter walked through my room, and since it was very hot she undressed me and for health reasons had me lie stark naked on the bedspread. She knew even less about human emotions than my aunt. I didn't dare and wasn't able to resist, but as soon as she had left I called Alima to the rescue to dress me again. Not ten minutes later my cousin walked into the room again.

"What, is this child dressed again?" she said.

"Yes, *nona*," Alima said shyly. "But leave him be; that's what he's used to, you see."

Perhaps I was also in love with that beautiful cousin, all the more reason for my modesty.

Before we went back to Sand Bay I went to school for a short time. I must have been eight, because I was a little bit older than the others, but my position as a gentleman's son meant that I had to be protected from bad company: I was sent to the Ursuline School, where boys over ten were not allowed, because they were considered men. So I was one of the oldest. I was terribly unhappy when I was put in a class with all those other children. My mother had said she would stay outside to talk to the sisters. At the first recess I realized I'd been had. Nevertheless I kept calm and sat down on a bench. Immediately a little blond boy came up to me and, sugarsweet, said in a bleating tone (but not really to tease me, I think), "Oh, what a darling little boy." His totally unexpected comment was the last straw. I jumped up and ran out of the schoolyard, between a couple of sisters who tried in vain to catch me, across the street and into the barracks on the other side. I was welcomed by the soldiers with laughter and applause, and the sisters who had followed me into the street retreated hurriedly. When they were out of sight I called a *sado* and told the driver to take me home. I was greeted with alarm and immediately taken back to school.

I was at the Ursuline School for just a couple of months. I remember only a few things. For one, I said "Yup" in my father's curt way, which they permitted when I explained that my father said it like that. And I told my favorite nun, Mother Josepha, all kinds of lies—for example, that each morning I wrestled in the carriage house with my native friends and that, just like real wrestlers, we only wore our underpants. To show her I drew a little man on my slate, much like I had seen in a book.

"But that's a grown man," the nun said, observantly.

"Yes," I said. "But that's how I look."

I was not punished for this fabrication, probably because the nun was experienced enough to dismiss my lying as fantasy. I was a hero at school and once chased a whole class across the playground. A girl with blond braids and a pretty face, which I noticed for the first time, was looking at me from a bench with admiring and dreamy eyes. A sister suddenly grabbed her by the shoulder and said, "Do you think that's smart what he's doing there?" And she nodded ecstatically.

But we had to go back to the jungle shortly thereafter, and I got a new Miss who took me to school in the morning. I don't know why, but one day I had the feeling that I had lost her. I started to run along the street, very upset and hoping to catch up with her. I passed the "real" school not far from that of the Ursulines. A large number of older boys stood by the fence. They shouted something at me as I ran past and, frightened, I yelled back, "Have you seen my Miss?" That made the whole group burst out laughing. I was humiliated and had the painful realization that at that school I would not be a hero.

The new Miss was called Bertha Hessing. She was tall and white and the only purely Dutch woman among all my Misses. She intimidated me at first, but when I got to know her I loved her in a different way than the others. She talked to me much more; I had the feeling that just as with the "great friend" we had something to say to each other. She told me and Flora the most wonderful stories, which she claimed to have made up herself. Actually they all came from her favorite book, *Adam Bede*, with the characters disguised as princes and princesses. There was a Prince Adam, a bad Prince Arthur, a Princess Hetty, and so on. The fact that there was such a rivalry between the two princes made this fairy tale more fascinating for me than all the others. Through Miss Hessing (my parents never called her by her first name, as they did with all the other Misses), I almost lost my belief in Santa Claus, whose existence thus far I had not really questioned or maybe thought of as one Santa Claus among a thousand Santa Clauses. He wrote me a little note at this point in purple ink. He said that I would get something this year but not next year, "if the little boy continues to swear so badly." The purple ink gave off an unpleasant smell, exactly like the little bottle of purple ink with which Miss Hessing wrote her letters. But I solved the riddle by deciding that the present had come from Santa Claus, and the letter from her in order to scare me.

She went with us to Sand Bay and would walk on the beach with me. Our walks in the direction of the Tjimarindjung were as if we were entering a calm and dark enchanted land. In the other direction it was more heavily populated. First of all you passed the outrigger praos, the most primitive form of boat—a narrow, roughly hollowed-out tree trunk, with two wings on either side to keep it from capsizing. On dry land it looked like a seesaw. Fish scales, and here and there dead fish, lay on the sand, and at certain hours you could see the fishermen shove their boats into the sea. When my father had brought over his crew of Batavian sailors, I looked on these Balekambang fishermen with contempt. But at that time Miss Hessing and I were fascinated by their activity while we collected shells along the beach. She taught me to pick up the pretty ones and leave the ugly ones behind. She had me listen to the roar of the ocean in some of them, all the while talking to me. Sometimes she would tell about her fiancé in Singapore and show me his picture—a very handsome man, I thought, with his hand on his hip and his turned-up mustache. I was supposed to call him Uncle Edwin. "And what will I get from you, when Uncle Edwin and I get married?" I promised her a whole box full of shells, but these she could collect herself; then a box of stamps, because she wrote so many letters, but she wrote all her letters to Uncle Edwin, and once they were married he would be with her. By awakening my interest in Uncle Edwin and their marriage she defused my jealousy. I loved her so much that I neglected my mother.

"You don't like your mama anymore; you're in love with Miss," she said, and maybe it was an early sign of her hatred of "intellectuals." "And she's such a *tòtòk*, she never brushes her teeth."

Miss Hessing left and was replaced by a true daughter of the land, with a broad face, improbably long hair, and a strong Javanese accent. This girl's name was Fientje Flikkenschild and from the beginning I disliked her. She ran after me everywhere, as if I were a baby, and she answered all my questions with her ringing accent, "How should I know?"

One day I turned the half-full chamber pot over her hands. My father just happened to see this, and he beat me like he never had before. It's true he hit me with an open hand, but in his anger he struck me so hard that Miss herself thought he was going to kill me. From that day on any chance of rapprochement between him and me was gone. I ran away as soon as I heard his voice or whenever I saw him coming in the distance. I had always been afraid of him, but from this day on I considered him my nemesis. My mother told me later that I sometimes got on my knees and begged her not to tell my father something. I don't remember this but it could easily be true. Maybe he hit me out of pent-up anger toward his coolies, maybe also out of gallantry with regard to Miss Flikkenschild, whose hair was so long and thick it must have been a feast for his eyes. This last explanation at least was my mother's interpretation. She angrily took my side and would not rest until Miss Flikkenschild had been whisked away by prao. She may have left the very next day after my parents had a stormy evening, and my otherwise firm father failed to support her sufficently. I hid in the new prao shed by the Tjikantèh so I wouldn't have to say good-bye to her.

This was my last Miss. From then on, whenever my parents went to the factory, they took me with them. I always looked for a spot where my father couldn't see me. The engines were working now, as long as the waterduct didn't collapse. At home I had even more freedom because I had become too fast for Alima. I learned now to distinguish between people who would tell my parents where they had seen me and those who didn't pay any attention to me except to be friendly. When I had crossed the Tjikantèh bridge I felt I was in a forbidden land, but also safely out of sight; on this side of the river I could only hide in the servants' quarters. I always went barefoot and, thanks to my mother's countless chickens, the greatest difficulty was to move around without getting *tahi kotok* between my toes.

I had made a new friend in Ading, an aristocratic, rather light-skinned villager, about twenty-four years old, who wore his hair in a bun. He was Munta's greatest rival in all of Balekambang. He was less clever and eloquent but was lighter skinned and had a more delicate appearance. He gave me my first lesson in sex when I was about nine, in the same prao shed where I had hidden the day my most awful Miss had left. He first told me what a man and a woman had to do when they wanted "to become one body"; for the purposes of explanation he preferred to use the example of a boy and a girl. When I finally understood what he meant but was still staring at him in disbelief, he said, "All the boys of the village do it with their sisters when they go swimming." Then he expanded his teaching into a comparative study of the two of us. The differences in many respects were striking.

"But can two men never do something together?" I asked, less out of deviant tendencies than out of the notion that my mother couldn't do such things.

"Yes," he said. "But it's very difficult and it would be quite painful."

I didn't feel a personal friendship with this Ading as I did with Munta, and it was purely accidental that I sat with him in the prao shed that afternoon. One day the rivalry between him and Munta became so heated that they both drew their knives. Their fathers came running—Isnan with a gun, I think—and maybe this was what kept an accident from happening. Ading's father, a *mandur*, had impeccable manners and was always very dignified. My father hardly ever scolded him and often drew attention to his aristocratic, handsome appearance. In addition to Ading, the oldest, he had four other sons, all equally good-looking, with the exception of the youngest and most cheerful, who had been scarred by smallpox. But one day this dignified man was called in and scolded angrily by my father: as a *mandur* he had to see to it that all his sons left the area within twenty-four hours, because they only knew how to use one thing, my father said emphatically. For a moment I was frightened by these words, because I understood them now. But my father's severity dominated everything, so the next day I saw the sad exit of all these handsome young men. It wasn't until months later that they started to come back, one by one.

I don't think Ading was perverse in believing I should know certain things. His answer to my last question proves that this was the case, unless he was afraid "to harm a white child." But I found another teacher in Kiping, the head of the Batavian sailors. Kiping told me fairy tales in which such things were treated in the simplest manner. The fairy tales would begin, for instance, "Once-upon-a-time there were a man and a woman who liked very much to form one body together (Rabelais's bête à deux dos) and who therefore had many children." If I was shocked by sex it was not because of the natives; their lack of tact is made up for by their perfect naturalness.

When my father had gone to Sukabumi again, my mother suffered violent malaria attacks. She lay in bed, delirious. Alima, old Ma Umi, and all the other servants stood around her. She didn't recognize me, and for the first time in my life I thought that she was going to die. When she came to her senses again, she called for Kiping and asked if he could take her to Wijnkoops Bay in the prao. He lived with his men at the end of the island, close to the Tjiletuh, where he made our boats. The adventure was attempted in the biggest prao we had. Under Kiping's direction my mother was lifted, horizontally, across the foaming surf, into the boat. After that it was a matter of getting through the violent breakers as fast and as carefully as possible: each fast-moving hump would suddenly stand upright, then the green would break into stripes of white noisy foam. After we passed the fearful breakers, the following eight hours were only a matter of boredom and discomfort. We stayed in Wijnkoops Bay that night in the only (delapidated) hotel. The next day we spent hours in a cart, driving the forty-two *paal*[2] to Sukabumi; my mother was deathly pale, didn't talk, and often clung to me. My "grandma" lived in Sukabumi; she was really my mother's French aunt, who had brought her up. My father, who normally didn't like to go there, preferring to stay with *Hadji* Gedah, was waiting for us. He carried my mother from the cart to her bed, and I walked behind them, dumbfounded in my admiration of somebody who could carry such a heavy body all by himself.

13   Sukabumi

We stayed in Sukabumi for perhaps half a year after my mother's ill-ness. During part of that period I went to school for the second time. I figured out how long I went to school altogether and came up with a total of about three and a half years. I prefer to pass over the school in Sukabumi briefly. Once again I was put in the same lower grade as at the Ursuline School, but in this school there were bigger boys, as old as sixteen, already sprouting mustaches, who had stayed behind simply because they came from isolated places. I didn't think a single one of the children in my class was worth bothering about, and joined the big boys, who gladly accepted me. Compared to other schools, as far as I can tell, it was unusual that they didn't use foul language. One day the teacher called me in to urge me to play with the boys my own age. The result was that a couple of days later I was called in again:

"Are you the one who threw that big red rock at another boy?"

"No sir, it was a yellow rock."

"Well, that big yellow rock, then?"

"Yes sir."

"Then go stand by that pole over there for the rest of recess."

Outside of school I had a friend, a tall boy who no doubt was five years older and made me feel for the first time that I had a best friend. We traded books with each other. I gave him four books I had torn the illustrations out of, because I wanted to cut out the people from them, and in return I got one undamaged book from him. Years later, when he was "in long pants," he traded just about everything I had for imagi-nary books that were supposedly in a chest at his parents' house, but which he described to me, illustrations and all. He took all that I could give him, but I never saw the books he had described. That's how our friendship ended. And yet I was sorry, less for the books than for the friendship. The most painful moment for me was tearing up his letters, since I didn't want to keep a single reminder. I once had an equally painful moment, a moment of misunderstanding and indignation, when a friend refused to recognize me because he had just started the

HBS[1] and wore a cap with a star. But not being able to understand was perhaps worse in the first case.

Sukabumi was one of the nicest towns in Priangan, built against the slope of Mount Gedé, with a delightfully cool climate and many hills and valleys. It was full of charming houses and lush vegetation, and had a large *alun-alun* with character, and a clean Chinatown crowded with new *tokos.* The outskirts, with the native houses, were also idyllic and looked prosperous. The European colony consisted mostly of retired officials, who grew flowers in their gardens. It was in that part of town that my "grandma" lived, with her youngest daughter, Aunt Hélène. My parents didn't like going there, although the house—as far as its location, rooms, food, and servants were concerned—left nothing to be desired. My Aunt Hélène was a typical devoted unmarried daughter—somebody who was a well-read woman for the Indies, an excellent housekeeper, skillful, helpful, and charming when she wanted to be, unpleasant when she didn't. She was a tall, heavy woman with hair piled high, an open and sometimes hard, sometimes friendly face, fierce blue eyes, a *nez en bataille,*[2] a large mouth with thin lips, and a flowing, stately gait. For one reason or other, there must have been an old feud between my parents and her. Perhaps she couldn't forgive my mother for divorcing Otto's father, with whom she was on excellent terms. Later on I liked her a great deal because of her unmistakable sincerity. She may have been a difficult person to live with, but there was nothing false about her. In my childhood I was quite afraid of her. She thought I was badly brought up—a true child of my parents, probably—and the comments poured out of her when I happened to be near her. She also had an authoritarian, loud voice which only overflowed with friendliness when the doctor came to visit.

Her mother, who my mother said she loved very much, didn't do much more than read and sleep. She was completely shrunken, with a small waxen face, melting blue eyes, and a protruding mouth with yellow teeth. She called me "little boy" and made crackling, sometimes even terribly screeching sounds when she talked to me. At a later date Aunt Hélène felt responsible for my reading material and didn't want me to read a book by Hall Caine, though I had worked my way through all my father's books while he was at the factory. My father was an enlightened despot in this. When I was eleven he gave me the books I had already secretly read when I was ten, and when I was thirteen, he said nothing about my reading the *Decameron.* Only once did he take a book away from me: one called *The Belly of Paris*, no less. He could just as well have let me be, because I had already realized it was the most boring material I had ever tried to read.

Across from "grandma's" house there was first a telephone company office, then a movie theater. In a city such as Sukabumi these symbols of European civilization constituted an attraction in themselves. Before that the biggest attraction for me was the European *toko*, Luppe, and the Chinese *toko*, Beng—small five-and-tens, where I got marbles, mechanical dolls, decals, and even books. I still get sentimental about a beautifully illustrated book, though I only remember its poetic title because I didn't understand what it meant: *My Friend Left Bank.*

Wa Gedah lived on the outskirts of the city. This Sundanese lady who had become a *hadji* was peculiar in her way; she looked a little bit like Voltaire but more friendly. She knew the Koran better than most, wrote poetry herself, and told me the adventures of two great Arab heroes who, if she didn't corrupt the names, were called Amir Ambiah and Omar Maja. Amir Ambiah had a stick that was as thick as a lantern post, she said. This detail made the hero less attractive to me. She also knew some Dutch, and I suspect that she made up the stanza of Ta-ra-ra-boom-dee-ay which she taught me; the final lines went like this (it was about an organ grinder):

> If your children come around
> I will make the music sound.

When she spoke Sundanese she was exceptionally lively and eloquent. Whenever she saw us coming she would utter long and varied cries of ecstasy; she'd call her daughter *Dèn* Aïsah and all the servants together to see who was coming. This "hullabaloo," as my father called it, nonetheless always warmed our hearts. It was always delightful at Wa Gedah's house; you sat on pillows on the floor or on low couches, and in no time you were absolutely swamped with cookies, lemonade, and exquisite candied fruits. Outside was a big flower garden, which was all the more alluring because you looked down at it through heavily barred windows. Later I imagined the garden of Omar Khayyam to be more or less like this one—relatively narrow but full of Persian roses. The bars in front of the windows were a result of one of Wa Gedah's quirks: she was scared to death of burglars. Another was her pathological love of sweets. She'd put three spoonfuls of sugar in a cherry drink and eat dried dates with a thick sauce of sickeningly sweet Chinese *stroop susu*. Nonetheless, she also remained slim and active. Her love for sweets showed up mostly during the evenings of the *buka puasa*; I used to sit next to her and, although I had not fasted, I got more than enough to eat. She worshiped me, and she would pick me up, lift me above her head, and rock me to the beat of a Sundanese song: "Pang-tieng-'ntieng-pang-tieng-keung...." She did this to weigh me, and each time she would try again to see if she could still do it. When I had become too heavy I was replaced in this game: her daughter *Dèn* Aïsah, who had taken over her manner of shouting welcome and who loved to eat cigar ash, bore a son, Dudung, who naturally eclipsed me completely. She wrote didactic quatrains for him in high Sundanese, wherein he was advised, among other things, always to behave politely and not suddenly pull open his *sarong* when there was company.

I admired all the strange things in Wa Gedah's house, especially the pairs of overlapping triangles above each door, which were to keep out the evil spirits and represented either the name or the symbol of Allah. She pronounced the name Allah with all the exaggeration of the initiated: as "All-lòch," with three heavy l's, which didn't seem to blend together. Then there were long *krés* that had paintings on them of oriental harbor scenes in reduced perspective, using bright colors and much indigo and whitewash; also a faded flight into Egypt with a lot of landscape and very small figures. She was very pious, of course, and had a separate little room where she prayed by a bowl of water which we Europeans were not allowed to touch. Through the bars sometimes I could see her pray, stretched out on the floor. She always looked fresh, even shivering, when she came out of that room. I was allowed to lie next to her in bed among the colorful Madras pillows. I was particularly happy to be allowed to do this during the time when a fearful story spread through all of west Java. For the wedding of *njai* Loro Kidul, queen of the spirits of the southern seas, the spirits who served her did something strange: they printed mysterious marks on most of the china of the native people, which wasn't even all that strange, because the marked plates and dishes were supposedly needed for the wedding feast. In addition, many people fell into some sort of hypnotic trance or woke up in the morning to find their teeth filed down. It caused quite a commotion throughout the land. The newspapers either fanned the rumors or ridiculed them, but the real cause of this mystery, whether supernatural or not, remained unsolved, as far as I know. It was talked about as far away as Balekambang. We were in Sukabumi when this nuisance was at its peak. I didn't dare go to bed for fear of waking up to find my teeth gone, and a holy woman such as Gedah was the obvious person to protect me. But she was more practically inclined. First of all, she said, spirits are not interested in Europeans, and second, it would be best for me to eat ham before I went to bed, because they certainly would not go near that. I'm sure she wasn't teasing me, because she strongly believed in spirits. One day, when her clock struck more than twelve times, she ran out of the house screaming and did not dare go back before an old and perpetually drunk European, who tinkered with clocks and whom she called *Tuan* Siraèh, appeared and swore to her that it was something mechanical rather than supernatural.

Another old friend of my mother's was the wife of the *patih*. It was in her house that I had been so gravely ill during the eruption of Mount Kelud. She was an affectionate flirt with protruding eyes and a mouth she would purse over her glistening, blackened teeth. From her my mother had learned to play Chinese cards, which was considered scandalous for a European lady. Aunt Hélène would have particularly disapproved, because she was a woman who was so well read and who talked on the phone every morning with the district secretary's wife, or some other intellectual, about the latest novel in the book dispatch box. My mother played with the *patih*'s wife, sitting on the floor at a low table. The cards were glossy yellow on the back, black and white on the front, sometimes with red, and they were covered with fantastic angular figures, which could have been the envy of some recent abstract woodcut artists. My father allowed her this pleasure because she never lost great sums of money; most of the time she won, but since she immediately spent the money, it still amounted to a costly pastime. I always had to go along, not only to the *patih*'s house but also to the houses of the Chinese women, sometimes with the *patih*'s wife, sometimes not. The Chinese women were much noisier than the Sundanese; their cries of encouragement, joy, and bluffing were much more piercing. Every now and then there was a woman who was a sore loser. Their laughter, too, sounded completely different. "Eh! Gua kelepasan, gua bekakak ni!" they said about themselves ("Here I forgot myself and burst out laughing"). I remember the names of these card players: *njonja* Tja Hwat, *njonja* Yan Eng, *njonja* Bengala. They were fat and pudgy or lean and stiff, but always very ugly. When there were children in one of the homes I had to try to play with them, which seldom succeeded. They hit me, and one time all my marbles were stolen by a rude Chinese boy who suddenly and violently blamed me for pushing his little sister off her chair. Another time I fought with a much bigger Chinese boy who had a shaved head covered with pimples; I scratched his eye so that blood came out. On these occasions we were called in for a minute, scolded, and then the card game continued with passion, sometimes until late in the evening, by the orange light of a kerosene lamp. Sometimes I sat behind my mother's back and whined to go home until she finally agreed. But thinking about the presents I got when my mother won gave me the necessary patience, and the candy jars were not absent here either. The conversations with the *patih*'s wife were in Sundanese and those with the Chinese women in Malay. Their shrill cordiality didn't match Wa Gedah's histrionics, but it was clear that my mother enjoyed it more than conversation with European women.

My father also had Chinese and Javanese friends. First of all, there was Lie Po Hin, the lord of Pondok Dua in the Batavia region, who had helped him recruit our sailors. He was later assimilated in the European community and, though he didn't know a word of Dutch, was baptized Mr. Hendrik Lie. *Baba* Po Hin, Kiping told me, had a love amulet called *tangkur*, which made him tireless and "like wood." He was an ugly man who pushed his belly out in the arrogant way of all rich Chinese. He was a marvelous cook and he rivaled my mother in all sorts of secret recipes. He loved to pat his European friends on the shoulder. One day when he tried to do this to my father, his hand was pushed away rather brusquely. My father wanted to have Chinese friends, as long as they weren't too intimate. Po Hin's only son, Tjan Ho, was about twenty-five and suffered from consumption. He spoke and read Dutch, which is why I remember him, and also for one of the most shameful incidents I was ever guilty of. In order to get a Dutch book from him I buttered him up for an entire evening, saying I wanted a *tanda mata* (a "sign for the eye," a souvenir), although he only meant something to me because he spoke a few words of Dutch and possessed these books. At long last he gave me an ugly book with no illustrations, but there were two others that I really wanted.

When we stayed at Po Hin's—except for one time when we stayed in a *pondok*, which stood in the water on poles—I always felt a little depressed toward evening. I took no part in the conversations, which were about estates and rich Chinese, and I had plenty of opportunity to notice how somber the lighting of the big manor was. I was always happy when the carriage came to bring us home. The way back was also gloomy. We'd pass Rawa Bangké (the Marsh of the Corpses), where the Chinese cemetery was; the fireflies there were called "the nails of dead Chinese" by the natives. Po Hin had another equally somber house in the old city. It was not far from the monument where the East India Company had put up the head of the traitor Pieter Erberveld;[3] the skull, pierced by a lance with an inscription below it, had been plastered over many times until it was entirely cement. Nonetheless, its presence added nothing to the charm of the neighborhood.

Among my father's Javanese friends the old regent of Tjiandur came first; he was called *bung* (brother). Despite his brown skin and the fact that he didn't have a mustache, he supposedly looked like my uncle, the general. At any rate, he was a potentate, full of humor, it was said, but very conscious of his nobility and his power. He was a great hunter, and in his den he had two room dividers covered with hunting scenes; both had bleeding bulls painted on them, which shocked me greatly. I wanted to sleep in the room farthest away from it, and even there I lay awake half the night (this detail is significant because of the obsessions with murder that haunted me later). At the regent's house I had another totally different experience, one of troubled surprise: his granddaughter, a girl at least four years younger than I, was said to be engaged to the son of another regent who was then going to the HBS. I looked at her with a mixture of respect and horror.

The *patih* of Sukabumi, the husband of my mother's good friend, was alive but in the last stage of syphilis and was kept hidden in a dark room. I was once taken to him as he sat there wearing blue glasses. They yelled my name, "Toetoet," at him several times, because he had carried me often when I was a small child. He laughed absent-mindedly, repeated "Toetoet," and caressed me hesitantly, which I thought was creepy. Then I was taken away and never saw him again. His oldest son had lived at my parents' house when he went to the HBS and became *patih* in his place. When the factory in Sand Bay caused my father great losses, he tried to make up for them by applying for free land from the government. I think he wanted what were called long-lease contract lots, but they were only given to natives, so that my father had to work with strawmen, or rather strawwomen, one of whom was Alima. He wrote this openly to the young *patih*, trusting he would help him. But the *patih* put his career as an official before their friendship, and not only did he not help my father, but he showed the letter to the assistant commissioner. One day, when my father was visiting this Dutch official, the latter asked, "You're good friends with the *patih*, aren't you?" When my father said yes, the assistant commissioner picked up a letter from among the official papers on the table and handed it to him: it was the one my father had written in trust and confidence to the *patih*. My father thanked the assistant commissioner for warning him so loyally, had himself driven immediately to the *patih*, and explained to him, without mincing his words, what a European calls a "rat." It caused a rift in the friendship, but my mother and her friend continued to visit each other and play cards. A few years later the *patih* was arrested because he was caught with his hand in the till, and not only was he relieved of his post but he was put in jail as well. I add this so that the reader won't be misled by his supposed incorruptibility.

His younger brother Hussein was still at the HBS and sometimes came to have *rijsttafel* with us in Gedong Lami. He would be dressed like a Dutchman, with his HBS cap on, and would speak almost flawless Dutch. When I saw him again in Sukabumi, on vacation, he was reading a library book with the subtitle: "A Story of Cave Animals and Cavemen." It was marvelous, he thought. It didn't occur to me at the time that the subject could interest him because of the similarity to his own legends. After all, I considered him a European, due partly to his white skin. I also looked up to him because, when I was still a child, I had heard him praised by Wa Gedah, Alima, and all the others, as being extremely intelligent. But suddenly someone appeared who eclipsed him totally: Alibasa, the son of another ruler, who was a couple of years older and who always wore native clothes. He was a young man with an exceptionally handsome, petulant face, always cheerful, and with a way of looking at every passing woman that struck me even then. He was darker than handsome Ading of Balekambang, but more handsome, more masculine, and with infinitely more character. If one takes into account the difference between a Sundanese and an Arab, an adult and a boy, he strongly resembled my one-time enemy, Ismail Pakarudin. Although he spoke Dutch well, he would only do so with me. With my mother he immediately fell back on Sundanese, and he also used this language to run circles around the HBS student Hussein, who was in his last year. Hussein's admiration for him was obvious; I learned the real reason at a boating party, when Alibasa outshone everyone else. He was in charge of the rowers, had the Chinese lanterns set up, and jumped from one boat to another, while playing the guitar, which he played not like a native but like a very talented Eurasian. The women were very much taken by him, and my mother said, "That Alibasa is a real *brandal* (rascal)!"

We lived in two houses in Sukabumi. The first one was small and belonged to a couple of Eurasians who lived next door to us. My mother became friends with them, and after they had gone to Batavia later on we saw them there. They lived unabashedly in Kemajoran, a typical Eurasian neighborhood, which is always mentioned with disdain. But they were honorable people. Both were tall; the husband was a retired clerk from the Accounting Office with a talent for tinkering and drawing. He had monstrous enlargements of family pictures all over his house, done in black crayon, and perhaps he had framed them himself. He also wrote out multiplication tables for me, when I didn't know them yet, in a beautiful clerk's hand. Everybody called them Aunt and Uncle Majeu (this name too was undoubtedly of French origin). Aunt spoke slowly and with a drawl, and Uncle's voice echoed from his sunken cheeks. Her way of welcoming my mother was less excited but certainly no less sincere than that of Wa Gedah: "Ye-es, child, so-o sweet of you to think of us. We old people, ye-es, everyone forgets us...."

Uncle Majeu loved to propose a toast at dinner and he was, in his own way, very witty: "If you have trouble with gas some time, just go to the Gedé pharmacy and ask for Mrs. Dewal's powders; you'll see what happens. They're really called Dewal powders but I call them *obat* Vanderfart, ha ha ha."

Aunt Majeu's favorite story was about their falling in love. They had dreamed of each other long before they met: "Now, you won't believe it, but Uncle dreamt of a peacock... now, just like me, proud.... And, ye-es, I dreamt of a *tokè* (wall lizard); now, just like Uncle after all, always *nèmpèl* (clinging to the wall); everywhere I go, he goes."

Shortly before we went to Europe I took a picture of Gedong Lami when Aunt and Uncle Majeu happened to be visiting us. They stood straight, next to one another in the dome, although I had backed up at least twenty yards, and they yelled in turn: "So nice of him; he wants to take us old people to Holland!"

Those Indies are dying out, and in spite of everything bad you can say about it, I personally see this happen with a certain sadness. These two people must have died long ago, because when I left the Indies, Aunt Majeu, who was a little older than Uncle, was almost eighty.

We lived longer in the other, bigger house. Just as the house with the colorful decals on the windows was called "Turpijn's House," this was Mrs. Buffalo's House, a name that struck me because I was then reading my first Buffalo Bill stories. In the front yard, a small oval area, the only decoration was a large *kembang sepatu* in bloom: a flower of a damp, fresh red, in-between crimson and the bright scarlet red of geraniums. There was a drainage ditch around the house, where I floated colored blocks from my building-blocks set as if they were boats. I'd pick them up at the last moment, right where the neighbors' wall cut off everything, fishing them out of the water with one finger. Often all kinds of other things were floating in the ditch, but they didn't scare me away from my game. In the front yard was a tree called *ki angsrot*, another onomatopoetic word referring to its small yellowish pods, which had a strange smelling liquid you could squirt at somebody after biting off the top.

In Sukabumi I not only went to school but had my first catechism classes. The opportunity was too good to pass up; right across the street from us was a church with a presbytery. The priest was a jovial, somewhat coarse type, who would give me sweet Spanish wine when I stayed a little longer. It was strange that I saw the most disgusting boys from school gathered together in the church. I always found this to be true; later, at the HBS in Batavia, there was an appeal to all Catholic boys to join a Catholic club, and it was exactly the same situation. I went there once but withdrew as fast as I could, with only half-conscious, yet unmistakable feelings of disgust. That club had another jovial priest who did his best to make us forget that he wore a cassock, to be cheerful and act young with the boys. There was a sort of unspoken agreement to show each other that you can be Catholic and still like sports. They played pool and could even smoke an occasional cigarette. This priest, noticing that I didn't show up again and being perhaps something of a psychologist, asked me to come see him and gave me tea in his room, where the walls were covered with books. I rather liked him too, with his Napoleon chin and his bright gray eyes. He studied me while he talked, and he noticed that I was looking at the books. He said casually that he could lend me what I wanted, also that the Catholic faith was not just any faith but that I could find marvelous proof for it in his library. Even this argument, which no doubt was the best one to use on me, failed. When I left the library my curiosity waned, and what remained was a disgust for the man in the cassock.

One day my brother Otto showed up in Mrs. Buffalo's house. He jumped out of a *sado* before it had stopped, walked right through the red *kembang sepatu* onto the porch, yelled "Mama," and embraced my mother, who was waiting for him excitedly in a beautiful peignoir.

"And is that Arthur?"

It surprised me that he didn't say Toet; apparently she used my real name in her letters. I had sometimes longed for my brother, who was away in Holland, though I only knew him from pictures. I always called him *bung* Otto when I talked about him to my mother. Now I saw a well-dressed man in a gray suit who hardly looked like the pictures, with thinning hair and a blond mustache and who I was allowed to call by his first name. He was taken to "grandma" and Aunt Hélène, to Wa Gedah and the *patih*'s wife. Curiously enough, as a *tòtòk*, he had forgotten all his Sundanese. Although he would regain command of it later, now he only laughed a little and didn't know what to say. This, combined with his blond hair, made him seem strange to me. Despite all the warmth he had for all of us—he also got along well with my father, whom he called Mr. Duke—I needed time to get used to him. My first rapprochement, I'm afraid, was fostered mostly by the money he gave just about every time he left—"to buy a book"—and so I almost longed for his departure and was deeply disappointed when he forgot to give me this tip.

When he later came to Balekambang he taught me to swim in the waterduct, beginning with a board between my legs. I was also allowed to go hunting with him, but most of the time I returned before the real excitement began. He turned out to be not only an excellent planter but also a passionate hunter. When he finally returned to Europe he had killed over five hundred boars. As an employee—later as a manager—he kept a whole pack of dogs. He loved them according to their hunting instinct. He had many pictures made of them, and he would tell long stories about the ones which had been killed in action, about the old guard and the rising stars. His second love was birds: wood pigeons, woodcocks, and the like. After a while he got rid of whole collections of animals, only to start up a new hobby with equal intensity. I talked to him about books, and he listened to me patiently until one day he asked me how it was that I hadn't become a book myself. Still later on I was able to play tennis with him, but verbal communication was always difficult. I had the feeling that to interest him my only recourse was to tell him more or less colorful, preferably funny anecdotes.

Otto showed his preferences and his peculiarities in a cheerful and winning way, but underneath it all he was very stubborn. He worked hard and was very pleasant; while I sometimes thought he was superficial, this was perhaps due to the fact that he was attached to his own life, which remained closed to strangers. I once had one somewhat deeper discussion with him, in Grouhy, about my mother. I told him that I had offered to go back to the Indies with her if that was the only thing that would make her happy—as I presumed then—sacrificing what I called (for lack of a better word) my literary career. But she had refused, although I was completely serious and had told her that I had remained very attached to the Indies.

"Why did you propose that?" he asked.

"Because she complained so much."

"But she always did," he said calmly. "In the Indies it was exactly the same, don't you remember?"

I had to admit that I didn't.

"Sure," he said. "I never knew Mama to do anything else than complain. As long as Mama is complaining I'm sure everything is fine. You can count on that."

My mother was disappointed by him in Brussels and in Grouhy, too. She had held on to Grouhy so that he could stay there with his wife and four children as comfortably as in the Indies, but he rarely came. The truth was that he was bored in Europe. Once, in Holland, for lack of anything better to do, he went on a rabbit hunt, but it was a joke. In the Indies he sometimes spent weeks in the Bantam area hunting bulls or perhaps more boar. The exciting part of the boar hunt was not so much the kill as the chase the dog gave the boar and the fierce fight once the boar was cornered. The hunter came only after the dogs had overpowered it, and then he dealt the final blow without much trouble. After that the dogs that had been killed were buried and the wounded ones were sewn up.

In Brussels, a number of times Otto came to visit us unexpectedly. On the road to Anderlecht he had found a kennel where they ordered special dogs for him: "Griffons bassets vendéens,"[4] he said enthusiastically. They were really meant for other game, but he wanted to try them out in the Indies on *bantèngs*. The concern was whether they would get used to the climate; they were not supposed to have too much hair but, of course, if necessary, he could have them shaved.

I liked to listen to him when he talked like this, because of the enthusiasm in his voice, although my mother noticed once again that he hadn't come for her but for those dogs. Nonetheless, she praised him in front of me, mostly because of his careful manner of contradicting her. "He's at least not as blunt as you can be." (Answer: "But then, you left him alone so much more.")

When the telegram came to inform us of his death, we had just moved to Meudon and were half in the hotel, half in the apartment. I had come from Paris with a heavy suitcase; my arm was still stiff from carrying it. I had to write a telegram and a number of letters. The light in the room was pink. From a corner came the harsh voice of the manager's wife. I gave the telegram not to her but to her husband with the glass eye. In my mind all this has fused with the news of Otto's death. Outside it was dark and cold. While Jane was in the room, I walked around and thought about him. The news of his death didn't come entirely unexpectedly, but not long before they had written that the doctor considered him cured. My main reaction was that an honest person had died—one that I didn't know very well, though I was proud, nonetheless, to be attached to him "by blood." I never knew exactly what he thought of me; I didn't much care. We never had any run-ins, and I was certain that I could count on him if I had to. Toward the end we had written each other occasionally. I had tried to tell him what I felt deep down about him, despite all our differences and the great distance. His last letter (which I answered, but he couldn't have gotten my reply) was full of courage and sincere warmth. He wrote that he soon was going on a grouse hunt, and although that wasn't really much, it gave him the feeling he would be "at least half a man" again.

14   Dreams and Notaries

June. When I was in the Bibliothèque Nationale with Viala, I met a man in his forties with an intelligent, delicate face and completely gray hair. However, as soon as he put his monocle in, I noticed an unpleasant complacency around his mouth. Viala didn't introduce us, but took him aside and talked to him in a way that was both obliging and distant.

"He has all it takes to be a decent scholar," he said when the man was gone. "He really knows a lot, has good taste, and many a publisher would be happy to have him work for him. But he ruins everything for himself; he lies as if he thinks everybody else is a fool and he promises things he doesn't deliver. His laziness makes him unpredictable; it's all because he used to be rich. His wife is Russian and she used to get money from her family. At that time he was a great collector and lived in a fantastic house full of fantastic furniture. After the revolution it was all over, and he has never been able to get used to it. If people still give him any work, it's because of his wife, who does all the tiresome chores for him."

Viala's words sounded like an admonition to me; he spoke as quickly as always and yet he seemed to emphasize certain words. We spent the whole day together, and that evening I brought up the subject of the man, saying that he seemed to be nice. Viala gave me other details that were not very interesting, after what he already had told me. I got home at 12:30 and, contrary to my normal practice, I fell asleep immediately.

Dream: I was locked in a dark cave which was perhaps the Hereafter and I was told I would see horrible things—monsters' faces, murder scenes, perhaps all manifestations of the wrath of God. Nothing happened. There was nothing but the dark, which became more and more oppressive. But although I *knew* that nothing would happen, I was still scared and I screamed as loud as I could, "Let something happen, godammit! Show me something!" Nothing happened and the scene turned into another one I can't remember.

In the morning my first thought was of the man with the gray hair.

What will prevent me from becoming just like him one day? You can convince yourself that you can get used to anything by exerting a little energy and a little willpower. You can change yourself into another person, if necessary. Nonetheless, some things in us are unchangeable, and different circumstances turn the same human being into either a decent person or a misfit. I think I have some courage and am not lazy, but it may turn out the same way, because I have weaknesses, depressions I can do little about and which might very well give the impression of laziness to somebody else—an "employer," for example.

I jumped up wanting to talk to Viala about this, but he would probably tell me that I don't have to worry at all about resembling someone who was a snob when he was rich and who was impressed with deference, expensive restaurants, and a medal on his chest. Perhaps I was mostly worried about a possible future resemblance between Jane and the Russian's wife, who has to do so much for him.

Of course, all this comes out of self-distrust, my ever-growing distrust of my ability to resist the notaries. Every night, if I don't stay awake till two or three o'clock, I dream. The dreams are not that bad in themselves and, as far as I can tell, they don't mean anything, but *every* morning the feeling of being threatened comes back. If the room is already light, I realize immediately that life goes on as usual but in an atmosphere of fear that sleep prepared so irrevocably. It sometimes takes half an hour before I have enough optimism to push aside this atmosphere. If it's the "enemy forces" that overwhelm me unknowingly in my sleep, how can I fight these "forces" for which the notaries are gradually becoming the symbol?

Last night's dream: I had to visit a dignified bourgeois family (a notary's family) to arrange a marriage, if possible. The family lived in an upstairs apartment of a stately, dark house. I took the elevator up. When I entered the drawing room I noticed that I was wearing orange silk pajamas for the occasion. The parents of the girl in question noticed it too, but they didn't think it was strange; quite the opposite, it made a good impression—perhaps they were worried about marrying their daughter. There was a piano in the corner of the room, and the daughter suddenly appeared out of the same corner. She wore a black evening gown and had a rather unfortunate, severe hairdo and an unfortunate smile that was meant to be charming. She took my hand clumsily and distractedly, and while I thought that she was not my type, I had the feeling that she had exactly the same impression of me. Suddenly a cousin was also in the room, vague and blond and hovering in the air somewhere behind the daughter, who had sat down on a chair somewhat apart from the distinct, massive dark group formed by her parents and me. The parents went on talking politely to me, and I even had the feeling they didn't consider the matter lost. As for me, I was thinking, "Never will I marry the daughter; I'd rather marry the cousin." A son also appeared in the room—a boy of eighteen or twenty who soon dominated the conversation. I thought he was unbearable, but suddenly he took me out of the room and we were on the way to an archeological monument—a temple or a museum or both. In order to get there he jumped over rubble and stone blocks; agile as a cat, he landed on the corner of one terrace after another, and I followed him, but I was irritated because he was so much younger: I only barely made it each time, and I felt stiff and heavy, while he jumped easily, as if there were nothing to it. In the temple or museum we found a knight (perhaps it was a large stone that gradually became a knight on horseback); it was, or at least I thought it was, Richard the Lion-Hearted and he declared he had to go to the young man's house, because he had to settle a feud with his cousin. We took him back with us; in a moment we were back in the drawing room, but now it was completely flooded and the whole family, including the unknown cousin, turned into some sort of gilded finger bowls. They floated on the water in the drawing room; the knight on horseback entered and became something like a tall ship and would fiercely stab his lance into the finger bowls, which were taking on water. The son and I looked on as if it were a performance intended for our pleasure. The father-finger bowl bravely bore a couple of lance stabs and was half flooded; other members of the family were also stabbed. At first the cousin seemed to want to hide, but when it was clear there was no way to escape and the whole family would be destroyed, he became very brave and took such risks that in a moment he filled up with water and sank.

How significant those finger bowls must be for a Freudian "interpretation"! I myself see only that in my subconscious a notary is equal to a gilded finger bowl. Is the knight connected to my feelings of resentment? It's almost too logical to be true. Somebody will explain to me how dreadful all this really is, according to a psychoanalyst's rulebook.

After my father's suicide I dreamt about it over and over. In this I was more fortunate than my mother, who complained a year after his death that she still hadn't seen him in a dream, and she considered this a sign that he was either angry with her or that he "wasn't free yet." In my dreams I went over the suicide many times. Sometimes—perhaps when I was more conscious—I'd succeed in stopping him, just as I wanted to do in reality. Sometimes he'd already be dead, but he'd not always use a revolver. Once I dreamt I was called to a hospital after my mother had had a car accident. I reproached her bitterly for doing such a thing to me—to go driving when there was ice on the roads and just after my father had hanged himself. While I was talking, the room changed: the bed on which my mother was lying disappeared. She was still injured but stood in her fur coat next to me, and in a corner of the room was a corpse wrapped in a sack. I knew it was my father, even though I couldn't see his face. "Just look," I said indignantly to my mother. (When I told her the dream she didn't dare take the car out for days.)

Sometimes my father killed himself before my eyes, but only as a presence; I never really saw him. Only in one dream did I see him clearly: after pacing for a long time in a shed or barn or something like that, I suddenly stood still in the dark with an open door leading to a courtyard in front of me. The opening was no larger than the width of two tiles perhaps, but the sun was shining, and standing in the dark I could clearly see everything that might pass by. Somebody took me by the arm from behind and asked, "Do you want to see your father?"

"Of course," I said without hesitating.

"Do you dare, even if he looks ghastly?" (That's exactly the question I would have asked myself.)

I said yes, and right away my father passed slowly in the lighted opening. He didn't look at me, but he was exactly as he was before the decline of his last years. He wore a light green cap, pulled almost over his eyes, perhaps to hide the deep gunshot wound in his head, and a light gray coat which was rather loose and a bit too long. The coat was open on his chest and was fastened by only one of the lower buttons. His hands were in his pockets and he shuffled past me slowly, though in a perfectly natural manner, as if deep in thought.

Fear, a feeling of being threatened: is it a Kierkegaardian problem or a simple case of passing hypochondria? "Artistic temperament," said my old doctor in Brussels. A remnant of Christian guilt? No, it may be true that deep down I am irrevocably a Christian, but my fears can be localized: they stem from the "notaries," whether they are big political bullies, capitalist gladiators, or bureaucrats of the liberal society where our "artistic temperaments" still feel most free... until they come into contact with this species, until they are fleeced by their justice. What a humiliating realization for the "artistic temperament" then, that he will never be able to stand up to those people who have sacrificed everything to the formulas they have learned, which make them invulnerable in society. This is the most despicable type of invulnerability. I'm not impressed by the notary-bully any more than I am by the others, since I have rejected my fantasizing about the pecking order in that profession, since I have one incontrovertible sensation: the ugly pettiness of it all. But this reaction, this inability to distinguish, would it also have been the reaction of a small storekeeper who thinks he's robbed by the law? So be it: the same pure feeling then, which I share with the storekeeper for this illustrious occasion. I still remember how one day the attorney, whose eagerness now has cooled so much, walked by my side through the garden of Grouhy after my mother had told him I took so little interest in business that she had to do all the managing alone, and so on. "But you must do something more than just meditate," he bellowed pompously.

The daydreams of the man with the "artistic temperament" fix upon the worst—the courage of the vulnerable. Bomb throwing: there's no more attractive revolutionary than the terrorist. If only you could throw bombs at the notaries. . . . No matter how you look at it, this dreaming about bombs is a typical form of compensation for the impractical, the people who are unable to carry out any act. It's all too bourgeois a dream of heroism. Actually, the greatest heroism for people with "artistic temperaments" is total withdrawal, disdainful resignation to the victory of the notaries, with contempt and resentment. But it's an essentially Christian resignation: "Look, I'm not even defending myself. I don't feel like it. I have no time for it."

When real resistance sets in, even in impractical and impossible forms—for example, the cold-blooded murder of a constable—unreality has already taken over. And yet, I've seldom indulged myself in anarchistic drivel for the mere pleasure of talking. But, as part of my "artistic temperament," I have an anarchist's hatred of all notaries, a hatred that dates back to my childhood. I would really be doing myself an injustice if I denied that I very quickly recognized how unsavory this practical group of people is. My hatred of almost anything that has to do with officials and policemen, with all bureaucrats, is not "literary" at all. I would admit it here if it were the case. You can only be sympathetic to representatives of this group if you feel they are victims themselves or exceptions, if you know their human side, stripped of their invulnerable formulas.

There was nothing special about the sincere feelings of hate I noticed in myself as I sat in the attorneys' room in the Palace of Justice in Brussels, waiting for the attorney who was going to help me sign the benefice of inventory for my mother's estate. The faces around me were really repulsive. There was a law clerk with slicked-back hair, adenoidal growths, open mouth, and bad teeth, who had the same air of learned cleverness that hung over all these collars and robes. There was also the dignified old barrister with a gray goatee and jaundiced eyes, who looked around over his glasses as if to convince himself that no colleague in the room had made it as far as he had. My attorney, an elegant man, maneuvered with supreme indifference past his colleagues. He was six feet tall, in a rustling black robe, a signet ring like a shield on his finger. There's one thing that must be more horrible than the barely concealed hate and jealousy of these creatures kept together in one room, and that is their occasional feeling of friendship for each other. While I sat at their large table, disgusted in every fiber of my being, I hope, I looked for two possible friends in this setting.

My father was thought to be a difficult person, even in his early years, because he would gladly sue anyone. He knew the law quite well. He had studied this means of fighting and he had attorneys among his friends, not by accident but because he had learned to appreciate them in the courtroom. One of them, an Armenian who was famous in Batavia, was on such friendly terms with him that he completely neglected his case, and as a result my father was suddenly put in debtors' prison. I thought about this in the attorneys' room in Brussels, but at the same time I was naïve enough to believe that my thick-skinned rascal from Namur would fight the other notaries tooth and nail.

For a whole hour I can look at pictures of Deterding or Zaharoff,[1] their idols, and know *nothing* about these animals, confronted with a mystery infinitely deeper than you can see in the eyes of an alligator.

15 Pelabuhan Ratu

The road from Sukabumi to Wijnkoops Bay was full of curves, with ups and downs, and in particular one big bump, as the planters said, where my mother closed her eyes and mumbled the incantation "*Bismilah*." The carriages were not the ordinary open *sados*, though they were also very light, but deeper and closed-in at the back. We were awfully tired when we arrived in Wijnkoops Bay after a bumpy eight-hour ride. The local name for this place was nicer: Pelabuhan Ratu, Kings' Landing. It was what is called a small town in the interior, which is not really wrong, if you equate a *kampong* with a village. It was rather deserted, with almost nothing except native houses, a *pasanggrahan* (a government house, used mostly by traveling officials), and one private hotel.

It was at this hotel that we usually stayed. It used to be run by a *hadji*, but he died and his widow neglected it. It was really not much more than a large native house with bamboo walls that had been plastered over to give the appearance of normal walls. But it had a *kolong*, and in place of stilts it had masonry supports, and in front a stone patio. On this patio the guests liked to put their rocking chairs, not just to take advantage of the cool air but also because it was safe. Once inside the real porch you had a floor of woven bamboo under you, here and there a board underneath. But the floor was so irregular and the boards so rotten that sometimes your foot went through it, right into the *kolong*. On the walls were the same advertising posters you saw everywhere else, a planter's joke scribbled here and there, the picture of Governor-General Van Riebeeck[1] with his curly wig, standing next to the bat cave which was supposed to be somewhere in the neighborhood and which he had visited in seventeen-something, and, of course, the inevitable color pictures of the steamboats of the Royal Packet Company in dark blue water, which also hung in our house in Balekambang. My mother said that her first husband and his friends one day wrote Sundanese graffiti on the Japanese engravings of a newcomer who didn't catch on at all; on one engraving representing a Japanese lady in a pa-

lanquin they wrote, "Euj, eureun, euj, hajang kiih!" ("Hey, stop, I have
to peepee"). The humor of the Pelabuhan Ratu planters—that is to say,
those of the surrounding plantations who sometimes got together in
the hotel—was always in this vein. They sat together on the patio, a
German, a Eurasian, and a Dutchman, sunburned after forty years in
the tropics, and they talked about planting and profits, if they weren't
talking about "broads."

I occasionally joined them and heard one or two talk about the novels of Sir Walter Scott, which I had read from my father's book collection. They maintained that these books were too hard for me and gave
me fruit and peanuts. My father didn't seek their company. I heard
him tell my mother that the German was a scoundrel, the Dutchman a
whoremonger, and only the Eurasian a decent fellow as long as you
kept an eye on him. The Royal Packet Company agent sometimes
joined them. He was a tall, lanky young man who had a reddish mustache and a crew cut. On one of our trips to Sand Bay my father had a
discussion with him which I was never to forget.

We were going to be transported by a Packet ship instead of by our
own sailing prao. The agent decided, however, that we had to take a
raft first to where the tender would pick us up. We agreed under protest, especially my mother, to this unnecessary complication. The raft
went out into the sea, past the breakers, stopped, and then bobbed up
and down, which made my mother and me terribly seasick within
minutes. I was on top of a sack, clinging to something that would
steady me, and lying as quietly as possible; next to me my mother complained, as much as she still could. My father, who was never seasick,
walked furiously back and forth on the raft. We saw the ship we were
supposed to take floating calmly in the distance, and no tender in
sight. My father angrily informed the agent what he thought of this
new arrangement. The agent, apparently also getting nervous, responded, "Shut up or I'll box your ears." He uttered these words with a
casual growl, in a haughty manner. As sick as I was, I lifted my head to
see what would happen next. I saw my father take one step and jump
on him, as he called it, and I heard him say, "Just try it! You just try it!
I'll throw you off your own raft!" The agent glowered down at him, because he was more than a head taller, after all, and on my sack I almost
hoped he would hit him, so certain was I that I would then see him get
knocked into the water. But he didn't. Instead he apologized, first
somewhat rudely to my father and then more amicably to my mother.

My father was almost fifty at the time and when I think about it now, I'm certain that he would have done what he said. Once, in a warehouse in Pelabuhan, I saw him pick up one of the heaviest weights from the floor and lift it with some effort and a somewhat trembling arm, but still faultlessly, above his head. He put it down and said to Kiping, who was the strongest of our sailors, "Your turn." Kiping lifted the weight to his shoulder, smiling sheepishly. I don't know whether he smiled because he really couldn't lift it any higher and was laughing at himself, or because he didn't want to outdo my father and was laughing for that reason.

Kiping was usually very friendly; nonetheless, he killed a fisherman from Balekambang one day, because the man had cheated and then ridiculed him. It happened on the beach, and even though Kiping hit him with his bare fist, the man collapsed and didn't get up again. He was a young man, named Usmèn. He was carried to our house on a stretcher so that my mother could tend to him, but it was too late. Moaning all the time, he lay unconscious, his temple crushed and blue. The blow was so hard that the court suspected Kiping of having used a hard object. The natives (and my mother too) thought he had a charm that could turn his fist into iron whenever he wanted to. Later there was a similar incident with one of the Batavian *buajas*—I think it was Quartero. During a brothel brawl the owner shot at him and he responded by crushing his skull with his bare fist. At the trial he split a coconut in two to prove he really hadn't had a weapon. You acquire a strong hand like that by practicing on a banana tree; the side of the hand eventually becomes so hardened that it leaves deep furrows in the tree.

Perhaps this was what Kiping's magic was all about. He was arrested a few days after the incident and, handcuffed between the village chief and the Sundanese policemen, he walked smiling into our yard. He quietly asked my father to help him; he hadn't done it on purpose, he said, but in a fit of anger. My father did help him all he could. He sent a petition, saying it was manslaughter and not premeditated murder; he went to the inquest in Sukabumi and pleaded for his sailor like an attorney, and he assembled all the witnesses who could testify that no weapon had been used. It was no doubt his efforts that kept Kiping from getting more than one year. Toward the end of our stay in Sand Bay he reappeared and took up his position as captain of our praos as if nothing had happened. He had fled only two weeks before his release, a fact that caused my father to go around the house cursing violently, but Kiping was let off for this too, after my father submitted another petition. My father sincerely liked Kiping, just as he did old Yung, and Kiping would have gone through fire for him, but then Kiping was a Batavian and not a Sundanese.

I haven't finished yet with this intermediate stop of Pelabuhan Ratu. For us it was the edge of the civilized world. The sea there looked less deep than at home because the bay was wider: the water looked smoother, grayer, without the shadow cast over it by the mountain range which gave Sand Bay such a dark blue color. There was a belvedere by the warehouses, where we used to sit sometimes with the only planter my father really respected, a former naval officer, Evert Reedijk. Sometimes he also visited us in the hotel; he was a tall, heavy, bald man with clear eyes, an amiable open face, and a thin blond mustache (he looked exactly like the Flemish writer Cyriel Buysse, whose pictures I saw later). Everybody at Pelabuhan called him a idealist, and when the planters were sitting on the patio they laughed as they watched him pass by on horseback. He was always working on new ideas, trying to get government support for them, hoping to increase the prosperity of both the harbor and the little town. He came up with numerous plans to improve trade and navigation and then went ahead on his own plantation as if the improvements had already been implemented. The result was that he always miscalculated and suffered great losses. But the Sundanese loved him so much that he was always protected, even in times of poverty. When he had money he would pass out expensive cigars with pretty bands among his coolies and the *desa* people; when he was poor they brought him as much free rice, fruit, and fish as he needed. One day he rode his horse through a swarm of wasps and was attacked by them. His horse bolted and threw him off. Having been severely bruised and stung, he was taken in and lovingly nursed by the natives, as if he were one of their most honored chiefs. The strange thing was that he always spoke high Sundanese, the language which a *desa* man uses with a superior. In the hotel you'd know that Mr. Reedijk was there by the way he asked whether the old servant, who was more or less in charge of the hotel and who looked a little like our Yung, had arrived yet: "Bapa Rusni parantos sumping?" he would say, with a very strong *tòtòk* accent, as if addressing a regent.

Bapa Rusni wasn't there very often; in the morning he would get us a can of condensed milk, put the knives and forks on the table, and disappear, usually till six o'clock in the evening, when he would come back to light the lamps. My parents didn't mind because they always had their own train of servants. The bathroom was in the yard, close to a well where you had to draw water and pour it into a tank, from which it flowed through a hollow piece of bamboo into the bathroom. If you wanted to have a continuous supply of water, you had to first fill the tank outside, after which you wished almost agonizingly for the appearance of Bapa Rusni, who was the only one who really knew how to operate the mechanism. First you stopped up the bamboo with a rag which had become so slimy it was disgusting just to look at; the bathroom floor had the same sliminess. In those days I was already writing short stories, mostly based on the fairy tales Kiping told me, but in Pelabuhan the satirical spirit struck me and one day I wrote down every accident I could imagine happening to a traveler staying in this hotel. It was a great success with my parents, and even my father laughed.

One afternoon we discovered a cake in one of the Chinese *tokos* by the beach—a canned cake, of course, between all the other cans of sardines and vegetables, and which cost a lot of money. We cut up the cake for tea, and I was scolded for wanting too much and not knowing the difference between "food" and "delicacies." At that moment Mr. Reedijk rode into the yard. Since my parents were alone with me, they were dressed in their bathrobes, and so they went inside. From behind the door my father told him to help himself. He drank two cups of tea, ate the expensive cake, the "delicacy," right down to the last crumb and so quickly that I watched with shivers running up and down my spine, not daring to say a word. My father noticed it immediately when he returned: the previous scene with me heightened the effect. "The poor man must have been starved," he said to my mother as soon as Reedijk was gone. "He is every inch a gentleman and would never have done such a thing otherwise."

As a matter of fact, Evert Reedijk really was a true "gentleman." For the natives he was also a *mitra nu tani*, but not the kind who mostly helps by populating the *desas* with white, blue-eyed children. He wrote articles in English about the future of the country, and sometimes it seemed that Chinese syndicates were interested in his expansion plans or that the government would build a railroad from Sukabumi to Pelabuhan. But he died like one of Conrad's romantic, lonely, misunderstood heroes, considered a fool to the bitter end by the other planters, loved by the Sundanese, but pulled down to their level. There have been other Europeans like him—more intelligent than the whites around them, shut out in a similar way, happy and unhappy, proud and resigned, who died in a *kampong* hut.

I remember two crazy women from Pelabuhan: a very old one who said she was the *ratu* and who would spin around like a dervish in the street when the children taunted her, but who would sometimes quietly tell stories for hours to my mother; and a young one, rather plump and giggly, whom I thought pretty—certainly for a crazy person. Our sailors thought her pretty too; one of them, the bow-legged Rahim, told me he would like to take a walk with her, for although she might be crazy, she wasn't so in all places.

It was also in Pelabuhan that my friendship with Barna, the son of the *lurah*, flourished and died. He was a bit older than I and went to school. He always accompanied me on my walks and beat me at marbles in the front yard. Because he could read and write and was not one of the servants' children, I considered him a friend and an equal. One morning I saw something written very neatly on the hotel wall: "Mr. Ducroo's son is nuts." I was so indignant about the insult that my mother herself started an investigation. Barna was present and yelled that he personally wanted to thrash the culprit. My mother suddenly looked at him sharply, asked him to write something on a piece of paper, and the culprit was caught ingloriously. He confessed, and my mother sent him away with a scolding. I was too crushed to do or say anything; for the first time I had the feeling that both truth and revenge are worse than the crime, but I cut him bravely out of my heart. When I went for a walk again, he was waiting for me in the street and swore to me that he still was my friend, but I walked past him as if I didn't know him. He came after me, talking loudly all the time, trying to make me laugh; at that moment he really ceased to exist for me and I went on without any qualms, feeling that everything had turned out for the best.

I want to record an incident that took place on the road from Sukabumi to Pelabuhan, which was to ruin this stretch for me for years and evoked a real resentment in me for the first time. I was riding ahead with Alima and another servant, not having Misses anymore. Our little carriage was far ahead of my parents' and we stopped somewhere at a store, maybe to water the horses. I got out and was eating a banana in the store while a child of about four stared at me with big eyes. When I held out the last part of my banana to him, the storekeeper suddenly said, "You don't have to give *my* child a piece of your banana; *my* child has enough bananas here." And to the people standing around he said, pointing at me, "This is the son of someone who beats people up and follows them into the village!"

The fact that my father hadn't exactly done that was irrelevant to me, but to have a native talk to me in this way was very serious indeed, and for a moment I stared at him as if petrified. But when I spoke I found the necessary words, even though he was a man with graying hair and a severe face, lean and fearsome, and looked to me, at that time anyway, like some Sundanese policeman.

"You're rude and insolent," I said to him in my best Sundanese. "I'll tell you this before my father gets here to teach you some manners."

Then I turned my back on him and went back to the carriage. He jumped up and followed but didn't try to stop me from getting in. When I was sitting next to the driver he ordered the man to drive off quickly or otherwise he would really go after me, which he would have done already, had I not been a child. The driver was going to comply, but I firmly told him to stay, because I wanted to see what my father would have to say to this impudent fellow. Alima was scared to death but didn't dare interfere in such a serious matter. The man kept walking round and round the carriage, rolling his eyes and holding his hand on his hip as is done in *wajang*, and as some natives do when they want to scare somebody. I looked at him fearlessly from my seat and happily anticipated the arrival of the other carriage. Finally it came rumbling up and stopped when its driver saw us standing still. But on hearing my first words my father got very angry with me, asked who I thought I was, and ordered my driver to move on immediately.

When we arrived at the hotel in Pelabuhan my mother asked me what had happened and then told me the rest of the story. My father got out of the carriage without paying any attention to the man, whereupon he said something rude to my mother and she got angry in turn.

"It doesn't surprise me that my child had to teach you some manners," she said, and my father was forced to interfere. He didn't hit the man but gave him the choice of leaving immediately or being forced to do so. The man slunk away but arrived in Pelabuhan at almost the same time we did and filed a complaint with the *wedana*. He was Bapa Tjiing, known to be a troublemaker. My parents went to see the *wedana* and since my father hadn't hit the man, the matter was dropped.

While they were talking inside I was standing by the fence with a young pockmarked clerk, who told me in detail what his two girl friends looked like, their names, and how they were in bed. That seems to be in contradiction with the proverbial oriental reticence, but thanks to Kiping, Ading, and this man, such disclosures were made to me before I was ten, and clearly the man enjoyed making them, much more than Ading.

When I heard that my father would not be fined but that Bapa Tjiing would not be punished either, I felt a violent resentment welling up in me because my father hadn't hit him, and I plotted silently to go look him up later and to thrash him myself. I went to Sukabumi again perhaps twice; each time I looked in the store to see if he might be there, and each time he was. "Wait another year or so," I thought to myself. "I'll come back and eat a banana."

In my fantasy he wouldn't recognize me; I would give a piece of banana to one of his children and ask if he knew who I was. When I had refreshed his memory, I would take care of what my father had failed to. I know that nowadays it would look much better if I felt differently about the "poor native," but I'm not up to such feelings yet. I hated that poor native for at least four years as if I were a native myself, and even today I could draw his lean face with the mustache. I talked about him to nobody except Alima, who kept telling me he was an evil person (*djahat*) but using a tone that seemed to indicate it didn't make much difference to her.

16 The Last Years in Balekambang

When we were back in Balekambang my father became my teacher. The Misses had failed; he was going to do it himself. He had gone to a schoolteacher and asked for a list of textbooks. The rice factory was running well now, and every morning before he went to work my father gave me lessons. Luckily I wasn't slow to catch on, because he would probably have mistreated me and then left me on my own. He taught me everything: French, Dutch, history, geography, math. While he was at the factory, I was supposed to do a lot of homework; in the evening when he came home, tired as he was, he would go over my lessons and check my homework. For his tenacity alone he deserves all my gratitude; later I knew his hatred of teachers, his temper, his pent-up anger toward the Sundanese, but here he really was a father to me. He sometimes threw the books at me and called me a dunce, but he stuck to it, which must have been more awful for him than for me, although at the time I thought he was a bully and a pedant, and as a pedant even more of a bully. Sometimes my mother interfered and asked him not to make me work so hard; he should not forget he was giving me private lessons, she would say, and so on. To reward me he would give me books which for the most part I had already read in secret. He held back two or three Sir Walter Scott novels which were less chaste than the others, but I read them anyway. I poked around in all his boxes and chests when I had no more books of my own to read, and one day I found an illustrated catalogue from a publisher of semi-pornographical material. One of them showed a farmer's son trying to throw a farmer's girl on the grass and the caption read, "Oh, Tony, if your mother only knew!—Don't worry, she knows more than you do!" This picture remained a mystery to me in spite of all the natives' lessons. What was it that mother knew better, I wondered. Why was the boy struggling with the girl and on what occasion would my mother have had to wrestle like that?

Sometimes my father called me to him, outside of the lessons, like before, when I was still allowed to play with his watch chain. But it wasn't the same. Ever since the day he beat me I considered him the enemy. Once when I was supposed to read a poem from my reader, I sang it because I happened to know the tune. My mother heard this and said, "You must read it." To my surprise he said, "No, let him sing." But I didn't trust this either. I felt that my mother was right and that I was betraying something by singing to please my father.

In my spare time I organized a group of native playmates. The most important were still Enih and Entjih, the daughter and son of the stableboy. The girl was very imaginative and would built houses out of my books. We even made them with more than one floor; cut-out dolls were used for the ladies and gentlemen who visited each other. Enih made up long stories about the Ducroos and the Rengers, where her father had served previously. My imagination soon outdid hers. I believed I really had known the Rengers family, particularly *Sinjo* Rentie, the son, who was a good ten years older than I and who I knew only from Enih's descriptions. I told her in all seriousness that I had experienced all sorts of adventures with him, that I even chased *tjuliks* with him.

"And did you shoot too?" Enih asked, with mock seriousness.

"No, but I walked behind him and carried the gun."

When I was older and painfully aware of my sexuality, I thought I was actually in love with Enih. This also started with the dolls game. She had to play the role of one of the dolls—it was a lady out of a fashion catalogue—and I played another one. I had these two dolls get married, despite her laughing protests. One day I suggested that she really marry me; she understood what I meant but said there was no place to do it. I suggested several places, even a pit on the beach. She then told me that it was impossible because I wasn't circumcised and so to her I was the same as a Chinese. The natives' disdain for the Chinese, combined with my own, convinced me immediately; it seemed irrefutable to me that Enih would refuse me if I were the same as a Chinese.

Her little brother Entjih's circumcision had made an impression on me. He told me that they had put cold water on him for half an hour so that he wouldn't feel the pain. Moreover, they dressed him up royally and let him ride around on a little horse. A few days later he took me to a corner of the yard and showed me how "it" looked: it was unrecognizable, with red and yellow welts and swollen like a pig's bladder. I thought it was fine for the natives but beneath me, yet at the same time

I understood that he had deserved something for undergoing all this.

It had become obvious that I had to be in love. All the knights in Sir Walter Scott were, and eventually they even married. I fell madly in love with a picture of Isabelle of Croye, which showed her giving her hand to Quentin Durward to kiss. The presence of the kneeling Durward stood in the way of my love until I came up with the idea of identifying with him. Perhaps that's how I came to identify with at least one of the heroes in any book. Sometimes the choice was difficult, but in *Ivanhoe* and *The Talisman* I chose Ivanhoe and Sir Kenneth without hesitating—in spite of Richard the Lion-Hearted—because they were the younger ones who married in the end. In *Guy Mannering* I was faced with a dilemma, because the hero of the story became old, so I had to wait for young Bertram, who didn't appear until the middle of the book and who, I felt, was the real hero. In *The Fair Maid of Perth*, one of the books I wasn't really supposed to read, the choice was the hardest: Henry Gow, the blacksmith, was undoubtedly the hero and also married the fair maid, but he had a full beard and was thirty, which as far as I was concerned made him old. Looking at the pictures I felt much more drawn to two beardless young men, Conaghar and Robert of Rothsay, but the former was defeated as a child by Gow and the latter didn't fight at all. I had inferred from Scott's works an attitude toward life which I wanted to see reaffirmed by each new book. Before I started another one I would ask my father, "Who is the hero? Who is his friend? Who is the enemy?" Finding a real friend and a real enemy was sometimes rather difficult.

In Sukabumi I cried over a book for the first time. It was Farrar's[1] *Eric, or Little by Little*, which even my father called a marvelous book. He said to me, "Don't you think that anyone who is a good writer suffered a lot to become one?" The idea that there was any connection between the writer—who was probably a man just like anybody else—and his heroes completely surprised me, but such a sensitive remark coming from my father made me stop and think. After that I began to look for the writer's suffering in a book. I even found an example of it in a story about American Indians: a passage about the death of an old beaver hunter, which I read with a catch in my voice to my mother, who, much to my surprise and irritation, was unmoved by it. Scott gave me little satisfaction in this respect, nor did my other favorite writer, Captain Marryat. But another marvelous book I got for my birthday, *Uncle Tom's Cabin*, offered a rich harvest. And strangely enough, either because of my father's compassion for Uncle Tom or his dislike of Legree, I never identified him for a moment with that slave driver.

When Enih refused me, I decided I had to fall in love with somebody else. I thought about all the European girls I had seen at school in Sukabumi, and I hesitated between a girl who was a few years older, thin, but with beautiful black curls like Scott's heroines, and another one about my own age named Polly, with whom I had once played hide-and-seek at the club. I chose the latter because I had a better chance of success, told Enih about her, and tried to convince myself by repeating "Polly" affectionately when I was alone. But the wives of two *kutjiahs* who came to live in Balekambang offered me a better choice. I fell in love again, this time very secretly, with a real woman—first with the one who seemed prettier to me in the beginning until her habit of chewing betel nut repelled me, then with the other one, whose white unfiled teeth attracted me.

I played tag with the Sundanese boys, fantasizing that we were knights like Sir Walter Scott's. We called each other Ivanhoe, Kenneth, and Richard, which they didn't think strange. Later, when I had a new book about lion hunters, I wanted to change the names and have them call me Marandon, but they objected to this because they thought the old names were easier and they were used to them. In reality their names were Entjih, Hatim, Sanub, Ahim, and so on. Ahim was a very quick dark boy who felt more my equal than the others. His father had taught him *pentjak*, a cross between dancing and fighting. One day I suggested that he try this art on me. First he modestly refused but I forced him and grabbed him. Within probably less than five minutes he had thrown me on the sand twenty-one times. Only once did I manage partly to pull him with me. Each time I fell, the other children, boys and girls, jumped up and down and cheered. Finally I was dead tired and dripping with sweat, but more surprised than humiliated, because I thought that it would be different if we had fought in earnest and I was allowed to hit him, instead of just pull at him. But for the others my prestige had been shaken; I was now their superior only because I was the son of a *blanda*. Later when Ahim was gone, Entjih told me maliciously that Ahim had said I was a real *blanda* because I smelled like an *andjing basah*.

The father of this Ahim was called Pa Sahim and probably was crazy.

Once a couple of coolies ran away, but they were caught and brought back by Isnan on horseback. All three squatted in our yard next to one another; my father yelled at them and then beat them one by one. The first two did not resist and were hit only a few times, but the third jumped up and sort of wrestled with my father. I had seen this sort of wrestling ever since I was a child, but now that I saw my father roll on top of this coolie, who lost his headcloth and was pushed against the ground, it aroused me sexually. I tried to ignore it, but the feeling was both frightening and thrilling at the same time.

While my father was hitting the third man, Pa Sahim suddenly came running up from his house and hit one of the two other men from behind. My father immediately let his victim go and told Pa Sahim to leave. The strong stocky man stood before him and looked at him with red eyes. Looking back at it now, I think that this scene could have ended in murder. If my father hadn't dominated the man with his will, or if the other had pulled a knife, my mother and I might have seen him murdered by the four men in a matter of seconds. It's quite possible that next they would have turned on us. Such things did happen. But Pa Sahim left, and the three coolies who had been beaten followed him. My father lay down on a lounge chair, and my mother brought him some tea and spoke to him soothingly. I wonder now what I would have done if I had seen my father murdered. I think I would have run out immediately, through the *kampong*, straight to the mouth of the Tjiletuh, and hidden where Kiping and the Batavian sailors lived. Or would I have wanted to defend my mother?

Another time, when Ahim wouldn't play with me, I went to look for him in his house. He was eating, with his face turned toward his father and his back to the door. Half in anger and half in fun, I pulled him off the *balé* to the floor before he saw me. He refused to come with me, and his father began to yell at me as I had never before heard a Sundanese do. I left to tell my father. While I was crossing the Tjikantèh on the bridge—because the coolie houses were on the other bank—I could still clearly hear the man screaming, "Just go ahead! I'm not afraid! I'm not afraid!" When I got home and told my parents the story, my father scolded me, but he seemed inclined for a moment to do something about the screaming, which we could hear even in our house. He could have been murdered that time, too. My mother held him back, saying the man had to be crazy; you could see it in his eyes.

A few days later he was sent away, and so I lost my friend Ahim as well. My resentment toward him was similar to that I had toward the store-keeper on the road to Pelabuhan. I was determined to hit him in the face the very next time I saw him, because he had compared me to an *andjing basah*.

In spite of all this, my father's treatment of the natives made me less than happy. I felt it was inevitable, but I shivered when some such thing was about to happen. From time to time my mother warned me to leave because somebody was certainly going to be hurt. My friend Munta, the Don Juan, once got a beating, after which he quickly ran away, renewing my hatred of my father. Once he hit an old, rather fat villager who brought our mail from Pelabuhan by prao. The man un-doubtedly deserved it, because he had opened a certified letter to see if there was money in it, but that afternoon I was filled with compas-sion and indignation. My immediate reaction was to run up to my room and break a piggy bank where my mother sometimes put a dime. I came up with about one guilder. I was sure my mother wouldn't scold me, but I was scared to death of my father. Behind the *djarak* hedge, I doubled over so as not to be seen and ran very fast to catch up with the man. He limped as he walked, pulling up his *sarong* and straightening his headcloth. When I caught up with him—he was al-ready between the double hedge leading to the *kampong*—I quickly gave him the money and sneaked back, my heart pounding, trying to hide behind the shrubs.

I write down this "good deed" just as I did my feelings of resent-ment, as almost irrational compulsions and nothing more. I had such an impulse again, ten years later, when I was a beginning journalist at the *Nieuwsbode* on Kali Besar in Batavia. On a hot and sultry afternoon when I was waiting for the streetcar to go home, a native stepped in front of me and offered me a wooden table with all the paint worn off. I asked him if he thought I was going to take the thing with me on the streetcar. He looked at me imploringly and whispered, "You can have it for just one guilder, sir, or for whatever you have," pointing to his mouth. "I'm so hungry." Starvation was a problem at that time in the Buitenzorg area. I had barely half a guilder on me, but I experienced the same reflex. I told him to wait and ran as fast as I could across the bridge of the Kali Besar back to the newspaper, where I might still find the chief proofreader. I did and quickly asked him for a guilder. Then I ran back and found the man waiting for me. All the time I had only one fear: that he had left because he didn't trust me. When I was sitting in the streetcar, which luckily came right away, I felt indescribably happy and yet surprised at myself.

Like every other colonial I myself later hit natives, mostly *sado* coachmen. Several times I forced them to drive when they didn't want to by giving them a jolt in the back with my fist. But all this came from a mistaken notion of machismo, in imitation of others, without real conviction. Once, after I had slapped a man and he walked away without saying a word, I was filled with disgust, pity, and anger at myself, and all I really wanted to do was to find him and apologize. Another time, however, in Tjitjalengka when I was seventeen, I fought with the houseboy Piin, who wouldn't obey me when my parents were gone. He was unusually tall for a native and had been surly toward me for weeks. I jumped up from the table where I was having dinner, chased him into the hall, and hit him. He turned around and grabbed hold of me, and we rolled over one another down the hall till we came to the wall. I got him between my legs exactly the way I had seen my father do; his headcloth had come off and was lying on the floor, and I could have hit him because he suddenly stopped resisting. But I didn't. I pushed his head against the wall, got up, laughed, and let him get up. I went back to the table feeling quite pleased with myself. He continued to serve me, and when my parents came back, neither he nor I mentioned what had happened. After that he was always at my beck and call and was extremely attentive. One day, when I hurt myself with a short sword, cutting my ankle to the bone, I limped inside, my slipper full of blood. He turned gray and hurried to help me. It was a short blade from a sword stick I had just bought and he had sharpened it for me. This may have been the reason for his concern, but such pangs of conscience strike me as too subtle for a native. What a nice topic for Freudians: the "bond" of master and servant resulting from a thrashing. I would like to have watched my father's face, if we had talked about such feelings.

Let me get back to Pa Sahim and to Balekambang. Perhaps the man wasn't crazy, but he certainly was cruel. One day Isnan shot a *binjawak* (a small alligator) in the Tjikantèh, and it was brought on shore while still alive. Pa Sahim put his machete between the jaws of the animal and split it open as if it were firewood, exclaiming "Ha" with each new blow; each time the mouth of the animal opened further, although it had already been split to the stomach. Such a sight strikes the natives as funny.

When Otto came to visit us in Balekambang he shot a *lutung* (a black monkey) for his collection. The animal was still alive when he came home with it. Munta came to me and said, "Go look at the *lutung* your brother shot. A *lutung* is like a person; if it's in pain it cries." I went to look at the animal. It was moaning like a human being and it did indeed have tears in its curiously human eyes. All upset and tearful, I went to my mother and asked if the animal couldn't be kept alive. She was afraid it couldn't; besides, Otto wanted the skin for his collection. During the night the moaning body was taken to the servants' quarters. The next day, as soon as I was up, I went over there. The animal was still alive and looked at me. I petted it carefully on the head and gave it my hand, which it grasped fearfully. Isnan came to skin it. I resisted, saying that perhaps it could be saved. "Not possible," he said. He had received orders to have it skinned, and it was taken away. I looked all over for my mother, but she had gone for a walk with Otto and my father. By the time they came back, the *lutung* had been skinned. For a whole day I refused to talk to them; I would have hated myself if I had spoken to such people. But the most painful thing I learned later from my friends: the *lutung* had been skinned alive. When all its skin was gone it still moaned, and only then, said Enih or Entjih, their father, the stableboy, had crushed its skull with his machete.

I try to recall that pain while I write this, but nothing.... It's gone, or the act of writing replaces it. And yet for years I would think about these things and experience the feelings of hatred and pity with just as much intensity. I sometimes reminded my mother of what had happened, to punish her for not having prevented it. That *lutung* skin remained in Otto's collection for less than a year. He was sorry that he had shot the animal, though it was probably more likely that he was sorry he hadn't killed it outright.

This event alienated me from Isnan. I really waged war with two adult servants when I was still a child in Balekambang: one was Isnan and the other Pieng, the kitchenmaid. Maybe Pieng was just hysterical; she would scream wildly when I had done something to her daughter, my playmate Amsah. This "mistreatment" was never serious: a ball would hit her foot while we were bowling or I would make fun of her, saying that she had prettied herself up for Normin, one of the Batavian sailors (when she had been chewing betel nut, which I couldn't stand).

When my parents were at the factory, Pieng would come yell at me. I felt inclined to fly at her, old as she was, but soon I succeeded in wounding her with words and that was much better. She'd hurry back to the kitchen, and among her pots and pans she'd beat her breast while she screamed, and although she didn't quite pull out her hair, she came close to it. I would open the little door to the adjoining room where Isnan was sharpening the knives and say, "Look at that crazy woman." He would look as if he weren't interested, but in reality he enjoyed the spectacle. I can no longer remember what mean things I managed to come up with—it would be interesting from a psychological point of view.

Isnan would say, "Allah, your tongue is sharp!" whenever I was fighting with him. It was good that I had a sharp tongue, since there was no other way I could get to him. He was the great animal killer in our house. He shot cats and dogs, which were thought to be a threat to the chickens; one day he caught a dog in the chicken coop and hit it with a bamboo stick until he broke its spine. The animal howled terribly. I heard it and came running. It was a chaotic scene: the dog was lying in a corner on the floor, moaning and powerless, while Isnan was wielding his bamboo stick, and I was tangled in Isnan's legs, pushing and pulling wherever I could—all this in a small space with chicken droppings and feathers and the door closed. It's a miracle the dog didn't bite either one of us. Isnan pushed me aside, or almost ran over me, while he finished the dog off with the bamboo stick. I screamed, "Just you wait, Isnan, till I'm big; then I'll do the same thing to you!" I hated him more at that moment than I ever hated Bapa Tjiing.

The animal stories are the strongest memories of my Balekambang period. The chicken coop was in the backyard, and the chickens ran everywhere, sometimes even inside the house. There was no place you were completely safe from their droppings. But they provided meat and eggs, the only variation in our diet of fish, since cows were seldom slaughtered there. If somebody gave you water buffalo meat, you had to be careful, because the animal might have been sick. We had water buffaloes ourselves—ordinary gray ones with some albinos mixed in. Those were the ones I liked to ride, after my friend Sanub had taught me how to get on them. My mother's favorite cow, Sajati, which didn't have any horns, had pushed me in the river mud, but the water buffaloes with their big thick horns plodded on mindlessly, with Sanub and me on their backs.

At home I had a little chick which ran around peeping, even over my books. One day somebody—I don't know who—stepped on it and it died. I was overcome with grief when I buried it in the yard, right next to the scales that were used for weighing the grass.

My friend Hatim gave me a *perkutut* which he had raised in his family's coolie house. With great pride I put the bird in a cage and asked Amsah to feed it along with those of my parents. But a week later it had died from starvation because Amsah had forgotten about it. It was during a time I was snowed under with homework from my father, and I had not paid any attention either. When I saw it was dying and my mother figured out why, I was furious with Amsah, but also with myself. The fact that the bird had been raised in Hatim's poverty, that he had fed it out of his mouth, and that it had to die in our rich home like this, gave the story the melancholy quality of a fairy tale, but this aesthetic element increased rather than softened my pain. Hatim could have beaten me up, if he had wanted to, but he took it calmly. He had a dumb face with buck teeth. After the chick's death my mother gave me a big yellow rooster that was in no danger of being stepped on. It was my rooster only in name; he was totally independent, except for the few times he let me carry him around a bit. This rooster was nothing but a joy to me. One time Otto sent my mother half a dozen fighting cocks, all with their combs shorn, but my unshorn rooster chased them all off. I had a vague idea of proclaiming him a fighting cock and of winning money with him—the *kutjiahs* even suggested it to me— but when I tried, it became clear that I was his master only in name.

The animal that was really mine, although it supposedly belonged to my father, was the fox terrier Lulu. His breed and markings made him a real white man's dog in this village—ambitious, energetic, and dauntless. Since his mate Lili had died early, he lived in our yard with his daughters, which didn't keep him from regularly exercising his droits de seigneur in the *kampong* among the common native dogs. He fought incessantly and always won. The villagers respected him, for he had to be an *Ardjuna* among dogs. Nonetheless, he sometimes came home wounded. Once there was a round hole in the middle of his head, so sharp and deep that I couldn't understand how it hadn't penetrated into his brain. My mother dressed his wounds and nursed him with *cajeput* oil and iodine, just as she took care of the wounds of the *desa* people. Lulu was always there when we played tag. Although he was very obedient to my father, when my father and I both whistled for him at the same time, he would turn around in a circle and finally come to me, although cringing for fear of my father. My father sometimes beat him with a whip, but I didn't. I wrestled with him, I pulled his ears or lifted him up high and then threw him against the ground, but always playfully. Like most children I was cruel to animals, but it didn't amount to much. I would only hurt an animal in order to experience a strong feeling of pity for it. We had a lot of cats, almost all of them calicos, and I let them sleep with me, one after the other. I tormented them by throwing them gently against a wall-hanging, so that they caught themselves on it high above the floor and hung there miaowing fearfully, not daring to jump down. And if they finally did, I threw them back up again. When they were dead tired, I felt I should be nice to them. This naïve sadism I remember only from Balekambang, though later too I always took cats to bed with me. I clearly see the wall hanging, dark red with a white pattern. Near the bottom it was draped over a low wooden bench, and the whole thing had a beautiful name from that time: *alkatief* (*alketiep*, the natives said), a word that to me meant wall hanging and bench and the whole corner of the room.

Fox terriers have a violent dislike of monkeys. Just beyond the cowshed was a thickly overgrown pond, dark green behind curtains of vines with white flowers. Lulu spent a whole afternoon there, trembling and barking; he smelled the monkeys that we knew were there because the branches creaked and swung back and forth. One afternoon I went to a coolie's house to look at a little monkey that had just been caught. It was sitting on a stick, making frightened chirping noises. I had forgotten about Lulu, who was standing behind me and looking up at the stick, trembling. The monkey saw him and crawled up against me like a child, but with one jump Lulu grabbed it by the waist and pulled it with him through the yard. It had happened before anybody realized it. I got to him fast enough, hit him on his ribs as hard as I could, and pulled at his jaws, but he stood there motionless, probably till he was certain that he had squeezed all the life out of the little monkey. And then he dropped it contemptuously. It was dead; a little bit of blood ran out of its nostrils. I picked up the little corpse and brought Lulu along by the collar; when I got home I tied him up, put the little monkey in front of him, and hit him with a whip till he was moaning. But even after that, I was inconsolable and I went down to the beach. The only that would have assuaged my grief was if I had hanged Lulu.

Lulu died of rabies. For a few days he had been grumpy and listless, and I sometimes pulled him by the ears, lifted him up, and dropped him again. But he simply left silently and unsteadily. My father noticed he was sick, because of his walk, and had him chained in a cool place, where he lived on for two days. I wasn't allowed to go near him, but my father went to see him every day and petted him on the head, and Lulu would give him a glassy-eyed look when he left. "Sullen rabies," my father said. "A good animal. He didn't even think of biting any of us."

I had some other run-ins with animals, not just of the cockroach and centipede variety that make Dutch women shiver when they think of the Indies—cockroaches I saw every day in Balekambang; some snakes were even killed in our yard. One day when we were playing "hide the handkerchief," I put my hand in an empty birdcage and was groping around when suddenly Enih screamed. From under the tin roof of the cage appeared, like a green arrow, a *bungka laut*, a deadly snake. Another time, when the bridge across the Tjikantèh had collapsed, Entjih and I rowed people across in a small prao. When we were coming back by ourselves and were right over the crocodiles' *kidung*, we were attacked by furious wasps. We flailed at them with our paddles so that our little boat capsized, and we found ourselves in the dark water right above the *kidung*. Otto had taught me to swim, so I wasn't afraid of drowning, but I was more frightened than when the snake shot out of the cage. Entjih and I swam ashore, leaving the boat and the paddles behind. I thought of Djasilem and could almost feel the teeth of the crocodile in my leg. Afterwards, imagining what it would feel like to be dragged under water by a crocodile became an obsession, and I added to my evening prayer: "Don't let the crocodile get me."

There was the glorious day when my father came home with a tiger —but he hadn't shot it himself. As usual, they had lured the animal with a goat which it had killed but only half eaten. A lantern had been hung above the bait, and my father and the *lurah préman*, a former village chief, were sitting in a tree waiting for the tiger. My father had taken the newest gun from his arsenal, a double-barreled rifle. The *lurah préman* had an old gun of his own, perhaps one of the first breechloaders brought into the Indies. When the tiger stepped cautiously into the circle of light, the *lurah* touched my father, who pulled the trigger twice, but both times his gun jammed. The other, having waited politely, now shot, and the tiger fell instantly. It was skinned, and this time I went to the prao shed to look at its skinned body. It looked strange but still had something of a tiger. The villagers lined up to buy a piece of tiger meat—not to eat but to use as medicine, Isnan said. The head with the holes in it was boiled in a big kettle so my father could have the skull, and the water became a strong greasy soup. The skin was then stretched out on the wall on the back porch, where for months there was an unpleasant smell.

The only time my parents went away and left me alone on the island under Alima's supervision, I felt like a king. In the evenings I had the *gamelan* brought inside and asked Munta to give a *wajang* performance there just for me. I also asked Enih to dance with flowers in her hair and, although later in Europe I refused to learn how to dance, I *tandakked* without embarrassment among my native friends. I turned my father's book box nearly upside down on the couch, and during the day I read till I had a splitting headache, which Alima, Ma Umi, or somebody else had to massage away. Early one morning I was called out of bed because a gigantic turtle, the biggest anyone had ever seen, had been caught on the beach right in front of our house. I hurried over there in my pajamas and, as always, barefoot. The sun was barely up and it was cold on the beach. A large number of fishermen stood around the captured turtle. It was enormous. A little further on, it had laid a number of eggs that seemed three times as big as the turtle eggs I had seen up till then. The men were talking about dragging it to the village and slaughtering it there, and for a moment I thought that this was a good idea until a boy wounded the turtle's eye with a stick. Without hesitating, I ordered the rope with which it was tied to be cut. It slowly crept toward the surf and entered the water in a stately fashion. It disappeared for a moment in the foam, but past the surf we could see it swim away in a straight line right into the middle of the bay, more on top than in the waves. You could see its head lifted up for a long distance, and the natives watched it as if it were a sea monster. I had the eggs brought to the house, and I felt wonderful. In the afternoon one of the *kampong* notables yelled over the fence that I should never have turned the turtle loose, that he would have dared (this was what he said) pay eight guilders for it! With the greatest disdain I had the man chased away.

I must have been about eleven then; it was perhaps during the last six months of our stay on Sand Bay. The rice factory's failure was becoming obvious; Royal Packet ships didn't stop anymore; the water conduit collapsed frequently; the rice that was promised never arrived; there were complications with two religious leaders, a *kalipah* and a *naib*, who were supposed to deliver rice but never did (my father called them crooks and scoundrels); and the coolies kept running away. Two Chinese foremen, father and son, appeared on the scene. The son spoke some Dutch and said he would do his best to "flatter" the coolies. My father asked, "Gow Hui, where is the stableboy?" and he answered, "Sir, he's busy peeling the dead cow." His father, a former Chinese *kapitan*, softly hit himself on the belly with a *kléwang* to show the villagers his invulnerability. A friend of my father's, my "Uncle" Van Kuyck, came over a few times with workers from another part of Priangan, and each time he brought bread, which was reheated over and over; we ate it with butter only, as if it were cake.

From this last period I don't remember much more than the mood. A young European planter came to live on the other side of the Tjiletuh. He had a phonograph and we would row over to listen to his music, which was far better than our symphonium. The waltz from *Coppelia*, *Tesoro mio*, Rudolph's aria from *La Bohème*—all remind me of this period. Sometimes we would row farther up the Tjiletuh to an old farmer, Pak Saïn, who had the reputation of being able to *teluh* people (put a spell on them, causing them to pine away) which, according to my father, meant he knew how to dispose of them with poison. He was a very small, lean, beardless old man with laughing eyes. We had to climb a steep bank with steps cut into the earth, which was especially difficult for my mother, but once we were in his garden it was paradise. Wherever you walked or sat, the vegetation was lush. There were tall trees everywhere and you could eat fruit and all sorts of tubers: *ubi*, *tales*, *ketela*—all you could want. It was the jungle in all its beauty; his house was surrounded by foliage. You could see fishnets, angles, and farming tools everywhere. All the bamboo was covered with betel. At dusk we returned: my parents silent, the oars creaking, Kiping at the rudder, telling a joke, and the sailors humming a rowing song. The sun setting over the wide Tjiletuh, the shadows falling quickly over the water, making the vines and the rattan on both banks blend together, the hollow dry sound of a bird called a *tukang kaju* (literally, woodchopper), and my hand dragging through the water—when I think of all this it brings back some of the happiness of those days when I was free of all schoolbooks. We also went to the *séro*, a kind of fish trap that had been put in the sea, with a series of compartments the fish couldn't get out of because the opening they entered through were pointed inward. These fishing trips were always great fun for my mother, but the slightest hint of seasickness was enough to spoil it for me.

When my father gave up the rice factory and applied himself to the long-lease lots in the interior, we went on long trips to other areas and slept again in villagers' houses. We would trek through the forest, sometimes across wobbling bamboo bridges, my mother and I in a sedan chair, my father, Isnan, and some village chief on horseback. And in the evening we would sleep on mattresses on the floor, with my mother's *sarongs*, which she put up as a *klambu* around us. I still remember the forest that had no equal except in fairy tales. You would literally enter it: it seemed to go on forever—a damp, leaf-covered path with leaves above your head, and trunks wherever you looked—and then, suddenly, you were out of it again. Blue sky and green fields lay beyond the last trunks. I would have to write pages to capture anything of these trips. There was the morning pleasure of breakfast, made up of weak coffee, the way the Javanese drink it, and turtle eggs that you had to tear open as if they were waxed paper sacks. Or there was the joy of coming into a little "town," barely the size of Pelabuhan Ratu, with a *pasanggrahan* where suddenly you'd find a stack of torn European magazines; then the market, where we bought all sorts of trinkets as if they were precious objects: red-lacquered Japanese boxes and for Alima a *kabaja* pin with rhinestones in place of diamonds.

In all this I forgot to mention my stepsister, Sylvia. Since my parents didn't have a daughter they followed the custom, quite common among families in the Indies, of taking in an *anak mas* (literally, a golden child). One day my mother came home with a little girl who had been left behind by a coolie; she was one year old, perhaps, with a pretty round face and big black eyes. She was called Bettina, after the operetta *La Mascotte*, because she was a mascot herself. My father played with her even more than my mother, perhaps, but after two weeks her parents came to get her. Her mother had been crying for her all the time and couldn't part with her. My parents were sad when they gave her back and announced in the *kampong* that they would like to adopt another child. A woman from the village high above the Tjikantèh showed up with a nine-month-old child in a *slendang*, its eyes closed, its face flat, and its cheeks puffy and feverish. It also had a sore on its forehead, because when the mother went into the rice paddies she put the child down on a rice block and one day it fell off. This child was much less attractive than the first one, but its unfortunate condition moved us: the mother was an older woman, the father a young man who was not her husband and denied that he was the father. After a few days in our house, the child had been completely cured by my mother—the fever had disappeared, the sore was healed; only the flat face turned out to be irreparable. The name given to this child, Sylvia, fit the *anak mas* tradition. I was about nine when she arrived, and she must have been about three when we all left Sand Bay. And yet I don't remember anything of her early years, except that she called me "Pappie."

I don't remember anymore how and when we left—my parents and I were suffering from malaria during that final period—but I think that they planned to come back soon anyway. However, in Batavia my father found buyers for his long-lease lots, and with the money he built small villas on the land surrounding Gedong Lami. The rent gave us enough to live on. The Balekambang adventure had cost a lot of energy and good humor, but in this way the financial damage we suffered was recouped. The rice factory was neglected and one day it burned down; the house we had lived in fell into disrepair; nothing was left but a messy coconut grove. We went back a couple of years later: everything was different, even the trip, because we took a car from Sukabumi to Pelabuhan and a motorboat from Pelabuhan to Balekambang. Enih had married a *kutjiah* who was much older and she left with him; the villagers called me *djuragan anom* instead of the familiar *nèng* as before. All I remember from this visit is standing alone under a big tree— the famous banyan tree, which so far I haven't talked about—looking in the direction of the Tjimarindjung, and listening to the sounds. It was there I had walked barefoot and hidden in the shrubs when we played Richard the Lion-Hearted and Ivanhoe. Before Otto finally managed to sell our land at Balekambang—to a Belgian plantation company, I believe—when we were already in Europe, I sometimes thought of this area as an ideal place to finish a turbulent life, with only a few books and, as I imagined, being great friends with the villagers. Some of our Batavian sailors had married, become Sundanese, and stayed on. Héverlé and I talked about the island. He asked me for it and so I gave it to him, and he called me "Mon ami javanais qui donne des îles."[2]

When we came back to Gedong Lami, Tjang Panel and Flora were waiting to embrace us. It struck me how cool the house was and how nobly high the ceiling. I went straight to a picture I had frequently thought of as if it were a symbol of recognition: a dog with floppy ears with a bird in its mouth, and I was happy it still hung in the same spot. But Flora was now a young lady of seventeen. She was slender, with her hair pulled back, and she wore a blouse and skirt. I had to find something to restore the old intimacy; I took a book I had received for my last birthday and put it on her lap. *"Peter Simple?"*[3] she said, stressing the last name. *"Loh*, that must be a nice story."

17 Practical Moves

July. I haven't written for three weeks now, because once again I was forced to deal with practical matters. One of the reasons for my paralysis is that you can't put something out of your mind and at the same time be passionately interested in it. Those who deal with their "problems" so well put body and soul, energy and cunning into their struggle. My greatest victory is being able to forget what has assailed me. I want to jot down what I just went through, but only as if it were already behind me, as if it has already become a story. If I had to describe my current feelings, I'd come up with such slop that it later would seem horribly exaggerated to me.

When my correspondence with the notaries soured, when I had made it clear to them that it wasn't I who had hired them but that they had forced themselves on me and that I looked upon them with neither friendship nor gratitude, they immediately announced that they were ready to turn the job over to another notary as soon as I returned the money they had advanced me for the funeral. In my indignation I tried to get a second mortgage on Grouhy, over and above the one my mother had already placed on it. Under the circumstances it turned out to be impossible. I accepted my defeat. I couldn't send the notaries their money and decided simply to wait and see how things would turn out, and at any rate not to write them anymore. Although Graaflant was not much of a businessman, he offered to take over for me, if necessary. I sent him a long letter with information and questions, but he thought it all too unbusinesslike, because there were questions like: "What can happen if the notaries substitute my mother's jewels with fake ones and sell the real ones?" The jewels had not been left in the sealed house but had been put in a safe. Graaflant thought that such a substitution would be too risky, even for a notary. Moreover, the Brussels notary had taken the jewels to a safe with a combination lock, and he knew the combination but didn't have the key, whereas the judge had the key but didn't know the combination.

In the meantime Grouhy had remained unsalable. The real-estate agent had turned down two bids which seemed ridiculous to him, because we should at least try to get me some money after paying back the mortgage. Viala, who had worked himself to death, finished his book. While it was being printed, Jane and I had already started addressing envelopes for the prospectuses. We sealed them and put on the postage. We worked on the envelopes a few hours every day: the names of all the doctors, pharmacists, and veterinarians from the telephone directory, postal zone after postal zone. In a short while there were more than six thousand addressed envelopes at Viala's. We thought we would also learn French geography through this, but that didn't happen. When we were through with the envelopes there was another period of waiting. "If Grouhy isn't sold soon and Viala's book doesn't make it either, we'll have to find something else," we said to each other. "But what? Still, we should realize first of all that we're lucky to have a job as Parisian correspondent. There's no work in the Indies, nor in Holland. It's not a personal question of inferiority; it's a time of crisis for everybody."

The last of our money went into the book. As soon as it came out and the prospectuses were mailed, the orders should have started coming in. In one month, Viala thought, we would recoup our expenses and the month thereafter we should start making a profit. I continued to work on my Meester-Cornelis recollections, writing hastily, barely rereading what I had written. The proofs of the book came in. With the vignettes Viala had included, the three-hundred and twenty pages of vellum paper, the carefully composed biographies of the rhyming doctors, it seemed serious rather than amusing, though still quite curious. We sent nine hundred prospectuses throughout the provinces because there might be bored doctors who'd respond more favorably than their Parisian colleagues. When there was not one order after three days, Manou confided to Jane that Viala was beginning to get worried about it. We waited a full week. The nine hundred prospectuses yielded three orders—not even enough to cover the mailing costs. Héverlé saw the book and said, "It doesn't surprise me at all; I thought it was going to be a collection of bawdy songs for doctors to remind them of their student days. Viala made a scholarly work out of it, carried away by his zeal!"

Viala's subconscious desire to experience the worst made him want to visit the doctors personally in each area, with a couple of copies in his briefcase. He called this taking the bull by the horns, but he was startled for a moment when I told him that I would do the same. He took me with him, however, and I worked one side of the street while he did the other. After two hours I had been admitted to see five doctors. The first problem is the concierge who has to explain which floor and which door would yield the doctor, but once at the door you're confronted by the maid or a nurse who does her best to fend off salesmen: "The doctor is out. The doctor can see you, preferably on Monday. The doctor is busy right now; please come back another time." Once I got as far as a waiting room, where I waited, with my briefcase, till four patients had had their turn. When I finally saw the doctor I didn't even get to open my briefcase. He was a man with a pinched yellow face and a beard, clearly worried about the Depression. Nevertheless, I said that "I had mainly come" to show him a book.... Perhaps he was interested. "Not at all, sir, not at all!" he said, and opened the door on the other side. I had waited a whole hour just to pass through his office. I met up with Viala in a little café. "This method is much too impractical," I said, after I had related my experiences, trying my best to make them sound as funny as possible. "How can we imagine that these people, absorbed in their work, would be interested in an expensive book, when perhaps they don't even read?" He had been received kindly a couple of times, he said, and they looked at the book and told him long stories about the bad times....

I suggested that we go to Brussels, where I knew a few doctors. Wijdenes wrote from Holland to ask for five copies, which he sold to his relatives. With this money I traveled to Brussels. The doctors received me well, were happy to see me again, and so on, but they also talked about the bad times. I got a few addresses of doctors especially interested in such publications. They talked about the bad times, too.

I went to Suzanne to tell her about the fiasco of the book and explain that I couldn't send her any money. She had an abcess in her mouth that disfigured her whole face. She was sitting by the window, her hair messed up and staring blankly with her half-blind expression. Without saying a word she took the compress from her swollen cheek and throat to show me how bad it was. Nonetheless I delivered my message as well as I could. I added that of course I would continue to send money for Guy, but that it might be better, both for him and for her, if he went to a boarding school, now that she would perhaps have to go out and find work. This time, due to the serious nature of the circumstances, my fear of my own cruelty, of breaking the promises she had always counted on, disappeared. With money, if everything had gone as it should, I would have taken care of things for her and Guy as I always intended, infinitely better than when my mother was still alive. Now it was only fair that she at least try to take care of herself.

She took it rather well—surprisingly well for someone who has lost everything, including her erroneous ideas about class, who is pushed back to the condition I have left her in. She has learned nothing in all these years, seems as helpless as ever—even more so because she had been thrown completely off balance. Only money could help her. Her reaction came after I was back in Paris. Her misspelled letters blamed me in a tone that not only hurt but made me bitter. If I learned anything from my relationship with her, it's that those bitter feelings which always look ridiculous and unfair in hindsight provide a hiding place that one seizes upon as a last refuge.

And then came the emergency measures. Aunt Tina, also sick and feeling the pinch of the Depression, took Guy to some sort of a vegetarian and theosophist school. She would pay for his clothes and from time to time find out how he was doing. I don't think they'll turn him into a theosophist very quickly. Suzanne went to the institute and found it to her liking. It's in the suburbs, with a huge yard surrounding it; the children she saw playing there looked happy and healthy. Until something better can be arranged this is the only solution. And all this took less than three weeks.

So Guy, impossibly spoiled by his grandmother, is now living with those vegetarians. I wrote a fatherly letter to the headmistress, trying to hit on the right tone. I got back a letter full of proper educational psychology: the child was less of a problem than he seemed, he was really very sensitive, everybody loved him already, and he would soon be completely adjusted. Every time his mother visited him he cried, but as soon as she was gone he went back to playing happily with the other children. Suzanne has moved to a small apartment and is trying to find a job. I'd like to see Guy again, but another trip to Brussels is out of the question. Suzanne's reports always stressed Guy's crying. He would tell her: "Be careful not to get run over; otherwise they'll come and tell me that you're dead too." I can hear the tone in which he must have said that.

Viala and Manou continued to work on the sale of the book, Manou with great courage and devotion. They're nicer to a woman and so she sold a couple of copies. An old doctor told her she had the loveliest eyes, "clear as Vichy water." He had taken her hand and stroked and pressed it a long time before he decided. I tried a new system with Viala, giving the prospectuses as letters to the concierges in Paris. It saved postage and provided a marvelous opportunity to document concierges' dwellings, their variations of filth, and the acrid, moldy existence of this sort of people. Result: three more orders. We have now given up the money as lost and have gone back to the newspaper as our only means of support.

Given Viala's character, I know that he thinks this failure is worse for us than for himself, although he's suffering three times more than we are, and even more so if you take into account all the trouble he went through. We see each other very little now. He's doing library work for others, and Manou is talking about setting up a waffle stand. Jane and I work on our articles as much as possible here in Meudon. It's vacation time and it's hot. We don't even have to go to Paris to find material for our articles; in every one of them we talk about the heat wave and how the theaters remain closed.

I received a summons for failure to pay the mortgage interest on Grouhy; I immediately forwarded it to the real-estate agent. He wrote back that he had requested and obtained a deferment.

18   The School and Baur

The nine or ten new villas my parents built on their property didn't change the old-fashioned air of the surroundings of Gedong Lami. This area was originally called *Kampong* Melaju and it was an extension of Meester-Cornelis, which in turn was an extension of greater Batavia. The highway to Buitenzorg went right past our house and there weren't many European houses anymore. Our own house was beyond Chinatown. The local train from Batavia to Meester-Cornelis had its final stop one past Gang Lami, which ran perpendicular to our house. At the terminal was an intersection, Gardu Tjabang, with the guardhouse and the *tongtong*, which a couple of years before had to sound the alarm so often. There the obsolete heavy locomotives, covered with dust and puffing mightily, were doused with water and allowed to catch their breath.

Apart from the schoolchildren, the people who took the train every day were mostly clerks and officials who worked downtown for the government. A *procureur-bambu*[1] with a handsome gray goatee, Mr. Yusuf, a white Armenian, gave daily lessons to whomever would listen: "And so I said, 'No, begging your pardon, Your Honor, that man was not a fanatic. He knew the Koran and the Koran does not say as people think: "Place a fan and a dagger next to you, even in prayer, to be prepared for the Christians at all times," but: "So that your prayer be cool as a fan and sharp as a dagger," which is not at all inflammatory. I have studied the Koran myself, Your Honor, and my explanation is also that of Professor Snouck Hurgronje,[2] which you can find on such and such a page.'" The petty officials listened, nodding respectfully.

Close to Gardu Tjabang were a few large houses—some set way back, much more hidden than ours, beautiful and alluring by moonlight, and sinister as haunted houses in the cheerless light of street lanterns. Mr. Frank Robertson lived here after he left our pavilion—but in a small house. At night sometimes I went to see him, to pick up a *Strand Magazine.* I'd look at the pictures because I couldn't read the captions. Our fence went so far in that direction that I felt I was already way down the street, when in fact I was only as far as our own *bungur* tree.

In the morning the ox carts passed here with a penetrating yet ponderous rattle. The attendants seemed to walk next to their animals from early morning to late in the evening. At night the Chinese food vendors came with a little flickering light in the boxes which they carried on their shoulders by means of a bamboo yoke, selling *bahmi* and *soto*, or the Javanese, who of course didn't sell any pork but *saté kambing*. If my parents happened to be sitting in the dome, we called these vendors over. This was one of the coziest moments of the evening. We sat in the dome in the dark, while the vendor stood below, next to the steps, with his portable kitchen on the gravel, taking care of the fire and the meat. Some Chinese also sold *bèko*, which I had to buy secretly because my mother thought it too disgusting; they were animal figures blown from a gooey, bright red substance which soon hardened and became brittle. It tasted very sweet and always stuck to your teeth. When the peddlers blew through a pipe, roosters and horses appeared while you watched, and since their breath was invisible, I didn't worry about it.

Chinatown had familiarized me with all the Chinese odors. It was located past Gang Bungur or Lammerslaan, which was parallel to Gang Lami, and directly in front of the assistant commissioner's house, which was only a little smaller than ours. Even closer to us, in a meandering hidden alley on a tiny overgrown square stood the Rehoboth church, where Flora went because she was Protestant, but where I was only allowed to peek in. The church was neglected, narrow, with many broken windows, and dusty and bare inside. The Eurasian children of the neighborhood played marbles around it on the little square. Lammerslaan wasn't as well paved as Gang Lami and much muddier after it rained. At the train terminal was a large field where the first traveling movies and sometimes a circus set up their tents. This was the place where Bek Yam Seng was murdered and thrown out of the *sado*. Flora liked to take me there; when it was free, boys or soldiers played soccer on this field. A poor European with a long spotty beard lived between the assistant commissioner's house and Chinatown. He had decorated his fence with egg shells painted with various colors.

Chinatown was by far the dirtiest and busiest neighborhood. Among shacks and cheap restaurants were a blacksmith and a junk dealer who put half his store out in the street; in between them were *tokos* whose only reason for existence was the uncertain hope of success. These were chock-full of shiny objects and were brightly lit by gaslight, which gave an air of luxury, compared to the reddish gloom of the dark houses. The smell of Chinese food enveloped everything—houses, streets, and passers-by—it was heavy, even inescapable. You could smell Chinatown before you came to the first Chinese houses.

Once out of Chinatown, not only the mood but also the whole appearance of the neighborhood became fresher and cleaner. The European school was here, across from the first movie theater, which a Chinese had opened. They showed the first French comedies and Pathé-Color with flower ballets, and horrible visions of green-colored devils with spotted bright red tongues. After that there was a sudden transition to the first full-length films: *Zigomar*, *The King of the Bandits*, *The Story of a Poor Girl*. Later on there were even more beautiful ones: historical movies about Rome—*Quo Vadis*, *Spartacus*, *Cleopatra*. A Javanese orchestra, mainly wind instruments, accompanied the movies with the same cheerful, sentimental circus tunes and in all seriousness played *Ach, du lieber Augustin* when the Roman warrior and the Egyptian queen took their leave of each other. The owner of the theater spoke Dutch. He was a relative of the Chinese who had placed the spell on my father. I thought about that when he talked to us: "Come back next week, boys; good movie, *The Last Days of Pompy!*" Right next to the theater was a filthy alley which would engulf the soldiers who had made their conquests in the native section of the theater.

When I came back to Gedong Lami from Sand Bay and was no longer restricted to our own property, this was the area I explored. Now that I'm talking about Gedong Lami again, I sense clearly that these chapters are all about the child from Balekambang. He's still a child, and I feel he's waiting for me to end his story. There he is—a little pale because of malaria, a little puffy, with big, black eyes, in the house where he was born, like a puppet you have to tend to, and I have to say "I" when I set him in motion again.

What did they do with me then? They sent me to the Brothers' School. My parents' old prejudices cropped up again. I had been allowed to play with native children as much as I wanted, but I was not supposed to be "contaminated" by the neighborhood Eurasians. So a Catholic environment, as far as my mother was concerned, was still the solution. The school was on Koningsplein, more than half an hour away from Meester-Cornelis by train. I had to get up early each morning, walk through Chinatown, take the train from the black, grimy little station to Koningsplein Station, walk around a large portion of that square, and go into a kind of monastery. It was my first contact with European children my own age, after two full years of island isolation. During those two years my father had made me work so hard that I could skip two grades. The books were not the same perhaps, but the brother who pointed out my seat to me looked surprised when he saw what my father "had gotten out of me": "Well, you really made the boy work," he said, shaking his head.

I was put with boys my own age, and even a little older, in the next to last grade. Then disaster struck. I was humiliated in every area. I couldn't keep up with what was going on. I was lost because I was confronted with completely different textbooks, using completely different methods. It wasn't a question of catching up but of not being able to pick up the thread, because I couldn't find it. My attitude toward all classroom situations dates from that moment. From then on it became a constant struggle between me and the system, with no holds barred. Each teacher, whether as an individual or as a link in the chain of teachers, was somebody whose will went against mine. He would try to teach me what he wanted to teach me, and I would keep up appearances with a minimum of submission, never letting him get a hold over me. I had to learn quickly and forget again just as quickly. I had to cheat and copy to keep up appearances—just appearances—and that way stay as free as possible.

The first year I was still working on my mode of resistance. But I didn't yet have my principal weapon of later years—my excellent memory. I circumvented obstacles clumsily. I didn't know how to avoid pitfalls. I flunked everything miserably, and although the pride of a good student was unknown to me, this failure humiliated me at the time and stripped me of much of my self-confidence.

Another humiliation was bloodier, and the fact that it happened at the same time added to the intellectual humiliation, although it should have counteracted it. I suddenly noticed that I was one of the weaker boys; the prestige I had among my native playmates didn't apply here. I was subjected to the typical fights of a European boys' school: there would be a big circle of excited onlookers, with three or four who were the really strong ones as judges, and two boys would pull at or hit each other with their fists until one of them would apologize. I fought a couple of times and lost; they hit me and twisted my wrists when I wouldn't say "uncle." But my case was unusual: within a few days it seemed the whole class despised me. I couldn't make a single friend, I had nobody to confide in, and one day I had eight fights lined up before school let out. One after another they came up to me to be put on the list. Among them I recall a boy with a stoop and slit eyes whose first name was Franklin. Hissing like the proverbial "traitor," he announced to everyone that I apparently didn't know anything about the boys of the Brothers' School. That day I snuck to the station behind the trees along the sidewalk; the number of fights gave me some sort of safe conduct. But from that moment until I got to the HBS three years later, my attitude was cowardly, almost without exception. I gave in as soon as there was any hint of a fight, as soon as words alone didn't work anymore. In words too I found my masters everywhere. I couldn't find the right ones for a large group. I told a boy in the highest class that I belonged to nobility. He burst into shrill laughter and said in Malay, to show his utter contempt: "Wah! Di-keruk, seh, nobility! Bapanja tukang sado!" ("Di-keruk," which means something like "scraped out", instead of Ducroo—"his father is a *sado* driver"). Everyone laughed in approval. Another older boy, the son of a French barber in Noordwijk, hit me in the face daily. Wrist twisting was another daily occurrence. The French boy was the only one I managed to get revenge on. The big gawky boy was in charge of distributing library books during recess, and once he refused to give me the new book I was entitled to because he said I was late. I wasn't late, and since this threat affected me more deeply than any other, I was suddenly reckless. I said that he had closed the library early. As he stretched his hand toward my face, I kicked him in the shin as hard as I could. He went pale and sat down. I didn't get my book, but I saw with pleasure that when he pulled off his sock his shin was bloody. He was too big to fight with me on the schoolgrounds, but after that he left me alone, much to my surprise.

Who was my only friend at that time? A half-wit. His name was Emil Massing and he had come from Sukabumi with his mother. Sometimes they lived in a guestroom in our house, and sometimes in a native house in our backyard. We went to the same school. Every morning we walked through Chinatown to take our little train. He was two years older than I but two grades behind me. Once we were in school I didn't see him again, not even during recess. So I ate my sandwiches by myself, hoping that everyone would leave me alone. On the train a group of children gradually formed a clique, among them some who went to other schools. We didn't pester each other because the trip distracted us, and we were very cheerful because it was still so early in the morning or because when we went home school was over.

I fell in love with a girl who was almost sixteen and a Nordic beauty. She was pink and robust—once when I was fruitlessly pulling on a window, she got up and opened it for me. An eighteen-year-old boy in long pants, who was perhaps a little bit in love with her too, incited us smaller ones to sing a song like "Sarah, your slip is showing," when she got out at her stop. We thought this was funny, and for me it was my only proof of love, my only contact with her, so we sang it almost every day. Since the half-wit Emil was my only confidant, I told him about my love when we were at home. I passionately embraced a *guling* (a cylindrical pillow) which I was holding between my legs. It didn't occur to me to be shy in front of this witness. Like the Javanese, he went to the movies just for the noise of the chase scenes and fights and was unable to distinguish between the characters. Once he went to see *Napoleon's Great Fall*, and when I questioned him, he was painfully distressed because he had not seen Napoleon fall anywhere. So he didn't betray me. He spoke even less to the girl than I did, and he didn't mention it to the other children, either.

Her name was Mary—May-ree, as I said it—and needless to say, she was bored by our company; as soon as the train reached the terminal she stood up and was one of the first to jump off. To be able to see her longer, to stand close to her and, to show her that I, little boy that I was, was her equal in this game, I did the same thing. I'd jump onto the platform, usually before she did. One day when the train was still going full speed and I was standing below her on the steps, she teased me, saying, "Why don't you jump now?" I looked at her and laughed, but she only shrugged her shoulders. I thought this was a test I had to pass, while she was absolutely sure it was only a joke. With my book bag in my free arm as usual, I jumped out. I felt as if I was picked up from behind, somewhat similar to the time I jumped off the bridge into the Tjikantèh, and had the sensation not of falling but of being swept up in the air. Something happened to my feet, my elbow got under my face, and the gray concrete platform scraped hard against me. I realized I was lying next to the train. I saw the wheels turning and felt the wind from the cars passing above me. People were yelling, "Orang

kegiling!" (somebody run over!) because I didn't get up. At this screaming I jumped up, very much ashamed, and saw everybody hanging out
of the train; my lunch box and books were scattered between the
wheels. While an official with a cap ran toward me, scolding me angrily
and asking my name so he could write to my father, I saw Mary among
the people who had gotten out, looking at me gravely. When the man
with the cap disappeared I laughed nervously as if it were all a big joke.
Emil helped me pick up the contents of my book bag from under the
train. Walking along the street, I had a hard time keeping from crying,
and I was scared all day for fear the man with the cap would write my
father. At one o'clock I saw Mary back at the station; I wanted to act as if
nothing had happened, but she walked right up to me.

"So," she said. "Didn't you hurt yourself? You squealed like a stuck
pig."

That was the only moment of closeness between us. I saw her again
ten years later as the wife of one of my older friends. She didn't recognize me and I pretended not to recognize her.

The tall eighteen-year-old was named Alfons Ramond. It turned out
he lived close to the Rehoboth church, and soon I looked him up in the
afternoon to spend some time with him away from the train as well. He
liked the same books I did. There was a rage in all the elementary
schools for thin books with bright colored covers, which contained the
adventures of Lord Lister, Nick Carter, and Buffalo Bill. I didn't read all
of them but wanted to own as many as possible. Emil's mother sometimes gave me a dime, which I immediately turned into one of these
books at the Koningsplein Station newstand. The bookseller was an
old Javanese who wore glasses. We developed great skill in picking up
two books when we bought only one. We would thank him politely,
which a Javanese was very sensitive to, while we put away our booty
hastily but with an affected casualness as we left. It never occurred to
us that we were harming him in any way. We thought that the station
bookstore was rich enough not to notice these small losses.

It was Alfons Ramond who gave me all his detective stories when he
had finished them, and he called me by my last name or said *amice*,
which always pleased me. One afternoon I brought him a Lord Lister
story to trade, one that I thought was particularly good. I told him the
end of the story, which was shown in a color picture: the gentleman-
thief was escaping by means of a rope which was cut at the last
moment by a young lady in a red dress. She was caught by the police

instead of him, but she loved him. "Here she is," I said. "Miss Edith Wharton." Alfons looked at the picture thoughtfully. "And had they already...?" he asked. He said it very calmly and I was shocked. How could a gentleman-thief and a girl in love in a detective story stoop to such things? "I don't know," I said hesitantly. "Oh, then it's not worth reading," he said in the same reflective tone. "That's the only thing that counts." I went home troubled by this attitude; it shocked me more than all the native stories had. It was as if someone had pulled my fantasies down into the gutter, because a book was something so very special. Some time later Alfons told me a story which was going around the neighborhood: a girl and a boy in love were thwarted by her parents. One night she climbed out of her window and he snuck into her yard. On a lounge chair on her parents' own front porch he deflowered her. I could see it happening and thought it was terrible —not sensual but disgusting, somehow inevitable, somehow catastrophic. "Yes, on their very own front porch," Alfons said. "If a man and a woman agree, there's nothing you can do to stop them... nothing! Then it has to happen!" he repeated, as if he knew how this story affected me.

Emil's mother, who was not really his mother, was called Mrs. Sachs. She was a widow, and my stepsister Sylvia would later be her namesake. A small round woman with fat lips and a stoop, she was in her way a great lover. She had adopted Emil out of love for his father, a planter from the Sukabumi area, who wanted to take him away from his real mother, a Sundanese. This planter sometimes came to visit his son, and before long Mrs. Sachs and he became lovers. He had once promised to marry her but for one reason or other, perhaps out of fear of Emil's real mother, he always put it off. When we left the Indies, Emil was grown, and Mrs. Sachs had paid for all his education out of her widow's pension. She spoke bitterly about "Emil's father," as she always called him, who had recently married somebody else. In a long disapproving discussion, Wa Gedah, my mother, and Mrs. Sachs all agreed that he shouldn't have kept promising her for so many years. He was a planter with a big mustache just like my mother's first husband, but he was apparently of lesser quality. Mrs. Sachs idolized Emil, who in return tried every nasty trick on her that his miserable little mind could think of. She slept in the same room with him and would dress and undress in front of us or use the bathroom behind a room divider while we were playing in the room. She sometimes kissed me to show my mother how much she loved me, or perhaps because she really did love me. When we had Brussels sprouts I would say, "Just like Mrs. Sachs's kisses." She chain-smoked native cigarettes and had read one book, *The Arabian Nights*, which she took as gospel. She was a medium and had heard and seen many ghosts; this was all she talked about with my parents, and with me it was the Arabian spirits in the bottle and, for a lighter variant, Aladdin's spirit. At the end of every sentence she said, "You see," for emphasis.

"And then I clearly heard a voice screaming in my ear: '*Bobo!*' (sleep), and when I turned around there was a pitch-black man standing by my window, you see."

My parents, who at the time readily believed in anything related to the spirit world and had bought a four-volume work by a certain Van Hien about all the spirits of the Indies, were not convinced by all her encounters with the spirits.

At the time Emil was my only friend, because I had lost Flora. She married a clerk in the Accounting Office and gave me her wedding picture, which did little for me. She left Meester-Cornelis for the old city and soon had a number of children. Tjang Panel, whom she had left behind, was shortly thereafter no longer welcome in our house. I think she had become the victim of her rivalry with Mrs. Sachs. It didn't matter who was right and who was wrong; it was a simple natural law that no two people could be in my mother's favor at the same time. But one day Mrs. Sachs left too and took Emil with her.

I was relieved, despite my fear of a new school, when my parents decided that the Brothers' School was too far for me to go alone and entrusted me to the public school in Meester-Cornelis. It was a chance for a new beginning, and since I had learned that acting tough wouldn't work for me, I started out prudently—something I had learned in the meantime. A number of boys seemed again to hate me instinctively and my attitude was certainly just as cowardly, but there were far fewer run-ins, so I didn't stand out too much. One boy in particular was my enemy. He was handsome, with broad shoulders and curly hair, and was obsequious to anybody who was a little bit stronger. But he was stronger than I. I think he became an officer in the merchant marine. I met him in the street one day, even before I went to that school. He laughed at me and asked the question that just about everybody asked at that school: "How big is yours?" It took me awhile to understand what he meant, and from then on there was bad blood between us. Later when I passed by a yard where he and some other boys were playing, he said something that I didn't understand, but it must have been insulting, because the others laughed. So I responded and he came toward me slowly and threateningly. I was standing alone in the street with a little whip in my hand, and while he slowly walked toward me, I thought I would come home dirty and beaten up, but I knew I had to stand my ground. The boys followed him, eager to see what would happen. I counted his steps and repeated to myself: "When he's just one step away I'll use my whip and hit him across the face as hard as I can," although I knew that was against the rules. He advanced slowly as if in a dream, and I said over and over to myself, "as hard as I can." But when he was about at that spot where I planned to hit him, somebody jumped in between us. It was the boy who lived in the house where they were playing. Maybe he felt sorry for me, maybe up till now he had only wanted to see if I would run away, or maybe he was afraid of what his parents would say if there was a fight in their yard. He grabbed my enemy by the shoulders and pulled him so hard that he almost fell down. I saw the surprised face of my assailant and was amazed how casually someone else could deal with the situation; moreover, the unknown boy wasn't any taller than I—even thinner.

Another boy once hit me so hard I had a bump on my head the size of an egg. But at another time he said to me, "Why do you always read books about fighting but never fight?" I couldn't answer him and wondered about it myself. When I had read *The Three Musketeers* I dreamed up a game that was a variant of cops and robbers, in which we fenced with bamboo swords. We also shot air pistols at each other, replacing the little darts used for target practice with gravel. I excelled in this game. I always played D'Artagnan. Whether he inspired me or not, I was one of the best fencers, but my books could not make me any stronger than I was. Only much later would I force myself to box and join stronger friends when there was going to be a fight. Naturally I grew in self-confidence—just as every new student in boxing school learns to overcome his reluctance, not so much to be hit but to hit hard himself. The road I had traveled by the time I was eighteen and had hung around with the strongest boys of Bandung, Arthur Hille and the two eldest Odingas as my close friends and equals, seems more amazing to me now than it did then. Perhaps even then "the mind" brought some superiority, but when I think of the conversations we had, I realize this trump card was still negligible. And intelligence was never able to protect somebody from the names my friends of that time could make up for others. The two years my father spent as my teacher and the four years I spent changing from a coward to an aggressive young man—those are two conflicting but equal accomplishments of self-discipline. I was so overwhelmed by my first humiliations in school that I might well have avoided any violence to the very last. I would have been an honorable and pleasant character as far as many people were concerned, even for a woman like Jane. If I had been in Europe it would probably have gone like that, but, to quote Stendhal, a strange *espagnolisme* remained with me, for which my tropical upbringing can be help responsible.

I was such a coward that I betrayed the class to my teacher, even though I hated him for using me as a special target for his taunts. Sometimes he left the room for a moment and would ask one of the boys to write on the blackboard the names of those who talked while he was gone. The boy would do it and look threateningly at the class, but when the steps of the teacher announced his return, he would quickly erase the names. Whether it was a pedagogical trick to learn more about the boy's character, I don't know. One day I was given the chalk. I wrote down the names of two boys, and when the teacher came back I left their names on the blackboard. A murmur of disgust went through the class, and at recess one of the boys threw himself on me and hit me on the head. I didn't hit back; I felt he was right, and yet I didn't fully realize how despicable I really had been. Maybe I wanted to prove to the teacher that he could trust me though he was my enemy; maybe I wanted to prove to the class, too, that I felt no solidarity with them. It was confusing and complicated, and only later when I thought about it did I see it as a despicable act.

In the second year I became friends with a boy two years older than I; he was both the strongest one in the class and probably the biggest coward. He was a Eurasian who looked like a full-grown man when he was only fourteen, and his name was Baur. As soon as I came to the school I heard from various sources that he had a big one, which he would show proudly under his desk. His scapegoat was a skinny little "assimilated" Chinese whose legal name was Theo Gouwe. Baur took him aside every now and then and told him with the greatest disdain, "You're just a dirty Chinese, and your name is not Theo Gouwe but

Bok Seng Gow. You understand?" The little Chinese looked at him murderously with his slit eyes, and when Baur was gone he said, "I is equal to a European!"

The Chinese were ridiculous in school, because of their desire to be considered Europeans. In contrast, the behavior of the Javanese was all the more striking: they were serious, applying themselves as if it were a matter of life and death, and if they were the least bit intelligent, their determination put them at the head of the class. It was equally important for them to prove to themselves that they weren't inferior, and they always seemed to keep a certain distance from the whites. They were the only ones for whom even the elementary school was a means of competition, while the European boys would have laughed if anybody had suggested such a thing. Baur's way to shine was to be terribly rude to the teacher. His cowardice cut him off from any other distinction. He never fought, showed off what he had, and was by far the worst student, as if this were what a tough guy should be. In this last respect I was a kindred soul. The only reason I was less cowardly than he was that I wasn't as strong, so I tried to outdo him in being rude in class; and although in elementary school he was the champion in this game, I had caught up with him by the time we got to the HBS. There our competition became more clearly defined because there were different teachers: I dared talk back to two teachers, where Baur did not.

When he was fourteen he had an affair with a married woman who lived close to the Rehoboth church. People talked about it, but when they asked him he denied it. Later on he came to Gedong Lami and asked if I could let him sleep in a room in one of the pavilions because his father had thrown him out of the house. He and a couple of natives had been sleeping on the front porch of the land office. His father, a European with a gray mustache, absolutely despised him and beat him with a whip. One day as I came through the alley by the Rehoboth church, Baur was walking out of a house and almost ran into me, all the while screaming behind him, "Well, drop dead then, if you don't want to." I asked him if this was the house of his supposed lady friend, but he quickly changed the subject. In school we always talked about sex but mostly in a trivial, scornful way. Most boys hadn't gone as far as Baur had, and the most profound conversation I remember from this time was about whether a woman could enjoy it as much as a man. My particular enemy at that time was very rational about it—"Of course it's the same!"—but we looked at him incredulously.

Baur didn't talk much about such things; his experience as a man showed up in a different manner. One day we had a substitute teacher, a woman who had come straight from Holland and who usually taught a class of younger children. She was tall and looked rather angular and somewhat masculine. Since she didn't know our usual seats, we had changed around before she came in. I was sitting next to Baur. Apparently she had heard of his reputation, because she stood next to his desk while she addressed the whole class: she was "only a woman" but she was "very strict," and so on. It was hot and she was perspiring heavily, and from time to time her voice cracked unpleasantly. Suddenly Baur's rumbling voice cut through all this: "All that's fine and dandy, but the *bau ketiak* (smelly armpit) is about to kill me." While the children held on to each other to keep from screaming with laughter, she bent over him and said, "What did you say, Baur, you rude child!"

"I said it's terribly hot here." He looked at her calmly, almost underneath her arm, which she had lifted; her white blouse must have been drenched, because her face was shiny red. She didn't dare ask if that was really what he had said, and during the whole period his presence must have affected her as that of a man. She assigned extra work as punishment to him and me and some others too. For the rest, during the hours until the regular teacher came back, she was nothing more than Baur's helpless victim.

After Baur had slept in a lounge chair in our servants' quarters for a couple of nights, I told my parents about it. They felt sorry for him and had him come into the house. I went to see his father, whom I had met before, and asked if his son could live with us. He said he had no intention of paying room and board for him. "And if I may give you some good advice," he said, suddenly serious and confidential, "Don't associate with him. He's my son, but if you run around with him it will rub off on you."

I left insulted, but Baur came up with something new. A couple days later a young architect visited us; he, unknown to my parents, was reputedly a homosexual. He said he was interested in Baur and was going to take care of his board. Baur got a room next to my father's so-called office and had long telephone conversations with the architect. When he had visited him, he always came home with books. I hadn't met the man, and Baur acted as if he were almost afraid for me to meet him. Nonetheless, I didn't in the least suspect an abnormal relationship, and I greatly envied Baur his friendship with an adult. He even called him by his first name when he talked to him on the phone. But even if Baur had such inclinations, either this was the only time or I didn't attract him. Toward me he never made a suspicious move, though he had inexplicable fits of resentment as if I had suddenly insulted or betrayed him. He would fly into a rage of jealousy, as often happens among boys, and when we were not mad at each other he liked to show how much stronger he was. He would half-strangle me, saying it was "Old Shatterhand's iron fist."[3] Once when we were swimming in the river behind the house, he held me under water so long I thought he really wanted to drown me; another time he threatened to throw me in a well and dragged me half over the edge. But if it was my turn to get mad, his cowardice won out immediately. One day I showed him a postcard with a couple kissing and said, "This is you and the lady from the alley." He took the postcard away from me, but I had three of them and I showed him the other two, making the same remark. He took away all three; that night when we were doing our homework, I remembered them and asked for them back. He refused. I was slowly getting mad. He said he had torn them up. I took his watch, which was lying on a corner of the table, and threw it on the floor. He picked it up, saw that the glass was shattered and that it didn't run anymore, and said he hadn't torn up the postcards. "Now you can keep them," I said. The next day he gave them back to me.

Another time he told me excitedly that he had met somebody who had warned him about my father. "And also about you," he said. "Because you're a chip off the old block." I attacked him furiously and we fell against a large clay flowerpot that broke into pieces with a loud noise. My parents came running and scolded us, ending the fight I had started in earnest. We didn't speak to each other for a week and this time it was easy for me although he was much better at sulking. When we had these fights, he said, "I know something that would really get you. One evening I'll go to your bookcase; I'll open it up, no matter what precautions you take, and I'll tear a page from one of your books. You can't check all the pages, and I'll take a book you really love." This plan struck me as so diabolical that it kept me awake. I was certain he was capable of doing it, and I was particularly worried about a book on the Franco-Prussian War which he wanted. Eventually I gave him this book, as a sort of ransom for the others. Not long after, something happened; I can no longer remember what it was, but it made my father decide he didn't want Baur in the house any longer, and one evening he left for good. Perhaps my father had heard something about the architect's reputation and kept it from me.

The next morning I met Baur on the train. I didn't remember whether we were mad at each other or not, but he pushed me aside and quickly sat down on the seat I wanted. This made me furious, but I was reluctant to start anything on the train. As soon as we got to school I looked for him; he was standing by the door of a classroom, telling in great detail what he thought of me and how he had treated me. I walked right up to him, but he stopped talking and pretended not to see me. I called him all the names I could think of, for a Eurasian and for him in particular. He was livid but kept staring at the sky. Everyone listened to these insults with amazement. This was to be our last conversation.

When I was twenty I saw him in Meester-Cornelis in the same old movie theater from our school days. He had stopped Sylvia in the street and told her that he was Baur (but she had been too little to remember him) and that he had known her brother very well. When I recognized him, I looked at him closely; he had become fat and slow-moving, while I had slimmed down. He was married to one of the many insignificant Eurasian office clerks and lived in a small house across the street from us. I didn't feel the slightest resentment toward him and thought he'd talk to me as he had to Sylvia. But when I looked at him I saw the muscles of his face stiffen and his gaze turn to the sky, just like the last time I had spoken to him.

Aside from Baur, I had an account to settle with a completely different sort of friend, the only one who reminded me of my Balekambang days. He was the son of my mother's personal maid and his name was Mahmud. He knew all my books by their Dutch titles and shared my enthusiasm for the musketeers. I taught him how to fence, and when my schoolfriends came over I never sent him away but let him play with us as an equal. Since he seemed so smart, his mother sent him to the native school in Gang Lami, where he learned to pray in Arabic, and very soon I noticed a distance between us. I became the *blanda* to him, and he came up with all sorts of excuses not to play with me anymore. I tried to ignore it, until one when I was sick and in bed in Baur's former room, I asked his mother to get him. He refused to come, but when I looked through the window I saw him hanging around the fence as if he didn't dare leave, either. I called him but he looked up and shook his head. I jumped through the window and walked up to him barefoot. He was scared and didn't want to answer my questions. I suddenly felt that my father was right when he called the *guru kampong* a corrupter, and I said to Mahmud that from now on he was free, but I beat him up on the same spot. Apparently his Arabic prayers had not made him brave enough to hit a white man. He got up from the gravel and ran into the street. I stayed behind, crushed, and with a much greater feeling of regret and sadness than I ever had felt in my quarrels with Baur. And yet it gave me a great pleasure to have beaten him up; honesty seemed to demand it, since he had needlessly begun to look at me as his enemy. I climbed back through the window, afraid my mother would see me, and went back to bed with my fever.

During the same period my parents were enjoying the peace after Balekambang. The money was coming in from the villas that were always rented. My father bought two big gramophones, and every day he would listen to a number of records that were sent on approval. Mlle. Néo's voice in *La Frêle Parisienne* (on the Odéon label) made him dream about his old Parisian days. Whenever he played the special record with Mme. Melba on it, the women in Gang Lami would say to each other, "Listen, listen—she's in labor again!"

From this time also dates a letter that arrived from The Hague, from my father's favorite sister – not Aunt Tina, the only one who was still alive when we came to Europe – but the aunt who had thought I was so suspicious as a child. Its style now seems to me terribly antiquated; what inimitable phrases these people used when they wrote to each other about what concerned them, and how easily a cliché, an inserted foreign word, an attempt at humor betrays them, and not only them but the whole class to which they belonged! About her daughter, who had once undressed me when I was a little boy and who was so worldly and yet so pious, my aunt wrote:

> Her independence, and most of all her personality, plus her thirty summers make it possible for her to get around very well on her own! She is pretty, dresses well, and is slender, which is very important here, because of the constant walking we do; and yet she has filled out as you never saw her before. Her life still follows a different course from what is usual, absolutely under the direction of and always in obedience to God's will! It's hardly noticeable to the outsider, only to those who see her as we do and who

also are able to follow God's guidance—most people ignore or struggle against Him without any awareness of the Truth.

And speaking about her sister in Brussels:

Our relationship with Tina has considerably cooled. She's doing fine, she's very happy in her own way of life. She's such a *spirite fervente*[4] that all the rest has been pushed aside. I think that her notions have become too one-sided, however much can be gained from them, that is to say, not from *the spirits*[5] but from a life in constant communion with the Father and the Savior. Nowhere does God demand that you shut yourself off completely from the world and lock yourself in with *les esprits.*[6]

Then there was a four-week interlude that was explained as follows:

When I do too much around the house, I always have an *outburst*. Pain everywhere, and a heavy millstone in my stomach, so that I'm truly sick. *Pour comble,*[7] the first time I went out after this, I fell head over heels down the stairs and landed so hard that I'm still very sore from this additional exercise, and although I came through in one piece, I would like to have been spared all of this. A stiff Dutchman would not have gotten off so lightly, and certainly not one of sixty-two summers, but we land on our feet and we are flexible like an accordion.

And finally:

And now we're sitting again under the coconut trees and I follow the path back to all your beautiful villas in Kampong Melaju! It seems to me it's a safe feeling as far as the money is concerned, and a steady warm stream to your pocketbook! This property, Charles, will give you a lot of work, but you have your dear wife beside you, who has shown you love and devotion on other occasions. As I always say: without that able mate your little boat would now be lying *on the bottom of the sea*, and for this she's dear to all of us.

I believe my father must have thought that such a letter was full of wit and wisdom and that it reminded him in a very pleasant way of what a good family he came from.

19 The Child Continues to Mature

The elementary-school principal in Meester-Cornelis didn't want to recommend me for the HBS, which meant that I would have to take the complete admissions exam. He was curious, he said, to see me take the exam and pull a rabbit out of my hat. This expression was new to me, and it humiliated me. I repeated it to my father, who became furious and said that I would take the exam simply to please him. He was unlike other fathers, in that he didn't say he would beat me if I failed. On the contrary, he sent me to the same Ursuline school I had gone to four years earlier, to have me "coached" by the nuns in the afternoons. The same Mother Josepha who used to be my favorite teacher tutored me, and when I went up for the exam a candle was burning for me in the chapel. I took the exam quite calmly and passed it in spite of the broad range of material; when my father went to ask for the results, he learned I ranked second among the students who had taken the complete exam. With great disdain for those who had been accepted without taking the complete exam, my father went to my former teacher, who supposedly didn't look up from his desk, to tell him that I had pulled the rabbit out of the hat; he also added a few off-color remarks. This triumph didn't satisfy him, however, and that same evening he sent me to my former teacher to thank him as politely as I could for my education. No doubt the man wanted to throw me out, but he seemed disarmed by my politeness.

I also went to thank the nuns. They were proud and happy, and completely certain that it was all due to the candle in the chapel. I was now thirteen, and it hurt my father's pride that I was going to start the HBS a year late, but considering my years in the backwoods this was forgiven.

Unknown to the rest of the world, I had made a greater vow to God than the burning of the candle. I had promised in a prayer to give up my most secret sin forever, but my willpower failed after about three weeks. Fortunately there was confession, and I also went faithfully to catechism to be able to receive Holy Communion and to be confirmed.

The day of my First Communion I went to my room as soon as I got home, to find out if I could really feel Christ's body in mine, but I didn't notice anything different. Grace had not touched me in the least. After an hour I was certain I wouldn't feel it, and I turned my devotion back to D'Artagnan.

My confirmation was more impressive. I had to go to the cathedral in Batavia; my parents went with me and I wore a dark suit. I staggered to the altar and knelt before a real bishop. He smeared oil on my fore-head in the form of a cross, after jerking up my chin since I had felt the need to bow my head. When I felt the oil (this at least was unmistak-able) I wanted to bow again, but a gentleman in a morning coat gave me a push from behind; I tripped down the other side of the altar and was caught by a young priest who quite kindly wiped off the oil with a cotton ball. Despite the presence of my parents and a bishop, the cere-mony disappointed me. From then on I felt more and more convinced that I had paid my dues to the Church. When my father confessor was replaced by another priest, I didn't think I had to tell him as much as I had told the old one, whose list of questions I knew by heart. He had only two hard questions: "Have you talked about dirty things?" and "Have you done dirty things with yourself or with others?" Whatever my answer, he said, "All right!" and followed this with a gentle ad-monition. He was gray and fat; the new priest was thin and much younger. In an incredibly short time and without any inner turmoil or crisis, I lost my faith and straightened out my relationship with the Church. Since my parents insisted that I go to Mass every Sunday and there were always friends of theirs who would see me, I took along lit-tle books to read instead of my prayer book. A pocket edition of *Les Misérables* in six or eight volumes was ideal for this purpose—and inexhaustible.

Nonetheless, I did experience three or four days of real piety, al-though I no longer remember exactly when that was—perhaps just before I was confirmed. My mother had come home with a crucifix, a cheap figure of white faïence nailed to a shiny cross of brown wood with black edges. The cross itself fitted into an ornate stand that looked like a table leg. I thought it was marvelous. I stared at the Christ figure for a long time, convinced that it looked very much like Him, and carefully studied the curls and the cut of the beard. My mother had given me the crucifix as a present, so I asked if I could buy her one in return. She was very touched and gave me some money and the address of the store. I went there and discovered that my crucifix had cost two seventy-five, so I bought my mother a larger model for four fifty. The figure on it, although bigger, was almost identical to mine, but the cross was richly sculptured and perfectly matched my mother's old-fashioned bed. She placed it on her night stand, while I took my crucifix off the stand and hung it on the wall by my bed, and for three or four evenings I said my prayers with real fervor at the foot of my crucifix. I didn't realize for a moment that this piety was mostly aesthetic in nature. But after a few days my prayers declined in fervor as the novelty of the cross wore off.

After I passed the exam so satisfactorily I went to the HBS and soon came to the painful realization that I was virtually a mathematical moron. I tried to compensate for my stupidity with my flair for writing; I turned my answers into short novels, answers that were sometimes correct despite long digressions. The unbelievably short answers some handed in, while still making high grades, always amazed me. How did they dare do this, I wondered, in a subject that was so difficult; why weren't they scolded for their laziness and why was I not encouraged for my serious treatment of the subject matter? My answers amused and irritated the teacher, perhaps in the same way that my recent business letters amused and irritated the Namur attorney.

My fear of teachers disappeared at the HBS in a few days, because I could deal with the constantly changing teachers with elementary psychology. I kept a low profile during recess; nobody seemed to know I was a coward. My last outburst of anger against Baur, which had taken place there, even gave me a good name, and in class I was soon the one who would talk back the most to the teachers. Nonetheless I did my best, better than in elementary school, perhaps because my unsuspected success on the exam had spurred my ambition. I almost made it, even in math, when, as a result of either my puberty or the many detective novels I devoured or some other cause, something unforeseen happened.

One evening while looking in the *Weekblad voor Indië* (*The Indies Weekly*), I found some pictures of a murder case that was a cause célèbre—the murder of Fientje the Phoenix. She was a Eurasian prostitute, the friend of a Eurasian named Gramser Brinkman. Her disfigured body had been fished out of the *kali* Tanah Abang, floating in a gunny sack; her breasts were cut off and her feet, tied together with rope, were sticking out of the sack. A native prostitute, Roanah, came forward with information. Fientje lived with her lover in an isolated *kampong* house. One evening Raonah was going by, heard strange noises, and looked inside through the bamboo wall. By the light of a kerosene lamp she saw Brinkman grab Fientje by the throat and throw her on a bed. Two natives helped him cut off her breasts; yet, even after that, Fientje managed to get up and stagger to the door, where one of the natives hit her on the head with a blackjack. She fell; the others checked to see if she was really dead and started to pull the bag around the body. At that moment Raonah ran away, scared out of her wits.

The pictures showed the victim, the murderers who soon confessed, and the reconstruction of the murder, with Raonah peeking through the bamboo wall, an attorney at her side. She re-enacted everything exactly as she remembered it, refusing only to lie down on the spot where Fientje had fallen. The picture of Fientje was extremely suggestive—a Eurasian girl with her hair up and the eyes of a doe, eyes that seemed to invite murder. She looked a little like Flora but she was prettier, with a softer, oval face and a more suggestive mouth.

I was impressed by the article, but it wasn't until that night that I noticed how deeply it had affected me. All night long, till about four o'clock the next morning, I kept seeing the drama unfold over and over again, and quite vividly. It wasn't so much like a movie, as I said at the time, but like something going on inside me, clearly a product of my own mind but one over which I had no control. I began by imagining the *kampong* house in the middle of the night, with only a little bit of light shining under the door and through the cracks. Then I put myself in Raonah's place; I walked down the quiet path, saw the light, went to the bamboo wall, and looked in.... When everything was over, and the body had been put into the sack and thrown into the river, when I saw it floating away in the water, the house of the first scene would immediately come back into view and everything else would recur in the exact same sequence. This was not a dream, because I would be wide awake, but it went on night after night; as soon as the lamps were lit, my fear of what I would go through that night would return. Alima's presence didn't help at all. I asked if I could sleep in my mother's room; this quieted me for a few nights, but then it started all over again. The fact that I didn't know what Brinkman looked like, since his picture hadn't been in the paper, didn't hinder my fantasy at all. I saw him from behind or imagined him as another Eurasian. I had to stop going to school, because I'd wake up exhausted, having had only two or three hours of sleep. They took me to a psychiatrist, who talked about puberty and stress and gave me a very salty medicine. I had to be taken out of school to rest for six months; otherwise, the doctor feared that I would become feeble-minded. At these last words my mother burst into tears, and I had to comfort her, although I myself was tormented by the fear that I might be crazy. For whole days I sat on a lounge chair in the yard with children's books I hadn't read in years and which I had to borrow from a friend. I read them as medicine, in the hope of becoming a "normal boy" again as soon as possible. The only books I enjoyed were the two volumes of *Chickenfeather or The Abducted Girl*, a parody on spiritualism that made even my father laugh. The cheerful students in it distracted me for a while. I thought that the cure would come from stories of student life, and I tried to read everything about it. Because of the pictures and the subject matter, I even succeeded in liking Klikspaan's sketches of nineteenth-century Dutch student life;[1] deep down I thought they were boring.

When the "visions," as we called them, subsided, I was allowed to go to the movies one evening. A harmless film had been chosen, but hanging outside the theater was a brightly colored French poster advertising a detective film that was coming soon, with a grinning, masked man dressed in tails, sneaking away. The movie was called *Le Pouce;* it was about a criminal who left behind bloody fingerprints. I had only noticed the face of the man in tails, when my friend Rudy van Geen pointed out his hands: one was dripping with blood and the blood had been made to look as marvelously red and thick as one could possibly imagine. That night I couldn't sleep, even in my mother's room. I thought of the old Darma murder case that took place when we were living in Sukabumi in Aunt and Uncle Majeu's house. The night light on the floor behind a screen in my mother's bedroom lent itself to this very well. I saw the Ambonese butcher Baludi appear from behind a wardrobe and cut the sleeping Darma's throat right in his bed, with his wife lying next to him. My father had gone off grumbling, to sleep in another room, and my mother lay by herself, not far from me. It wasn't that I imagined I was Darma, but I thought, "This is more or less the kind of room in which it happened"; and the man in tails on the poster merged with Baludi, who also had been caught by a bloody fingerprint he had left on the wall (he had a scar on his thumb). Only a fully lighted room could chase away the "visions," but my mother couldn't sleep with the light on. When I didn't dare wake her anymore and continued to torment myself next to her, afraid also to admit that even her presence didn't help, I sometimes lay covered with sweat.

This condition lasted about two years. The *klambu*, which in itself is such a pleasant part of life in the Indies, for a long time aroused a vague fear in me, which went unrecognized at the time but which dates from this period. Pulling it down around me seemed to define the space where I would be tortured. We left Batavia for the cooler climate of Bandung. My father's old friend, "Uncle" Van Kuyck, lived there and took us into his house. The trip, staying with other people, and then the new house distracted me. I was forbidden to look at any newspapers, but even the slightest provocation caused the visions to return. The Mayerling drama, which I happened upon in some memoirs, turned out to be neither too removed nor too far above my head to affect me. But the best was another murder committed by Brinkman, who had been acquitted in the case of Fientje the Phoenix, in spite of all the evidence. Now he had done in a native woman, Aïsah—to torture me personally, I thought. This time he was convicted, but he hanged himself in his cell. I got to see his picture now, because no matter how much I fought it I had to look at the newspapers. I hated this Brinkman as my personal enemy. I assured my mother I was not afraid of him, nor of murderers and thieves in general, for that matter—that I would even enjoy seeing such a person executed, and that I myself would gladly shoot someone like Brinkman. But my father must have scorned me in that period, because to him I was destined to become feeble-minded or, in any case, a kind of lap dog.

Shortly after my fourteenth birthday old Alima died. She had given me some money for my birthday to buy books. I showed her the books I had bought, but she paid no attention. She shoved them aside and looked at me. Her eyes were somewhat cloudy and around them were a thousand little wrinkles. "Ma Lima sudah tua," she said, as in the song. I had paid little attention to her lately. A few days later my mother said I had to take her to a female dentist, because she was complaining that her mouth hurt. Alima was shivering, and I helped her in a dos-à-dos. The dentist turned out to be a heartless person with a face like a shovel; she took one look at Alima's poor teeth and decided to pull them all. She threw the thin little woman into the chair before I could interfere, pushed her head back, opened her mouth, and started working on her teeth as if she were cracking nuts. Alima only moaned slightly. When she came home she felt worse than before. The brutal treatment had been totally unnecessary; what she thought was a toothache was certainly a symptom of something else. Two days later she was dead. It was the first corpse I had seen. Her face had changed beyond recognition. Her mouth was black and twisted into a rigid smile; her face wasn't brown anymore but yellow. She had died in a coma, without saying good-bye to anybody. I went along when they carried her to the native cemetery. The Sundanese deny the fearful aspect of death by acting as natural as possible, and so the pallbearers were joking among themselves. I got angry and asked them to be quiet, and we walked quickly and, at the end, somberly, to the grave. I don't remember anything else; hiding somebody away in the ground never represented the final good-bye for me.

When I had rested for about a year, my father thought it was time I did something productive. There was no HBS in Bandung, so I was sent to a gymnastics school and was also tutored in English, French, and bookkeeping. I learned French and bookkeeping from the nuns again, and English from an English businessman who happened to know my father and who looked a great deal like Mr. Micawber. He told me not to read so much, because I would go through all the great books right away and would have nothing left for later. He had a good sense of humor. One day he was challenged to a duel by another businessman; having the choice of weapons, he said, "Well, then I want to duel with full chamberpots."

Later the representative of the British and Foreign Bible Society taught me; he was a quiet man with red hair and a bright mustache and many children. One afternoon I had a profound discussion with him about fat and obese women. On the way over on my bike I had seen a Jewish woman of really formidable proportions; it was such an overwhelming experience for me that I arrived at the Bible house as if possessed by the desire to be drowned completely in all that flesh. Since I couldn't talk about anything else, I told him about the encounter without analyzing my feelings. He suddenly flared up and spoke about "the horridness of such beings, oh horrid, indeed."[2] But while we had conflicting notions about this (I wasn't really disinclined to admit the "horridness" in principle), for an hour we spoke in English about this subject. And after that, whenever I was riding my bike, I tried to find someone equal in size to that Jewish woman among the planters' wives who drove around Bandung in open cars. But nobody ever came even close. I never saw anyone her size nor her type, nor the lady herself, however much I wanted to renew this obsession.

Without question, the erotic aspect of life tormented me, but I didn't know any girls, so to speak. At the elementary school in Meester-Cornelis I thought all the girls were horrible. At the HBS I imagined I was attracted by a wisp of a girl who actually looked very common but who had very bright teeth. There was a prettier girl in the class, but she was very conceited and had yellow teeth. Baur laughed at my choice and at her name too, which was indeed impossible: Sabine. I defended her dispassionately, because I had hardly spoken to her and was only responding to the schoolboy's custom requiring everyone to have a girl friend. Moreover, all those loves were purely platonic. But finally I met a girl who was two years older (she was sixteen and I was fourteen); she knew all the French and English songs and looked like a young woman. She was dark, with small eyes and a round nose, but quite pretty, particularly in a *sarong* and *kabaja*. In the Bandung club she allowed an officer to court her, and just to tease him she shared a drink with me. I was never really in love with her, but I was flattered by her interest and—the day she taught me how to kiss—proud that I finally had a real "girl." She said it bored her to kiss the officer; to show me how unpleasant and annoying it was, she decided to demonstrate on me. The first time it seemed both pleasant and, as she said, disagreeable. I thought kissing was only a form of teasing or some sort of indecent game, but we slowly came to the realization that maybe the officer had actually found something here. I wasn't really jealous of him; I had already decided that I was only a playmate who was allowed to tag along, but Trudy and I saw more and more of each other. We went out together almost as often as we wanted, and one day she said that as far as she was concerned, the officer could drop dead.

"Why?" I asked.

"Stupid, because I love you! And you act as if you don't want to know."

I still don't know what perversion drove her to prefer a child over an officer who, she herself said, was an excellent dancer. When he walked he stuck out his behind a little too much, but all in all he was quite attractive, with his pink face, his hair parted in the middle, and his small blond mustache.

"I don't like mustaches," she said, with a flippancy that was becoming more and more the fashion. "Besides, he thinks he's irresistible and he talks too much about his good family. He told a friend of mine

that it would be a great honor for a colonial girl to marry someone like
him."

She wanted to teach me to dance but I refused. I was determined
never to dance, because I thought it was unmanly and because my
parents always talked to me about it. Gymnastics was enough for me:
after I got over my initial distaste I became very much involved in it. I
also played basketball with great enthusiasm, but I asked Trudy not to
come watch me. I was embarrassed when she suddenly appeared, in a
dark tailored dress, smiling at us children playing basketball. But after
all it didn't matter to me. I played well. Besides, she had chosen me,
and not the other way around.

Her father was the manager of a small movie theater, so we could get
in free. He put no restraints on his daughter. She took bookkeeping lessons from the nuns, just like me, and that's how we got to know each
other. One day she said I had to give it up, because I would never do
well in it. Not long after, she came to visit me when I was sick. Our
bookkeeping lessons provided the excuse, and she brought me flowers. I had a high fever and I looked at her, still bristling with indignation about her remark. My parents thought she was very attractive and
didn't suspect anything more than friendship between us. My father
began to flirt with her, and she repeated to him what she had told me
about the bookkeeping lessons. While she sat by my bed with the flowers next to her, I couldn't utter a word of thanks. I thought she was forward and extremely ugly. When she leaned over to fluff up my pillow, I
even imagined that she smelled bad. She was hurt, most of all because
I didn't thank her. When I felt better again, my disgust had disappeared and I went to see her. She greeted me with what was more than
sisterly coolness—emphasized that her only feelings for me were
those of an older sister, that I was a thankless boy, and so on. I knew
she was partly right, but I could still recall my disgust so vividly that I
couldn't apologize. I thanked her clumsily for the flowers and left. We
were distant acquaintances for the next three years.

Trudy's visit had convinced my father that I wasn't learning anything. Around that time a HBS was founded in Bandung. I was now fifteen, but I had to go, even if it meant starting over in the seventh grade.
This decision humiliated me, and I decided to flunk out as quickly as
possible. My stupidity in math had increased, and I was now so bad
that my father asked that I be exempted from this subject. So I was
no longer a regular student but more like an auditor. This time I in-

tended to play a different role toward the boys. I was no longer one of the smallest and the weakest, I kept telling myself; gymnastics had done me good. The first month I anticipated fights even when there was only a vague threat, and during recess I knocked a few people around, which made it clear I should be left alone. Once this was established, I withdrew into myself. I knew that I would never be popular. My attitude toward my teachers changed too. I was no longer rude but ironical.

"Mr. Ducroo sits there," one of them said, "as if he came to take a look at the HBS to see how we do things around here. Mr. Ducroo, I notice, learns a whole lot outside the HBS and nothing here. The only question, then, is what Mr. Ducroo is doing here?" He called me Mr. Ducroo out of disdain but also from a certain powerlessness, because I never gave him a chance to rush up and pull my ear as he loved to do before he sent a boy out of the class.

I had two friends among the teachers; all the rest were my enemies. These were the Dutch teacher, who liked to predict that I would be a writer, and the French teacher, who liked me even though my work in French was not the best.

"Ducroo," he said, "you still know more French than anyone else. Why is that?" I told him I had had lessons from the nuns, and he called it atavism. He liked to have me read French poetry out loud. He had an imagination that went beyond his subject. He would dream up stories to connect our themes with some sort of a conversation lesson. He was amused when I pushed the story in a grotesque direction. At the worst he'd say, "Ducroo, mon ami, ne faites pas le mauvais plaisant."[3] I really felt we were friends (much more than I did with the Dutch teacher, who fed my vanity), because he was human and engaging, because I felt he liked me more than just as a student.

There was also a bully with watery blue eyes, a former officer who called me to the front of the room. He yelled at me terribly, made everybody tremble when he raised his voice, which was indeed very loud, and wanted me to look him in the eye, he said, "because we have to understand each other right from the start," and other such nonsense. I looked straight into his little blue eyes, which didn't show a trace of danger. I went back to my seat as calmly as I had left it. He also threatened to knock me through the window "with this hand," which he held up, if I would disturb his lesson for so much as a moment. If I caused any trouble, he would pull every hair out of my head. Was that completely understood? Later I met him in a barber shop, and it struck me again how ridiculous he was. I was always certain that I wouldn't let him hit me either. Since I was back in the HBS, I had the feeling I had overcome my old cowardice, and I had decided that no one but my father could raise his hand against me. What struck me about all those teachers—with the exception of the one I had half-consciously accepted as a human being—was the role they played, a strikingly false pose that at the time I couldn't explain.

Once again I was on the lookout for a girl friend. For a couple of days I rode my bike after a sweet skinny little girl with curly hair and soft eyes, who always knew her lessons very well and left school in a *sado*. The HBS was housed temporarily in an old villa a little outside the city, across from the Tegallega race track. The girl was sweet and said childish things to me while I hung onto her *sado*, but I was vague and hesitant because she didn't attract me all that much.

I noticed then that there was always a swarm of boys riding around another girl who rode her bike quite sportily. She had an ironical long nose and a mass of dark blond hair that spread full in the wind. I had made friends with a boy of strong character, Edo Junius, who was two years younger than I; he was a Eurasian, but his skin was almost white. He was a whiz in school without any apparent effort, and outside school he kept to himself, living according to a code of honor which he stuck to stubbornly. He was the one who had the best chance with the girl with the nose, as I called her at first.

"Why don't you ride along with us," he said. "You'll like her."

So I did, and within a few days I was really in love with this sporty girl, Leni. She had a most engaging smile, which pulled her upper lip a bit cruelly, and strange blue eyes, almost like marbles. Suddenly Junius withdrew from the group. He didn't see the point, he said, since she didn't want to ride with him alone. I was sorry, because I liked his company, but already I was too much in love to follow his example. Although I felt he was right and that to some extent I was betraying him, I kept on riding my bike as close to Leni as I could. When Junius was still part of the group, this habit had caused me some trouble. One day, so as not to give up my place, I pushed so close to her that our handlebars and pedals locked together; within a matter of seconds we were both sprawled on the ground. I felt awful about it and almost wished she would hit me, right then and there. But she took it as a point of honor not to act like a girl, and she smiled at me to show she was a good sport, although she limped and Junius had to help her back on her bicycle. I was too crushed to do anything and I stayed behind, saying that my bike was broken. Subconsciously I wanted to punish myself for my clumsiness and yield to Junius his rightful place. But strangely enough, it was as if everybody forgot about this horrible incident overnight; when Junius disappeared, Leni was as friendly to me as ever.

Another boy and I were most in her favor now. His name was Joost Beyling; he liked to come to my house on Sundays and called me his best friend. He was older, with a more manly build than most of us, and he had fair skin and almost pure white hair. Both of us wanted to win Leni, but we tried to keep it an honest friendly competition. In the morning I waited for Leni, and when she chose a certain path we were sometimes alone for a long time. After school there was always a large group. But even when she and I rode alone we talked about the same things the group did.

One afternoon I came home and found my mother sobbing. My father wasn't there. It looked like the classic aftermath of a catastrophe. This was the crazy episode in which my father spent a whole month in debtors' prison because his friend the attorney had failed to do a thing in his case. After I had comforted my mother I rode my bike to the prison. My father paced up and down an almost bare, rather dark room, and he didn't look one bit surprised when I came in.

"You see," he said, "what can happen to you." The attorney finally came by and expressed his distress at what had happened, but it took some time for him to get my father out. My mother went there every day. She had our little Ford stop at the jail and told the chauffeur she was going to see her husband in the hospital, which was behind the jail and where you couldn't take a car. The chauffeur pretended, of course, to believe her, even though my mother usually didn't take one more step than was necessary. During this time my father felt the need to tell my mother in a special way how wonderful she was and how indebted he was to her. Although otherwise he always professed a dislike for poetry, he now remembered the verse he had read in his school days and expressed his gratitude in trivial poems. I saw his writing long afterwards—fifteen years later, perhaps—in Grouhy, and I found it painful because of its clumsy rhetoric. But my mother was as touched by them as the day she first read them, so they served their purpose completely. She even used to quote them: "I who am 'great of soul,' as your father once wrote."

Within two days my mother changed the atmosphere in the jail-room by bringing in lounge chairs, pillows, room dividers, and something to cook on. She was never home when I returned from school. I ate alone, quickly, and then went to join my parents. In a few days we became friends with the guard. Sometimes my mother got food from him so she wouldn't have to go home, and sometimes the three of us had tea at his house. It would have been almost pleasant there if it weren't for the occasional screams of a prisoner who had tried to escape and was being whipped behind the walls. The guard was a European who looked like an Ambonese. Later on he became my father's supervisor in Meester-Cornelis. One night he let my father go home. We told everybody that the doctor had given him permission.

My mother said to me, "Never, ever tell anyone in school, you understand, because it's a disgrace." I was romantic enough to think that indeed it was shameful, and so I felt the urge to tell Leni that I was the son of a jailbird. This was of course more out of a desire to be interesting than to be honest. When one morning we were alone together, I told her the secret—not emotionally or childishly but with the dignity of an adult. She said that it didn't matter and that she was still my friend.

It bothered me that none of us made any progress with Leni. I decided that Junius was right, that she ought to have just one boy to ride with. If she wouldn't make the choice, we would have to do it for her. I called all eight of the rivals together on the schoolground and suggested we draw lots; the winner would bicycle alone with Leni. The others would promise never even to talk to her, and whoever broke the pact would be beaten up by all the others. As strange as it was, they thought the plan was marvelous. Not for a moment did I think I would be the lucky one; in fact, it seemed more dignified for me to withdraw. Perhaps I had come up with the whole plan to get out of it honorably. I wrote our names on slips of paper. Joost Beyling put them in his school cap and took them over to Leni. We stood a couple of steps away and laughed a little; Leni laughed too, as if it were a joke she didn't understand. "I'm not going to be part of this," she said, but she picked a slip out of the hat and read the name, "Schuytema." She almost screamed when she said it, threw the slip of paper back in the hat, and went away. But nobody followed her that afternoon except Schuytema. He was the least eligible of the group, a quiet little Eurasian with a strangely protruding upper lip. He was apparently excited by his success, whereas somebody else would have been embarrassed. Every morning and afternoon Leni now rode alone with Schuytema.

My friendship with Joost Beyling grew. We laughed about Schuytema's luck, and we often went out together. One afternoon in Bandung's main street, Braga Road, we met Leni. She rode right up to us. "Who thought up that stupid idea," she said, laughing but mad. Beyling pointed at me. "Thanks a lot," she said. "What am I going to do with that horrible Schuytema? Will you ride with me now?" We shook our heads and laughed. Beyling pointed out that this would go against our honor. She got on her bike again and rode away, pedaling harder and harder.

The next day Schuytema came up to us. "I've had enough," he said. "Why don't you ride with Leni again?" With clearly hypocritical compassion Beyling asked him what the matter was. He pursed his large upper lip. "Nothing," he said. "I just don't want to anymore. Why don't you go ahead?" And he walked away with his hands in his pockets. When school let out, Leni rode alone.

Gradually we started riding with her again, but it was now clear she was only interested in Beyling and me. Sunday evening at the club we found her with her friends. The one who was the most fun was a general's daughter named Hetty, who had arched eyebrows and ladylike manners. At the time I was probably the one who was least afraid of her quick wit, and I was sometimes so caught up with her that I forgot about Leni. Junius watched from a distance and never joined us. He was a boarder at the house of a cavalry captain who once said to Junius that I really knew how to handle girls: "That boy is solid. He's not going to be taken in by love." In reality I longed terribly for the end of this situation. I took Beyling aside and told him that one of us had to make a statement to Leni that very evening. We drew straws and the lot fell to him. So I stayed behind with an ugly girl with glasses while he talked to Leni. After we had taken the girls home, he gave me the following report.

"She thinks we're still too young. In a few years I may come back.'

"And me?"

"I asked about you and the same thing goes for you."

"Then let's wait a couple of years," I said.

From then on I no longer rode with Leni. Beyling did, however, more than ever. Sometimes I saw them together downtown in the afternoon. Maybe Beyling didn't want to tell me that she really had chosen him, I thought, but I didn't feel a twinge of jealousy.

Around that time another boy was showing off a ring which Leni had given him. Beyling told me about it. I told the boy he was lying, and he showed me the ring. I asked him for it because I didn't want him to show it off anymore. He laughed at me; at one o'clock we wrestled in the mud, but that didn't really solve anything. I wanted to keep on fighting, but he jumped on his bike, saying he was late and didn't want to be punished for it. The next morning I was waiting for him. As soon as he saw me, he rode up, waving the ring, and gave it to me as he rode by. "My parents don't want me to fight over that," he said. I gave the ring to Beyling and asked him to give it back to Leni. The next day I got it back from him with Leni's message that I could keep it. I shrugged my shoulders, put the ring in my pocket, and kept it till I lost it, like everything else.

This was the moment for me to get close to Junius again. We separated ourselves from almost all the others and talked about more important things than girls. I was sixteen and Junius fourteen, but we nonetheless felt the same about everything. "I wish I didn't need anybody," Junius said. "If you need somebody, that shows you're weak." Besides me, he went around with one older boy who had an Italian father and the reputation of being the strongest boy in school. He liked to show off his large biceps, but he also often calmed us down like an adult. He had recently had his first experience with a woman, and he told us about it in a serious tone. We listened as if we were being initiated. What he emphasized most was the expression of surprised pride with which the woman had looked at him, as if to say, "See, you did that." We didn't laugh; on the contrary, we thought Belloni was our superior because he had gone beyond our silly games. There was only one thing, Junius noted, that was strange about him. He made it sound as if he were always successful: if the woman was receptive, it was obviously because she was in love with him, but if she was unreceptive, she was no less in love with him; she just didn't want to show it. Once Belloni asked me mysteriously if I knew Trudy. He had danced with her at the club, and she had talked about me. I hadn't seen Trudy in months. He wanted me to tell him how firm and soft she was and exactly what shape certain parts of her body took. I told him I couldn't really say.

"I can tell you," he said, "because I always pay attention to such things when I dance with a woman. They must be big but very soft." He pretended that he only went out with a woman who would let him do everything he wanted. The strange thing was that I also took him seriously, partly convinced by Junius, even though his friendly face and thick lips always reminded me of Mrs. Sachs.

I avoided the girls in school and hardly noticed that they avoided me too. Beyling came to tell me that Leni was now his girl. I wasn't surprised and was happy for him. At the club one Sunday evening I got close to Hetty again. She was very cheerful. It was catching, and we laughed as if we had never avoided each other. Suddenly I got serious and asked her what she had had against me before.

"I don't have to tell you that," she said, and then wanted to leave. I stopped her and said I didn't know anything about it. "Come on, Ducroo," she said, stamping her foot. I got angry too and insisted she give me an explanation. Blushing, she said that she had heard from Leni that I had called up Joost Beyling to say that I knew very well that..., that.... Oh well, I knew the rest, didn't I.

"I don't know anything," I repeated. "Please go on."

"Well, then, that he and Leni had done... intimate things with each other, don't you know."

Since there was absolutely no experimenting with the HBS girls, such an accusation was serious. What intimate things she meant I understood quite well. I left her alone for a moment to go over to Belloni and ask if he perhaps had started the joke.

"With such children!" he said indignantly. It couldn't have been a joke, Hetty said, when she saw from my face that I was really hurt, because Beyling had gone straight to the telephone office and asked for the number of the person who had called him, for I had refused to give my name. Like a detective Beyling had learned from the telephone office that it was my number. He had then gone to my house and had taken me brutally to task, and then I had confessed.

Like another such detective I now wanted to know how Beyling had gone to the telephone office. On his bike, of course. I asked Hetty not to tell anybody yet that she had talked to me about this, and she promised. The next day at one o'clock Belloni, Junius, and I caught up with the group formed by Leni, Hetty, and Beyling. I asked Beyling to tell me the story of the mysterious telephone call in which he had played the hero and I had played the villain, unfortunately without knowing anything about it. He didn't hesitate a moment. He tapped on his forehead and said I should try to remember. Just as with Baur, I then told him what I thought of him, but much more tersely and without raising my voice. "I thought you were my friend, and all you are is an ass." My father taught me this was the worst insult for a man; when I said it, I put my handlebar right next to his.

"I have never been your friend," he said disdainfully.

"If you were not my friend and still came to my house so often," I said, "you are not only an ass but a hypocrite too." I expected him to hit me, and I kept my eye on him. His face was red, but he looked straight ahead over his handlebars. I suggested he go right to the telephone office with me; this he could hardly refuse. In the meantime Leni talked to Hetty, who had been won over to my side and later reported to me what she had said. Not for a second did it occur to Leni that I might be telling the truth. "Don't you think it's rude of Ducroo to say such things to Joost?" This cowardly female reaction was new to me. The girls turned away, and Beyling and I, followed by Belloni and Junius as witnesses, rode to the telephone office. The four of us went up the steps. A telephone operator, surprised by the appearance of a group of boys, came up to us immediately. "I would like to talk to the operator who's here in the afternoon," said Beyling. It was clear what he was up to. I cut him off.

"Is it possible, Miss, that somebody who gets an anonymous call would come here on his bike from Dago Road, which is at least a fifteen-minute ride, and still learn the number?"

She began to laugh. "You have to realize that we make sixty connections every three minutes, so after one minute we don't remember anymore." It came out so quickly that Beyling went back down the steps with us without a word. In the street he tried to explain something to Junius, who was walking closest to him, but Junius turned his back on him.

Four years later Junius traveled with Leni by train between Bandung and Djokja. One afternoon when he had returned from his vacation he asked with a knowing smile if I still remembered her. He was now on very good terms with her, and he had explained what had really happened. She had been upset and wanted to talk to me. It was unnecessary and all in the past, as far as I was concerned, but I couldn't refuse Junius this satisfaction. So Leni and I saw each other again. She asked me a couple of questions. "How could anyone do such a thing?" she said. We had little to say to each other anymore. Junius walked happily behind us. He dismissed Leni as if she were a remnant of his past he needed to get rid of, and when all was said and done, she was the only one who was still hurt. His bringing this up again for his own pleasure could only be out of a sense of justice. For me it was also a taste of what "real life" had in store for me. Beyling's treachery had struck me more than Leni's disfavor. Yet, when I'd given her up I felt that I had given up all girls. Until I left the Indies I cultivated the image of a spiteful person who, with a few exceptions, was even more unpleasant in the presence of girls. It was the beginning of the period in which we examined every emotion, and whenever we hadn't seen someone for a month we would say, "You won't know me anymore; I have changed enormously."

Shortly after the little melodrama with Leni and Beyling, I left school for good. There had been a clash between the history teacher and me, and we both complained about it to the principal; this ended with my being punished twice over, even though the teacher had lied. I tried to get the class on my side as witnesses to the real course of events, but the letter I sent around was intercepted and given to the principal, who didn't appreciate its wording and suspended me for two weeks. As a result I lost valuable time I really needed at the last moment to catch up for what I had neglected all year. My father received an angry letter from the principal, which he didn't like at all; when I had told him what happened, he silently supported me. The principal probably expected his letter to have more effect, but I was readmitted with another scolding and a vague compromise, although I still refused to apologize to the teacher, as I told the principal, since he was the one who had lied. But I didn't succeed in making up the lost time. My weakest point was German. My father went to talk to the German teacher, and the next day he gave me a letter for him. I sensed what must be in it, and I was unable to deliver the letter. After some hesitation I tore open the envelope and read the words that my father had my mother write in her neat handwriting. An appeal was made to his own fatherhood. I think my face suddenly became bright red. I tore the letter to bits and scattered them behind me on the road. When I came home my father asked if I had given the letter; I said I must have lost it, because I couldn't find it anywhere. Immediately he slapped me with the back of his hand. I was dizzy, but I didn't think it was too great a price to pay. Deep down I wanted to fight my teachers on my own. I flunked horribly, but only when I went to say good-bye to my friend the French teacher did I suddenly burst into tears. He comforted me by saying that since I hadn't completed the first year in Batavia, there was a way out: I would certainly be allowed to take the year over. He didn't understand; I had no intention of going back to school. I felt defeated, but I was worried about what I would do next.

Around that time my parents had rented a house in Tjitjalengka, three-quarters of an hour by car outside Bandung. It was a quiet town with only a few Europeans—twenty or twenty-five, perhaps—a controller, the stationmaster, the doctor, and a couple of retired planters. Alone with me in the car that took us there, my father was seething— to use one of his words. He insulted me the entire trip. "You've read about dropouts in Klikspaan. Well, that's what you are now. You're a dropout." I didn't say a word, but as soon as I saw my mother in Tjitjalengka, I said I wanted to pack my suitcase and go off on my own. I knew a distant cousin in Bandung who was about thirty-six—part businessman, part adventurer—who had been in the circus as a child and was now a representative of an Australian movie company. If he didn't have any work for me, I was sure he would let me sleep in his office. My father said I could go. I took my suitcase, and my mother put a ten-guilder bill in my pocket. I was probably the only one who was serious about this. Before I left, my father said that I should stay because he could perhaps do something for me. He took me to the Dutch teacher, who again spoke very highly of me and felt that private lessons would not be wasted on me. Following this route and with his recommendation, I could perhaps get a teaching certificate in Dutch. I think he also mentioned to my father something about a doctorate you could get in Liège; this brightened my father's face. So I would soon begin to commute between Bandung and Tjitjalengka to work toward a diploma.

At that time I received a letter from Junius, who had gone on vacation and whom I had not seen again: "I made it, and what a report card! I wish I could split my grades with you." It touched me and restored a disturbed balance. If Junius wrote something like this to me, he must mean it twice over, since he was not at all sentimental. It reinforced my notion that friendship can do a lot to protect you from society and its laws. What happened to be impossible now might be possible under other circumstances. I flunked only because Junius couldn't split his grades with me.

It was in those days that my father told me that if he had to, he would still whip me when he was sixty and I was twenty-four. I didn't doubt it. He was my father, and I was a slight sixteen-year-old who had barely conquered his former cowardice in school. And yet I asked myself why I remained so afraid of my father, when in all probability I would not be at all afraid of this man if I met him on the street. An old woman of local nobility, ugly but coquettish, said to me a year later in Tjitjalengka, "Once you've been with a woman, everything will change. You won't be afraid of anything, not even your father." Intuitive psychology, but the test wasn't made, because her appearance terrified me even more.

20 Joies de Meudon

August. There comes a moment when you think: so what if I lost my last penny. Suddenly the fear of being cooped up in a musty little room and suffering from the cold disappears. You realize that you won't know anything until you're in the middle of it, and in the meantime it's better to be happy with what you've got. The emergency measures have given us a better perspective of our circumstances. Suddenly it seems that everything could have been worse, which makes us certain that it won't stay like this.

How could I have written so desperately to my sister-in-law? She sent a little money for Guy; that's the most important thing at the moment. As for us, we'll find a way. This morning I mailed an article full of details on my old friend D'Artagnan, the romantic figure as well as the historical one—an article I hope some boy will enjoy, one who finds the problem of whether or not this hero actually existed to be as tormenting as it once was for me. What a strange basis for a boy's fantasy! Recently I saw a little girl reading on the doorstep of a house. A little boy a few years older in a sunhat came up very close to her on his scooter, took off his hat with a flourish, and said, "D'Artagnan, capitaine des mousquetaires du Roi!"

I put tomorrow's copy in the mail and have a cup of coffee at the Feuilleraie and feel really happy. It's only when I think of Jane working next to me or of Guy being at the vegetarian boarding school that I feel my mood disintegrate. A cup of coffee is now an extravagance for me, but I'm perfectly willing to sing praises for the small pleasures I've earned for myself, which are ten times as delicious. This is the big vacation month. Gerard Rijckloff passed through town on his way to Italy and spent an evening with me on the Boulevard Montparnasse after my return from Brussels. He talked about Hitler's madness and the latest scandals of The Pit, telling with his solemn voice about "how a young man, who still had a backbone and enough character to recognize when he's been attacked, had been dragged into the swamp by somebody else." His voice, along with his deep blue eyes and square chin, works its effect on women. As for that, he talked about his approaching old age and acted very calm. It used to be, when we were together in Paris, he was always on the lookout for women, hunting in the Métro and the bus, loving hard, sleeping badly in spite of all that love and a huge supply of barbital tablets he had collected little by little, and too tired to talk when he appeared again. At three o'clock in the afternoon he was in the arena with a Moroccan "black panther"; in the evening he was incapable of anything except a date in the Dome with a Norwegian intellectual whose virtue he was going to try to overcome. Once I took him and Héverlé to a Chinese restaurant. Héverlé was at his best and was brilliant, but Rijckloff had come straight from the panther. Later I asked him what he thought of Héverlé. "Oh, he's undoubtedly very intelligent but extremely tiresome; his voice betrays his irritation with the silence of the universe." I asked Héverlé for his impression of Rijckloff. "Eh bien, à vrai dire, je n'en ai pas! Il a l'air gentil, mais il est endormi, votre ami Rijckloff."[1]

It would be senseless to bring them together again; moreover, without any warning, the Héverlés have left for Greenland to see how the midnight sun plays with the shadows of the polar bears. Wijdenes has gone to Engadine and Genoa in search of the shadow of Nietzsche and now sends a picture of himself, sitting next to the rock at Sils Maria, with his sharp laughing face under a Basque beret, unharmed by the idea of Eternal Return. He's sitting on the grass in the sun as an illustration of its final chord: "Doch alle Lust will Ewigkeit."[2] He's happy, he writes, that he didn't find a Nietzsche cult in Engadine and that an electrician lives in the house in Sils Maria with a shamelessly ugly advertisement next to the entrance. There is a picture of that, too. He announces his arrival in two weeks. I plan on putting him up in this hotel.

The Brussels notary is also on vacation. The seal on the furniture has been removed, but the auction can't take place until later.

La Feuilleraie has now become the greatest attraction in the neighborhood for us; it replaces the vacation spot we had to forego elsewhere. The terrace with the garden behind it well deserves its name. We carry out wicker chairs under the trees. We avoid the poor village square named after Rabelais, with its two unsightly little hotels, and all of Bas-Meudon with its sleepy little streets, its unpainted garages and small shops, and instead we look for summer in the direction of Bellevue. Seen from here, Paris with its white minaret called Sacré Coeur on top in the afternoon light can make us dream of an oriental city, the Damascus we will never see.

There are small intimate streets around La Feuilleraie, where I used to point out "the Indies" to Jane over and over again, with little villas in different colors, which you can look into as you walk by and see old family portraits hanging on the walls. You get to know the dogs that bark as soon as you stop. Sometimes we go for a walk by the light of a full moon, when the buildings become shadowlike and a fallen tree trunk is like the center of a dreamlike engraving. The forest is what attracts Jane. She sees much more variety in it than I do, and she can be amused by the squirrels we meet; one or two run away roguishly, wagging their tails like tiny dogs. For me it's the houses. Trees only begin to interest me when they stick out above the walls surrounding the buildings; the ones in the gardens are usually tall and full, while those in the forest look rather sparse.

I have my favorite villas in Meudon-Bellevue. The house I like best is tall, at the corner of a lane, covered with ivy, and always empty. The walls are painted to look like wood, but the paint is so faded it all looks like cardboard: a cardboard house that's too cheap for the neighborhood, a mystery. On another corner is an old-fashioned villa, with vine-covered garden walls and many chestnut trees, painted light yellow, with faded Italian green blinds which are almost all closed. "The House of the Quiet Old Women." It's hidden behind an iron gate with fierce spikes and a high crest of ivy. Inhabited but always dormant, it is guarded by a shaggy black dog which is also usually asleep. Further on down is the "Roman Palace," grayish-white and cool in its huge garden full of romantic trees; when you pass close by the other side, it becomes an ordinary building with too many steps and a terrace which has as many pillars as the back porch of Gedong Lami. And standing apart from these, in all its massiveness, is a red convent school for boys, with a saint's statue on the porch which at night, with the hall light behind it, looks like an enormous priest. A month ago the boys were still playing in the yard, some with their arms around each other, which always gave me goose pimples and yet seemed so innocent and vulnerable. The bell rang, they went inside, and I said to Jane, "There is perhaps one boy who will never forget this hour, this bell, this light, and a part of the building as it now catches his eye." I thought of myself and of Guy at the same time.

Apparently La Feuilleraie is an old villa too. Fortunately for us, there aren't usually many customers. Lately there have been too many children, though, who make a racket playing croquet in the garden. It's strange—there are people who generally like children. In the little faces around us that come to look at us either shyly or boldly, we have found one child who may turn out to be a decent human being. The five or six others already show clearly the signs of a future brute, businessman, and old maid. We sit under a spruce with low spreading branches, but the pride of the garden is a tall acacia and a linden tree that's just as tall. It's a flowerless garden but colorful, thanks to the variety of trees and shades of green. Two busts of unknown gentlemen from the Louis-Philippe period have been put up in the ligustrum hedges on either side of the garden path; they stand exactly in the middle, a bit hidden, yet looking at each other reassuringly across the garden path. All around are plane trees and chestnut trees. Most of them are in the surrounding private parks, but the design is such that, seen from various points, they appear to be a continuation of this garden.

"Even when we are really and truly poor," says Jane, "I still think we will be able to give a different color to our surroundings than what people are used to in Paris. For the same money we could rent a sunny one-room apartment with fresh air and perhaps even a little balcony, instead of two or three dark rooms at the back of a courtyard, and with a musty staircase where your last bit of courage dissolves when you come home."

I think so too as I sit here. Something like that must always be possible.... I look at the lantern on the other side of the iron balustrade that juts out above a road; an arm, painted green, holds the lantern, and the light burns fresh and greenish. It's clearly a street lantern, but one that seems to be intimately attached to the little house that sticks out above the wall—probably a gardener's house of the luxury variety. The two front windows are the same old faded green as the closed windows in "The House of the Quiet Old Women," but these are open. We can clearly see the curtains hanging there, in a strange fashion, almost like mosquito netting. The rest of the façade is covered with a lattice painted the same green as the windows. If I could paint with my pen, I'd like to make a picture of this scene: the character of such a wooden blind with the old paint on it, its shadow and intimacy that can make everybody say, "I've known it for a long time; as a child I stood under it so often." By the lantern at the edge of the façade are a couple of patches where little light red stones have been inlaid, and while I look at the old paint on the wood, I think I recognize it too, as if all these things, including the mosquito netting, create another realm, probably Gedong Lami—the huge windows on the street side: there were two dwarf palm trees next to them, which I forgot to mention in my inventaire sentimental.[3]

It is the house that represents the happiness of our childhood, even more than our parents. Parents themselves are perhaps only part of the realm we explore when we are searching for nothing but our earlier selves. The house remains faithful, at least if it's not redone. It can always stay our friend the way animals do, but it's bigger and more intimate. It doesn't contradict the impressions you want to retain, the way parents do. Later, when I was on a trip, I sometimes thought, "How nice, there are no quarrels here," and then, when I came home again, it was also unexpectedly pleasant at my parents' home, because for a few days we all lived in the old realm. But after a few days it was all over again. They were once more as they really were: egotistical and petty. A house is as immutable as "nature," "steadfast nature." It's the realm of the house you long for, and which for me will always be that of Gedong Lami. Wherever there was a similar situation, in Tjitjalengka or Grouhy, I rediscovered Gedong Lami, but not in other places—for example, Bandung. Balekambang was isolated enough, but the houses were too different. Maybe the house is also the reason why somebody with a religious childhood asks for a priest at his deathbed. I won't; my environment wasn't all that religious, but if religion had been an important part of Gedong Lami, I'm afraid that too would have left its mark. It's normal for a child to love his parents: after all, they love their child the most. But there are children who hate their parents and transfer their affection to another living witness of their early years—a grandmother, an aunt, a maid. The house is still the most complete witness and, what's more, the storehouse of our memories. Without consciously realizing it, we trust so much of ourselves to the house from our childhood.

And yet our parents sometimes take that atmosphere with them when they leave, and it seems as if they were the only ones to create it and that, in some way or other, we love in them what still exists of it. Even before my mother's death I knew that the whole realm that took shape in Gedong Lami would die with her—the smell of the food from the Indies which she cooked in Europe from the very first day and sometimes almost every day in Grouhy, the blend of *cajuput* and oil with which she was massaged, and the incense which had to be burned Thursday night in front of the kris collection to placate its spirits and which was then taken around through all the rooms, because of the possibility of other spirits.

I was looking at this same lantern when I first remembered the emotional game my mother and I played, the "Toet, when Mama is dead..." game, and I wished she could know how strangely it moved me to think of her that first time after her death and how moved I was when I wrote down that passage. Thanks to her, Guy might also have the memory of a house. Grouhy can be his Gedong Lami, even if he's living with the theosophists now. When she was spoiling him and I would point it out to her, she answered, "I want him at least to remember me fondly." How amazingly desperate, this seed of immortality planted in a child of five or six. I'm inclined to underestimate Guy's memory, but after some reflection my trust increases: she cannot have been wrong here.

I would like to talk to Guy, now or as soon as possible, to bridge the gap between us and to know that the differences between us are not the same as those between my father and me. When will I be able to do that, and what will he be like then? Sometimes I think I would rather talk to my father than to my mother now. I could ask him so much I didn't dare put into words before, if I could have found the words to do so. You are a child of your parents, whether you like it or not. At the time the last thing in the world I wanted was to resemble my father; however, I sometimes caught myself acting exactly like him, biting my nails and glancing over my hand, which must have looked exactly like him.

On one of our trips from Sand Bay to the interior when I was ten, they let me ride a *desa* chief's horse for a while. It had the habit of moving politely to one side of the road, because it was usually ridden in the company of the controller, who was given most of the road. When I had to cross a floating bridge, the horse moved to the left, just as on the road, and the horse and I fell into the water. My mother yelled; my father turned around in his saddle and saw that I had not fallen off my horse. When my horse was dragged out of the water and I rode on as if nothing had happened, I had the vague sensation he recognized with some pride his ability as a horseman in me.

After I was nineteen he left me alone for the most part. For somebody with the reputation of an autocrat this was peculiar, to say the least. When I was an adult I sometimes tried to get closer by talking to him. Perhaps I've always appreciated his strong independent streak and his aversion to wasting time. After Stendhal everybody can openly be in love with his mother and hate his father. When I was reading Joyce I came across the little boy who didn't like his father's smell, and I immediately recalled a similar reaction in my own childhood. But later, when we were in Europe, I also noticed a pleasant sense of joy in him, when I would come home from a trip. I think I could now address myself to his sensitivity, if I saw him again. I would at least be aware of it. For some time, shortly before we left the Indies, I felt a sort of hatred in my mother toward me. Why? Was it a result of her change of life? Or the feeling that I was pulling away from her for other women? What kind of women were they after all.... In those days I instinctively grew closer to my father without there ever being a real intimacy between us. He never told me anything personal about himself, the surest way to win me over if he had wanted to, and if he had known me well enough.

And yet, when I was eighteen or nineteen he was my rival, although perhaps unconsciously. When we had girls over for dinner, he would ridicule me or scold me, as if to make it clear he was still the boss. Had he been a better psychologist, he would have used something else, since this just gave him the reputation with the girls of being a grumpy old man and provided me the opportunity to benefit from their feminine pity. In this too I can clearly see that I am his son. Couldn't I have done the same, and if I noticed I was mistaken, might I not have persisted? In the moments when I consider my parents most critically, I want to know how many of those same characteristics have carried over in me, altered only through practice and intellectualization: such as my father's temper, which according to a psychiatrist showed his weakness and was perhaps a forewarning of the neurasthenia he developed, or my mother's tenacity in certain respects and perhaps even her conviction that she was always right—these characteristics only made manageable and kept under control by intellectualization, who knows? Sometimes Graaflant maintains this, and I have never seriously contradicted him.

How little interest this must hold for somebody who is not one of my "friends," but how much do I really count on a certain tone to chase away that reader? When Wijdenes is here, I can put my childhood in the Indies before him as a counterpoint to his liberal Christian up-bringing in Eastern Holland. "We would perhaps never have become friends if we had met each other a couple of years earlier," he says sometimes.

Every once in a while we pass by La Feuilleraie and follow the road that leads down to the park in Saint-Cloud. Here Jane quickly steers away from all sign of human contact, even if there's hardly anybody to be seen. She won't even look at the lemonade and beer stands with the wooden benches and the folding chairs, whether or not there are people sitting on them. We walk along leaf-covered winding paths of hard clay until we come to a pool with many steps and a whole array of views. Here we stop to look in the water and to look all around us. A little further on we will walk on the grass along soft, attractive avenues. They form a big star. A tunnel lures us as a variation and, at the same time, a continuation of another tunnel. Sunlight falls at sharp angles, as if the tree groupings intercept the rays in a special way to make them oblique and reflect them sideways. When the honking of the cars on the road to Paris doesn't reach us, we almost expect to hear the soft rolling sound of a carriage. There is also a terrace somewhere, with a stone balustrade that has deep cuts in it, where the presence of others no longer bothers us. At dusk we sit there alone, the voices of other people muted. Just like us, they sit half-hidden on a bench or walk soundlessly along the large flowerbed in the center. The flowers lose their color in the approaching dark. Behind them, where Paris begins, there's still a pink glow as the first lights are turned on. We walk back along the Seine, and in the dark we start to talk about something which is no longer related to the decor.

Sometimes, confronted with this paper, I think I'll never write down what's really important, because it's too close and too vivid for me. Only the past allows its parts to be grouped together, and the present, which I sometimes take on, always hides something. Life can swindle you worse than the notaries do, and it's not only the ultimate cer-tainty of death that gives you the feeling of being swindled. Sometimes you're swindled without even being present, defeated in unknown places without being able to realize that it's happening. Only later do you notice how irrevocable it was, leaving you more powerless and more deeply humiliated, because it didn't happen in a world you can despise.

21   A Young Man in the Indies

For almost two years we lived in Tjitjalengka, but since I had a commuter pass to Bandung, I stayed there whenever I had a chance, most often (and most comfortably) with "Uncle" Van Kuyck. He was my father's old friend, who had come to the rescue in Balekambang with a team of coolies. But he had done much more. Before the failure of the rice factory could be turned into the success of the long-lease property, my father had had to borrow money. Gedong Lami was even on the verge of being auctioned by the court. Uncle Van Kuyck had really been our savior, which led to the rumor that he was in love with my mother, that he must even be her lover. Actually, his increasing friendship was based on something entirely different and much more spiritual: the spiritualism into which my father had initiated him. He was the type of planter who came from a good family and was proud of the fact that he remained European in spite of earlier predictions. Even so, twice he had married women to legitimize the children he had had with them; the first time it was a native woman and the second time a Chinese. Both women had died. The daughters from his first marriage were grown and married. Although he was goodness personified, he thought it perfectly natural to curse one of them for marrying a Jew. It made no impression whatsoever on Van Kuyck that his Jewish son-in-law had studied in Germany and had scars on his cheeks from dueling; just the opposite—he said he was convinced he had inflicted this decoration on himself while shaving, or something similar. For me his daughter's name became synonymous with a child *cursed* by her father. After the death of his second wife, to whom he was devoted, he felt lonely and left the cinchona plantation where he had proved himself to be a genius of a planter, and he moved to a house in Bandung. His youngest daughters stayed with him or with a Chinese aunt, or with my parents when they were back in Gedong Lami. He had a great number of edifying proverbs he repeated to these girls; moreover, he impressed upon them that they should never forget that they were Van Kuycks. These admonitions irritated my father sometimes, since Van Kuyck talked all the time about the importance of selecting cinchona seeds but, in my father's opinion, had failed to be selective in other areas.

In Bandung he went every morning to the club, where the goodness he radiated made him very popular; and every day at dinner he could report that he had been talking so damn pleasantly with his friend so-and-so, whom he had known way back in the year such-and-such, and who had told him damn interesting things about damn crazy events. In the meantime he would carefully spread a slice of bread with a personal concoction for himself or for a guest who wanted to have a taste. In the afternoon he sat on his front porch, reading in his pajama pants and *kabaya*, with a *sapu lidi* in his hand, which he used to kill flies and which he called his scimitar. He read *De Telegraaf*[1] almost from the first to last page and found "damn good articles" again and again. Or he would read some history book, preferably Streck-fuss's *World History*, translated, as he was always quick to add, by Ter Haar. This work with its many volumes and the bound volumes of *De aarde en haar volken* (*The Earth and Its Peoples*) formed the core of the library that he had brought with him from his cinchona planta-tion. This reading showed his undying interest in "events." Two pas-sages from Streckfuss became classics for me. One, that it was damn strange about those old guys, but when they had enough prisoners they simply burned all of them alive; and, two, that it was no less strange that Czar Peter the Great received foreign ambassadors while he was sitting on a chamber pot with naked women on either side. He had two kinds of pictures in his house: those of sailboats, pref-erably on stormy seas, and those of battles. The latter were mostly from the Franco-Prussian War, such as *The Charge of the Hussars at Gravelotte*—"That was a toss-up, young man." And, as for *The Defense of Longbuyau*, he said, "Those French were beaten all the time, be-cause they used those damn old *chassepots*." During the Great War, color supplements from *L'Illustration* increased his collection, and he continued to speak with the same cheerful insight about those *soixante-quinzes*, which got rid of damn many people. It was exactly the same tone he used in talking about anchovies—"Watch out, young man, they're damn salty." "And at Verdun, those Germans were so stupid they attacked in closed ranks; that was simply terrible; whole regiments were wiped out!"

He had an aristocratic, long and heavy face, with small round eyes, a bent nose, and a gray grenadier mustache. Equally striking was his enormous belly, which suited him, given his character and his stature. He had three topics of conversation: "events"; deep tillage, that is, his stroke of genius by which he had his soil worked with forks rather than spades, which made his cinchona the best in the world; and third, once he had found spiritualism, his "reports from Above." Not only had my father allowed him to read all his spiritualist library, but they had seances with him at Balekambang. My mother proved to be a writing medium, and the presence of a common guardian spirit sealed the alliance. This very high spirit revealed itself under the unembroidered name of Mary. They talked about Mary's advice even in my presence, because I wasn't supposed to be able to guess who that might be, but since the term "from Above" was also used a lot and seemed so comforting, and since it was connected to the native spirit world I had always been so familiar with, it led me subconsciously to the explanation. I was soon used to Mary accompanying us everywhere, like an invisible house guest. My mother became almost an extraterrestrial being to Uncle Van Kuyck—somebody who had at least had unfailing premonitions and was consulted again and again outside the seances.

"What are your feelings about this, Maddy?"

"I don't think it's good, Kuyck."

"Then I won't do it, Maddy."

One day I saw him enter the kitchen, hesitantly, while my mother was cooking.

"What's the matter, Kuyck; you look as if you've lost something."

"That's right. I'm really upset because the ring I got in '83 has disappeared. And Sahari can't find the damn thing anywhere."

"Then you must pray to Saint Anthony."

"Saint Who?"

"Saint Anthony."

"Saint Anthony? I'll do it, Maddy; you can count on it. You know, when you say something like that, I don't take it lightly."

And the next day Sahari found the ring.

His relations with the Above were not at all terrifying. Soon he was discussing them with everybody, so that the club always knew when old Kuyck had received reports again. Discussions about this with my father became so breathless that sometimes, even though my father considered his pupil his only friend, he would carefully avoid him for some time. But on occasion, when the discussion became intimate, an almost suffocating joy reigned in the room. I was called in then and had to promise that, if necessary, I would support the children of Uncle Van Kuyck, because it was only thanks to him that our fortune was restored. I promised this all the more readily since I liked him personally, even if I got my dose of edifying proverbs from him.

"But I owe your father no less," he said. And to him, "I shall never forget, Charles, that you brought me to the Above."

Unfortunately, down below the friendship didn't last forever. Uncle Van Kuyck went with us to Europe, but from the moment we arrived it seemed the relationship had changed for good. The old friends became critical of each other, and only rarely did he come to visit us. He consoled himself in Brussels with new friends, and his daughter Ida, the cursed one, who had lost her husband and came to live with him, begging his forgiveness. He now wrote endless letters to his children in the Indies about what happened on earth and elsewhere. When I met him, he was as amiable as ever, but the proverbs took on a certain bitterness, when they were applied to my parents. A letter I found among my mother's papers must date from that period, that is to say, shortly before my father's suicide. It is so typical I want to quote it verbatim:

Dear Maddy,

I received your letter of May 5th in good health. *Merci*. It's very good of you to keep my letters and to reread them from time to time. If you, and Charles too, want to read reproaches and anger into everything, that's your problem, and I wash my hands of it. It's never *your* fault, always someone else's. And you fool yourself when you think you're perfect; it's time for your friend to tell you what's wrong with you. If you want to consider this a reproach, that's your business; I have always kept my mouth shut, thinking, "They have good brains and know how to behave themselves." If you ever said anything to me that was anything but kind, I always kept silent because I believed we are all imperfect and shouldn't judge one another. So much has happened that, when things got worse because you couldn't control yourselves, I only stared at you when you went too far. But you thought, "That old dummy Kuyck, we can tell him anything, he won't mind." But I think all the more, and while thinking I kept saying to myself: are they blind, don't they see that everything in nature takes its revenge?

Even Mary reproached me that I kept my mouth shut too much, and I did that to spare you. Neither one of you has the slightest self-control, and it's about time that your eyes are opened, that you repent. You always reinforced Charles's stupid idea that everyone must bow to his will, and since the poor bloke has got his fortune, he's simply gone crazy with vanity and pride. He has been warned enough by the Above, but he never wanted to listen to good advice when it conflicted with his own ideas, and somebody else always had to bend to his will. I'll never forget those scenes at Tjitjalengka. Maddy! I know all too well that we are nothing. I'm grateful to Charles for bringing me to Him and I have tried to be a true friend and unselfish. I have not forgotten Mary's words and lessons and I reflect on them all the time. I want only to mention this, it's what makes me strong, think about it: would He, the Almighty, be so mistaken in a person He has blessed—even a nobody? Both of you have completely forgotten that. Mary always said I was *blessed*. She also said, "We like to be where love, peace, and satisfaction reign." Well, Maddy, Ida is here now. She didn't know me before; she only said, "Dad, I didn't know you were like that." This I receive through affection and love. You feel, and you know full well, that what I say is the truth. We will not break off our friendship; I'll simply wait for the time when Charles will come to me for help, and that time will come, just as it did twenty years ago, but it will be for spiritual help this time. Don't forget what I told you about what has been told to me: "God's punishment is five times more severe than that of a human judge." I hope everything is well with you. When I have money again, you'll be the first ones I'll repay.

                                                    Your true friend Kuyck

Six months later, the help he wanted to give my father here below was unnecessary. But after my father's death, he told me that he often went to the "poor bloke's" grave to pray for him. "How he could do that, young man, is still a puzzle to me," he said. They had often talked about the terrible punishment for suicide, in connection with a Persian princess who had done something similar and who later revealed through a medium that her soul had been chained to her rotting body until the Above granted her deliverance.

But in Bandung and Tjitjalengka the friendship was still strong, in spite of what was perhaps the first friction. In these "scenes" my parents were usually the combatants and Kuyck was the peacemaker; he never failed to compare them to our parakeets. When I was at his house, he treated me like a son and he let me stay out at night as late as I wanted. I didn't abuse this freedom. I even walked as if deaf and blind past the native prostitutes who, after eleven, would squat in fairly large numbers along the street where he lived.

One evening at the fairground behind the movie theater Trudy's father managed, I saw her again. There was some sort of a carnival with American or Australian attractions, the most important of which was called the fun wheel. Anyone who couldn't hold on to the center of this wheel would be thrown off by centrifugal force. Natives, schoolboys, and adolescents would crawl on it together, pushing each other away as soon as the wheel started to turn. If only one was left, he could sit there quietly, although he would become dizzy and not be able to see anything, but he would still laugh as if challenging the rest. Eventually one of the bystanders would jump on the wheel to pull him off, and like big insects locked together they would then fall off. Sometimes they'd hit hard against the wooden edge when the wheel was going full speed. A couple of times I had managed to stay on by myself and had become more and more excited, until I began to feel the pain in my shoulders and elbows. People would take off their shoes and when I looked for mine, I couldn't find them. There were at least forty pairs in a pile. So I took a pair that didn't fit very well and stumbled off. Then I saw Trudy, who had been laughing at me for maybe half an hour. She was with a tall Dutchman (Dutchman was what I called every *tòtòk*, every imported rival), a man in his thirties, who walked respectfully next to her. She whispered to me, "Please come talk to us." I said I didn't want to intrude. She pinched my arm viciously, "Come on, he's so boring." My vanity was flattered. I walked with them along the stands and finally to Trudy's house. I hadn't seen her father in a long time; he was a jovial man with a face red from the sun, and he liked to sit in his house in as few clothes as possible. The four of us sat together; Trudy's Dutch admirer was indeed obviously in love and boring. Her father conspired with me to make a fool of him and poured us a lot of port, which the admirer couldn't hold at all. It became a point of honor to me to drink twice as much as he did and show that it didn't affect me. He left at eleven and I was invited, with the typical hospitality of the Indies, to spend the night. The fact that I was staying at Uncle Van Kuyck's house was not the point; after all, why should I walk through the whole city so late at night, when there was a room here. After that I often spent the night at Trudy's and I could drop in whenever I wanted.

In Tjitjalengka I went hunting with a double-barreled shotgun my father had given me. Because my mother was so fond of the meat I shot a great number of birds—at first only woodcocks, *tekukurs* mostly, and later the little green parrots called *bètèts* or *èkèks*, of which there were so many in a banyan tree in the local cemetery. A Sundanese went along with me to pick up the fallen birds, and if they were still alive he would stab them with the quill of one of their own feathers, or he would wring their necks. I saw the little fat tongue of one of the parrots come out twitching even though its neck had been wrung. It took all my will power to control my disgust, mostly with myself, and not to go home immediately. After that, I shot every bird twice, although this was against all the rules of hunting and also wasted a lot of buckshot. And yet even this hunt had something exciting about it. Sometimes I spent days on end in the Tjitjalengka forest and made a whole *kampong* happy by exterminating the squirrels that damaged the co-conut trees. I came to hate crows because they were smarter than all the other birds and flew away screaming when you just pointed at them. My greatest hunting adventure consisted of shooting a long-eared owl. It came down from a tall tree, flapping its wings slowly, and, with the blood that dripped out of its open beak, it looked more fright-ening than the biggest game. Our Javanese chauffeur trembled when I brought it home. He thought it came from the world of the spirits.

Tjitjalengka's few Europeans had a small club with a pool table and even a stage where the stationmaster would give a recital every now and then. On the *alun-alun* between our house and the controller's they sometimes played tennis. The controller sang too. In the evening his voice came across the *alun-alun* to our front porch. He sang Schu-mann's "Die Grenadier," which I thought was the Marseillaise. It was a nice peaceful little town and people saw each other too rarely to gos-sip extensively. I rode the train with Chinese, Arabs, Eurasian railroad officials, and schoolchildren. I hardly ever spoke to anybody but some-times enjoyed listening to the conversations around me. Eurasians love proverbs, which with their accent really take on a new lustre. A railroad official once said, in a gallant voice to a bulb-shaped lady who rode the train only rarely, "Eh, Miss, you're really getting too fat, say."

"Yes, what do you want, sir, I am now again boarding with other people and the food is good and they say, 'Dainty pigs never grow fat.'"

The young man, his eyes shining and his smile full of mischief, replied, "Yes, and they also say, 'It's easy to get fat on another man's milk.'"

The accent falls heavily on the last syllable, particularly in the last two words. Although these conversations were lacking the operatic quality Stendhal was fascinated with, he would have loved them for their geniality as much as he did Italian conversations.

We rented the former *patih*'s house, a luxurious native house. There was a large garden surrounding it, and the tin roof rattled sometimes because the property was once a cemetery and was not completely free of spirits. We held *sedekahs*, in which the spirits are satisfied with the aroma of the dishes while the food is eaten by the natives. One night after prayer the roof rattled mightily. We all stood in the garden to watch. This was proof that the spirit was satisfied, thought the person who led us in prayer. In those days my parents and Uncle Van Kuyck had seances till late at night, and in the morning my father went over large sheets of paper with big letters written in pencil— apparently Mary's handwriting—and he fidgeted when I got too close. Sometimes I also looked in his spiritualist books, but I liked only those that had real ghost stories. I can't say whether or not I believed all this. I probably thought that this world existed for some people because they wanted it to.

Not far from the Tegallega race track, a couple of houses down from where my future friend Eelco Odinga lived, was the house where Darma had been murdered. This was the murder that had kept me from sleeping three years before. I couldn't believe it when I discovered this; it was as if something from a fairy tale had suddenly become real and concrete. It was a relatively small house. In the morning a native school held classes there, but at night it was empty because nobody dared live in it. The story went that two sailors of the Royal Packet Company had spent a night there and had run out into the street crazy with fear. Eelco was an excellent boxer, and he and I taunted each other so much about our fear of ghosts that one evening we decided to go there. We had visited the house before, but during the day. In the murder room we looked for the bloody marks on the wall, but all we found were betel nut stains and smears of mud. There were so many of them that it looked as if everyone in the neighborhood had wanted to leave imitation bloodstains there. It was just after dark, about 6:30, when we went back. We had left home talking animatedly, but when we got near to the steps we didn't utter another word. We walked carefully over the gravel. The door to the center room was wide open, and we could see a table with dishes and a candle, but not a soul in sight. It was like a small *sedekah* but only for the spirit of the murdered man without any humans to consume the food. We stood still in the semidarkness and silence when suddenly a voice roared from further back in the house, unmistakably a European speaking Malay. We ran out, happy that our expedition had come to a sudden end. Clearly, some former sergeant or other had moved into part of the house, and his native concubine tried in this way to soothe the occupant of the other part.

Honesty demands that I relate the stories of my own three ghosts. The first one visited me in Gedong Lami at the time of my murder visions. I had finally fallen asleep that night from fatigue, when I woke up again and through the *klambu* saw Alima standing next to my night stand. I asked her to give me a glass of water, but she walked back to her own bed. I waited a few seconds and suddenly heard her quiet breathing. I jumped out of my bed to look at hers and saw that she was sound asleep. When I woke her up she said that she had been asleep all the time. Moreover, she was wearing a dark *kabaya*, and the woman I had seen was dressed in white. My bed stood by the only door of the room, Alima's bed by the window. I kept telling myself that I couldn't see very well through the mosquito netting, or that Alima was sleep-walking that night, which otherwise she never did. In my mother's opinion it was clearly Grandma Lami, who was a woman the size of Alima. She had certainly come to look at her troubled grandchild.

The second ghost appeared somewhat later. I was reading in the *kamar pandjang* when suddenly I felt that somebody was looking at me through the window on the river side. The feeling was so strong that for a couple of seconds I didn't dare look up from my book. When I did, I saw something—perhaps a little bird—move quickly away from the screen. In the frame of the window, the night was pitch-black. I realized that what I thought was a bird might have been the flap of a native's headcloth. Slowly but surely I went to the door and turned the key as noiselessly as possible. Then with a pounding heart I went to get my parents. My father opened the door. We looked around the house, in the garden, by the river and, of course, saw nobody. Given my tendency to hallucinations, my father wanted to give up the search right away, when Isnan came with a kerosene lamp. I suddenly had an inspiration which I owed no doubt to Sherlock Holmes. If it had been a native who had looked in and not a ghost (which my mother was already inclined to assume), he was certainly not tall enough to look in the window without hoisting himself up on the wall. So I called Isnan to bring his lamp to the window where I had seen the suspect thing and, indeed, against the wall there was a faint but clear imprint of toes stretched out. I was triumphant, convinced I had prevented a murderer from entering. Actually, it could easily have been the garden boy looking in out of curiosity.

The third time, I was seventeen and we were in Tjitjalengka. A friend of mine from the first HBS, Rudy van Geen, was staying with us. We had talked about ghosts at dinner, and for Rudy's sake I had told a romantic story by Captain Marryat, "The Brown Lady of Rainham." Captain Marryat was staying with some friends in a castle and had noticed that one room was always empty. In that room there was the portrait of a lady in brown, and although this lady wasn't part of the family and nobody knew who she was, she sometimes wandered through the castle. Captain Marryat asked to sleep in the room, and nothing happened. One evening he showed a pistol to one of the other guests. When he was about to go to his own room he saw a lady coming down the hall. Since he was in night clothes, he quickly hid behind a door. But when she came up to him, she did not walk on but looked around the door, straight at him, and smiled "demonically." The captain suddenly recognized the brown lady from the portrait. Her cruel laughter made him so angry that he took the pistol which he just happened to have on him and shot her in the face. With the sound of the shot she disappeared. Everybody came running, but all they found was the captain in his night shirt and a bullet in the wall. I told this story in all seriousness during dessert. After dinner I went to pick up a tomcat that had just come in, but he jumped away onto the dark front porch. There was some moonlight. I ran after him, and when I was just about to grab him, he slipped underneath a bench. When I bent over, my face was at the level of the seat, but when I straightened up again and looked for the cat which had run into the garden, I was a step away from the bench and I suddenly saw someone sitting on it, vague and white, yet clear in the moonlight. I turned around but I didn't budge. I would rather not see a ghost, but "I took hold of myself," stood still on the same spot with my back to the bench, and I told myself, "I must be seeing things; I'm still under the influence of the story I just told. I'm imagining this. If I turn around quietly now there will be nothing there." Then I turned around and looked, and more clearly than before there was the whitish creature, looking at me. Unquestionably it was a man, and there was nothing horrible about him. He sat there silently with his hands on his knees and looked at me with a kind of benevolent attention. His face was rather round, and everything about him was a sort of foggy white, including his hair, because he was neither bald nor gray and yet the color of his head was no different from the rest. Only his beady eyes and little mustache were black. More than anything else, he looked like a gingerbread man, but he was of normal size and his posture was as natural as could be. All this I saw in no more than two seconds, but later I tried to draw a picture of him and I was able at times to come up with a likeness.

I walked away slowly. I kept saying to myself that ghosts are seldom dangerous and I didn't want to run, but neither did I walk all the way around the front porch: I took the shortest route by stepping over the railing. Back in the room I had hardly come into the light, when Rudy said, "God, what's the matter? You're white as a ghost!" I told him quickly and we rushed back, but there was nothing more than the moonlight on the back porch and the bench was clearly unoccupied. "Was he a native or a European?" my parents asked. I couldn't say, due to the colorlessness, but I thought he was a European because he didn't wear a headcloth.

This was my only contact with a ghost. The *sedekah* during which the roof rattled occurred later. At that time I stood in the garden with the others and watched to see what the rattling might be, but I was just as indifferent as the first time. The explanation of these experiences I leave to others who will certainly be able to come up with one. Puberty seems to me the obvious cause here, particularly after what I told about the murder visions.

When I was seventeen I had still not gone through the change which the native noblewoman had prescribed for me. In Tjitjalengka my mother had a kitchen maid of about sixteen, with a most attractive, soft oval face. Her name was Nur. Standing next to my mother, I would look at her round form, which attracted me like no other, but I hardly dared talk to her. When she passed me in the garden on her way home, she always greeted me with great friendliness, but in my mother's presence she seemed mute; nonetheless, I never found the courage to follow her. To some extent this was perhaps due to the relationship between Europeans and natives. Everyone notices a young European walking with a native woman; moreover, Nur lived with her parents. It didn't occur to me that her parents could have yielded her to me and that something like that wouldn't have shocked either them or my mother. My books made me too European for this. A year later a native acquaintance of my parents said he would be happy to look for a "playmate" for me (literal translation of the Sundanese). My mother laughed but she consented, and one afternoon a sweet girl showed up at our house. She was from a good family, perhaps even vaguely related to the noble procurer, they added. She had a little note from him for my mother: "This seems to be the person we talked about."

"Don't you want to take a look?" my mother asked. I refused indignantly. I thought it was awful that my brother had a native housekeeper before he was married. My prudishness was strange but uncompromising. I didn't object in the least to going to native women when it was my turn, but living with such a person seemed almost criminal to me. You can never tell with such subconscious criteria where sensitivity ends and stupidity begins. There are two ways a native woman can be repulsive: with betel nut in her mouth and with coconut oil in her hair. The former could be forbidden or avoided, but the latter seems unavoidable, and that smell on a pillow could make a European realize how low he had sunk. But here too I was really only following a code defined by my friends. If Junius, Rudy, Eelco, and others each had had a steady *njai*, I probably would have made it a point of honor to choose one with great care. But for a boy our age to keep his own *njai* seemed so disgusting to us. The only ones who did so were the spoiled sons of nouveau riche Eurasians. When you were young, you had a *njai* only if you worked on a plantation and needed a housekeeper for practical reasons as well.

Furthermore, deep down I thought that the feminine mystique would have to be revealed to me by a European. And since a girl about my age was out of the question, I kept waiting for "one of my mother's friends" (someone like the lady who, when I was a child, let me sit in her room while she got dressed), and although my mother had no friends who even remotely fulfilled my dream, this expectation must have been some comfort in itself. One afternoon reality took the form of Trudy, as was only logical. She started seeing me again, but she treated me like a younger brother. Sometimes we talked about sex, me in a worldly-wise tone and she in a questioning one. Among her father's old books she had found one which she showed to me mysteriously and almost fearfully. We read some pages together, and I explained the literary descriptions she thought she didn't understand. The book was called *Women's Lives and Loves in an Arab Harem* and was supposedly written by a famous sheik. There were ten or twelve pictures of French nudes that were really most ordinary. But the hero of the story, a harem keeper with inexhaustible resources, relieved ten virgins of their "days of uselessness" within twenty-four hours, I believe. Trudy gave me the book so she could prove her indifference, and I passed it on to my friends. In return, one of them gave me *The Beauty of Women* by a Dr. Stratz, with a great number of illustrations and a set of criteria for the ideal feminine body. I showed it to Trudy, but the friend who had loaned it to me had to have it back soon. As a result she couldn't study the text by herself and had to ask me what she wanted to know about feminine beauty. I was able to answer almost all her questions from memory. This gave her great confidence in my scholarship, and she asked me if I wouldn't tell her all her blemishes. I said most seriously that I really couldn't judge as long as she was dressed. That same afternoon, when her father was out, she sent her little brothers to bed and came to my room wearing nothing but a *sarong* and a kimono. She had told me in advance of this scientific visit, so I had gone to my room early for the siesta. When I heard her approach, I caught myself straightening my pajamas in front of the mirror with the thought that perhaps I might not be such a bad lover; yet at the same time I decided I was being ridiculous. After she had come in and we had locked the door, she seemed unwilling to take even her kimono off. After all, she could pull the fabric tight and stand whichever way I wanted her to. A bathing suit might be better, I suggested, but she didn't have one. Then suddenly she threw off the kimono and started to ask questions. I sat on the bed, becoming more and more excited, but I answered her as calmly as possible and with a voice I tried to keep as normal as possible. I even cited various authorities, since what some repudiated was praised by others. She seemed too thin to me, and so I said her hips were a little too masculine, but I brushed this aside, saying it was probably due to her age. Her shoulders after all were a little thin too. Otherwise her body was not at all girlish. She was self-conscious about her breasts and said she knew for sure they were ugly. I reassured her as well I could, since they were covered by the *sarong*, but she continued to doubt and belittle them. This was the reason she slowly lowered the *sarong*. Finally I got to see one of them and, for symmetry's sake and the general perspective, the other as well. I could now reassure her completely, and the *sarong* went up again. The real examination was now over; without thinking she sat down next to me on the bed. Then a new chapter began. I got rid of the *sarong* by asking her to show me once and for all a woman's body. All I had seen so far were native women standing under a *pantjuran*. They'd sometimes laugh shrilly when you were still far off, and if you got too close they would modestly sit down in the water. Trudy's body was sensual and brown like that of a native woman, but taller. She first stretched backward and then, because I kept talking indifferently and didn't make any wild gestures, she decided to try to make me lose my composure. She said, "This is what I would do if I were wicked." And indeed she almost succeeded. The afternoon flew by. Finally I asked her if we could go "all the way"; she said she really still was a virgin and wasn't sure. I tore myself from her arms and jumped out of bed. I ran into the bathroom and took a ferocious shower for half an hour, got dressed, and went downtown on my bike as fast as I could. I thought she'd still be in bed and didn't really want to see her before I came back in the evening.

When I did see her again, she was sitting at the dining-room table with her little brothers. I greeted her cheerfully to show that everything was back to normal. She didn't look up and whispered abruptly that she was terribly embarrassed. I asked her if she was glad that nothing had happened, and of course she said yes. She was nineteen at the time and I was seventeen. It went through my mind that if I had deflowered her, at least it would have been a fair trade. But I would have felt I had to marry her. Even now I don't really know why nothing happened. My father told me later that he always had a distinct aversion to virgins, and I noticed a similar aversion in myself, but at the time I also thought what a betrayal it would have been of her father, who had always trusted me with his daughter. Instead of interpreting this trust as some sort of contempt which would have to be avenged, the "young man from the Indies" that I was lacked the courage and the freedom every European beginner has in abundance. And yet even now I can't say that I regret not having acted in a more sophisticated manner.

I lost track of Trudy when she married her Dutch admirer. She was in fact almost engaged to him that strange afternoon. Neither one of us was anxious for a repeat performance. Her fiancé had a long bony face and close-set blue eyes. His full lips made him look like a dumb Sherlock Holmes. She told me frankly that she often felt more for other men, but that he was at least a simple young man (which her father thought too) and he had a good job. One day he almost got mad at me, because I had lent Trudy a detective novel. There are so many good books, he said, and you're responsible for the literature you pass on to others. He had elevated—Dutch—notions about literature, and I thought of the sheik's book and I was too much amused to contradict him for even a moment. I was in Batavia when Trudy married him, and I got out of going to the wedding by sending a telegram. Shortly thereafter she went to central Java with him. She had told me that she intended to let days go by before really becoming his wife, but I made a bet that she wouldn't hold out for more than a day; she said at least three. We agreed that if she lost the bet we'd do what we hadn't done that afternoon. She promised to tell me truthfully, but we never saw each other again. It must be fifteen years since we had this conversation.

22 The Real World

When I finally accepted the idea of being initiated by just about any-body, I needed a psychological push. Arthur Hille and Eelco decided to go out on the town one night and didn't want me to come along. I told them I could accomplish the same thing by myself and I worked everything out. I was spending the night at Uncle Van Kuyck's. At eleven o'clock I took the first prostitute I met and helped her climb in through the window I had left open. My only fear was that Sahari, the houseboy, would see me. Once in the room I managed the erotic part with a cool and businesslike attitude that surprised me. Only when the woman was leaving did I notice something that made my heart race. On the bedsheet there was a small bloodstain. I pointed it out to her and said sternly that it had to be removed, but how it got there she didn't explain and I didn't dare ask. She picked the sheet up, took it to the sink and, squatting submissively, washed the stain away while I quickly examined myself behind a screen to make sure nothing had been damaged despite the advantage of male virgins. When I came back, even more surprised than before but at least reassured it wasn't me, she was still squatting there. The light fell on her face in such a way that she looked like a pathetic *babu*. I gravely paced back and forth until she had finished and the bedsheet was in place again. Then I quickly let her out the same window she had used to come in.

Then minutes later I jumped out myself and ran as fast as I could to find Arthur, who lived nearby and slept in a room accessible from the yard. I was deeply disappointed that he wasn't home yet. It occurred to me that my defilement was pointless if I couldn't have the pleasure of telling him right away. Actually, it turned out to be an advantage, for the next day I could tell my story with more superiority. I made the creature perhaps a little less repulsive than she had been in reality, and I emphasized how I had handled everything dispassionately, con-vinced that I could never underline this strongly enough. There was an implied reproach, as if to say, "It's no big deal." From then on I was allowed to go with them. And each time it was the same. We went to the slums of Bandung or Batavia; each expedition was a question more of proving my courage to my friends than of really enjoying myself. Going to native or Chinese prostitutes in a badly lit *kampong* house at night, walking through a dark slum with a revolver in my pocket turned out to be little different from going to the Sirene Park where there was always a chance of getting into a fight with *buajas*. In those days, if I didn't go wherever Arthur Hille went, I would have hated myself for good. For him and for all the rest of my friends who had more or less an appetite for these women, these expeditions were first and foremost a matter of courage. I was so indifferent to the danger of disease, and so lucky, that two years later in Surabaya, Eelco surprised me by giving me the most elaborate instructions. If somebody seemed to think a certain neighborhood was dangerous, another one insisted on going there. This fulfilled our boyish romanticism. We had to prove to ourselves that we were no longer children, that we were men, and already embittered by life. Although we didn't know it, our Byronic bitterness was the main theme when we talked to each other about ourselves. We were disillusioned, but at the same time dauntless, like movie heroes.

The world of European girls, with whom one could never go beyond a certain point, and that of the native whores were in conflict within us. With the girls it was never anything else than mere "idealistic" necking. You knew that when it started it would be all over within a short time. The girls themselves never talked about anything but going steady and breaking up, but they pretended it was forever. The most tender encounters took place in the back row of the movie theater. If you were too visible you just held hands. I soon became known as a young man of strict morals because I never indulged in it. Eelco, however, was very successful. He was as much a dancer as a sportsman and could tell exciting stories, making them up, if necessary. He was the best built young man I ever saw. He had no trouble with his double life: he was just as much at ease with the daughters of the Bandung bourgeoisie on the dance floor as he was in the cheapest native brothel. He wasn't particular about the compliments he dished out to the European girls and he didn't have to be, but when I sat next to him I sometimes felt resentment well up in me as if he were making fun of me. I thought he was really naïve to think that the girls would take such nonsense seriously, and I felt the need to balance his behavior with a sarcastic remark. All I got out of it was a reputation for bitterness, which only made Eelco's savoir vivre look all the better. In contrast, his younger brother Taco was an extreme example of a young man whose romanticism had no restraint. Taco's respect for girls must have been without bounds. In their company he blushed, stuttered, and was even rude. At his best he was silent, with an occasional outburst when he talked to them as if they were little boys. After he had reproached Eelco for repeatedly drifting in the direction of European girls, he pretended to consider this tendency as an incurable weakness in his older brother and he didn't talk about it anymore. The Odingas, who would be insulted if you considered them to be from anywhere but the Indies, were in fact of Frisian descent, on both sides. They were strong and fair, particularly Taco, who had an exceptionally handsome face and wavy, sandy hair. He read a lot and had an unusual appetite for adventure, but he completely lacked Eelco's mythomania.

One thing in particular brought me closer to them than to my other friends. Their father was a bully who would tear into his four sons with enthusiasm, calling them God-forsaken queers or whatever came to his mind, with the result that all four of them trained as hard as they could to become stronger than their father, as quickly as possible. He could only do front planches on the rings and no back planches anymore. As soon as they had gotten good enough to do both front and back planches, they could risk standing up to him. After Eelco had found a job and would talk to his mother, he always referred to his father as "your husband." I sometimes went to his house and talked with his father on the front porch. Eelco would walk by with his hat on and come back later to pick me up, pretending not to see who was standing next to me. His father was used to this and seemed to think it was funny, when he wasn't angry. He talked about his sons in a coarse, humorous fashion, and his sons used the same tone when they referred to him. When Taco rebelled, he threatened to knock his father under the table. His father asked who was the boss in his house, and Taco said, "You are, when I let you." The father walked out of the room, grumbling to himself, because Taco had become red and fuming and he suspected that the rebellious youth might be right to feel that he was stronger. After such scenes Taco always spent the night with friends, but first he would urge his younger brothers to protect their mother because together they were strong enough to resist the bully. The mother was a sweet, soft woman who always trembled at the sight of her husband. Over the years her sons had placed her on a pedestal, a position which probably embarrassed her more than it pleased her. All four of them were crazy about her, and yet they could joke about their father's character, which they recognized in themselves, once his tyranny had been sufficiently opposed.

Eelco's mythomania, which did not prevent him from doing strange things in reality; Taco's pathological adoration of girls, which he transformed into a tireless and spontaneous association with native women (Taco always has the best addresses, we used to say); Edo Junius's principles, which he held to ever more stubbornly; Arthur Hille's belief that he should never pay for love, not even with whores, which got him into one fight after another—all this was nothing more than a late colonial version of the romanticism that Europe had "overcome" long before. Rudy van Geen was the most normal, the most self-controlled of all of us, and yet he shared all our traits. He was completely trustworthy, and although I might have admired Arthur Hille the most and was fondest of Taco, whose character and enthusiasm I felt was the most like mine, I unconsciously began to consider Rudy as my most dependable friend, as the brother that Otto could have been if he hadn't been so much older and if I had known him better.

About this time we discovered a book whose naïve tone so completely fit our attitude toward life that I was the only one who didn't believe that it was infinitely superior to *The Three Musketeers*. It was an English story with all the ingredients of adolescent dreams and boys' fantasies, a book of wandering, boxing, and loving, although the hero lived chastely with the woman he had saved from the hands of an attacker. One stormy night she had happened by the little hut in the forest where the hero lived quite happily all by himself. Written in a quasi-literary style, this book was a delight for the average British reader; its repressed sexuality, so characteristically British, unconsciously struck a chord in us. We all wanted to be Peter Vibart, the hero of Jeffery Farnol's *The Broad Highway*: his way of quietly sucking on his pipe, his clumsy manliness, his ideal of earning money as a blacksmith in the countryside rather than as a pompous gentleman in London, the contrasting gallantry with which he never failed to protect a woman—for us it seemed as true as it was beautiful. This is the best proof that at eighteen our sexual activity with native women had affected us very little. At the same time, Taco could tell us with relish about his adventure with the *njai* of an old planter. He had been surprised by a sudden visit of that planter and hid in another room. From there he could see through the bamboo wall how the old man took the young child on his lap, undressed her, cuddled and pinched her all over, and then simply left. After this Taco took up where he had left off. Taco was just as much in love with Peter Vibart's Charmian as the rest of us. And undoubtedly his romanticism made him search for this woman, even among his native girl friends, if they reminded him of her even remotely, because his shyness had closed the world of girls to him. I was the most like Taco, since my association with girls was at best friendly and never intimate. I sometimes succeeded in talking to one just like Eelco, but only if I had classified her in advance as fairly low, and then I talked in an ironic tone; the words were meant for her and the tone for myself.

Junius had an unfortunate love affair with a girl who loved him but who wanted to break up with him out of pity for another, as she told him. Such crazy cruelty made me get involved too. Junius wouldn't leave his room, and once I noticed he was crying. That a boy with his character could come to this right in front of me was the last straw. I looked the girl up, told her everything, and asked her to go to him. "Is he really unhappy?" she asked, holding her breath. She went to him, and Junius was ecstatic for a whole day. Then his rival, who was somewhat older, came to visit. When Junius heard his name, he thought happily that it might come to a fight, but the person who appeared looked much more upset than he was. He burst into tears and begged Junius not to bother the girl anymore because he couldn't live without her. "My life is in your hands," this twenty year old said to Junius, who was barely eighteen. Junius finally shook hands with him like a friend, although he didn't promise anything.

During that same period Rudy was terribly unhappy because at long last he had found a girl he could really love, but she had a young stepfather who was in love with her. All the classical entanglements came into play, feeding and poisoning their love at the same time. The girl wrote letters to Rudy; he'd read me parts of them at the time he was most afraid of losing her. Even then I was struck by the influence of Dutch novels, because she wrote that it had been so beautiful and that now she had the feeling it was all over. Her stepfather, who was sometimes given a speaking role in her letters, seemed to express his feelings in the same style. Both Junius's and Rudy's experiences made me angry, but it was a cold-blooded anger. I thought it was stupid, exaggerated, ridiculous, and needlessly cruel. Taco is right, I thought: with the native whores one is blissfully spared all this. I especially sympathized with Rudy's hatred of the older man who, moreover, seemed demonical because of his sham fatherhood. We hated the potential rivalry of all older men so much that I almost accused Eelco of treason when he got a job and boasted of his thirty-year-old friends. In Tjitjalengka, when officers were quartered in our house and dutifully courted my mother, I left the room or treated them with the most insulting indifference.

In Bandung I made friends with someone, however, whom I soon adored and who had the greatest influence on me. He was an old assistant commissioner who had missed out on a professor's career only because he was poor. He was seventy-five, stood tall and straight, looked like a patriarch, and was sarcastic and aggressive. He had one glass eye; since the other one was also impaired he sat in the dark or wore dark glasses. He couldn't read anymore, but he still remembered a lot. When he heard I could read Middle Dutch he took an interest in me and let me sit with him for hours on the balcony of his room in Uncle Van Kuyck's house, where he lived. He had made a lot of enemies in his life, due either to his temper or to his bitterness. He didn't like my parents, whom he ran into occasionally. My father's voice was too harsh for him; as for my father, he said he had left when old Ströbl pulled faces like a tomcat squinting into the light. He had first ridiculed me when he happened to hear that I like to read Shakespeare. Later he asked me to learn some passages by heart for him, which I did. When I recited them to him, the friendship was sealed.

"I must say, you have a felicitous memory, young man," he said, as if to himself. He asked me if I owned a good Shakespeare edition, because I shouldn't ruin my eyes as he had done on those damned Diamond editions. He went to the closet and groped for a ten-guilder bill, which he put in my hand.

"Go buy yourself a good Shakespeare," he said, and added, resting his hand on my shoulder, "I'm not giving you money; I'm giving you Shakespeare."

He answered all my questions and talked with great contempt and quiet superiority about teachers and army officers, considering them the dumbest people in the world. His vast learning, his sarcasm, and his loneliness, which turned my visits into the high point of his day— all this made me go to him as if visiting the greatest man in the Indies.

He had once clashed with Governor-General Van Heutz,[1] and I didn't doubt for a moment that compared to him, this Van Heutz was no more than a pygmy. Old Ströbl became the intellectual justification for all my rebellious instincts, for my irreverence, and for my youthful bitterness—all at the same time.

He had broken off his studies in classics because he didn't want his married sister to have to support him. Then he had quickly passed his exams for the colonial service and had left for Java. He was old for a controller, and as soon as he was assigned to East Java, he caused so much trouble that his assistant commissioner was transferred for disciplinary reasons. He immediately made a name for himself in the colonial service as someone who was far too intelligent and much too difficult to be made an assistant commissioner. Since he had already translated several Javanese chronicles and had published several significant archeological studies, they gave him a special assignment with the archeological service. For eleven years he traveled all over the archipelago, describing every statue he could find. He filled many thick volumes of the *Reports of the Archeological Service*, which I later tried to read out of admiration for him but which turned out to be too monotonous. Throughout the Indies his reputation grew as someone incorruptible and witty but also, in the final analysis, as someone insufferable. He could be gallant and improvise toasts, but only outsiders liked his epigrams about other officials. Whenever he had to deal with a superior, a conflict was inevitable. Once he told me about the time he was an examiner at the administration school and had given all the favorite candidates of the teachers a hard time; for this alone I could have hugged him.

After he had an eye operation, the doctor forgot to tell him that he shouldn't sneeze. He did, of course, and his eye spilled out, as he told me grinding his teeth, as if half of his head had been splashed on his coat. The doctor was in a panic and wanted to give him an anesthetic and clean out the eye socket, but old Ströbl, who was then in his sixties, refused. Now that the surgeon had proved that he couldn't do his job, he said, he wanted to get his money's worth. "So I was awake," he said, "when all the nerves were cut, and only then did I have some idea of what Edward's children must have felt, which you can read about in Shakespeare. But then it was too late to read it again."

Almost blind, he had gone to live with a cousin by marriage, who was an officer in the Army Ordnance Corps. "And you know, of course," he said, "that the greatest minds in the world become officers, but the greatest of those go into the Ordnance Corps." He explained what great analytical insight you need to write down: "Cotton, white and red, striped, kitbag," or maybe even "bag, kit," who knows. He knew all the military punishments by heart, and he counted them off on his fingers in a tone that made it sound like a ritual.

"But if a lieutenant knows something a colonel doesn't," I said, "is he still not allowed to contradict him?"

"Of course not. Imagine, just imagine," he repeated slowly, "a colonel saying something stupid and the lieutenant adding another stupidity to it."

When he couldn't stand his military cousin any longer, he went to live with Uncle Van Kuyck, whom he liked to tease but whose attentive ear and sincere goodness didn't fail to have their effect on him either. In addition to my language lessons in Bandung, therefore, I could also profit from his learning whenever I wanted. But soon my parents disliked my going to see him.

"You've changed completely," my mother said—which made me proud of myself—"Arthur Hille made you arrogant and impossible, but old Ströbl is perhaps even worse. He has, I don't know.... He has turned you into a cynic."

But it was a European girl who ruined all this. She did nothing more than pass by, and quite literally. She had just come off the boat from Holland and was passing through Bandung on her way to a job as a teacher in East Java. She was two years older than I was. I hardly dared believe that she had noticed me, but I wrote her that I loved her; her answer proved that the improbable could nonetheless come true. A passionate correspondence started up between us. Here I was in my element. "This is my first real love," I thought. I told nobody about it, except Taco, who went to Batavia with me when I decided to take on the real world. Unexpectedly I got a job, through Uncle Van Kuyck, surprisingly enough, with Wouter Doornik's newspaper, *De Nieuwsbode*. This infamous character had started as a muckraking journalist and was now one of the richest men in Batavia. Everybody knew his puppet's profile with Roman pretensions from cartoons in other newspapers. "If you don't satisfy him, he'll see to it that your career is finished," an old Batavian told me when I said I had just become Doornik's youngest editor. I wanted a job, any job, so I could get married, and I would have accepted anything, but at the time I thought journalism was just about the perfect career for me. For someone who didn't have a diploma, the possibilities were limited, particularly in the Indies, and they needed a romantic color to be tolerable to me. Journalism gave me just that. Just as being a bohemian later, journalism made it possible for me to become a writer. I had never before considered being just a writer. Journalism combined my idea of the man of action, or rather of adventure, with what was perhaps my only gift, namely writing. From D'Artagnan via Sherlock Holmes and *The Five Sous of Lavarède* I had recognized the figure that seemed to fit my ideal best: Rouletabille, an eighteen-year-old reporter.[2] A reporter could be some sort of detective, and even if this were not true, he had a world of adventure in front of him.

When I started at the newspaper in the dusty office where the sun shone even hotter than elsewhere in Batavia, or when I was first put with the proofreaders in the same back room where the native typesetters worked under a Chinese supervisor, when I got to translate the Aneta[3] telegrams into newspaper Dutch, always in the same characterless formulas, and when at night, as a special favor, I was allowed to report on a car dealership's opening or a missionary's lecture on New Guinea or a fairy tale program for children in the theater—I realized my mistake. But I continued to hope for better things, and my press card and my police badge and my free entrance to the Deca Park still impressed my friends. I used my literary talents on a fashion show of evening dresses in the fanciest dress shop in Noordwijk; after all, I had to show somebody I could write.

Mr. Wouter Doornik encouraged me and sometimes put my initials at the end of a worthless article. He had wavy gray hair and a glass eye, just like old Ströbl, but there all comparison ended. Mr. Doornik's other eye was always wide open, and his hair stood up with a forelock that suited "the first polemicist of East Asia." Under old Ströbl's sarcasm there was no doubt a great soul, but Mr. Wouter Doornik (known everywhere by his initials W.D.) had no more soul than was necessary to play the muckraker. Quick-witted and a "character"—and a continuous advertisement for himself—he was nonetheless reasonably well liked by the establishment. In many respects he was a vulgar version of Multatuli; however, he fought the governor-general in the name of the colonials who were his readers and would be the ones to support his newspaper. His polemical inclinations were mostly directed at his fellow journalists and, given their worth, he was perhaps a somewhat more decent man, in some hidden layer of his being. The other people at the office I'll pass over quickly; I've already written enough about "notaries." They were magnificent in their handling of press telegrams, and they were completely at home in the source of all knowledge that they referred to all the time: *The Encyclopedia of the Dutch East Indies*. Apart from that they wrote just about as badly as I did, a fact that was brought home to us a couple of times a week when Mr. W.D. appeared from his office, stamping his foot about some error or other, spitting out his "goddammits," and using explicit sexual language when he found gender mistakes on the proofs, because he read the final proof of the entire newspaper. His voice would penetrate through the doors: "Verlaan, that sister of yours—does she walk in the streets or is she a streetwalker?" Which brought forth the prompt answer: "She walks in the streets, Mr. Doornik." I couldn't say he wasn't a "notary," but he was an unusual notary, who tried very hard to convince himself that literally everybody was afraid of him. One day I made the mistake of saying, "There's someone who wants to speak to you." Like a lion he raised his head:

"Who wants to speak to me? Yeah, goddammit, if I want to speak to him."

Just as with my teachers I thought this kind of outburst was funny more than anything else.

"Shall I tell him that, sir?"

"No, goddammit, let him come in."

One time he danced into our room, all excited about a report he hadn't wanted to be published but that had appeared anyway. I put down my work to take a better look at him. All the editors who suffered from his rage bent their heads further down over their desks. It was a disguised pro-German report; his pro-French feelings were so renowned that the Legion of Honor was sure to come his way. Another time he amused us by pretending not to notice an actor who had extended his hand, a former Austrian officer who, of course, was known for his success with the ladies in the Indies and whom he had called a scoundrel. The man stood there smiling, all dressed up in a shantung suit, his hair parted in the middle, with his obsequiously extended hand, partially bent over. Old W.D., in shirt sleeves and his forelock brushed back, said, "So, Mr. Graff, is that you?" and looked down on him through his glasses, while he wiped his hands on his pants.

His life was full of curious incidents and heroic deeds which would fill a minor *Chronique scandaleuse*. Because of his aggressive journalism he had gone to jail a number of times. It was said that he had once driven his car straight through a passing battalion, because he didn't want to wait any longer. The old proofreader told me with relish about the time an angry husband had attacked him with a cane in front of the office, and how they had heard him cry for help even in the typesetting room, but nobody from the editors' room bothered to get up. I was allowed to have lunch with him and the others, and to laugh at the dirty jokes he came up with when he was in a good mood. One of them was to the effect that he would soon have a Russian secretary who, he said, snorting enthusiastically, was reserved for the manager's office. "Only on very special occasions," he said, looking at me, "will she be allowed to go into your room for a few minutes and seduce Ducroo." And the whole group laughed with delight, of course. Although I didn't object to this in itself and continued to believe that these men were strong and basically had the interest of the Indies at heart, nonetheless I despised them unconditionally as a group.

When there was something unpleasant taking place in the manager's office, our door would fly open so that he could call on us as witnesses, saying, "Gentlemen, here is...." One afternoon there was a pitiful individual who had just been released from jail, and to whom he had advanced twenty guilders out of the goodness of his heart. The man now came in to say that the doctor thought he needed a cooler climate, and therefore he wasn't coming back to work. He was returning ten guilders, but he had spent the other ten and would repay them later. The explosion from Mr. W.D. is hard to describe. After having called on all of us as witnesses, he said the man was a thief and would always be a thief. Grabbing his shoulders, he restrained himself and screamed, "Get out of here, before I let you have it." His brother, a man with an incredibly vulgar face, the likes of which have never been seen again, had just come back from Holland; he jumped up from his desk and ran after the man into the street, yelling, "Crook! Thief!" Mr. W.D. stopped at my desk. "You see, Ducroo, I'm a kind man, but I can't put up with that." No doubt it was because I was new at the office that he felt he owed his youngest editor this explanation.

Later, in Brussels, I met somebody who had been at Doornik's newspaper after I had left. But he was six feet tall and was as self-assured as he was tall, and he had left Holland on a three-year contract specifically to work for the newspaper. Mr. W.D.'s nervous fits didn't have the slightest effect on him. "We'll talk about it later when you're calmed down," he'd say, and go back to his desk. The first time he got a little note from the manager's office that said, "I order you to come here immediately." This was the tone Mr. W.D. used with a stocky six-foot editor of local news, who would let W.D. fire him as often as four times in an afternoon, and who'd sit and wait with his hat on his head until the boss would forgive him. The man with the three-year contract burst into laughter which could be heard as far as the manager's office. An hour later Mr. W.D. came up pale and trembling and bent over his desk.

"Do you know what you're doing to me? You're killing me. I have already swallowed two tubes of bromium. You're killing me, I tell you."

"If it's only the bromium tubes," said the other, "I'll pay for them from now on."

And whenever W.D. had another fit he would call the native attendant immediately and give him a tube of bromium which he kept in his drawers: "Abdul, bring this to *Tuan* Doornik."

In Brussels we laughed together about the funny stories of that office, but he had been there for three years and had played his role of colonial newspaper satrap to the hilt, whereas I left disgusted, a failure after four months.

After just two months I could only fight off the disappointment of my new existence by thinking that I was working for my "girl." For the first time a woman had said that was what she was. I lived in a pension on Koningsplein with Taco, who had got a job with a life insurance company. We each had our own room and our own little porch. The unhappiness of this period comes back to me sharply when I hear the chimes of so-called Windsor bells that ring every fifteen minutes. In the dining room we sat at a separate table from where we threw challenging looks at the older young men who sat at a larger table and whose acquaintance we carefully avoided. We were lonely and unhappy. Probably in reaction to this—I can't explain it very well otherwise—we proposed to race each other from the fence where we were standing to the backyard. We had to go through a gate, which was nothing more than a dark hole, next to which was a lighted front porch, where a lady sat quietly doing her needlework. We rushed toward the gate, when Taco suddenly made a turn which he was never able to explain and, like an insect drawn by the light, threw himself on the porch between the lady's chairs. He fell flat at her feet, jumped up again with a bright red face, and furiously uttered two "goddammits." This crazy incident stays with me, along with the melancholy Windsor chimes, and I only have to think about it for a minute to feel the fit of laughter coming on again. But the melancholia won out by far, because my "girl," who rightly thought it was unforgivable for me not to have visited her right away in East Java, wrote to me soon after to say that she had fallen in love with a married man. He was someone who didn't sleep at night, who suffered terribly in his marriage, but who wouldn't get a divorce because of his two children; therefore, in his terrible loneliness, he had been driven into the arms of my understanding girl. I replied immediately that I understood, and when I had gone back to my room after mailing the letter with Taco, I apparently looked so bad that he suddenly came back and knocked on my door. When I opened it I saw he was really worried. "You're not going to do anything stupid, are you?" he said hurriedly.

"What do you think! No woman is worth that," I said and tried to laugh. But after this the real reason for staying at the newspaper was gone.

I stuck it out two more months just to stick it out, but since Taco had gone back to Bandung, I was alone at night at the pension, where I hardly talked to anybody. The worst thing was that during the day at the office I felt so put down that at night, in the Deca Park, I couldn't think of myself as an aggressive young reporter. I no longer saw the slightest trace of a Rouletabille in myself—nothing but a melancholy "young man from the Indies," whose girl had dropped him for a married man and who now had no reason to stay at a pension on Koningsplein. When one day Mr. W.D.'s brother said "goddammit" to me too, I decided that afternoon would be my last at the newspaper. I leaned against the windows in the dusty office; although there was nothing outside except the even dustier streets, the paintless warehouselike buildings, the dirty river, and the whole shabby huckster spirit of Kali Besar, I was suddenly filled with a longing straight from *The Broad Highway*: "Now, as I looked out upon this fair evening, I became, of a sudden, possessed of an overmastering desire, a great longing for field and meadow and hedgerow, for wood and coppice and shady stream, for wide, wind-swept heaths, and ever the broad highway in front. . . ."[4] The phrase sang within me and almost pushed me out the window. I forgot the toiling newspapermen behind me, and I was completely helpless in the face of this bad literature. My parents were at Otto's plantation; I thought I could get there on the money I still had. If they didn't want to have me home again, I'd be obliged to wander like Peter Vibart, and I didn't doubt that Java would take me in as hospitably as the country of Kent had taken in that simple gentleman. For a young man of nineteen, this mental confusion was really something. The next morning I left, forfeiting my salary; even in the train I was still uncertain about how I would be received. When I arrived at Otto's place in the Garut area, my mother greeted me with open arms, of course, but what pleased her most was that my wedding plans had now certainly fallen through.

I pointed out to my father that I'd never be a good journalist if I didn't see more of the Indies first. It occurred to me that the journalists' trips complemented their ability to use the encyclopedia. There was of course politics, but that seemed ruled out in advance, because I thought I would never understand it. I had accepted the political outlook of *De Nieuwsbode* as I had that of my father and every other Dutch citizen in the Indies: a rebellious Javanese was unquestionably the enemy. Not that people like my father thought the Javanese were wrong if they rebelled. On the contrary, it was proof of one's open-mindedness to admit that the servants of the East India Company had been thieves and that we still had no business being in Java. But having said this, they could treat any native who would not bow to their superiority with the greatest indignation. When *Hadji* Hasan and a number of relatives dressed in white had been killed by our men in uniform, a number of red teachers, as they were called, and also some native Communists organized protest demonstrations.[5] On a wobbly stage behind the Deca Park, a couple of leaders spoke, among them Abdul Muïs, who all the newspapers thought was behind the murder of Controller De Kat Angelino.[6] An older colleague from the newspaper had taken me with him; we stood among the native Sunday crowd of Koningsplein, among the *soto* and *tjintjao* vendors. I carried the same little revolver that I had taken with me on our expeditions to the dark side of town. Abdul Muïs spoke with one hand in his pocket, waving the other around him violently. After that, another Javanese with a sagging horse face, the scarcely less famous Dr. Tjipto,[7] gave a somewhat long-winded, satirical description of the so-called fight, in which a handful of barely armed men had been exterminated like a nest of mice by soldiers who were armed to the teeth. Every now and then a speaker would ask, "Isn't that right?" and the crowd around us all screamed, "Right, right." When I noticed how much this resembled a normal public gathering, which the Sunday atmosphere also contributed to, I thought mainly of Antony's oration that I had to recite for old Ströbl. When Mr. W.D. said that a certain regent was a crook and that some communist leader or other was a scoundrel, who would soon take the money and run, I didn't doubt him for a minute. Politics didn't concern me in the least, I thought, and when the Javanese were ready to kill us Europeans, they'd do so indiscriminately. Philosophy would then be put aside; it would simply be a matter of fighting back the best we could. I even admired one of those stupid and gradiose phrases pronounced by a general in the National Council[8] in answer to an accusation from a native, who was considered rude just for making it: "I hope to return the gauntlet thrown at me here, wrapped around a bullet." This tough talk had been avoided too long by the humanitarian faction. It sent, as everybody said, a shiver through the National Council, and soothed the insulted souls of citizens like my father, Mr. W.D., and just about everyone else.

Perhaps I should define my present position while I'm writing these memoirs. Basically I'm just as removed from politics as I was then, although out of friendship for Héverlé I'd like to have the same concern for the Javanese that he has for the Vietnamese. I believe even more than I used to that the Javanese are completely right, and I clearly see that words like those the general used are the heroic language of a "notary." But then what? Even my parents never questioned the fact that in many respects the Javanese are more appealing than Europeans. But even now I don't believe that they are superior in every respect and that, therefore, it's our duty to be sympathetic to every Javanese. All I know for sure is that if I ever go back to their country, I will have infinitely more sympathy and attention for them than I used to have. That may not seem like much, but it means more, perhaps, than a preconceived political program.

23 Farewell to the Indies

My last two years in the Indies went by quickly. My father gave me money to take a trip across Java and Madura as far as the Kangean archipelago. There I became friends with the controller and a native doctor who was a grandson of the last ruler of Roti. They were using neo-arsphenamine to combat yaws, a disease that affected practically the whole population. Normally the natives would rather die than go to a doctor—whom they called *tukang potong*, something like "saw-bones"—but here they saw their horrible sores close after a few shots, and they came back in droves. Because there wasn't enough medicine, large numbers of untreated natives had to be sent away. The little government steamboat that sailed between Kangean and Madura was at the disposal of the controller for a couple of days a month so he could visit his other islands. I went along. We rode horseback or we sailed the boat, and the doctor and I went swimming off a coral reef and saw the most varied vegetation just below us. He was a modest young man who lectured the controller at great length about hygiene but who forgot all those lessons himself once he was among the sick. He ate from the dishes they brought us without a second thought and he laughed at the fears of the controller, who showed that he had taken the lessons to heart. In his laboratory one evening he showed me the heart of a murderer who had been krissed by the people. It was a blue, rubbery piece of flesh that felt like a hard sponge. The liquid it was preserved in was irritating to the touch, and also to the eyes when you tried to look at it close up. "One kriss thrust went through three of the heart chambers," he said admiringly. "You couldn't do it any better if you took careful aim. The man must have died instantly." With his brown finger he stretched open the hole in the three heart chambers so I could see better.

I suddenly felt very strongly the aftermath of my unhappy love affair in this lonely place. I would have liked to stay there. The only woman who had ever understood me lived in East Java, and she was now beginning to understand another man, perhaps simply because I hadn't seen her. And the train I had taken to get here went right past her. I saw Java as the land of corrupting civilization, and I stayed three full weeks in that isolated spot. The controller talked about the chansonniers of Montmartre and about Hindu-Javanese art, particularly at night on the deck of the steamer, when darkness surrounded us. He had an interest in things nobody else had ever discussed seriously with me, aside from old Ströbl. On my way back I visited the Borobudur[1] for days on end and knelt down at each relief in order to understand better the story it told. I read books about these subjects, and for the first time I began to understand the number of art treasures Java possessed.

When I had come back from my trip and my parents went to Gedong Lami to sell their property, I discovered the Batavian Museum and crawled around the statues in the archeological collection. This proved to be the strongest point in my favor when there was an opening for an assistant at the library. The librarian had seen me studying and had given me all the books I thought I needed. He chose me out of a large number of candidates.

For the second time I had a regular job. Every morning at eight I had to force myself to get dressed and go to work for no other reason than the salary I'd receive at the end of the month. But the work here was infinitely more pleasant than at the newspaper, and the boss I had now, despite the difference in our age and position, made me feel the same warm human affection I had felt for my French teacher at the HBS in Bandung. Moreover, shy and lonely as he was, he was clearly one of the most genuine human beings I have ever met.

Everything that was noble in the Indies seemed to come together here, that is to say, all those who were concerned with the noble things worth talking about. I read all the articles in the journal of the Archeological Society, even the oldest ones, translations from Javanese and Chinese—it was all part of one world for me, wherein art and science mixed together as I had never imagined. Everyone I asked a question answered me kindly, and sometimes even with pleasure. Some had more character than others, but they were without exception a cut above the newspaper people at *Kali Besar*. Obviously there were rivalries among colleagues here too, but I was not affected by them, because of my insignificant position. Here I also saw the peculiar characters who had furthered the cause of knowledge in the interior and who came back only for a short while to recuperate in a center of culture;

these were men who had lived in the jungle for years just to study a language or who wandered around all the time risking their lives so they could send a few articles to the journal. I had liked a story old Ströbl once told me about a famous professor, the only one capable of writing a *Kawi*-Balinese[2] dictionary, who had gone to Bali to do so and then seemed to have disappeared from the earth. A member of the Council of the Indies who went to visit that island decided to track the professor down and arrived at his gate wearing the top hat that was the symbol of his illustrious position.[3] He saw a European in a *sarong*, naked from the waist up, crouching like a Balinese but with a half-eaten Edam cheese lying next to him. So he concluded this was the professor. He asked if that were the case and the half-naked man answered, "I'm not at home."

"I am So-and-so, member of the Council of the Indies," said the other, "and I wanted to visit you to tell you that your book. . . ."

He hoped by talking in this way he would get through the gate, but the professor repeated that he wasn't at home, this time acting as if he were about to throw his Edam cheese at the visitor's top hat.

I met a scholar myself in the library who originally was a planter in East Java but who became so interested in archeology that, just like old Ströbl, he had climbed all the volcanoes of Java in search of Hindu art objects. He was big, had a large potbelly which was striking even for his dimensions, and had a wide patriarchal beard. He seemed to be able to consume incredible amounts of food and drink, and his carriers adored and feared him because they saw him as a keeper of the temple. They called him *tuan butó*. I asked him if he had known old Ströbl.

"How could I not have known Ströbl?" he said, in his deep heavy voice. "When we were at the club in Magetan and there were twenty people there that day, we would take on all twenty."

One of the adventures he told delighted me. He had been in Sumatra and had to pass through an area where anti-European sentiment was riding high. The controller had warned him and had even tried to keep him from going. "The next day," he said, "I landed in such a village, of course, and I couldn't understand the controller's stories because the *tuangku*, the village chief, was extremely amiable and promised me twice as many carriers for the next morning as I had asked. I slept very well and was ready to go at eight o'clock. At eleven not a single carrier had appeared. At noon I was so angry at the *tuangku* that

I knocked him down. Within half an hour the whole village had rushed up to help me carry. When I was back, the controller showed great surprise at the speed with which I had accomplished everything, and he wanted to know my secret. 'It's very simple,' I said. 'After the first lesson I understood that you had to knock down the *tuangku* and so I followed that principle in all the other villages. And you see the result.' " The controller laughed but asked him to keep this part of his experience a secret; otherwise he would be obliged to report it, however good the method might be. "I'm telling you," said the scholar, "so you can use it yourself when you go on your next inspection tour in that region."

I left the museum when my parents succeeded in selling all their property, including Gedong Lami. They wanted to go to Europe and take me along, thinking they owed it to me because of my neglected education, and also because they had more than enough money now. I spelled out my conditions: absolute freedom in Europe and no reproaches later, because here I knew I could get around but over there perhaps not. Not long before this I had stood up to my father for the first time. Taco was staying at our house and from a friend who had been to Australia had picked up the habit of staring fixedly without saying anything; we called these faces "hard as nails." During dinner my mother gave one of the servants a long scolding. A few cheerful words were in order to save the evening, but Taco pulled his "hard as nails" face. My father exploded, saying he would not put up with such faces at his table, and so on. With a calm voice I heard myself say that he could yell at his own friends at his table if he wanted to, but not mine. We were all scared by this first act of resistance, particularly because I had chosen my words so well. My father turned scarlet and screamed at both of us to leave his table. We got up, and I said as we passed by him, "Not just your table but your house too." My mother ran after me, and while Taco and I were packing our suitcases she asked me if I'd gone mad to talk to my father like that. She was still talking when he rushed in like a storm. My mother no doubt thought he was going to murder me, and she clung to him, imploring him not to hurt me. He tore himself loose and came up to me, saying, "Where is that boy?" as if he didn't see me. I stood up from my packing and looked him in the face ("You looked really mean when you stared at your old man," Taco said later). He was standing there with his fists clenched, but he stopped. I asked him if he didn't think it would be better for us to say good-bye with some dignity. If he had hit me I would have fought back with all my strength. At that moment I saw in him nothing but the old enemy whom I was finally forced to fight. It was possible that he was still stronger than I, and I was aware of the force of his anger, but I also relied on my own hatred, on my greater agility, and on the boxing techniques the Odingas had taught me. And yet I was afraid that Taco would pitch in, which would have been too painful for both my father and me.

But he probably saw that the old fear was gone. "I think you're right," he said and, again like a storm, he left the room.

When our suitcases were packed, I said good-bye to my mother, while he looked on and said I was still a would-be D'Artagnan and a Don Quixote. I told him coolly that I wouldn't shake hands with him, and he asked if I had understood that I would never set foot in his house again. "Oh yes," I said, "and there's enough of you in me for you not to have to worry about that."

Then Taco and I left with our suitcases. We had to walk through all Chinatown before we found a *sado*, because it was about eleven o'clock at night. We went to the boarding house where I had lived during my newspaper days and slept on a bed without any sheets.

The next day I made all kinds of arrangements and got a room with Rudy van Geen's parents, where I had always been treated like one of the family. But within a week I saw our little Ford in the front yard; someone had come to pick me up because my mother was sick. I found my mother indeed in bed. My father didn't appear. My mother said that he had forgiven me for everything and would let me come home, for her sake. Of course I ended up agreeing, but first I had a long talk with both my parents and demanded certain concessions. My father was extremely indulgent. My mother always won out in the end, but in this case, he may also have realized that he loved me, once he saw that there was a chance of losing me. At any rate, from this point on our relationship was different, and perhaps he was secretly proud that he was wrong when he used to think I was a doormat.

When we decided to leave for Europe, I resigned from the library so I could be free the last two months; while my parents remained in Gedong Lami to wind up their affairs I went back to the empty house in Bandung. Taco came along to keep me company. Arthur Hille and Rudy had left for Europe, the former to go to the military academy and the latter to go into business. Junius was working hard on his engineering degree at the first technological institute to be established in the Indies. Eelco was making a frightening amount of money with a British firm in Surabaya. He later had the strength of character to leave that life and go back to his studies at the Civil Service School, finishing at the same time as his younger brother, who came after Taco.

For Taco and me, our freedom in Bandung, combined with the realization that these were my last days in the Indies, was reason enough for renewed debauchery. Our house was kept by an impoverished, middle-aged Sundanese noblewoman, who also prepared our meals. Taco gave her money to run the house and had to go over her accounts, which always got him very upset, because as soon as he found something wrong, she would start to speak Sundanese instead of Malay and he couldn't understand a word. They became best friends, however, when she offered to find women for us. She had a couple of pictures of friends and nieces in her room. Taco chose first, then I, and she got a day off to bring back the originals. But it never worked. The desired women were always gone and all she'd come back with was a new selection of pictures. After a few days Taco got mad and yelled at her that he didn't want to see any more pictures and that he didn't want to be bothered until the women showed up themselves. Finally one day she called us in with mysterious whispering; squatting on the back porch were two ugly little women who didn't look at all like the pictures. They were probably two ordinary prostitutes she had picked up off the street in the hope that this would get her a few more days off. We had waited so long that we accepted this meager offering. The difficulty was choosing, because each of us would rather have given the other both women. We yelled to each other through the wall about our experiences, which confirmed every bad omen, but we did so in English out of charity to the creatures who might have understood Dutch.

After this Taco again put all his energy into the search and found recourse in some of his old addresses. During this period of debauchery our greatest (and my only) girl friend was a Eurasian who was considered a native and lived in a fairly well-to-do *kampong* house in Padalarang. Her name was Onnie and she was called An. She said she was nineteen but she was probably twenty-four. She was tall, stood straight, and had a sharp profile, which she certainly owed to her European father but which gave her something of an Arab look. She was different from all the others. Taco took me to her place, when I complained that all this to-do with women wasn't anything like what I'd found in books. My biggest disappointment was that I thought "the earth had to move." "With An it will," said Taco, grimly. The earth didn't move, but she was really better than anyone else we had had so far. When it came right down to it, she was a prostitute like all the others, but she was one who didn't accept money from the Europeans she was attracted to. Sundanese women are praised for their sexual talents, particularly by planters, but I found them without exception to be cool and chaste toward Europeans. They became affectionate only when the *persèn* was brought up. If anything, their erotic behavior was the opposite of passionate; they seemed to keep up a maximum of feminine dignity in the face of the enemy. An said that it was her European blood that made her feel attracted to us. She had been married to natives a couple of times, and she had also been a planter's *njai* for awhile. She was open-minded enough to sleep with Chinese, but she made them pay extra. She was so impressive when she was dressed up, with her sharp profile and the way she carried herself, that Taco and I sometimes took her in public with us, even in Bandung when she was staying with us. Our middle-aged housekeeper was not very happy about An's visits, because she swept through the house like a queen, examining all the furniture and the pictures. When they were alone together, she tried to tell An that Taco and I usually slept with her. Nevertheless An felt little inclination to give her the respect of an older wife.

She was truly cheerful, and when we were in Padalarang and the three of us walked through the village, all the villagers greeted us. She was a courtesan of importance, an importance the Sundanese never doubt. To underline this for us, she asked, "An *losse*, yes?" which made me laugh because I thought that she was using a soldiers' expression that she was a loose one. But she meant that she was the best in her profession; the best seats in the movie theater were called "*loges*." On the outskirts of the village there was a swimming pool which was almost always deserted. We took An swimming there. She threw off her *sarong*, and we took as many pictures of her in the nude as we wanted; this we considered not only risqué but artistic to boot. Taco and I competed with each other in taking pictures of her, and we soon had a collection as varied as it was numerous: An in *sarong* and *kabaya*, An in *sarong* with a blouse, without a blouse, An with her hair down, An wearing Taco's sweater, An with a guitar, like a Hawaiian beauty. She put up with us good-humoredly and didn't even ask to see the pictures when they were printed. We sometimes gave her a small present, a veil or some fabric for a *kabaya*; only her mother took money from us to buy food when we stayed with them, whereupon she would modestly retreat from the room to the back of the house to be the kitchen maid.

It surprised me that An never asked us for money, and I subconsciously expected that it would come to that some day. Once, after we had been swimming and I had to pay the man in charge of the bathhouse, I gave him a ten-guilder bill, which was all I had. He went to get change, kept two quarters and gave the change to An instead of me. My immediate reaction was that I wouldn't have any money, not even for the train home. But she gave the man a generous tip and let the rest drop jingling into my pocket without even looking at it. A little further on we passed a man whose face had been partially eaten away by syphilis.

"If you're not careful, An, that's how you'll look some day too," Taco said.

"Of course," she said and slapped her hip as if to say that was a long way off. Then she put her hand into my pocket that had the loose change and went up to the man and gave him a generous gift.

For us An embodied the romanticism of the courtesan. She was so well known in Padalarang that the man who had sent me a "playmate" once stopped me in the street with the subtle remark that he understood why I didn't want to hunt any pigeons, now that I had captured a peacock in Padalarang.

Whenever Taco and I would say to each other that European girls were inferior, we would cite An as the ideal woman. Experience also showed her to be superior to her European colleagues. Taco's friend Biederman, a grass salesman who had been in Australia and was the one that pulled the "hard as nails" faces, told us in a restaurant one evening that he had an unusual address. We got into a car of one of the rich planters who was still inside the restaurant, and Biederman gave the chauffeur an address close to the Tegallega race track, along with the necessary tip. We drove up to a villa which turned out to be next to my second HBS and looked just like it. The chauffeur honked his horn into the night, beacause the house was completely dark.

"If a woman comes out, it's all right. If it's a man, drive off in first gear," Biederman said. A small white woman in a kimono came out. Since I was the only one who could speak a few words of French, I had to ask the question which I had carefully prepared: "Est-ce que c'est ici que demeurent mesdemoiselles Hortense et Zize?" "C'est ici," it turned out.[4] And we could come inside. We were taken to a long table, where we drank champagne with the first woman sitting next to Biederman, while another, almost identical little woman sat between Taco and me. Then we spent half an hour going through the most murderous negotiations. The bottle of champagne cost thirty guilders; Biederman had only twenty-eight with him. Taco and I were hard pressed to come up with the other two. Since all this happened in front of the little women, they wouldn't give us any credit. Biederman, speaking Australian English, wanted to use a check, but that was out of the question. He then tried to pull the first little woman onto his lap for just one kiss, but he was told that this would cost two-fifty. I was so disgusted I tried to think I wasn't part of it. In particular I tried to look past the little woman sitting next to me, but when I saw Taco not saying a word and not moving a muscle, I noticed he was blushing violently just as he did when he was around European girls. Biederman consoled himself by emptying the whole bottle of champagne, and as soon as he was finished we got up. As we were walking down the steps, I said in French, quoting from a record, "Salut demeure chaste et pure." "Ah, vous avez tout le chemin devant vous pour rester chaste et pur,"[5] said one of the women behind us.

The car was gone, so we walked along the race track and Taco and I praised An to the sky. In the house we'd left behind they were used to rich planters and Arabs. The latter paid any price for white flesh, and these little women, probably from a third-class Marseilles brothel, must have made a fortune in that Tegallega villa, because they dared to be expensive and because they were French. What Biederman regretted most was that he hadn't noticed any trace of the many secrets these women were said to possess. While he was still talking, the combination of night air and champagne overcame him. He fell on the road, and we had to drag him by the arms till we met a carriage.

On the boat to Europe, an American who came on board at Padang showed me pictures of the *njai* he had left in Sumatra. I reciprocated by showing him pictures of An, whereupon he exclaimed that there really was no comparison. From Paris I sent her a reproduction, via Taco, of a drawing made by a Spaniard living in Montparnasse; it was done from one of the pictures I had taken of her. Her reaction was "Masa ini An?" (Is this An?).

The boat trip was boring, particularly in first class, which my parents thought was a necessity: the stupid jokes of planters on leave, the ceremonious inanities of retired officials, and all the bourgeois rivalry of the ladies. Not one of them had a presentable face, so that even a couple of ugly commissioner's daughters with glasses were courted with fervor. I sat by myself as much as possible, held back my persistent but vague seasickness, and I read—God knows why—a translation of Dante. My American friend looked like a German cook and was undoubtedly well into his fifties, but his stories were at least somewhat entertaining. In Port Said we went ashore together and took a rattling car to the seedy side of town. We stumbled up a staircase and entered a narrow room with red velvet sofas, where eight women were lined up to do a belly dance at the request of the American. It consisted of an obscene swinging accompanied by screaming, but no music. "That's all," said the American, after he had hurriedly prevented me from caressing a little dog sitting next to me and watching the swinging; "I don't think we want to stay, do we?" And we went back on board, where the sailors were being entertained by male dancers who made just about the same gyrations.

Only in Marseilles was my curiosity about European women satisfied. The one I found looked young and even seemed witty, but I was disappointed by her flat figure, bad manners, and false little voice which she used at the last moment to ask me for something extra to buy something for a friend who was having a birthday. This was the old dream of "Oh, a white body!" that had become flesh; not only that, this was a French woman, prized above all others. The four bound volumes of *Le Chat noir*, which I bought as soon as I arrived on the Canebière, came closer to what I expected from Europe. Marseilles didn't impress me at all: I had seen multistoried buildings in the movies. But I enjoyed going to a movie theater whose full-length feature was the boxing match between Carpentier and Dempsey, though no more than I had expected. The greatest difficulty was not saying "Monsieur" to the waiters. The more French women looked like the René Vincent or Hérouard pictures in *La Vie parisienne*, the prettier I thought they were, but their excessive makeup bothered me; it seemed as if they were covering up a disease—not anaemia but something like syphilis. A few months later, when I was in love with Teresa and found it easy to save myself for her in Brussels and Paris, I some-times thought that my chastity was only worthy of a provincial. After my failure with her, I made my sudden switch to "the European way" with all the more conviction. I excluded other possibilities, resigning myself to the way the game seemed to be played in Europe. In so doing I may have showed a ridiculous respect for the latest fad, but I was completely dominated by the need to prove to myself that I could play that game too.

24 Wijdenes Comes to Visit

September. I cut short the previous chapter because of Wijdenes's arrival. It's as if my pen went faster once I decided to reveal this period of my life to him. The manuscript is now in his room in the Feuilleraie, but after his pilgrimage to Sils-Maria he seems preoccupied with many things. He read *Der Anti-Christ* and the *Braunbuch*[1] on the train. The fact that the Nazis invoke Nietzsche, that their misunderstanding has devoured his hero only to regurgitate him disfigured as the father of such a vulgar ideology, offends his intellectual conscience. He's three years younger than I and a doctor of philosophy, though a renegade, or just about one, since he has turned his back on Kant and Hegel to join the ranks of those who attach only a poetic value to each truth, convinced that the philosopher is always more important than his system. In the four years I have known him I have seen him move more and more in the direction of a relativistic positivism. I have had to laugh at him and yet admire him for his thoroughly polemical nature, with which he tries to convince himself and others over and over again that he doesn't believe in the existence of values anymore, doesn't even need to. He doubts everything except the flow of his own blood and his own self-interest, and he opposes what he considers the last idolatry: the absurd adoration of the spirit. He had a liberal Protestant upbringing but had fallen away from the Church as soon as he learned to think for himself, and rejected even more strongly, with a Protestant's stubbornness, whatever seemed to be liberal.

While we look out over the garden, which is no longer appealing in the gray light, our wicker chairs next to each other (the *Braunbuch* is on the third chair), and while I drink the coffee I had been longing for, he slowly loosens up. At first he brings out a string of sarcasms in a monotonous voice, behind which he seems to want to hide the fact that actually he is a bad speaker. "Are Dutchmen always bad speakers?" I've often asked myself when I've been with him. The contrast between his letters and his conversation is striking. With Gerard Rijckloff, who is certainly witty, you can spend days without ever getting beyond a kind of superior—that is to say, stylish—gossip, but then he suddenly comes up with a story about himself which he tells in his own trenchant, masterful way. With Wijdenes I sometimes think, "Why in God's name do you regale me with those facile paradoxes, as if I didn't know you any better, as if I were just a bourgeois who has to be terrorized by them." By stubbornly contradicting him in a different tone, by negating his sarcastic tone, I usually manage to get him—after some retuning—to the level of his written word. It would really be a pity to have to accept the fact that his letters are more alive than he is.

"You understand, I hope," he says, "that I see Nietzsche's weak points too. His Eternal Return may be profound, but I consider it to be a more personal theosophy. His Superman is perhaps his weakest point because he created a myth but pretended that he was only giving a formula; the result is der schöne Adolf, Übermensch for every barbarian who never doubted that he himself was such a miraculous creature. Tell the riffraff that the meaning of life will come from the über-riffraff,[2] and they go home convinced they always thought as much. But I don't understand why they don't see from their own anger toward Nietzsche that that's not what he said. . . ."

Héverlé has the habit of picking out the verbal mannerisms of people. Sometimes he finds some that are almost unnoticeable, and maintains they are the most important; he insists that everybody has some. Wijdenes's is: "I don't understand," which he says at the beginning of a sentence and which is indeed revealing. He pronounces it hastily, at a slightly higher pitch.

"They aren't angry," he continues, "because they simply don't know him. They have listened to Zarathustra as an opera, but they never got to the tragedy of his letters. For many, moreover, a great man is always a great actor. This one, however, explained himself clearly: 'So wie ich bin, in meinen tiefsten Instinkten allem, was deutsch ist, fremd, so dass schon die Nähe eines Deutschen meine Verdauung verzögert. . . .'[3] One thing is clear: that he himself is first-rate."

"You make him almost a contrast to his Übermensch, and in that at least I agree with you. But it's understandable that he could not preach the first-rate man, to replace the God he had lost; he apparently had to come up with something unusual, as if a first-rate man wouldn't be unusual—more unusual than the Überfeldwebel[4] which that formula always produces in Germany. To replace God with man was obviously going too far for him, so he came up with this compromise, this kid brother of a demigod. It was others who messed up his formula later."

What bothers Wijdenes most is the political significance of all this. When it comes to swindling, political swindling is always the worst kind. This suddenly makes him the indignant defender of the Spirit. According to him, the current horror is that every decent human being—whether he wants to or not—seems to think and speak in terms of politics; every human statement takes on a political meaning. You're almost tempted to betray yourself and, what the hell, clamor for a dictatorship, with the understanding that you would be left alone, at least to the extent that you wouldn't have to give a damn about all those political experts. "I say this, of course," he interjects with sudden humor that shows on his pointed face in a broad, playful grin, "because I know that as far as I'm concerned I will never feel the need for wilder gestures than those a dictatorship would allow."

"Nonetheless, you do protest?"

"Of course; when all is said and done, we intellectuals tolerate least of all what threatens our freedom of thought. I know I'm not an exhibitionist, and I have to hope that a dictatorship would prevent me from turning into one. I know, or presume, that I'll never want the freedom of anarchy, the freedom to disturb my neighbors after eleven o'clock. I'm not an anarchist and neither are you; we can't imagine, not even for a moment, that we could live in anarchy. We no longer have the skills of a primitive tribesman for that sort of thing. But we won't put up with a few hoodlums, whom we despise for their ideology, telling us with the help of a stick what we must think. And so in this period of political tension, we suddenly realize that we're fierce anti-Nazis, that we prefer anything to a fascist falsification of Nietzsche."

"So you don't want a Master morality to be applied as a slave moral. But that's not the only thing, because you could try to become a Master in the new society."

He picks up the *Braunbuch*.

"Since they go through this dime-store novel in Germany," he says, "I know the only thing I can do is resist. There's no choice anymore; it must be done. In such a world you wouldn't even want to be tolerated. You would lose everything, including your last inner certainty, the idea you may have of yourself as a decent man. I've never felt before that inferior creatures could be so intoxicated with their long-awaited revenge. When the Communists took over, they murdered the czar and his family without the slightest concern for 'human dignity,' but it still wasn't as bad as this. There was a lot of hate, but not this typically German systematic humiliation. I don't delude myself about the decency of the Red Army, but in the first place the Whites were not exactly saints either and, secondly, this German stench is worse. You smell it and suddenly you realize that you're a 'liberal,' not in the stupid sense this word has come to mean in Holland, where a 'liberal' is someone so indifferent that he won't even shrug his shoulders when he hears that you belong to a different church than his, but in the absolute sense, that of being concerned with freedom of thought. Man will never achieve any greater freedom than *that*. I'm not exactly surprised, since I've spent a lot of time reading Marx and the newspaper. But for the first time I feel forced to take a political stand, and it's against Nietzsche's precept once again, which I find most humiliating of all."

"But is it absolutely necessary? You can put all your dignity into remaining an outsider. Of course, the others insist that you've got to join them. That's how it is in war too. Politics is civil war: the political soldier has the same blindness, the same stupid herd instinct, as those who are decorated on the battlefield. The man who is really against the military proves his courage when there's war; the man who is really against politics proves it now."

Suddenly he looks at me a little more intensely, with his narrow, slightly slanted eyes behind his round glasses. Then he smiles to himself in a scoffing yet hesitant way.

"You can say that, since you live in Paris, but I live in Holland. You won't escape your political fate, however, and if you try to run even further away, if you go back to the Indies, you still won't escape your fate as a European."

I answer that I don't really understand what he's getting at. If being liquidated is inevitable, no matter where or how, you can always try to make it a point of honor to die on your own terms—or at least to make it seem like that.

"You don't understand me," he says. "For you, too, everything you do or think has a political meaning; to escape your fate as a European, you would have to be Chinese or Hindu. I now accept the fact that I must defend my liberal individualism, and I will do so until I'm liquidated for being obsolete, decadent, pessimistic, and so on. As soon as this foul wind from Germany blows over Holland, they will kill me or put me in a concentration camp, unless I emigrate. I'm curious what a human being would still be able to do then; I mean, as an intellectual, with a Dutch degree, who writes in Dutch, that funny vernacular the angels used to speak, according to some author or other."[5]

I take up the joke, but I can't get him off the subject of politics. Maybe I don't want to, either.

"They're all crooks. Once you get involved in politics, you notice how horribly true that cliché is. The principles and the ultimate truths, the symbols, sound great. The lies operate at a lower level, at the practical level, just like the carrot and stick approach. If a Nietzschean didn't look any further, he would truly be enchanted with becoming a fascist, with joining those who have such contempt for the soft life and, of course, for death. But those are the gestures of crooks—even a child can see that, fortunately—calculated to stir the masses into action. That is war, as you rightly call it, and a war that is ten times dirtier, morally."

"Nietzsche praised war, but I'd like to think he wouldn't do so now. At the time he didn't know that the greatest heroes of today would be the chemists and that those who used to be war heroes would just be a mass of poor boys who expose their bodies to chemical experiments. But there are people who say that *now* Nietzsche would have been in politics; do you go along with that?" (He shrugs his shoulders.) "As for myself, I don't believe it at all. Now, Nietzsche would see the falsification that politics brings about, of all ideas, all spiritual values, all areas in which the intelligence acts without self-interest. You can't be a decent man and a politician at the same time, because you can't act nobly in a fight with unscrupulous technicians. One politician makes another—his deadly enemy—unscrupulous."

"Yes, sure. Be that as it may, it is also unconscionable not to get involved in the battle, and then to be done in by the unscrupulous politicians, because that's what it comes down to in the end."

"Possibly, that may be the most courageous thing too, or the most difficult, because it's easier to take sides than it seems. Belonging to a party means taking risks—as if an outsider didn't run any risk—but also great support. I dare say that Nietzsche would have had that courage. And you can imagine what book *he* would have written au-dessus de la mêlée;[6] something other than antiwar journalism, something that would have emerged from *his* particular courage, but which would have justified that courage, and how."

"If he had had something to eat," said Wijdenes sharply. "You know that I have learned something from Marx, too. Unfortunately. In the end all of Nietzsche's honesty and courage boils down to the fact that he had a pension as a former professor."

I wrote the previous pages while he and Jane went to Paris. I wonder whether he talks to her about these problems too, and whether they still have something to say to each other. It's somewhat hard for me to realize that it was through him I met Jane, that I once believed they must have been more than friends, that for six years or longer he had every opportunity to fall in love with her and never did. She was the intellectual comrade he was very fond of. For her he was one of the most stimulating minds in Holland. But you could have predicted that at a given moment they would go their separate ways, as if nothing had ever happened, that they would consider their friendship as a thing of the past and "hanging on" as sentimental and beneath them. Wijdenes is capable of formulating something like that in all seriousness, even if he maintains that he understands my feelings of loyalty to my friends from the Indies. But for Jane everything past is immediately forgotten ("Because I don't like my past," she often says), and she behaves as if that were the obvious thing to do. For her too, Wijdenes is one of the most genuine men she has ever known. She defends him against anyone who mentions his arrogance, but she has been on the verge of giving him up, "because somehow the rapport had diminished." There was a moment when he became her friend again, because he was mine. When I feel critical, that's what I tell her. She says that it isn't true any longer, but that the fate of married people seems to be that you can't have a friend of your own. In certain respects, then, Wijdenes is now a pleasant vestige of a happiness that is gone, but she doesn't go out of her way to enjoy these vestiges. It's as if it has become my task to encourage her in that direction, such as when, not without tact, I put them on the faithful little train to Paris this morning.

When they got back, I asked Jane whether their rapport had been reestablished. "Oh yes, it was very nice; he was enchanted by your childhood recollections. And everywhere we went he talked about how it will look after the bombing that's sure to come."

Politics then. But today he didn't bring it up again. He has devoured my childhood memoirs, he says, and is full of praise for the results of my Brulard method. "It's as if for the first time I have a clear picture of the Indies. In other books it was always too pretty. And I understand your parents completely now, their . . . fate here in Europe."

He had met my mother, who compared him to an animal, just as she did all my friends, with the exception of Rijckloff; one was a rabbit, another a turtle. "And Wijdenes, he always makes me think of a snake, so long . . . and with that mouth which suddenly *tjaploks* you, don't you think so?"

"And yet," he continues, "I miss the satire which you need to have when you talk about your childhood. Despite a few confessions you don't give enough of the clammy, stifling nature of it, or of the complete dishonesty of the future social climbers, those clever people who already want to be practical at age twelve. 'Sir, what good will this do you, . . . 'Sir, my father says that people with ideals lose all their money.' . . . Maybe you saw your friends in too romantic a light, while you handle the rest so unromantically—although not without poetry!"

Stretched out in the low room, his shoulders twitch and he picks up something from the table which he fidgets with. He grins as he looks at it. "There's really a whole lot of poetry in it, if you can read."

He puts the object down, and looks out the window. His hands are in his pockets now, which raises his shoulders, and again with the voice of a schoolboy, he says: "'Sir, I go along with you because you are my teacher, but I know better, of course!' What a memory you must have to remember all this."

"You may have forgotten the poetry of your own youth, because of your different perspective of youth as a teacher."

"No, I just don't have your memory. I would have to force myself to recall even half of it, of my liberal Protestant childhood. At home we would read an edifying book at the table—not the Bible, because that is too 'fundamentalist' for liberal tastes, but the imitative drivel of some minister or another. A meditation about one or two pages long, every day, after which we children were allowed to give our opinion, since we were supposed to participate; it wasn't stuffed down our throats. My mother was very good at this liberal education, and in all probability I owe my libertarian rebelliousness to this. My father, a doctor, sat through it as if he didn't want to disturb the peace. My youngest brother, Otto, could never sit still as a little boy, and so therefore he was locked in the closet—for hygiene's sake, not in the bathroom!—

where he began to sing, and he came out beaming, 'Oh that was fun; I want to do it again tomorrow, even if I don't have to.' My mother was at her wit's end and my father didn't dare laugh, mostly because of her, I believe. Later when Otto was twelve he saved his best tricks for when we had guests. The edifying reading took place then too, even if we had total atheists over for dinner—to each his freedom, and certainly in your own house. While my mother was reading, and she did better than usual, Otto stared at the guest who didn't know where to look, and when my mother closed the book and asked as usual, 'And . . . what did you think of that?' Otto burst out, 'Awful!'"

Jane and I were doubled over with laughter, even though she had already heard the story.

He goes on: "You have no idea of the delights of a liberal Protestant boys' camp. Was there anything like that in the Indies?"

"As far as I know, only the Boy Scouts. Everybody who was called 'white mouse' or 'cheese' by the local boys joined the Boy Scouts, but I don't know anything about it because I never did."

"A liberal Protestant camp is nicer, particularly when the leader, usually a student, takes his girl friend with him. In such a case a couple of young women, preferably teachers, serve as counselors. In reality it's a Dutch version of the pre-World War I German youth movement like Geist und Sonne, Wandervogel, and so on. And at night around the campfire it's confession time. Really! You wouldn't believe it, if you hadn't experienced it yourself. Once the leader suddenly began to tell what life had in store for us, as if our own awakening sexuality wasn't trouble enough for us. We were sitting in a circle with our hands on our knees when the leader jumped up in the center and talked about the dangers he had already gone through. I never did understand what he really meant, whether he had had syphilis or what. But at a given moment, when he was choking on his sentences, his girl friend came up behind him. She had taken off her glasses and now put her hands on his shoulders, then her head against his cheek and sud-denly, before you knew it, she started to sob violently. It was awful. None of us quite understood the point of the story, but the rest of the evening we were left with a disgusting feeling as if you hadn't brushed your teeth in years. Later that night we were so edified when we hud-dled together, that we didn't say what we all thought, which was something like: 'There's no air left to breathe...'"

"You really ought to write those things down!"

"You do it, then. It still makes me shudder. You'll never be able to show those people what piss-ants they are, to use Nietzsche's term. The Wandervogel at least has been wiped out by the Great War. But Holland remained neutral and so all these people saw only the need for more drivel. All this makes me think.... What did you experience of the war in the Indies, really? It's curious that you don't mention it in the story of your childhood."

"Well I did some, I thought, but maybe you haven't gotten that far. I was fourteen when the war broke out. As far as I remember, my family's main reaction was to run to the bank, but that was only in the first few days when everybody thought that communication with Europe would be broken off. 'After all, we have enough rice here,' people said, 'if only the Javanese don't rebel and if we can hang on to our money.' Slowly people began to take sides: a naturalized German wrote pro-German war articles and had them printed and distributed at his own expense, because the newspapers were all anti-German; he signed these sheets 'Paul.' Some people put up would-be advertisements on all the trees revealing his real name: Tänzer's toilet paper, Brand Paul. There must have been deeper conflicts too, but I didn't notice any of them. For me the war was something wonderful, just as I had always read in my books. France would finally have its revenge on Germany. A little twelve-year-old boy said solemnly, 'I'm only against big power.' We gave him a shove and said he didn't have to imitate his father—as if we didn't. My family, of course, was anti-German. My father was the last reader of the magazine dispatch box, which meant he paid less but got the magazines two months late, and consequently I had a better chance of swiping the pictures I liked. I carefully tore the big colored pictures out of *L'Illustration*. The first ones still showed the French in their red trousers: "Le Salut au Commandant blessé,"[7] and a beautiful *poilu*[8] who pressed a Gretchen with an Alsatian cap to his heart. Best of all, I had a collection of blue notebooks I had bought, in which I pasted reports from the newspapers and illustrated them with pictures from the magazine dispatch box. I thought if I continued I would assemble a complete history of 'the war to end all wars.'"

"How pathetic your faith in newspapers is. Having seen the Belgian refugees, we had lost that faith. But in Java didn't you worry at all?"

"No, it was a paradise for people who wanted to stay out of the war. Only when the Sarekat Islam[9] and some communist groups started to crop up did we worry a little. You couldn't be sure with the Javanese because, whether communist or not, any agitation could easily lead to a holy war and then all the whites would be put to the sword. I wonder if it's any different now. Once, in The Hague, I talked to a *Bendoro* something-or-other, a relative of the court of Djokjakarta, who studied in Holland. He admitted readily enough that the Javanese would like to throw every white man out of the country.

"But if that happens," I asked him, "do you think the Javanese will keep their princes or will Communism take over?"

He smiled as condescendingly as possible. "Communism, impossible, sir."

"It sounded funny, but I'm not completely sure he's wrong. The Javanese is a born slave, just like the German. He's unhappy without a tyrant."

"But you've been away from the Indies twelve years," Jane reminds me. "You don't know what has happened since then. They have got the Digul[10] concentration camp, for example."

Wijdenes turns up his short arrogant nose and sniffs. He skips a few steps around the room. "Yes, yes," he says, rubbing his hands together. I wonder what he's thinking about. "In the Achterhoek," he says, "we took in German children suffering from malnutrition."

This seemingly insignificant remark is full of meaning. Among those German children was a pert, seven-year-old blond girl. A couple of years later when Wijdenes was a student, she still sat on his knee. And three years ago when he saw her again in Berlin, he suddenly felt the call to get married, strangest of all because he thought that my relationship with Suzanne was the solution to the problem of marriage. What escaped him completely was the pay-off aspect of my marriage, or making a virtue out of necessity. He saw an intellectual living successfully with someone who was passivity personified, and he thought that marrying a dumb woman was the clever thing for an intellectual to do. (During the same period a Polish painter who was staying with us in Grouhy said to me, "Tha-at is the worst type of concubine!") Wijdenes didn't even consult me before he became engaged to the former boarder, who immediately felt she was a Frau Doktor and quit her job. The result was a catastrophe: his aversion to living with a woman became greater than ever, and she sent him a telegram saying she was about to commit suicide. Frightened, Wijdenes took the train to Berlin and read *Beyond Good and Evil* with greater interest than ever before. In Berlin he still had to play a role in a pitiful but exhausting drama to prove he was a "man of honor." He agreed to pay her an allowance to make up for the job she had quit, which cut his teacher's salary in half for a whole year.

Today, his third day here—he plans to go back to Holland tomorrow—I showed him the area. He told me that he sat up late reading my "whoring stories" and that my ghosts kept him from sleeping very well. "As far as those whores are concerned, it's a good thing you see through your own romanticism."

Romanticism means something like deception to him. He dislikes the same thing in it that he dislikes in religion, just as he ought to dislike the parliamentary system and all deception that passes for freedom. But compromise lies in wait for all of us: this apparent freedom leaves us free as individuals. Wijdenes's purity accepts this compromise with pleasure, because it doesn't affect him. Romanticism, on the other hand, does indeed affect him just like religion. He deludes himself with this compromise.

Rijckloff and I used to say to each other: "Unfortunately, what he needs to become completely human is a 'vamp.' If we were really his friends, we would get one, a specialist to work him up and squeeze him out." But why these drastic measures? He's not without feelings, but first he has to comprehend intellectually what his feelings are trying to tell him. He is like those writers who don't seem to notice anything at the time something takes place and afterwards show they consciously have recorded more than those people who seemed completely involved. If and when Wijdenes marries, he will choose a girl from his own group of friends, preferably one who broke loose just as he did. She shouldn't really be an "intellectual"; on that score he is well-enough equipped for two, and it would just create problems. She would have to have some female intuition which will make him feel like her pupil, because he has to discover rationally what she realizes instinctively. He shakes his head about my romanticism; he thinks that having classified it rationally he can see through it. He won't see through his future wife's intuition that easily—if she makes their life together pleasant simply by giving him enough independence, by not hanging around his neck like the German woman, Ilse, and by using some tact. It won't be as difficult as it seems now, although he has already accepted the compromise here too. When I was about to leave with Jane, he said: "Since Freud we know what love is. I don't understand why people worry about such things. The sexual urge first appears as falling in love, but after you've been to bed with each other twenty times, it's all over."

While I walk next to him up the steep hill to the park of Saint-Cloud, with mud and rotten leaves on our shoes, I already taste a sweet revenge. When he finds the woman he can live with, I'll ask him whether the twentieth time really... cured him.

"The whores," he brings up again. "Yes, we're different on that score too. Although less than I would have thought. The division between silly romanticism and sexual urge was exactly the same for me; it's just that I had a different upbringing that fostered a real disgust for prostitution. It stems from simple, traditional notions of morality and a revulsion for filth, but then, I don't have much of a sexual urge, so that my abstinence has never caused me too much trouble. So my contact with whores consisted mostly of barroom conversations when I was a student, and later when I went to The Pit. Only once when I was drunk did I go along with one; two friends pulled at my sleeves, but I absolutely insisted on getting into a taxi with that girl. My friends were very worried, since it was me. When they came home—we shared a house together—they saw me sitting on the stairs, almost sober again. Later it was very funny, but at the time it almost destroyed my self-respect, because I hadn't even tried to touch her and had run away disgusted, leaving ten guilders on an antimacassar. My adventures have been with so-called decent women and... Ilse. All in all, not very interesting for a Casanova. But even now my vanity is too great to admit it completely. Out of pure vanity I felt that something was missing from such a life, no matter how consistent it was with my nature, and what I'm telling you now so easily, bothered me for a long time, because it was an insult to my vanity. The Pit morality insists upon your having a little black book; mine contained no Pit members and was short. I listened with admiration to a great ladies' man, who said dreamily: 'Those girls... oh they're so sweet, you know... they lie next to you... and draw off your vital fluids.' Once one of those Pit women had me. She was, of course, much too artistic to be called a whore, and I realized I had lost and took the lesson to heart. It was far from pleasant, although maybe that too I have turned into vanity. The Ilse incident was the end of all those complexes, I believe, the last spasm of somebody who wants to think (to some degree) that he's a Pit hero, when deep down he isn't."

I feel close to him during this conversation, but I know that soon he will say something to put me at arm's length again and I'm irritated by his competition with the Pit members.

"It's senseless to speculate," says Wijdenes again, "but still, I would like to know what would have become of you, if you had been brought up by my parents in the Achterhoek, and what would have become of me under the tutelage of the squires of Gedong Lami. Our basic impulses were the same, at least in contrast to a Casanova's zeal...."

This time I interrupt him: "It's strange that you still want to associate me with the Pit mentality, and that you accuse me of would-be heroism. It's as if you're saying you actually have some respect for the goons in Nazi uniforms, because they know how to use a blackjack better than you do. I only had to visit the Pit two or three times to figure out what self-styled artists look like in Holland. I used to think that it was different in Paris, but on such a level people are the same everywhere. It's not just in The Hague or in Amsterdam that you encounter these revolting Pit types; you can find them all along the Boulevard Montparnasse, in Berlin, and everywhere. Through a somewhat vague preoccupation with art, the Pit sort has earned the right to an artistic tradition of sham, spinelessness, and the gall to be an absolute creep. Every exchange is carried out in quasi-subtle moves, in banalities that are considered terribly original, in dumb jokes that are three-quarters stolen, and in cheap psychological games—Dostoyevsky in one pocket and Freud in the other. Each of these misfits knows what a Karamazov he might have been and when his inferiority complex is acting up. In reality they don't even attain the level of a vaudeville act. This can harden your heart, but they have no heart; they only call it up when a poem has to be concocted. They are the inverted bourgeois par excellence, and the inverted bourgeois are full of superior cowardice."

"Indeed," he says, "if you turned a couple of Nazi hoods loose among those heroes, their inferior courage might be preferable."

"I really believe it. It makes me think of my friend Arthur Hille, and of the merciless beatings he could have given a half-dozen of these heroes any day of the week. What a monster from another world he would be for your vital fluids friend, despite how blasé he might be. 'My girl friend is a lesbian? How delightful!... She wants to go to bed with another? What a marvelously funny idea!' This really comes down to being too cowardly to be jealous, and to the stoicism of 'what-can-you-do?'"

"But not without some belief. To have a raison d'être, the inverted bourgeois must believe in the inferiority of the regular bourgeois."

"Every swindler will end up believing his own counterfeited documents, and sometimes even the one who was swindled believes it too. We shouldn't underestimate the indoctrination of the female Pit member."

"What do you mean? This indoctrination can work both ways, just as when you're learning to dance, a girl can lead."

"No, the female Pit member is much more emancipated than that. Even if she is too dumb to come up with three coherent sentences in a row, she still flatters herself that she's very understanding. She also justifies herself by means of art and the intellect. As for the inferior courage and the strutting she's so unused to, she either doesn't notice it or turns up her nose at it. That's precisely the way it should be. After all, there are still enough females to go around for all the soccer players and other jocks, who, when I think of Arthur Hille, become more likable. This has to do with my contempt for heroism as *theater*; I still prefer an officer to an actor. And then, those females think they're giving themselves to their men. The female Pit member does so too, perhaps, although she hides the feeling under a layer of ethical considerations. It's a matter of social style. The Parisian variety is so much more aware of what's 'in' that she almost defines her raison d'être as not giving herself. Rijckloff, with all his experience, once told me, 'A woman is still different from a man in such things, and language makes it clear right away: a woman gives herself.' Poor Rijckloff, with his reliance on language! The really emancipated Pit woman does not give herself, and you would get her dander up if you suggested it. Women used to give themselves a hundred years ago. Now a woman is a man's equal, even to the extent that she can betray her real nature and do something she doesn't want to, with an expression that says: 'you-never-thought-I'd-do-that.' She is submissive out of a false shame allowing herself to be put into the Pit mold. She thinks she's a bourgeoise as long as she's true to herself; she's frightened to death of not being 'in,' so she 'goes to bed,' even if she really is giving herself, sometimes, deep down, laughing and crying at the same time for having been had so easily. I say 'sometimes,' because after a couple of years

of concentrated Pit indoctrination there is nothing left of all this...
romanticism."

"I still don't completely understand what the norm is for you," says
Wijdenes, and his voice sounds very cool compared to what it was just
a moment ago. "I also don't believe that a woman gives herself. She just
goes to bed with someone; what do you expect? Somehow you still put
women on a pedestal, which I don't understand."

"It's my provincial upbringing—colonial, if you prefer. If it keeps me
from losing my last bit of moral fiber, so much the better. Suddenly you
make me realize what it was I didn't lose to those common whores,
why I have instinctively refused all histrionics with so-called understanding and thinking women."

"Where do you get such ideas?" he says after a pause. "Did you have
so much to lose? I don't understand. Could you possibly have had so
much at stake? Let me tell you something. When I was about fourteen,
I fell in love with an ordinary little girl at my school, from afar, without
ever telling her. And the feelings of that early love, of what I invested in
it, I never experienced again. It proved to me that a woman is only
a symbol, a lightning rod for feelings we have within us. At that time
I didn't read much, or I read only superficially. There was certainly no
place for literature in my feelings. Whatever genuine romantic feelings
I had were completely wasted on that one symbol. I realize that will
make you laugh, but what I'm telling you is as real as... the flowers in
that flowerbed."

We've come up to the terrace with the deep corners where I've sat
with Jane at sunset. But it is lighter now; the sun shines warmly on the
stone balustrade. We sit down on a bench. It's the most disturbing fact
he has ever revealed to me. "The idea of being romantically exhausted
for good." ...He's no fool and only thirty years old.

"When I had this thing with Suzanne," I say finally, "which inspired
you so strangely, it wasn't out of romanticism or respect for women,
only out of... decency. It's stupid to use such a word about myself, but
it will simplify what I have to say. I wasn't fooled for a moment by an
interesting situation—as you were with Ilse—rather, I resisted anyone who might possibly be interesting, even the desire for such a woman; a woman who wouldn't appear, who probably didn't even exist,
as I used to think. It was also a reaction to my own Pit tendencies.
I thought I could be decent to a woman who did everything I told her

to do, who had a hysterectomy when she was twenty-three and whose only child I had so foolishly fathered, and which was practically taken away from her by my mother. I thought I could give her back that child by renouncing the future woman who was perhaps only a figment of my imagination. I told her all this, but I might as well have said nothing at all. All she understood was that we'd get married. Life was no better after the ceremony, except that she was no longer an unwed mother. But it may be that even now I see all this through rose-colored glasses. It wouldn't surprise me if you thought that I still give myself too nice a role, because you can't know how humiliating and miserable the preceding period was for me. I was probably dumb enough to think that the situation would improve—hope springs eternal. What was real in all this was not my romanticism about the people, about the mineworker's daughter, as I sometimes used to think—it was a tremendous compassion for something as half-blind and vulnerable as she was. Or, to put it more precisely, I was suddenly totally disarmed in the sterile atmosphere of the hospital. I had seen her being carried into the room, as pale as death, her hands clinging to the sheet across her stomach, and then the doctor in all propriety showed me a little tray with what he had removed on it. That night sleeping on Graaflant's sofa, I woke up with a fever, feeling as if I had been operated upon myself. The next morning I said to him, 'Why shouldn't I marry her?' And he wondered too. There was also my protest against the bourgeois attitude of my mother, who thought it was perfectly normal to turn Suzanne into her child's nursemaid. That's a colonial attitude; it's what you do with a native concubine."

Wijdenes is listening attentively now: whenever you're just relating facts the intellectual sparring quickly comes to a stop.

"And, what I wanted to get to: my romanticism turned out to be so ineradicable that one day the woman of my dreams became real. Because, as you say, one day somebody did become a lightning rod for the feelings I still had available. They weren't renewed; they had been there all the time, and my romanticism knew it all along! So my romanticism played a trick on my decency, and if it had only been on my decency.... No matter how you look at it, I know I was right and I would do the same thing all over again. I would probably even marry Suzanne again the way I did as a pay-off, and because of the child. But I wouldn't dare think about all this if I had to see it from Suzanne's point of view."

"And yet, it doesn't hurt you?"

"It's cruel to base your life on something you can't justify anymore. And that's fortunate: it doesn't do any good to say you were wrong, just to help somebody else. You still can't put up with the other person being right. If you try, you'll see where it ends. Thus, I comfort myself with all the pain I have suffered. Graaflant watched me go through almost all of this, and he says it's not to be underestimated. If I had money, Suzanne would be better off now, if I had money.... Well, it always used to be a matter of money, but my mother used to have it and now it's gone."

Wijdenes gets up. "I can understand why you write," he says, while we're walking back. "But shouldn't you really write about this rather than your colonial past? It may be more clear to me than it is for others that your childhood in the Indies explains everything. But where does it end? What will be emphasized in the end?"

I want to say, "I don't care, because what really concerns me most I can't describe. Absolute impossibility; translated in your terms, that book would be called *Romanticism for Jane*." But what I say is more pointed and more superficial at the same time.

Wijdenes was satisfied with his hotel, but for me our last meeting was a disappointment. The cold weather constantly interrupted our conversations to chase us inside, out of the garden, into an uninviting hall with old, ugly lithos, and criss-crossed by old women. This fourth day I went with him to his train in Paris, understanding nothing of his enthusiasm for Bellevue and Meudon, or even for Paris, where after just half a day he always felt like a different person, and so on. "He's lucky to be able to enjoy a vacation even if he's worried about politics," I thought to myself.

We talked about politics again, but it was mainly a repetition of the first day—these subjects are always quickly exhausted. "Nowadays I classify the people I know as to their fascist or anti-fascist sympathies," he said. A year ago such a criterion would have surprised me; I easily accept it now. He's decided to fight a German-style fascism with every means at his disposal: articles and speeches, if it becomes necessary. In the taxi I look attentively at his tall frame again—his broad yet pointed face with the sharp arrogant features which can suddenly dissolve into a smile, his eyes screwed up behind their glasses and twinkling as if out of guilty fun, and a broadly laughing mug rather than a mouth.

"I have been meditating a little more about your veiled defense of women," he said. "But I can't go along with it, at least not totally. It goes without saying that a woman wants equal freedom...."

"She would have to want it *as a woman*, not *as a man*."

"But the distinction you're making is perhaps based on prejudice too. We say 'as a woman,' from our masculine perspective. Everything is prejudice, you see—love too. In the ideal couple neither one needs freedom. That is their prejudice and their right."

"It's true that you can't be both bound and free at the same time. But outside of love a woman would also have to follow other inner laws than a man, for those things that are really important."

"Utter nonsense. Everything in these matters, even more than in other things, is purely a question of temperament. Your romanticism will be your undoing, and romanticism has always been good for that."

"You can be undone by lesser things."

"And what best represents my attitude toward these problems is that they are not really problems. You're going to think I'm a rabid Marxist, but I really believe that anyone who is still bothered by such problems simply doesn't have enough to do. That military friend of yours is wrong to beat up another man because of a woman, unless he just likes to fight. Let's suppose I'm in love with a woman. Either I marry her or I don't, but at any rate I consider her my wife. One day she wants to exercise her freedom and to try it with another man. I would either accept that or not; I could leave or not, hit somebody or not—in all probability I wouldn't, but not for a moment would I think about her female *quality* in all that. You can throw plates at each other's head without posing a problem. Posing the problem begins only when you're looking at values that are in one instance reinforced and in another invalidated. When, as the philosophers say, you start to manipulate your values."

We walk along the train. Every few minutes we look at the clock, whose deciding hand has reached the last number but one.

"You're so goddamn clairvoyant," I say. "You've always seen through all the falsity in this world. A clean world . . . you don't believe in; if necessary you'd call that romanticism too. All right, the country you live in is just as corrupt as the rest of the world, maybe even more so. What values do you come up with if somebody asks you why you pay taxes to a corrupt state?"

"Not a single one. In Holland I can live—and thus my temperament—more easily than in another country. That's all. I will pay taxes to a state which basically leaves me alone."

"So it's self-interest, then. Fine. Will you put that in your articles if you defend that state?"

"No, because then my articles wouldn't be effective. I'll have to treat my self-interest as a problem in my articles."

"But isn't it a problem?" I say, as he approaches the train. "Have a good trip and write soon. Now that you have the time till Amsterdam, devote yourself to the problem of whether problems really exist. The problem of whether or not somebody will try to ease his hunger at any cost may be merely a question of temperament too."

I leave the station with the image of him grinning behind a window, tapping on the glass with two fingers, as if to say he had enjoyed playing that role in the dialogue and seeing me play the other role. When I'm in the street, the thought flashes through my mind that I'll have to ask Graaflant whether the auction is finally going to take place. All the way back I keep thinking, "Don't forget to write him," as if I could have forgotten at all, but I don't write Graaflant. I think, "Why bother him. He can do no more than I, and he has gone through enough trouble because of it."

I'm worried where the krisses might be that we used to burn incense for every Thursday night.

25 Double Portrait of Arthur Hille

Now that I've talked to Wijdenes about Arthur Hille, I realize how small a place I've given to him in my adolescent recollections. I know why: from an intellectual's point of view this friendship seems almost indefensible, the fact that I was proud of it is incomprehensible, and so on. When I now think of the brutes in their Nazi uniforms, I wonder how that fits in with my old admiration for Arthur Hille, who might have made a wonderful S.A. leader. But this is no place to gloss over contradictions—rather, to explain them or, if that's not possible, just to present them as they are. Besides, with some intellectual effort one can reconcile all contradictions.

Arthur's father was a petty bureaucrat in Batavia, but in the clubs he was a big man. He was gymnastics leader and president of Hercules, a gymnastics, music, acting, and fencing club that gave party after party in the Municipal Gardens. He was very fond of his only son, who as a child was not very strong. Since Arthur wasn't interested in gymnastics, his father emphasized his other gifts. By accident I saw a series of pictures of Arthur as a six year old in the dramatic monologue, "The Pickpocket." He was dressed in a tuxedo with an enormous top hat, which was much too big for his round head, which in itself seemed too big for his little body—a child with sad eyes and his lips pinched together—a touching example of the trained animal showing off his tricks. On each picture his father had written a couple of lines from the text of the monologue in his fanciest handwriting. "A Doctor of Law, an Attorney? I wrap them around my little finger. —Do you know how I do it? They can't keep their mouths shut. —I'll see you at the exit." The audience in the Municipal Gardens must have roared with laughter when the child said that, with that same melancholy face and his thumb pointed impudently over his shoulder. You can almost hear the remarks people made as they walked out: "Watch out now for that little pickpocket."

There was a telling story that went around about Arthur when he was twelve. In his first year at the HBS he fought with a native boy, Tjakra, and was beaten decisively. He went home crushed, and from that day on he started to practice gymnastics seriously; he accepted his father's coaching and, as in a dime-store novel, exactly one year later he went looking for Tjakra to have a rematch. But by now he had built up his body tremendously and he had a reputation in gymnastics, on both the bars and the rings, which resulted in his being considered the strongest in the class without ever having to prove it. Tjakra said with a humble smile, "Oh you don't need to; you're stronger than I am." But Arthur was not satisfied unless Tjakra would announce to the whole class that he was too much of a coward to fight him again. Tjakra did so. That was the beginning of Arthur's great reputation, which spread all the way from Batavia to Bandung.

Even before I met him I had heard all sorts of stories about him. One afternoon he had picked some fruit from a native's tree; when somebody told him he couldn't do that, he knocked the *pitji* (Batavian cap) off his head. When Arthur was going back through the *kampong*, it seems that all the men had gathered. Without hesitating, Arthur grabbed the first one, lifted him up, and threw him into the group standing around, saying, "Who's next?" The group shrunk back. After that he was known as "*sinjo* Tir" to all the natives of the neighborhood, and he could get away with anything. He fought with three drunk soldiers one night in a small street; on that occasion he pulled a stick out of the *pagar*, which he smashed to pieces on his three opponents, and walked away unhurt. He was seventeen then. One evening, when he had accosted a native prostitute in a *sado* and wasn't going to pay for his love, as he always used to say, the coachman, who turned out to be the pimp, interfered at knifepoint and forced him to pay two and a half guilders. He looked at the man carefully, and some time later he had the good luck to see him again. He got in the *sado* as if he didn't recognize him and told the man to drive him to a remote spot. There he asked if the coachman recognized him; before the other pulled out his knife, he beat him up with the piece of wood that was used to support the *sado* when the horses had to stand for a long time. The man cried for *ampun* and Arthur left him for dead on the road. In the Municipal Gardens one evening a young man knocked his hat off his head; he was a young man who thought Arthur had danced once too often with his girl friend. The young man had a friend with him and Arthur was obliged to put both of them out of commission. The two men went home muddy. Arthur, having only a damaged hat, smoothed his clothes and asked the girl for the next dance.

I don't believe all these stories to be completely true, but a nineteen-year-old boy whose friends are around all the time does not get such a reputation for nothing. When he came to Bandung, where he would prepare himself in a classroom of the HBS with a couple of others for the Military Academy in Breda, my old friend Belloni was still the universally respected leader and the president of the HBS club, which, according to Arthur, gave shamefully few parties. He talked about it to Belloni, who said they also needed time to study. "I see what you're like," said the newcomer. "You're so goddamned goody-goody you'd kiss the principal's ass." If his reputation had not preceded him we would have been astonished that anybody dared talk to Belloni this way. But it turned out Belloni was informed too, and his only reaction was a smile.

In a matter of moments Arthur founded a new club which closely resembled his father's; without much ado it was named for a recently defunct sister club: Sparta. He announced there would be one party a month, and immediately half the HBS signed up. The Odingas had known him in Batavia and were enthusiastic about his intervention; they told me to be sure to make his acquaintance. One afternoon, when school let out, I met him, walked along with him and the Odingas. I was disappointed with his appearance; he was only a little taller than I was, although twice as stocky. He had an ordinary, rather round, slightly arrogant but mostly good-natured face. Words streamed out of his mouth in a tone of detached contempt, and he seemed supercilious, as if he stood above the petty concerns of everybody else. It's the same attitude you get from a swaggering Parisian street-kid. I barely said a word.

"Say, Eelco," he said, as soon as I had left. "Why does that friend of yours shoot his goddam mouth off all the time?"

When Sparta was founded I made a discovery: although I was by no means popular I seemed to have a certain reputation. I went to the first meeting reluctantly, mostly to please Eelco. The first permanent officers were to be elected. Arthur Hille had announced, in his usual cocky tone, that under no circumstances would he be chairman, only captain of gymnastics; when, nonetheless, his name was read off once as the votes were being counted, he said, "That is really stupid."

Much to my surprise, my own name was proposed several times, even though I had nothing to do with setting up the club. Afterwards, I was elected secretary by a large majority. I think it was only when I became an official of the club that Arthur Hille started to pay any attention to me. The most surprising thing was that most of the members were people I didn't know, because not many were from the HBS. Most of them came from other schools, or were older and worked. They were mostly Eurasians, along with some Ambonese and Chinese. I must have made an impression as an "intellectual," which assured me the job of secretary.

From the very first meetings I watched Arthur's behavior among the members. He stuck his nose into everything and seemed to have a particular silent disdain for the groups he took no part in, music and fencing, for example. To take a foil in your hand seemed ridiculous to him. "And when you are an officer," I asked later, "and you're challenged to a duel?" "Me? Duel?" he said, pulling a face, "How will that happen? By means of a calling card? I'll spit on the card and stick it on his face. And when he's lying under the table I'll ask him if he still wants to duel." This kind of coarse humor made everybody fear him, and everyone in the gymnastics group kowtowed to him. Except for a few people who he accepted as friends, he always treated the members in a friendly but scornful manner. The born leader, in a word. That's why he could have become an S.A. hero.

"Goddammit, Van der Tol," he said to somebody who had laughed out loud at one of his jokes. "With those miserable teeth of yours, why don't you keep that trap shut, because I hate to look at it when I've just had my dinner."

He could do German giant swings on the high bar and the Iron Cross on the rings while keeping his face expressionless, as you're supposed to. The anchorman of the gymnastics team, a Eurasian who worked for the railroad, had larger biceps than Arthur and could do a better "Cross," but Arthur was the recognized leader because of his verbal superiority.

Our friendship began in his room one afternoon. I had come to see him about some club business, and he took the opportunity to chew me out for the first time. He had just heard about something he didn't like and told me to be sure not to do it again. I answered that it was none of his business and I'd do as I pleased. He frowned and raced angrily around the table where I was sitting. He would like to see how long I would be secretary in that case, he said. His face became red and so did mine, but suddenly I laughed at him. "As far as that's concerned," I said, "I'm not crazy about it and would turn the job over to you." He then said he hadn't meant it that way and we made our peace, but the fact that I, who cut such a sorry figure (that is to say, no figure at all) on the bars or rings, had dared talk to him this way was reason enough for him to like me.

"I've never seen anyone with as little spunk as you talk so big," he said.

He himself had conquered his feelings of inferiority in one year after Tjakra beat him up, but he didn't know that mine were still fresh on my mind from my first school years and could have tormented me at any time. If he had beaten me up and I had fought back, I would have felt better about myself than if I had had to admit that I was afraid of him. If later I was proud of my friendship with this bully, that was partly due to the value system which had been ground into me at the Brothers' School.

He didn't live far from us and soon we saw each other almost daily. The fact that we both were called Arthur amused us when we started to call each other by our first names. We discussed in advance most of the business to be decided at the official meetings, because in reality he was the boss of the whole club. When the chairman suddenly resigned—the *praeses*, as he always said—Arthur came radiant to the next meeting and said, "I already have a new *praeses*." We looked up amazed. With the same smile he put his hand on my shoulder: "You, of course. Any idiot can be secretary. As far as I am concerned we can make Jan Tek Li secretary (he was the worst of his gymnasts). So, we all agree that Ducroo will be our *praeses*." I told him it was all right with me, but on two conditions: one, that I didn't have to open any dances because I couldn't dance and, two, that I didn't have to make any speeches from the podium because I didn't want to. He thought that was fine. "The only people who want to bullshit on the podium are those who think they can act. You're damned right to refuse. And you don't have to dance, of course. When that nonsense of the polonaise begins, you walk around the hall twice with one of our sweeties on your arm. You can do that, can't you? And then you hand her over to somebody who wants to take a spin around the floor with her."

But the next few weeks we had many differences of opinion. He called me impossibly stubborn, stormed off in anger, and slammed the door. He came back in the afternoon at teatime, wearing his friendliest smile to tell me he could never be as impossibly stubborn as I. Once he gave me an ultimatum. The music director and he would both resign if I didn't do as they said. It was just before a party so I said in all earnestness, "Having you resign would not be in the interest of Sparta, but I can't be a rubber-stamp president either. Therefore, in the interest of Sparta, I resign."

He walked away saying that it was just fine, and I didn't see him again that day. The next day he came back hot from a quarrel with the music director, who had taken my offer seriously and wondered who should be elected in my place: "'Are you out of your mind,' I said. 'Either I'll party with Ducroo as *praeses* or I won't party at all.'" This particular conflict was resolved by flipping a coin.

The performances were given in a small military club because we couldn't afford to rent the big club and because Sparta was discriminated against compared to the HBS club because of our "inferior elements." The Indies' first militia had brought together a large number of twenty-four-year-old men in Bandung. They came from everywhere and used the anonymity of their uniform to raise hell all over town. Arthur insisted on strict discipline; consequently, hardly an evening passed without the stronger members being called on to throw out loud militiamen or drunken visitors. I would like to know whether he remembers these events as being as farcical as I do. It always surprised him that I took part in these quarrels, even though he stood next to me ready to fight. One afternoon he told me that I had a lot of enemies.

"If I were a weakling like you I'd try not to have so many," he said. "But don't worry; if one of them wants to beat you up it would only be normal, given our friendship, for me to suggest he try me first."

I asked him never to do such a thing, however much I'd appreciate it as an expression of friendship.

Shortly thereafter I spent a few weeks at my brother Otto's plantation. As soon as I came back Junius visited me: "You should tell your friend Hille," he said (he couldn't stand him himself), "not to stand up for you in such a ridiculous fashion and ruin your reputation completely. He beat up Horstman in front of all the girls during recess for having said something about you."

The strange thing was that I barely knew this Horstman, a rather handsome fellow with a large frame and curly hair, but he seemed to have observed me in the club and had spread around that he was going to take me on one of these days. I really felt that what Hille had done was an attack on my honor, and I talked to him about it. I told him I hadn't heard of this threat before, but that in any case it was up to me to take care of the matter.

"Not so," he said, amused. "You didn't hear it and I did, accidentally. So it was up to me to teach him some manners. I only asked him if it were true and he took much too long to answer. Then I told him I never wanted to hear that again and to get the hell out of there. Horstman still had something to say, probably because there were girls watching. I said, 'If you open that big mouth of yours once more, I'll make sure that you won't be able to see Truus van Aken again' (Horstman's steady girl). He opened his mouth and I shut it. I hit him with a left, actually, because with Truus van Aken in the vicinity I thought he might try to throw himself at me. My right hand was ready for him. But all he dared to do was turn around and leave, with his face still smarting. You wouldn't want to bother with someone like that, would you? It makes you feel damn low to have a cad like that cut such a poor figure. You don't know how ashamed I was for him."

"Did you have something against him personally?" I asked, trying to understand.

"No, nothing, except that he wears his hair like those movie jerks, you know, like Francis Bushman[1] or something. I always get sick when I see such monkeys."

He himself wore his hair short, to make sure he didn't look like a movie jerk. In his own arrogant and obnoxious way, he really was sort of chivalrous and had what was perhaps an instinctive set of values. Although he used impossibly crude language when talking about girls, describing graphically the various parts of their bodies he claimed were damaged ("Dolf Eckers once told me that when he wanted to feel up Willie Lament, he discovered that everything had already been felt up by De Geer"), nonetheless, at other times he accused me of being cynical when I sneered at the type of timid, sweet girls he preferred. Shortly after he had come to Bandung and they didn't know about him yet, the witty general's daughter, Hetty, tried to conquer him. It was more a matter of ambition than affection; at that time she was very aware of the impression she made. He danced and flirted with her and whispered to me after every dance, while Hetty looked around triumphantly, "I don't understand how you can talk to that creature." At the end of the evening he collapsed in a chair.

He didn't ask her to dance again. He acted as if he didn't realize what she expected and responded to her chatter with absent-minded grunts. To recapture his attention, Hetty danced enthusiastically with a young man who had a reputation for being very funny. And when Arthur didn't seem to pull out of his collapse, she moved her dancing partner close to his chair as if unintentionally, and then spurred the other fellow on by responding to his jokes exuberantly. Arthur lazily turned his head and said over his shoulder in an entreating voice, "Well, Hetty, are you dancing or not? If you're not, then sit down and if you are, please take that affected fellow with you."

"You're so goddamned cynical," he said to me, although I never went into graphic descriptions like he did. "I don't like that cynicism of yours, come to think of it." And he explained the difference between girls and girls to me. I don't remember a word of it, but it must have contained most of his philosophy of life. Somehow he wanted to draw the sharpest contrast, because he wanted to honor in some girls what he despised in others. But the girls he liked were really too dull for me. Let me give one example. A girl he had played with as a child arrived from Batavia. She was blond, fat, and drab. She worked for a government agency, and he almost never saw her. She didn't live far from us, in a side street, in the house of two very dark Eurasians who had just won 100,000 guilders in the lottery and now suddenly had two cars to drive around in. I've forgotten the name of the man, but he was called Baron Saté. One day the girl came up to Arthur in tears to ask him to find her another room. The couple had insulted her for no reason at all, probably because they wanted to get rid of her. Arthur accepted his responsibility to take care of her, since he was her childhood friend and her only acquaintance from Batavia. He first found her a room and then went to see Baron Saté. The conversation was heated from the beginning.

"Get out of my house," screamed the baron.

Since the front porch was very close to the street, Arthur took two steps and positioned himself at the fence, where he commented further on the couple.

"Go away," shouted the baron, "or I'll send my chauffeur after you."

Arthur thought that the chauffeur by himself would be able to do very little, but that the baron might come with the chauffeur. The baron called him a bully. Arthur said, "I'm a bully but a good one, and you're just full of shit."

Mrs. Saté came out on the front porch and tried to draw her husband away. "Don't talk to him," and to Arthur, "*Tjies, tjies*, that doesn't stand."

"Lady, why don't you go to the kitchen and see if your dinner is burning? And if you don't know any Dutch, don't talk about standing, since to judge from the old shit next to you, he hasn't stood up for ages."

This picaresque episode was witnessed by a large audience which gathered behind Arthur when an office across the street let out. When the Satés slunk away Arthur marched up the street as a hero, surrounded by the mob, and came immediately to tell me how he had avenged his childhood friend.

I have told these stories about him frequently, and I always notice that people find them quite distasteful. Their naïveté seems to escape people who can't see his good-natured face despite his fundamental arrogance, nor his real honesty and goodness. There was probably a consistently repressed sensitivity, too. It wouldn't surprise me if he ended up killing himself, just like my father. He became an officer because he thought there was no better choice for a man and because he probably thought, subconsciously, that he would be club leader there too—a strange misconception, but I'm not trying to show his subtlety. After my conversation with Wijdenes I wanted to evoke him here for the purposes of contrast, to try and figure out what common ground we might share and what I have in common with the one person among all my friends who is completely the opposite of the intellectual I brought to the train yesterday.

I lost sight of him when he became a cadet. He went to Europe two years before I did. I visited Holland once while he was in Breda and saw him only briefly. He had sent me pictures of himself in uniform, and in the beginning he even wrote me long letters. In Port Said he had knocked down a guide just before the boat left. The guide had grabbed him because he wouldn't give a tip. Then he had run up the gangway without giving the man a second thought, but the British policeman by the boat drew his attention to the outcome, "A really splendid knock-out, sir!"[2] From Breda he described his reception among the cadets to me. There were six or seven from the Indies, in uniform for the first time, and he was thrilled when he heard the cadet hymn. It was a feeble piece of poetry that he copied completely for me, and with great respect. These formulas after all have the same effect as the Achinese *klewang*-whetting war-hymns and prayers, the formulas that are used to intensify their fanaticism to the point where they run amok. And the self-deceit and romanticism of this, Wijdenes, you may best catch a glimpse of as you reverently play "Morgenrot! Morgenrot! Leuchtest mir zum frühen Tod. . . ."[3] on your piano. Arthur Hille asked to be sent to Achin, the only place in the Indies where a soldier could be a real soldier, where there is still some truth to the romantic image of the officer as a medieval knight, as another friend, who became an officer, wrote me once. A couple of years later somebody told me he had seen in the newspaper that Lieutenant Hille had been wounded in an attack, and had been decorated. I also heard from somebody else who knew of Arthur Hille through a fellow officer (who had made a brilliant career for himself at headquarters in Tjimahi), that Hille was terribly crude and a sadist.

I count the pages I've written about our adolescent friendship—if I keep up the pace, will I cut short the one long meeting we had later?

It's been three years now since I heard he was on leave in Holland, but about to go back to the Indies. I looked him up and found him sitting by the stove in pajamas, almost unchanged, except that his scalp shone all over through his crew cut. It was easy to see the scar an Achinese *klewang* had left on it. His wife, who had left Holland with him suffering from consumption, had died in the hospital in Kutaradja. He was staying with her mother but was bored, just like my brother Otto when he was on leave in Holland. "Even stuffing your face, as in a Chinese *bahmi* restaurant in the Indies, can't be done here." I suddenly recalled the huge meals he would order for himself and me sometimes, and the enormous portions of *bahmi* and egg *foo young* he could devour. My appetite would be dead and gone when he, after eating twice as fast as I, would attack a new dish with the same hurried gluttony. He had to go back in two days and was taking the train to Marseilles. I kept him company to Brussels. We sat close together, our knees touching, as in the old days, and I kept him talking, because my intellectual adventures wouldn't have interested him anyway. He had to shift abruptly and cut a lot short so as to give me an idea of all that had happened in so little time.

About the Achinese he spoke with the greatest respect. He called them *tuku bangsat* and the like, but when it came to their contempt for death he had nothing but praise, of course.

"A man like that looks right past you when you're standing next to him. You don't exist for him until he has stabbed you or you him. A Javanese, he doesn't see at all. When a troop passes they warn each other: so many *blandas* (Dutchmen), so many *blanda-hitams* (soldiers from the Moluccas): so many Ambonese and so many Menadonese. The *Kromos* (Javanese) he doesn't even count."

In the First World War the only men fighting alone were the pilots; the last knights found each other in the air and these encounters were a matter of life or death. For Arthur Hille in Achin, the art of cleaving, a technique from medieval romances, still existed. "I have tried my *klewang* on the head of some guy a number of times like that, and if you think of the knights who could cut another knight in two—you remember how half a knight falls off either side of the horse—you laugh yourself silly. Somebody tells me about a blow down to here," as he points to his nose, "and I begin to doubt him; somebody says down to here," and he lowers his finger half an inch, "and I think he's full of shit. A *klewang* is really just as good as a sword. In the old days, you know, our army was too rotten to use a *klewang*, and they were scared to death of the *klewangs* of the Achinese; they only dared to go out on an expedition in large numbers, if possible with artillery. But a *Kromo*, even with a rod in his paw, is very nervous. If he sees the shirt of an Achinese in the *alang-alang*—and a fellow like that sometimes wears a canary yellow shirt just for show!—then he shoots and you can be killed by your own men. When it's all over you have to make fun of them; that's better than yelling at them. You say: 'Goddammit, I can't get anywhere with you like this; you're much too sensitive. Next time I'll take your wives on patrol; they'll be more help....'"

I can easily imagine the embarrassed grins of the soldiers while they were getting such a going-over. It's clear from these two little sentences that he grew up in the Indies. The Javanese soldiers are as superstitious as any other soldiers. They called him Lieutenant Tiger; he brought good luck, they said to one another. If you went out with him you might be wounded but you'd come back alive.

"Do you know the history of our colonial wars? Not so well? There's a wealth of material. We now have our Army Information Bulletin, but I won't send you that because it's written by a bunch of suckers....

But, if you're standing in the war cemetery of Peutjut,[4] you know, and you see the names on the gravestones of men like Darlang, Webb, Scheepens, Vis, or Campioni, and you think how those men died, then you'll lose all your smugness, I assure you. You stand there with your medals and decorations on your chest and you say, 'Your most obedient servant, your most obedient, shitless servant.'"

"You should go back to the Indies," he said after a pause, "and look for material for a military book. You could do much better than Conan Doyle. They started to fight our soldiers' shitty fear of the Achinese *klewangs*, and for the first time they sent out a small troop by itself, without artillery, without bayonets even. That night, when they were sure they would be attacked the following morning, the commander spoke to his men: 'Children, tomorrow we get our chance. Remember that a man is only a man and a *klewang* is only a *klewang*. We have our men and our *klewangs*. Those of you who don't use your rifles, only putting *klewang* against *klewang*, those men I'll be satisfied with. But those who leave their *klewangs* in their sheaths and who strangle their enemies with their bare hands I'll be proud of and I'll rightly call my children. So can I count on you to forget your rifles?' And the answer went through the troop like a shiver, '*Berani sumpah!*' And the next morning for the first time an Achinese *klewang* attack failed and they were beaten at their own game. And there really were a couple of Ambonese or Menadonese who strangled their Achinese."

Ambonese and Menadonese are Christians. Is it possible that their faith contributed to their fanaticism and that it is more important than race? A senseless observation. I asked Arthur how many men he personally had killed.

"Eight, I'm sure of at least eight. Most of them with the *klewang*. A gun doesn't really work against an Achinese who has devoted himself to death. You shoot such a fellow with a parabellum, and he still climbs on top of you and sticks his *rèntjong* in your guts with his last gasp. Only when you shoot them right in the head is it all over. Then you see them spin around, wherever they're standing. But you can't aim that well during a surprise attack. These fellows sometimes jump out of the *alang-alang* just three feet away from you."

"When were you wounded?" I asked.

"The very first time. A week before Elberink was done in. A damn nice guy, thin as a rail but braver than anybody. If you just mentioned danger he'd say, 'You sit still; I'll take care of it.' But he was too careless.

He had picked a guide at random and they were walking about twenty paces in front of the others on the path. At a given moment the guide cuts him down with his *rèntjong*. He couldn't even defend himself. That was the signal and immediately the road was full of Achinese. We lost seventeen men. It was a fairly large patrol. The rest made it home only because a native sergeant held them together. Although he was wounded, he was the only one who hadn't lost his head. They had to leave behind the ones who had fallen, including Elberink, of course. You shouldn't ask what they looked like when we went to get them later on.

"We couldn't get over it. The Achinese think they're invincible after such a success. When I went out a week later I knew in advance I'd see them. I had only a small troop, eighteen in all. When we were attacked—it was early in the morning and the sun was barely up—it was like a dream! I saw those fellows appear very clearly but through some sort of fine mist, which was over everything, as if you were looking through a very thin mosquito netting. I must have shot twice. I don't remember hearing anything, but I know it from my parabellum's recoiling against my hip. Nothing. Then the *klewang*. Barely had I brought the first fellow down when a second one jumped on me. Since my arms were pinned, all I could do was fall on him. In the fall I got one hand free, but my *klewang* was underneath. So I had to thrust upwards, and I knew that I had to hold him just so because of the ribs. I gave him the full *klewang* and I saw his eyes turn and, dammit, at the very moment he kicked the bucket he smashed his blade down through my hat. You know, the kind of straw soldier's hat that's more for the sun than anything else. It was held on by a strap under my chin. I didn't feel the blow at all, but all of a sudden my whole mug was covered with blood. Well, I got up immediately, anyway. My men had done their work too. A couple of them were wounded, but none dead. Of the eleven attackers, ten were dead and one had fled. 'Finished, guys,' I said, 'let's go then: *Surak Manisé!*' That's the hurrah of the Maréchaussées;[5] they're not happy until they yell that."

"And then?"

"And then I got my medal. Oh, I really didn't deserve it that time; later I did better but nobody noticed. My captain was a bastard—a great gambler, a good talker, and brave, but rotten to me. He got out of me what he could without any feeling. I was some sort of animal to him. When he sent me out and Elly was in the hospital, he said to her,

'Your husband likes it, doesn't he,' and pointed at his biceps. He was a tall man with gray hair. Once I took my horsewhip down from the wall to use on him when he was sitting on my front porch. Fortunately, Elly stood in my way in the door. I had already had another unpleasant incident before I went to Achin, which also involved Elly. It was at the officer's mess in Batavia. A captain, fortunately not my C.O., flirted with Elly for three days. He must have thought he was honoring a newly arrived second lieutenant. For three days I watched silently. On the fourth day he didn't even see me anymore.

"'May I, madam? *Djongos*, bring a chair.' I jumped up.

"'No, you may not,' I said. '*Djongos*, take that chair away. And as for you, get out of here and fast, or I'll help you.' You should have seen his mug as he left. It didn't turn into a court-martial, and I had a couple of things I could have said in my defense, but Elly was white as a sheet, and that sort of thing never does you any good. Do you know what it's like to be an officer? When you're a lieutenant you think, 'I'm only a little fellow now but soon I'll be a captain.' And when you're a captain you realize that you're still only a little fellow. And when you're a major, of course it's just the same. I won't be a major. That's one thing for sure. Do you know what I did in Europe during this leave? I studied books about growing coconuts. If all goes well I'll retire as a captain. The retirement pay is a little more for a captain, and I'll start a coconut plantation in a region where it's safe. Come and visit me when you're back in the Indies. You can stay with me; I'll be all set three years from now."

(I don't know whether he's managed all that by now because I haven't heard from him.)

"But you wanted to hear about the captain in Kutaradja. He was a bastard, but he had guts. He led the troops, his *klewang* sometimes dangling from his ass. When the going got rough he'd say, 'Well, it seems something's going to happen; tomorrow we'll have to bring out the artillery.' The artillery was a revolver he wore just as nonchalantly. One day we had to go to a village because we had heard that the *mesigit* was crawling with *djahats*. We took a path over there that was so narrow that two men walking side by side pressed together would still scrape their elbows against the *alang-alang*. So you'd send a couple of men through the grass just like when you're hunting. We could have been mowed down at any given moment from the *alang-alang*. It was as if he enjoyed it. When we finally saw the square of the *mesigit* in front of us, we were all soaking wet. He walked straight toward the *mesigit*, with me right behind him. Everything was empty. So they had to be in the *alang-alang*, and we went in too. He turned to me: '*Mon cher*, be my guest,' with a courteous gesture. I thought, '*Mon cher*, drop dead,' but I said, 'Certainly, captain.' I hadn't taken two steps into the grass when they were jumping all over us. That time I brought down two of them without so much as a scratch. A guy like that is fast as quicksilver, and he's damned determined too. You don't have time to think of anything when you're dealing with him. But when at last he's lying at your feet and you see you were quicker than he was, that you did to him what he was trying to do to you, then you don't think about blood or murder or anything like that. You have only one feeling: pride. Such a man is no more than a predatory animal to you, and you feel you're a man."

"And why did you finally leave?"

"It was after Elly's death... and after all, this life took its toll on me. There was a time when they came every day to warn Elly they were looking for me. I sometimes turned off all the lights in the house because I was sure there was someone at the window. Once I went into the *kampong* alone with my parabellum in my hand, and I yelled 'Whoever wants me, come and get me.' All the time I imagined Elly horribly mutilated. When she finally died in the hospital, I thought, 'At least she was spared that.' You should have seen the men we picked up after they were mutilated, or the wounded soldiers who fell into the hands of the Achinese and had the British flag cut into their faces. There was another captain in Kutaradja, who had fled during an ambush. He heard his soldiers cry *ampun* behind him, but he was in too much of a hurry, having lost two fingers. He could have gathered his men around him and gone back. I'm really not such a hero as you might think, but if I had heard that *ampun*, I would have gone back. No doubt that same captain later proudly showed off his mutilated hand: 'Look what happened to me in Achin, ma'am.' When I was finally sent to Java my Old Man was proud of me, more so than when I was first leader of Hercules. But a life like that is hard on you. I am still quite strong but not as strong as I used to be. And when you feel like that and it comes to an attack again, you're dangerous. Then you're mean."

I suddenly hear Héverlé's voice: "Infiniment sordide, hautement déplorable!"[6] Courage is something you can learn, says Héverlé; he noticed it when he flew a plane every day. Air force pilots are without exception brave, but they're still "the dregs of society." I'm sure that when Héverlé is under fire he is just as brave as Arthur Hille; the rest is a matter of muscle. How elevating all this is when you think about military rivalry: the abuse heaped upon the hero who got the Order of William by the heroes who got a lesser decoration, or nothing at all. Now that I've also written down the Achin part, I realize with a certain satisfaction that the early portrait was only a prefiguration of what came later.

26 The Torment

October. The house where my mother died has been emptied. The contents, all the jewelry, and even the car, have been auctioned off. Yet I still wrote Graaflant a couple of worried letters about the krisses I suddenly realized weren't included in the lengthy auction announcement. On my desk there is now a whole stack of correspondence about this auction, which embarrasses me. Everything about my behavior has been "feverish and weak." If only I could have really convinced myself that one businesslike phrase would have been more effective than the pages of analysis I indulged in, trying to compensate for my inability to act, then at least my "image" would not have been destroyed in the disaster.

In a short jubilant note, sent special delivery, Graaflant reported how much we had made. It was one-fifth its value but much higher than we had estimated, given the times we live in. He added that he didn't understand why I hadn't been there.

I, who was proud to have forgotten the date of the auction! Graaflant's jubilation, which was slightly forced, perhaps, but with the best of intentions, put me off balance. His letter also praised the ability of the notary, who seems to have turned out to be the most selfless and maligned character in the drama.

During that same period I saw Viala again, who casually announced to me that he ate only one meal a day—"You get used to it very easily." Manou has abandoned her scheme of starting a waffle stand in favor of something like sewing patterns. Viala found a proofreader's job two afternoons a week. Manou now indulges in a stubborn dream, the national lottery. Why wouldn't they have a chance? She collects all the coupons in the stores, cuts out the ones in the newspaper that entitle you to a hundredth of a series number, and she laughs, her eyes shining, when Viala tenderly makes fun of her.

In the middle of October we move out of Meudon because our lease is finally up. It's useless to try to sell our furniture in the village where you can buy an iron bed for four francs. Part of it will go to the con-cierge in lieu of a farewell tip, which we can ill afford. Now that the money from Brussels may really materialize, Jane is traveling ahead to an inexpensive little hotel in Brittany which Guraev remembered from long ago. It's almost on the ocean and even has a "garden." It's inex-pensive because it's completely secluded and because it's now off-season. We plan on being away from Paris for a month and have been collecting data for our newspaper columns. For the time being we can store our books and the rest of our furniture (enough to furnish one room later) in Meudon. Worrying about these practical matters keeps us from unnecessary reflection.

Now I can go to Brussels to see Guy and talk to the real-estate agent. I received two threatening letters from the mortgage company for the past interest I can't pay. It is now essential to sell Grouhy at any price.

Those problems can indeed erase all others, and they give a writer the least satisfaction. All this is dull as soon as it's written down, and the passions they unleash. . . . I, poor intellectual, who am hoping to be able to keep them as dull as possible.

Back to Brussels. I'm incapable of describing the feeling of misery, of wasted energy and empty suffering, which comes over me when I step out of the station. If I consider this episode in a very general way, I see only one bright spot: my friendship with Graaflant.

My real-estate agent tells me that he still has only one offer for Grouhy, which isn't very high, but he urges me to take it, given the pressure of the mortgage company. I ask how long it would take to close the sale, since the money from the auction cannot be divided until the estate is completely settled. Since Grouhy is officially mine, they have promised me emphatically that they can take care of it in two weeks.

Graaflant also advises me to accept the offer. So let's do it. It's clear that he sympathizes with me completely, but he's sick of my self-indulgent bitterness and I'm sick of his attempts to cheer me up. Yet everything is going ten times better than it did by letter. He looks rumpled now, numbed, as if startled by the strange quirks of life and yet ready to confront them like a good sport. He inspires me most by being himself. He acts overly cheerful sometimes, as if he thought that otherwise he would depress me. But he is one of the few people who, despite all his seriousness, is still so warm that he remains a pleasant companion even when he's lying on the couch suffering from one of his migraines.

"I'm getting old and gray," he says, puckering his lips mischievously. "And yet, Arthur, my boy, I wouldn't give a damn if it weren't for all that shameful mess in Germany." And suddenly arguing with passion: "This is one of those moments in history when you can be poisoned by what's in the air of another country. They don't believe me when I say I'm sick about what's happening in Germany, but here in Brussels I'm absolutely miserable because of it. Every day I read the German news-papers that appear in Saarbrücken, Prague, and Paris, although I know ahead of time how they will affect me. And if you ask me if I believe everything I read, I'd have to answer, in hindsight, no, but while I'm reading them, yes. I swallow everything then, even what is patently false. Sometimes I think of myself as an old monk who wallows in the horrors of death to steel himself against the world. *Memento mori*, because this scum, with its barracks' stench of foul breath and sweat, deprives us of the only thing we really need: a modest amount of pure air. Never in my life have I seen anything that so clearly represented the enemy to people like us, like me, at least. Those stupid beatings! I have never been able to understand how any situation could be re-solved by violence. And maybe what I'm doing with those newspapers is cultivating my horror because I know my own laziness, my tendency to resign myself. If you are a coward out of the desire for some small happiness, you think, 'That's just the way things are and maybe there's some good in it.' This time I would hate myself for such an attitude...."

Of all my friends he's the one who is most entitled to happiness be-cause of the childish glow with which he savors the least little thing, because of his innate ability to enjoy life.

I cut politics short this time to look after my paternal duties. Guy's vegetarian school looks better than I had dared hope: it has a large garden, bright rooms, and a headmistress with a peaceful, pleasant face. The old doctor with his Leadbeater[1] beard is more or less the patriarch of this community, of course, and he is the one who pre-pared my father's body when he died. He receives me kindly and tells me about "the child" who had arrived suffering from persistent bron-chitis; he is treating Guy homeopathically, but he will have to lose weight before he is really healthy. Then he is brought in. He has indeed lost some weight, which is good; apart from that he looks the same. I look him over, unable to say anything that's even remotely satisfactory. The headmistress gives me a slip of paper. He has been here for three months now and this is his first report card. It says that he has moments of generosity but that he doesn't always tell the truth; he is talkative, boastful, and too easily self-satisfied. He has a good memory for the things that interest him, but he can't keep his mind on other things at all. A warm feeling for him wells within me, and I read the report almost as if it applied to me. In the meantime the old doctor jokes with Guy and strokes his hair. He is still a good child, he says, and the headmistress doesn't doubt that he will change. All they regret is that his mother seems to have so little trust in the school. I take Guy with me; while he takes my hand in the hall I see a list on the wall with his name way down at the bottom. It is as good as a prose poem, and it says which of the older children has to take care of the younger ones after school: "Denise s'occupe de Marcel, Monique s'occupe de Paul, Eliane s'occupe de Jules, Gaby s'occupe de Guy."[2]

"I would like a copy of this," I say to the headmistress, who laughs.

Outside I ask Guy who the Gaby is that takes care of him. His little clown's face suddenly goes into motion.

"Oh, she's really a little girl. It only says that she's bigger, but she can't help me at all, really; she's much smaller than I am."

That's all I remember of what he said. In the streetcar and in a café sitting next to me he just stares blankly and doesn't say anything, opening his little mouth over and over again, which is something I haven't seen him do before. He holds my hand very tightly as we walk. I don't know what to ask him and even less what to tell him. The only moment I don't feel awkward is when I buy him a little toy car. I want to give him a pistol with a target, too, but he says they don't allow any war toys in his school. He still has a very strong Belgian accent, but he doesn't sound so much like the gardener in Grouhy anymore. He knows how to get around in the streetcar as well as in the streets.

"Shall we go see petite mère?" he asks.

Why not? He takes me there. Suzanne's pale face seems hardly less swollen than the last time I saw her. She works for a friendly Scottish family a couple of days a week. She doesn't want to live in, because Guy comes home every weekend. Before this she worked for a crazy old woman who drank all the time. There are some people who won't have her because she's too much of a "lady." She can't do one thing, and she won't do the other. She has her own ideas about the auction, about the way the real-estate agent is handling things, about Guy's school and clothes. I force myself to explain to her calmly where she's being unfair, but the bad taste I used to have comes to my mouth again.

"We mustn't be enemies," she says, when I leave to take Guy back. "I wish I were rich and could help you." She has a brother-in-law who is a Communist, but a communist solution must be just as incomprehensible to her as a Moslem prayer.

Amsterdam. In the same bank building and in the same office where I came for information the first time, eight months ago, where I should have received 250 "grand," according to the statements my mother had made, a clerk figures out for me that not much is left.

"Yes, it was almost all American stocks, right, and there was about twenty thousand left after deducting what your mother owed us, of course. But since then the American dollar dropped by about one-third, right? Well, that's just about it: two-thirds of sixty thousand is forty thousand, right, and the debt doesn't devalue along with it."

"So, approximately how much is left?"

"Well, about two thousand, right? Plus a couple of little stocks. Yeah, you can't do much about it: could be worse, could be better."

I listen to this boorish talk, and look at his crewcut while he talks on and on, furrowing his brow to show me that those "little stocks" are very hard to convert to money, as if everything depended on it.

"What is the maximum?" I ask. "One thousand?"

"Oh no, not that much, right? If you get five hundred you'll be lucky."

"So at the most twenty-five hundred guilders instead of twenty thousand?"

"Yeah, that's about what it's going to be."

I really have to laugh. This is what all the notaries' efforts have come to. This shows how well they managed to protect the heirs from being dispossessed. The auction in Brussels managed somehow to produce about three thousand guilders more than we had pessimistically expected, whereas here eighteen thousand guilders went down the drain without anyone thinking of doing anything about it. My share of the loss is twelve thousand. A couple of months ago I would have thought that amount ridiculous, after the hundreds of thousands my mother always talked about. And now I think I could live on that amount for about six years, Suzanne and Guy included.

I spend the evening with Wijdenes, but the conversation drags and I feel a strong desire to leave. It seems absurd to me that I have a friend in this city. I don't usually pay much attention to my surroundings; sometimes I can even enjoy the celebrated character of Amsterdam, but now I feel an uncontrollable aversion to all these Dutch-speaking people. It is the place in Holland where self-conscious vulgarity shows up in all kinds of shapes: artists, businessmen, people on the street— they're all smooth operators here. Wijdenes says he doesn't notice it anymore, that he is able to live like a hermit here when he wants to. Moreover, he has come to the conclusion over the years that he is irrevocably Dutch, even an Amsterdamer.

In my clean little hotel there is a letter from Jane from Brittany:

"I am already intimate with the ocean, which is to say, it has become a continuous presence. The room is so quiet you don't even notice the old couple who run the hotel and there are, of course, no other guests at this time of year. The house, by the way, is an old French villa surrounded by a neglected yard with roses still blooming under the fir trees. There is a moss-covered wooden table which has one leg overgrown with ivy, and right under my balcony there is a huge shrub with silvery plumes, which also fill the vases in the dining room. Broom is all over the hills—completely crazy at this time of the year. It is autumn weather but mild; the only color to be seen is yellow. Not only the broom, but the poplars, even the cabbage fields, which are a venomous green, are at their best when the eerie light of a storm makes them yellowish-green and velvety. Did you ever notice that cabbage leaves can rustle in the wind, just like poplars? In the morning I can look from my bed through the arch window and see huge mythical black birds fly to an almost bare apple tree in search of the only golden apple that is left. This is certainly the prettiest season for the ocean, if you don't want to swim. The main beach is a bay, which is protected so well by the rocks that you can sit there and read for hours. There is one rock that is so white you'd think it had been bleached by the desert sun; it is weathered and looks as if it were covered with hieroglyphs. The coast in the distance makes you think of the Italian lakes when the sun is shining on the villages on the seaside, but when it is dark it looks like Scotland. Well, it all stirs the imagination so much and is so peaceful at the same time that I can even accept the presence of cows in a pasture on a plateau above the ocean."

I can't travel immediately. I have to spend a couple of days in Paris to get new material for the paper.

27   Contact with the Law

November. I've been in Brittany for a week now (this place is called Le Roselier-en-Plérin) and really, we have no right to complain anymore. In surroundings like this we think about the people who have *never* had even this much. For a whole week it has seemed as if the torment has abated. Couldn't we stay here, if we could make enough money without going to Paris to gather material? It often rains and the paths are muddy. We see more cows than people on our walks, and we also lie down and watch the ocean for hours. It changes colors more than any other I've ever seen. Some mornings when we wake up it's an ocean of milk with a blue fold here and there and a bit of faded blue at the edge. There are days when the surface is the green of a pale watercolor which turns perceptibly into a steel blue. On other days it's a blue that can compete with the bluest Mediterranean. We saw a rainstorm come across the bay: a gray striped bag which moved from left to right and changed the surface of the water with strong whisks. There were large purple stripes between the dark gray, which was all pushed away again by the incoming, slowly flowing green.

At low tide the bay to the right of the house dries up and becomes a small wrinkled desert, and the beach below us is wide, while at high tide it disappears completely at the foot of a small range of hills which makes up this coast. These rocky, overgrown hills resemble dolmens and are reddish here and there because of the dried ferns which, according to Jane, give them a Scottish character. In the rocks there are holes and grooves everywhere: beautiful tunnels that are round but short with slanted, threatening cracks you can walk about fifteen steps into. The dripping walls are a greenish gray with dark red spots, like slices of raw liver, on them: you feel like you're walking into an open wound. On a little rocky island there is a black cross for a philosopher who killed himself by swimming into the sea until his strength gave out, just like Conrad's planter of Malata. To make the cross visible they whitewashed the upper rocks; when the water rises, it leaves only this top of the monument which looks like a whipped-cream pie. The famous Brittany sailboats appear suddenly from behind a bight and disappear again like pirate ships: they're orange-red in the sun but within a few seconds a lull in the wind drops them into the shade and the boats rest in the same spot, disguised in plain brown. At night when the wind permits it, we sit in the garden and watch the light of Saint-Quay, to the left.

During the first week here I had another dream:

I was with somebody in a house that looked a lot like Gedong Lami but wasn't really, and we were menaced by demons. We were walking through a room when I looked into a large hall next to it and saw a kitchen ladder skip away. I went up to it and it stopped right away; it wasn't alone in the empty hall but was suddenly surrounded by all kinds of things: a pail, a mop, a broom, and so on. The ladder stood there in the middle, shamming, but I wasn't fooled a minute. I looked under it and there was something, all right—a doll, something between a plucked chicken and a clown, like some of Goya's etchings, with its thin legs spread wide apart. "Aha," I said, "here it is," and I picked it up by one of its legs. The thing was limp, just like a real doll, and I dangled it over my arm. At that moment I knew where I was: it really was Gedong Lami. I had picked up the doll in the dining room and walked to the servants' quarters, and the person following me was Alima.

When I got to the pavilions I said to her, "Go get my revolver." I had left it in the pavilion on the river side where my room seemed to be. I immediately threw the doll on a nearby garbage heap to the right, in the garden. It fell there and, true to its character, stayed limp. Alima went to get my revolver. I knew the demons would attack me now from the river side. I even wanted to confront them, once Alima had brought me my revolver. I waited with my back against the wall, next to a room which had once been my study. I looked straight ahead, waiting for Alima, and suddenly I felt a shadow with huge wings gliding toward me along the wall. I knew right away what it had to be, but I didn't want to believe it and didn't want to look. At that moment, as if to convince me, a dog sitting opposite me—which hadn't been there a second before—slunk away growling, his hair standing on end and his tail between his legs. I just had time to take this all in before the shadow fell on me.

It's the same vague, half-real fear that I should perhaps be ashamed of: it's always the same defenselessness, like that of a child, really. Two days later a letter from Graaflant brings me back to reality. He writes that Grouhy has been sold and soon they'll be able to send me that money, at last. The news was welcome, if only for the feeling that all my debts would be settled. Even the attorney from Namur sent in his bill a long time ago, and it's quite high, as if his zeal had never waned. I see the man in front of me, just as he was when he defended me for assault and battery in the courthouse in Nivelles. By the time I was thirty-two I had had three encounters with the law; each one brought a stronger feeling of repugnance, although it was a repugnance that had very little to do with fear.

The first time was in the Indies. When I was about twenty, my father and I were sitting on our front porch in Bandung, when a dos-à-dos drove up the gravel path. A slender young woman got out and casually sat down with us. She introduced herself as Mrs. Ruits and explained that she wanted to rent Gedong Lami, which was vacant at the time. She had come by train just for this purpose, she said. Her husband had a high position with the Royal Packet Company and was too busy to make the trip.

"My husband is your age," she said, at a given moment to my father. "If you knew him you would certainly like him. I don't like young men. What good are they?" And so on.

My father laughed a little uncomfortably, but he may have been flattered at the same time. She was somewhat strange but pleasant enough and really not at all suspect. She was loquacious and a little bit too forward, but then again, perhaps my father really did remind her of her husband. So Gedong Lami was rented to her. Eight months later the rent was still unpaid. When my father threatened a lawsuit he was notified that the lady had left the house. Finally he took the train to Meester-Cornelis and found the house in a shambles. Nobody at the Royal Packet Company had ever heard of a Mr. Ruits, and nobody had ever seen him in Gedong Lami. But, as a matter of fact, there had been several other gentlemen (obviously none of them married to the lady), who came to champagne parties that lasted late into the night, with all the lights ablaze. The neighbors across the street had been fascinated by it and couldn't remember ever seeing so much activity in our house.

My father filed his complaint and about a year later, shortly before we went to Europe, the lady turned up in Semarang. Her name was Ietje van Beek, and she was known to be one of the smartest embezzlers in the Indies. She had been convicted once before in Surabaja. Since I had been there when she first appeared, I was called as a witness. My father sat on one side of me, the lady on the other, just the way she had sat with us on our front porch. She had a face that was both dumb and sly at the same time. If she hadn't had such pretty hair and such a slim figure, she would have been just plain unattractive. While I was testifying to what I had heard, she stared at me with great indignation and said, "What a liar! What a lousy liar!" She sat less than an arm's length away from me, and yet I managed to avoid looking at her. I felt neither pity nor the slightest animosity for her. It was very important to determine whether she really had said Mrs. Ruits or Mrs. Reits; it seemed that a long time ago she had in fact been married to some Mr. Reits or other. At a certain point I had to take the stand. The president of the court was a friend of my father's, and had recently been at our house. Ietje van Beek's attorney had upon occasion defended my father, and he joked with us before the trial began. It all seemed so informal that I didn't stand when the president asked me to do as he did and raised his hand. "No, get up, get up," he whispered in surprise.

When the session was over and we were walking out of the courthouse, the former Mrs. Ruits, or Reits, came up to us with her attorney. Before we realized what was happening, she fell to her knees in front of my father in the almost empty hall and begged him to drop the charges. The attorney added in his meager voice: "Please forgive her, Mr. Ducroo; the child isn't really bad, she has a good soul." My father stammered something, clearly caught off guard, and attempted unsuccessfully to lift her up. Suddenly she got up by herself quite calmly. The only remaining question was whether the act was her idea or her attorney's. I went home with my first feeling of aversion to all these doings, including the good judge who seemed to be so startled when I didn't stand up to take the oath. It all seemed like a play. I had a particular aversion to one man, the bald district attorney, who had insisted so forcefully and so eagerly on a severe sentence for "this repeated offender." I had the chance to catch him at a grammatical error when he asked me a question. I pretended not to understand the question so as to force him to ask the question again and correct his grammar.

My second run-in I owed to Viala. To make some money, Viala and a friend had reprinted an erotic novel by Grant Oran (his real name was Dupuis or Dumoulin).[1] The book was entitled *Mademoiselle Javotte et ses cousines* and was later disclaimed by the author. Viala had met a customer who had complained about how boring Casanova was. He would like to read something like that, he said, but set in our own time and with young girls from good families. At first Viala laughed about it, but then he saw a commercial possibility. To give it an innocent air and also just for the fun of it, he imitated the book cover of the *Heures bleues*, a series of children's books published by Giraud. The joke wasn't repeated on the title page; there it said *Luxuriopolis*, in the mystifying tradition of erotic literature. Nonetheless, Giraud was deeply insulted and prosecuted the unknown perpetrators. One day Viala wrote me that they had surprised him and his friend. Twenty copies of the book had been found in their store, so it was proved they were selling it but not that they had printed it. Since I lived in Belgium and could not be investigated so easily, Viala's friend said he had bought ten copies from a Belgian dealer in pornography named Moulaert, who he had only met in cafés, and ten copies among a large number of other books from a Mr. Arthur Ducroo, living in Grouhy. Viala thought that would be the end of it, but to be on the safe side I removed from my library at Grouhy all the books which could possibly be compromising and brought them to Graaflant. But I left my Casanova edition. About two months later, when I had forgotten the whole thing, I was awakened in Brussels at nine o'clock one morning by two inspectors, who had first interrogated my mother at great length. She more than proved herself on this occasion:

"Who *is* this Mlle Javotte, gentlemen?" she asked them, "She's never been here."

"No, ma'am, it's about *Mlle Javotte et ses cousines*."

"Mais je ne la connais pas," repeated my mother fearfully, "Ni elle, ni ses cousines."[2]

"No, ma'am, it's a book by that name."

"Oh, a book, then you'll have to ask my son."

They came to ask me in my bedroom, looked through my cabinets and my desk, and then left politely. They had butchers' faces but lived up to the level of propriety suggested by their overcoats. That same afternoon our old gardener, Osé Béro, came from Grouhy fearful and upset to report that he had been surprised by the entire district attorney's office of Namur. The district attorney had been there, also the investigating judge, a clerk, a police sergeant, and two gendarmes. They had asked for my books, they had broken into the bookcase and into two metal boxes; they had searched through all my books and read my letters. A gendarme stood downstairs by the telephone, another one in front of the house, and the sergeant had stood at the window and helped read the letters. My mother was furious.

I also thought the joke had gone a little too far and went to Grouhy. It took two hours in the chilly house to put my books in order again. The lock on the bookcase had been forced. My metal trunks had been ruined. Moreover, the visitors had made the mistake of breaking into my mother's desk. Teresa's letters had been examined by the police sergeant and I tore them up. I wrote a letter to the Namur district attorney's office, and my mother filed a complaint at the Dutch consulate. I also wrote to Viala, indirectly, because his mail was being intercepted. "Votre mère," he wrote back, "devrait exiger des excuses publiques au roi Albert."[3]

In response to my letter demanding explanation I was summoned to Namur. It took a full day. I was interrogated in a dusky back room by an investigating judge, an insignificant, polite little old man with a delicate wrinkled face, a gold lorgnette and dyed mustache, who was obviously ill-at-ease about the unsuccessful expedition to Grouhy. His name was Maurice de Rougeville, which made it seem like a detective novel by Gaboriau, but that only moderately consoled me about the situation. I told him that my mother had filed a complaint at the Dutch consulate and was very upset about her desk that had been ruined. "Que voulez-vous," he said, "nous devons vous surprendre."[4]

A wild wind of chastity was blowing in Belgium in those days. They had put a former brothel keeper in charge of listing all the prohibited books, and his list was sent to all the bookstore owners, to their great amusement. Perhaps the district attorney from Namur saw the chance of his life with this transgression which was unexpectedly signaled from Paris. Just think how happy they would be if they discovered a wagonload of forbidden books in the basement of Grouhy. I forgot to ask Mr. de Rougeville if he had also looked in the basement. I was interested in what questions he might ask, but his eagerness made him start too quickly. First he used a subtle diversionary tactic, intended to catch me if I pretended not to know Viala.

"Do you know," he asked gropingly, "a certain Mr. Gaston Leprin?"

"Certainly," I said, "He's my friend Viala's business partner."

He was clearly disappointed. How did I know that person? I gave him a truthful report of my few encounters with Mr. Leprin. What did I think of him? An epicurean more or less, who knew all the restaurants where the food was good and cheap. While I talked he dictated a summary of my statements to the clerk; although it was of no importance, each statement was written down, simplified, and distorted. For example: "I thought Mr. Leprin was a rather materialistic person."

"Excuse me," I interrupted, "I didn't say that."

"But you did say that he knew where the food was good."

"Indeed, this seemed to me epicurean. I don't know a thing about Mr. Leprin's materialism."

"But you did say, didn't you, that he was uninteresting?"

"I said I didn't pay much attention to him because he interested me less than my friend Viala."

"Why don't you write down then," he said to his clerk: "'A fairly uninteresting person who liked good food a lot.'"

Did I know whether my friend Viala sold erotic novels?

"Absolutely not."

So I was surprised?

"Oh yes."

This was the case, unfortunately; he had been *caught* at it.

"Viala is poor. He probably needed the money desperately."

Did I know what kind of a book *Mlle Javotte* was?

"Oh, I've seen it in Paris in some bookstore. It's attributed to the author Grant Oran, but of course I never believed that Grant Oran would write such trash."

"It had to be," he said subtly, because they had discovered a Casanova among my books, "but that was of course something entirely different...."

"Indeed," I said, "and I also have read and greatly enjoyed the erotic poetry of Théophile Gautier, Verlaine, and Malherbe."

Did I think that *Mlle Javotte* had been printed in Belgium?

No, I didn't think so. I'd always thought that things like that were typically Parisian.

This answer was written down too. He finally thanked me for the information, regretted having had to disturb me, understood that the case was very unpleasant for me, if—and this he was ready to believe, he said with emphasis—if I were a decent man. When I left the office I was disgusted most of all by our common distress over the distribution of such unsavory reading material, as if we were both personally insulted by the literary disgrace which the publishing house Giraud and the author Grant Oran might have suffered.

But that wasn't the end of it. During the next days uniformed police officers came to visit me every morning because they needed some piece of information. The first one wanted to know who I could give as a character reference in Belgium, the second how long I had been living there, the third what my father's given name was and when he had died.... My reception became colder each time. I knew that Viala's mail was being read, and I was afraid mine was too. I felt that this trivial incident forced me into the same caution that a serious conspiracy would, and I felt like quarreling with every policeman I met. Tearing up Teresa's letters as a purifying gesture also bothered me. The only thing that comforted me in the whole process was a poem from Viala which I received when I was most annoyed:

> Il ne faut rien prendre au tragique,
> Dit la sagesse des Nations,
> Toutefois, faites attention
> Aux Sherlock Holmès de Belgique.
> Sur le terrain que vous foulez
> Un détective trop zélé
> Vient relever la molle empreinte
> Que laissent vos souliers Raoul
> Et vous n'abusez de vos feintes
> Qu'un limier crasseux et saoul.

> Prenez garde qu'une réponse
> Ne vienne vous clouer le bec
> Quand vous interroge un Alphonse
> Dans le langage de Schaerbeek.
> Car il sait bien, folle cervelle,
> Qu'il faut saisir la Muse telle
> Qu'elle s'exhibe au saut du lit,
> Le bras rompu, la jambe gourde,
> Et que sa conscience est lourde
> Du papier pur qu'elle a sali.

Mais j'arrête ici ma critique;
Votre nom n'est-il pas connu
Jusqu'au pays problématique
D'où le curry nous est venu?
Les indigènes, je suppose,
Tiendraient à couronner de roses
Le bel édifice indolent
Que vous promènerez dans l'île
Quand vous irez, d'un pas tranquille,
Pour y chasser le Grand Orang.[5]

(You shouldn't take anything too seriously, so says the wisdom of the ages. In any case, beware of all the Sherlock Holmes of Belgium. On the property where you are, an overzealous detective has just picked up the soft imprint that your shoes have left and you only abuse with your deception a drunken, dirty sleuth. Be careful that an answer doesn't nail your mouth shut when some Alphonse interrogates you in the language of Schaerbeek. Because he well knows, that madman, that you have to seize the Muse just as she jumps from bed, her arms and her legs tired, and that her conscience is heavy about the pure paper she has fouled. But here I rest my criticism. Isn't your name known as far as the problematic country from where curry comes to us? The natives, I presume, would insist on crowning with roses the beautiful, indolent body which you will move around the island when you go, calmly to hunt the great Orang.)

The third time was caused by the endless quarreling in Grouhy, in particular the endless feud between my mother and the staff. At a given moment there were for her no ruder individuals than her drivers. "What kind of people are they? They are *taxi* drivers," she would say. And I would be called in for the last round. Unfortunately, I usually got along with them quite well. "Yes, you like everything that is rude." The one time my mother got a real "chauffeur de maître" I didn't get along with him. His name was Omer and he must have thought he looked like the Belgian crown prince. He pursed his lips when he spoke, in a tone of barely restrained dignity, and looked at you with two angry fish eyes. He always dressed neatly and was inevitably late, though he always had watertight excuses. But he kept the car as neat as himself and he was such a careful driver that my mother preferred him to "all those brutes." One day he opposed her. It happened in her bedroom where she was lying ill. She was displeased with him and said so. He got angry and when she let him know that she thought he had tampered with his receipts, he screamed that she was the one who was dishonest, not he. I had followed the discussion with serene mischief from the couch, but at this point I asked him to leave the room. He said he wouldn't and demanded satisfaction. I stood up from the couch and held the door open for him, and when he refused to notice it, I felt obliged to push him in the right direction without any further discussion. It was really a scene from a movie. I handed my coat to the Austrian Frieda when the man picked up one of our heavy oak chairs to protect himself from my rage, as he later put it to the judge. He protected himself with that piece of antique furniture so well that I had just enough time to ward off the blow with my free arm, so that only the lamp next to my head was shattered while the chair flew very dramatically over a table and landed on the couch. He ran through the hall and down the stairs in such a hurry that an old hernia acted up. Later on he held me responsible for this, not because I had hurried him but because I supposedly kicked him down the stairs. He must have felt my intentions as reality because I watched him regretfully from the top of the stairs as he hurried away so quickly. When he was at the bottom he screamed at me, holding a hand over his eye, saying that I would pay dearly for this. To prepare his story he limped around the village till late in the evening, leaning heavily on the arm of one of our employees, a farm woman who was in love with him and whom he immediately took with him. His head wrapped in more than enough bandages, he informed everybody of what I had on my conscience. Only the village blacksmith reasoned that something must have happened to start all this, because "Monsieur Arthur never said anything to anybody."

When he submitted his bill along with many medical documents in the small courthouse in Nivelles, my lawyer screamed, "He said Mr. Ducroo would pay dearly and by God, was he right!" His glowing speech reduced the fine to about half. He addressed himself not only to the judges but to the whole audience, to ask: "Who among you gentlemen, who among you, I repeat, wouldn't have done the same thing as a son?" Before he began to speak, I had more than enough time to size up the court and to experience the atmosphere as expressed by the eldest judge, who held his head way back and his mouth as if he had tasted something unmentionable. Without exception the defendants who had been ahead of me had hung their heads, and there were great sinners among them, even somebody who had diluted his milk with sixty percent water. "Sixty percent," the judge said, smacking his mouth. "Why didn't you just sell water then?" Another old man sat behind me; he must have come to the courthouse as if it were a church. After each new misdemeanor he mumbled to himself, "It's disgraceful," and after this pointed remark by the judge, he said, "I agree. Why didn't he just sell water then?" The sentences were handed out liberally. When I was called, I was no longer sure I would get off with just a fine. It was the same thing again: I had the distinct feeling that even in a more serious case I'd behave about the same. My "artistic temperament" supplied whatever vulgarity was lacking in this courtroom. I was certain that more dramatic circumstances would only excite me more and would completely erase my good family background, which now allowed me to confront these older gentlemen as a gentleman myself. I stared at the mouth of the eldest judge as he addressed me now, and I contradicted him in a clear voice when he read the chauffeur's allegations and seemed to be personally completely convinced by them. The attorney behind me whispered, "Don't go into this; it's not important." He was afraid that I would compromise myself, perhaps, and ruin his defense before he had the chance to deliver it. So he expressed my regrets for me, which I didn't feel, and he underlined them by saying I couldn't possibly feel at home in a place which was so inappropriate for my social rank. I thought to myself, "Is he really so stupid or are these just the arguments he thinks such a stupid audience needs to hear?" It was evident that he spoke as much to the public as to the judges. He had a great reputation as a speaker to protect, even if it was only in Nivelles.

I think now that I was wrong about my capacity for armed resistance. If I could believe that those who create dramatic events were all big bruisers, insensitive and simply "dangerous," I might not fit in, but I know how vulnerable and impulsive some terrorists have been. I also know it would go against my nature to devote myself to politics, because my aversion to politicians would always be as great as my aversion to notaries. But the demarcation between the anarchist bomb-thrower and the anarchist like Viala is still unclear to me. I don't believe it's simply a matter of temperament, or rather, I'm sure that when circumstances reach a certain intensity, dreams translate into acts, and that after the act a whole new world opens up. So I really still believe that somebody like Viala (or perhaps myself) has the potential of being a terrorist. If we had been born in Russia and had seen our parents brought to the gallows, we might have helped each other throw bombs.

Héverlé apparently has a much more realistic attitude toward politics. "It's impossible to ignore politics at this point in civilization, to consider it as just politics," he says. But he hasn't started to write books for any given party yet. He is no doubt a revolutionary but in such a way that you can still agree with him if you give him all his due. Moreover, any book which reflects the author's *engagement*, which was not just written as a literary achievement, is perhaps an act of onanism, an act which is in place of another act. If you know an author's life well enough, you can always figure out what act, what unsatisfied desire, or what feeling of hate such a book replaces. And in spite of all my admiration for Héverlé I wait for the time when he will compromise himself as a revolutionary, although I'm certain that his real, individual value can only develop to its full potential in complete freedom. But as his friend I almost hope he will remain a writer and not become a revolutionary activist.

Just as sure as he is that he will never be a writer, Viala is sure that in the next war he will desert or be shot as a conscientious objector. "I feel more than ever that I'm an individualist," he said at the Héverlés', "I'm completely indifferent whether Hitler or Tardieu[6] wins. Let them liquidate me if they think I'm wrong, but then as quickly as possible and with no illusions for anyone. Nothing is worse than running the risk that they'll find your corpse on the battlefield and turn you into the Unknown Soldier."

"In principle I agree with you," said Héverlé, "and yet, if we had to take sides, I think it would make a difference to me whether Moscow won or not."

They said this during an extremely troubling conversation about the coming war, during which I had only one idea: to leave, to go back to

Java, hoping it would stay calm there, and live in a *kampong* house, if necessary, without books or any intellectual stimulation but with the pride of having rejected the political squalor of a new war for whatever cause. In this respect, at least, I agree completely with Viala. (The only question is whether you can get away from it all, whether you can find even one spot where isolation would be possible. This was perhaps the most disturbing part of the conversation.)

But to have myself shot as an example? I don't think I would join Viala in that, assuming he really would do it himself if things get that bad. The cowardly hope of escape would keep me from doing it. Eternal curiosity, too: to know what the new world order would bring, how we will have changed once the storm has passed.

We were supposed to come to Europe for a maximum of three years when I left the Indies twelve years ago. I had sentimental ideas about the French friends I'd have some day (in Paris itself!). I was entitled to French friends, I thought then, because I was so French. And at the same time I was afraid they would never really accept me, because I would never be French enough.

Today, in conversations like this one, when our friendship isn't doubted for a moment, my non-Frenchness gives me sort of a safe feeling. If some day I were killed next to them, it would only be out of friendship, and friendship cannot demand your being killed for something so external as war. And if I weren't killed and later felt guilty about this, it wouldn't be because they blamed me, just as in their place I wouldn't blame anyone who would take the opportunity to leave.

"As a Dutchman, you're the one with the best chances," said Héverlé.

But even if my guilt tortured me, I'd have arguments working against me: Jane most of all. If Viala had himself shot, what would this do to Manou? If I decided to go to the utter end of the world, would that have to be without Jane?

"If it doesn't have to do with principles, but only with feelings," says Jane, "no one can convince me that you have to sacrifice yourself for a friend, if you also have a woman you love."

How strange that you can trade one feeling for another! So I would have to say, "All right, I'll commit the cowardice of not being killed next to my friends, if you promise you will sacrifice your life to me."

There's one reassuring insight after all of this, namely that when the chips are down, circumstances will decide almost everything. All those who think they're following their heart of hearts when they talk may later question themselves wondering, "Is this me?" and perhaps not even that.

The weather is nasty; there isn't a corner in the garden that escapes the wind. Once in a while a brief rain lashes against the window; it's never much but it's annoying. Inside it's chilly because, even though this is the warmest room, the central heating is inadequate. I sit by the window to write; it's the only spot where there's enough light. The electric bulb over my bed gives off a reddish glow and is much too weak. In a minute, when it's completely dark, they'll bring in a kerosene lamp. I look at the trees in the garden. They're still green, but at this time of day they're almost black. They don't move, but the wind whistles as it blows through them. Behind me I hear Jane rustling the pages of her book.

The garden of Grouhy is far behind me, as far as I might have wished it when I was there. Sure, it was quite pretty, but I hardly ever found the right mood there. The grounds were more open around the house, with more grass, fewer trees, and less wind. It snowed and was wet in the winter. Here snow doesn't have a chance to stay; the wind from the ocean blows away everything unless it's collected in ditches, protected as if in a trench. There's a lot in this house that reminds me of Grouhy. I will end up longing for Grouhy here the same way as I used to long for Gedong Lami there. I used to think, "This happens sooner or later, no matter what," and when I went out or came back in the moonlight I would try to imagine that the present was already past. In the quiet of the night there was nothing waiting for me but the house, a black square with only one light surface in it against the enchanting motion of the sky. I wanted to experience it as if it were just a memory instead of the experience itself. The brown star in the grass was next to me or behind me; the tall flowerpots by the porch appeared suddenly before me, and they were so real they destroyed the illusion, like a dog jumping through a spider web. I rushed through the dark porch to find the lightswitch by the stairs.

It's too soon to long for Grouhy, but I wonder why I should go back to Paris.... It's a strange inclination to settle in some place, just for the charm it acquires as soon as you leave it behind. My father couldn't look at any spot that was the least bit appealing without wanting to build a house there. That's how it was in the Indies and also in Biarritz. When he saw Grouhy for the first time he felt drawn to it by a power that he later thought was satanic. When he became tired of life, he would walk around there and point out to me everything in the yard that had escaped his "blinded eyes": a couple of broken window panes in the grape hothouses, a couple of cracks in the wall: "Look at all the things I missed." In Brussels he had spent years going to auctions where he bought so many things that they finally had to be stored because they were about to push us out of the house. So it was really necessary to buy another house. He found Grouhy, and although my mother pointed out to him that it was quite far out, he wanted it so much that he couldn't sleep at night. Once he had bought it, he furnished it mentally and then using a floor plan. While it was being refurbished he bought new furniture, which was put in storage with the rest, and when they finally moved in, his illness caught up with him. He got no pleasure whatsoever out of it. It was up to my mother to carry on and to try to cure him with the new purchase. But he walked around the house as he walked around the garden, running a finger over all the furniture to see how damaged it had been by the move, how many cracks there were in the wood and in the leather, how many chips, how many broken locks, even how many unfortunately lost keys. He would sit in the living room among his beloved collection, among the things his only remaining passion had turned up or conquered in one end of Brussels or the other, like Job on the dung heap, and he sighed deeply and more often. My mother would bring him some flowers from the garden, dahlias and roses in a large bowl filled with water. She put the bowl in front of him. He sighed as he got up and put his finger in the water that had spilled over onto a small inlaid table.

Shooting himself was the logical end. He did it suddenly, but after thinking about it for months. The effect it might have on others no longer concerned him; he made the jump from a world in which he felt alone. Neurasthenia, world-weariness—those were words for what was living in him hour after hour and what turned him into somebody he couldn't live with. They called him a monomaniac too, and he was afraid he would end up in an asylum, having already been taken to a sanitarium twice. He was convinced he would soon be financially ruined... but when all is said and done, what do I know about him? For what strain on his nerves was he paying, for what drawn-out effort, what life-long repressions? And what did my mother and I realize of the humiliation he must have felt in his last year, in confronting the self-image he had lived up to all those years? One day a sixty-five-year-old man kills himself, as perhaps the final protest of his earlier self at thirty-five, on behalf of the latter, and because he had never thought he would have to experience life with dentures, a bad stomach, and impotence.

What is left for the others is a maudlin feeling which adds to the existing maudlin atmosphere. That's how it was with us, at least. For too long too much had gone wrong to be solved by my father's suicide—as, at first, everybody thought it would. It made everything worse. My ridiculous role of "young European," which I had taken so seriously, of the worldly-wise young man who could now turn everything into a game, had been seriously undermined for the first time by my father's sickness. After his death I was shocked into another state, perhaps not wanting to recognize it but unable to resist much. I became obsessed with death. A day didn't go by that I didn't feel death in me. Going to sleep was like a kind of dying. The particular taste of suicide was something else, but equally ineradicable. It was as if my father's last act had crushed me more deeply than any other. It seemed clear to me that in a certain sense he was also taking revenge on my mother. But why was there this last mysterious bond with me, who had so little in common with him?

He did it in Brussels. As soon as the funeral was over we went back to Grouhy. We had fled to a hotel the day it happened. The house in Brussels was sold, at a loss, and we went on a trip: my mother, Suzanne, and I, baby Guy, my adopted "sister" Sylvia, and also Aunt Hélène from Sukabumi, who had finally arrived in Europe and rushed in from Savoy. She had been staying with some old acquaintances from the Indies, but they weren't getting along very well at the time. My mother and she embraced with long-lost intimacy. The last days in Grouhy had been quite difficult; the trip would be an escape. In this way and with this company, we set off with forty pieces of luggage, which had to be counted every time: Paris, Basel, Lugano, Genoa, Nice, later Villefranche—my memory is of an unspeakably miserable, ruined trip, poisoned in every possible way. I tried to write away my obsession about my father's suicide in a story, even published it, but it didn't help much. The clashes between my mother and Suzanne were becoming violent. Sylvia played a mysterious but significant role in it. Poor Aunt Hélène, who had come to enjoy Europe and who had gone excitedly to all the plays in Paris to make up for those she had missed before, now had to draw on all her strength to remain neutral—as far as that was possible. She sympathized a great deal with Suzanne, but knew better than to contradict my mother too often. In a restaurant in Genoa I had a terrible fight with my mother. I had chosen it and she didn't think it was chic enough. She pouted and wouldn't eat anything. I got up in the middle of dinner, went outside, and took a ride to the Campo Santo on my own, swearing that this was the way it was going to be for the rest of the trip. Once in Nice, I installed the company in a hotel and went to Villefranche, but being independent was not as easy as I had thought it would be. My "soft-heartedness," which played tricks on me all the time, forced me to make at least a couple of visits; it was so close after all. A week later my mother moved into a villa right next to my hotel in Villefranche, and we played out a vaudeville act, with the rest of the company in the villa and me in the hotel with a mulatto girl from "Mâ-tinique" who had just become my bedmate.

In Nice we met the person who, outside of my father, marks for me the beginning of Grouhy as a madhouse. She was an old masseuse, whom my mother had known in the Indies; she was considered an adventuress and a harebrain. She was sitting a few tables away from us in a café in Nice, chewing on a crust of bread. She mostly ate dry bread which she brought with her and put mustard on to make it taste better.

My mother was surprised. "Isn't that Mrs. Starlette?"

"Maybe so. Leave her alone, for God's sake," I said.

I thought I remembered my father throwing her out of the house in the Indies. My mother said that was true, but that she had no quarrel with her and Mrs. Starlette gave such wonderful massages. So the old woman was invited to our table and soon she was talking up a storm. She was now seventy-three but still on the go. She had traveled around the world four times in various ways, and she still resembled the woman she must have been after the flower of her youth had waned. She was one of the first liberated women, a short suffragette, with wavy gray hair pulled into an untidy knot somewhere on her head, cheap dentures with reddish-orange gums which could have passed for real teeth, they were so damaged. Her face was once rather pretty and she still had the distinguishing feature of a nervous laugh which was probably the remnant of an earlier gaiety and still served as such. "That woman is so cheerful and can tell such good stories."

It turned out she could still give a massage like no one else, and so she was added to our group of travelers. But there was a quarrel even before we left Villefranche. I heard her scream that they could cut her open if they wanted to see how black she was on the inside. Again I was called on to show her the door. So she screamed at me and asked me what I took her for, and I felt obliged to say that I took her for an old shrew. She then left and my mother went over her background with Aunt Hélène: she had always been impossible and had had to flee the Indies, where they condemned her in absentia to eight years in prison for being an abortionist.

When we came back to Grouhy, it turned out that my mother was still corresponding with her; suddenly the plan developed to have her come live with us, because my mother's knee still troubled her and she had been the only person who could massage it properly. I protested, but in vain, as always. I pointed out to my mother the responsibility she was taking on herself by bringing an impoverished old lady from the Riviera where it was warm, to Belgium, when there was a good chance she would be chased away again. But a room on the second floor had already been fixed for her. She arrived, and soon it turned out that her massages weren't as good as they used to be. What she liked best was to lie in a lounge chair in the garden, and soon she had strained relations with the whole staff. She took the bus to Brussels when Grouhy started to bore her, and she said that at her age she could no longer give long massages. She started to cross swords with many of the people in the village, because she would leave her umbrella somewhere and then accuse people of trying to steal it when she came back to get it. She also lost a purse and had a maid fired because of it; all her money was in it, she claimed, so my mother had to reimburse her. The purse turned up a few weeks later behind the cushion of a chair; it had only five francs in it.

When I was living in Brussels she visited me one day and told me excitedly that my mother had thrown her out of Grouhy. My mother refused to give her money for traveling or anything. I gave her some money, but she didn't leave Brussels. I would see her sometimes, and she would come up to me laughing loudly. She sold shoe polish or accompanied a ballerina to Spa, just as she had been a Christian Scientist in Nice so as to be invited to tea by English ladies. In Spa she gambled and wrote to ask me for money when she ran out. She wrote long letters, mostly about the fact that she never wanted to go to an old people's home. This pride, along with her vitality, touched me. I sent her small amounts of money and suggested she write her memoirs, which I would try to have published. She filled many notebooks, but I couldn't do anything with them, although I would have gladly worked on them for her. Her life seemed to have been spent in quarrels and at dinner parties. She always knew exactly which distinguished person she had walked or dined with, what the menu had consisted of, and how expensive this or that had been. But apart from that, life had passed by her with colorless banality. This explains to me why the memoirs of burglars, hotel thiefs, and gangsters can be so intensely boring when you would think that such people would have something interesting to say.

I told my mother I had inherited Mrs. Starlette as her protégée, but just as in the Indies she refused any reconciliation. Mrs. Starlette belonged not to the snakes but to the thankless dogs. Every day she stepped through the veranda with her muddy shoes and was late for dinner, and when my mother locked the veranda, she protested loudly that was why she was late. This crime had no pardon, not to mention the fact that she had neglected her massages.

Viala once saw Mrs. Starlette in Grouhy and said after a couple of minutes, "Mais c'est une pauvre vieille folle." After that he would always ask, "J'espère que votre mère a toujours quelques folles sur ses terres?"[1]

My mother thought that all my friends were crazy—with the exception of Rijckloff—and that her looney friends were picturesque. Gradually everybody went crazy at Grouhy, the so-called masters, the servants, the guests, and myself. If you have to choose between the terms, "center of quarreling," "house of misfortune" (*rumah sial*), or "madhouse," for me the last one wins out, because it describes *everything*. And just as when my father would be sick and my mother would send for a *hadji* woman, now here too she tried to find occult reasons for the atmosphere in our home. The hate and envy of so many women put together was not explanation enough for her, so she always found snakes and adders whom she could blame for all the poisoning, just as in the Middle Ages they always found a witch to blame for the latest epidemic. Everything that Grouhy had to offer in natural beauty and domestic comfort was threatened at all times. Even with morning coffee in bed there was the fear that something was going to explode in a minute, and you'd wonder, "Can I hear anything yet?"

Uncle Van Kuyck came to spend some time with us. He would sit for hours on the veranda, staring blankly at the roses and the blue firs, and when I sat down with him I would try to recapture my old fondness for him, try to feel the quiet warmth of his presence again, as it was in our house in the Indies. He had the same potbelly, the same posture, the same eyes; only his mustache had been shaved off, and his long upper lip and weak mouth made him look like a rabbi. But it was all different; his comments about "events" didn't sound the way they used to. It was a senseless repetition of what had never been really perceptive, and now the good humor he used to emanate was no longer sufficient.

He never stayed very long. After my father's death my mother didn't want to have seances with him anymore. One day he broke off with her, by letter, and we couldn't really figure it out.

"Your mother knows why," he told me with a knowing look. My mother claimed she didn't, but since reconciliations were bothersome, that was the end of it; moreover, Aunt Hélène and everybody who had seen old Van Kuyck thought he had become pretty much senile.

Aunt Hélène was waiting to go back to the Indies. The stormy scenes at Grouhy between my mother, Suzanne, and me demoralized her, but my mother's constant fighting with the servants was perhaps the most insufferable for her. In the Indies she had always been able to get along very well with her servants, and she knew how my mother had been then. She now worried constantly about saying too much or too little and keeping up the appearance that she was on my mother's side, although in reality she wasn't at all. So while a new drama was unfolding with a kitchen maid or a chauffeur, she would sit stiffly in her chair doing some needlework, her face taut and disapproving, but you couldn't tell whom her disapproval was directed at. She would murmur, "Hm," when my mother told her something, as if she disapproved of the story rather than the one who told it. But mother expected something totally different and wasn't taken in by it.

"Hélène is against me," she said. "That's always been the case."

As for me, I was always on the servants' side, opposing her. I felt a great deal of sympathy for Aunt Hélène, and I thought how much I would have enjoyed making her regent of Grouhy if it were up to me. Her European trip had been a bitter disappointment in many respects.

"If you can't be free to do what you want, there's no point in trying to see anything," she said, as she stabbed furiously at her needlepoint.

She was dependent on my mother since things had turned sour with her acquaintances from the Indies in Savoy. She didn't have the money for the trip to Europe and back, and for living expenses during her stay on top of that. She was waiting for money from the Indies for the return trip and didn't want to go back to Savoy. She had left there after an extremely unpleasant difference of opinion when she maintained that Amsterdam was the capital of the Netherlands and not The Hague, as they thought.

After my father's death my mother needed support. It came unexpectedly from an old friend of Aunt Hélène's, a widow from Holland. She was also in her seventies, but what a contrast to Mrs. Starlette! She had always been a beautiful woman and was part of the best circles, which you could still sense. Her dentures had such small teeth they barely showed from behind her lips and she had a striking brown wig, which was betrayed only now and then by a gray streak over her ear. Above all, she must have had beautiful eyes, which still danced and glowed. Just like Mrs. Starlette, she was small and quick, but she had the appearance of a lady rather than a suffragette. Unfortunately, her craziness was just as unadulterated. After just a few days she would run after me in the garden, bringing me cups of coffee. I complained to my mother about her excess servility, and she told me that Mimi van Gerth had always been like that and what an excellent housewife she was: "She is somebody who *really* relieves me of all the work."

That was obviously my mother's intention and it worked immediately. Now Aunt Hélène was no longer needed. Mimi van Gerth easily surpassed Aunt Hélène's domestic abilities and was asked to stay in her place, which she readily accepted. Aunt Hélène was honest enough to warn my mother, even though Mimi van Gerth was her friend.

"You won't be able to get along with her, Madeline," she said. "Mimi has always lived alone because she quarrels with all her children. Above all, be careful of her gossiping."

But nothing could dim her domestic ability. Aunt Hélène left; Mrs. van Gerth stayed.

I disliked her from the first. But she was an old lady who did her best to discuss all sorts of topics and who talked to my friends about books and art at dinner and teatime, as best she could.

"It's a pity it isn't fifty years ago," sighed Rijckloff, "because she must have been very pretty, and then you could have silenced that annoying chatterbox with a kiss every now and then."

It flattered my mother that my friends thought Mrs. van Gerth was so terribly dumb, while she herself had the good taste to stay away from those dangerous subjects. Moreover, Rijckloff was there to assure her there was nothing he really hated more than talking about literature. My mother may have still been a little flirtatious in her way, but she thought that Mimi's flirting was not proper for a woman of her age.

Mrs. van Gerth loved to go to Brussels in the car with my mother to shop, but my stubbornness ruined her biggest day. That morning Rijckloff and I had set off alone with her for Brussels. We had a flat tire in the Soignes Forest. Rijckloff and I got out; while the chauffeur was busy changing the tire we walked up and down the road. When we came back to the car after fifteen minutes, Mrs. van Gerth was still sitting stiffly in the back seat, but she suddenly bowed to us through the open window and stuck her gloved hand out a little. With a mischievous look in her liquid eyes, she said affectedly, "And what's the matter...?" It was such a perfect fin-de-siècle caricature that even Rijckloff had trouble suppressing his laughter. Because the car trouble delayed us so long, she wanted to stay and have lunch together in Brussels. I said I absolutely had to get back and pressed her so relentlessly that she finished her shopping on time.

Of course, after a couple of months Mimi's treachery came to light. She took the servants' side but also my mother's, so she talked out of both sides of her mouth. Every morning she complained about a certain maid until my mother finally sent her away. At that moment Mrs. van Gerth came up to her with tears in her eyes and asked that the girl be forgiven just this once. When she proved herself to be a "snake," my mother and she exchanged some catty remarks. After that Mimi embraced my mother warmly again, but in the end Mimi ordered a taxi, because she wouldn't leave in my mother's car. I watched this from a distance. When I was at Grouhy, I would lock myself in my room for the whole day and read till I couldn't read anymore. When I needed a change, I would invite my own friends over, whom I would entertain as if nobody else were there.

But the struggle between Mrs. van Gerth and Sylvia, my adopted sister, made the air too heavy to be entirely ignored. Mrs. van Gerth was jealous of Sylvia, who for her part was no doubt jealous of Suzanne, and all of this jealousy came out during almost any meal, perhaps most of all at breakfast. Mrs. van Gerth kept picking on Sylvia and my mother chimed in, until she thought it had gone too far and her own feelings were hurt. But then it was already too late for a reconciliation. Mrs. van Gerth went around complaining subtly that Sylvia was not very clean for a girl and smelled quite bad. As for Sylvia, she never failed to notice when a gray streak showed underneath the brown wig.

Poor Sylvia wasn't all that enjoyable either, but there were extenuating circumstances in her case. She had been torn away from her native family and supposedly had been brought up as a European, but in reality she was treated more like a slave, more like a *babu*, than any European maid would have put up with. My mother was proud that she spoke a few words of French and had been a boarder for years at the Dames-de-Marie in Brussels, but after my father's death Sylvia was indispensable to her as a personal maid; soon nobody knew how to find things in her closet as well as Sylvia, who otherwise was the sloppiest creature in the world. As my mother's disease got worse, Sylvia was locked up with her more and more. She never had the safety valve available to every servant, which was a Sunday off.

The deeper cause of Sylvia's hate for Mrs. van Gerth stemmed from the following incident. One day Mrs. van Gerth had talked with the village postmaster, who told her that Sylvia received a considerable amount of mail that was held for her at the post office. She immediately disclosed this to my mother. So my mother sent her back with an autocratic letter to the postmaster, whereupon he turned the correspondence over to the intermediary. Mrs. van Gerth looked mysterious when she came back to my mother's room, the letters in her purse clinched tightly under her arm. She had them, she whispered. The door was locked and the two women inspected their booty. I was called in afterwards to find my mother in bed with envelopes torn open and sheets of paper with writing on them in front of her. She said, "Now look what I have to deal with." They were answers to a lonely hearts ad Sylvia must have placed and were written in very different styles. There was an office clerk who had enclosed a picture of himself in a bathing suit. He wrote that he wasn't rich, but perhaps she was and that he had other characteristics which women seemed rather satisfied with: "Du moins, c'est ce qui se dit; ce qui se pense, le sait-on jamais?"[2] He admitted he was a little bald, but the picture could vouch for the rest.

Among the other letters was one which consisted of a few grumpy lines from a retired man, a small farmer or something like that from the area, who wanted to know how much Sylvia would bring him and whether he could expect a picture from her soon. He was fifty-eight years old and would provide further information if the matter seemed promising enough.

"That's a grim one," my mother said, suddenly half laughing and thinking that even Sylvia was too good for such an old man. "But where did the child get such an idea?"

I was laughing too hard to be able to give any good advice. Sylvia's dish-shaped face and her defiant eyes, her mouth like a sawfish, and her smell which bothered Mrs. van Gerth so much—the whole thing was so funny I sat down to watch the sequel. Sylvia was called in and interrogated. They read the letters to her and spared her no commentary. During all this she stood next to the bed like a statue. She refused to answer and stared blankly, ready to deny even her own presence.

Some time later she was squeezed in all of Grouhy's nooks and crannies by a young electrician from the neighboring village, who was known throughout the area as a great lover. This was also reported to my mother, who invited the young man into the living room this time and asked him what his intentions were and what she should think about it. She had figured out by then that Sylvia also had a right to be married. But the young man politely explained to her that his intentions weren't very long range. He had loved once in his life, he said, and it was such a bitter experience that he had decided never to think of marriage again. Sylvia went off sobbing to her room but continued to meet the young man at the gate as often as possible.

The solution appeared to come in the form of a poor cousin from Amsterdam. He was in his late thirties and had a son from a previous marriage, but he won my mother's heart because he was good at all sorts of odd jobs I sadly failed at. His previous profession had been a band director, and he never talked about his wife; so she had cheated on him, gone crazy, or died. His name was Hubert; he had a strong Amsterdam accent and he addressed my mother as "Aunt" with each sentence. After some time he asked to marry Sylvia, and they were supposedly engaged. His stories amused me sometimes, because he really had been through quite a bit and had a rough sense of humor. But his continual presence in Grouhy, which after the "engagement" was all too easily justified, got on my nerves. I could see the pain that would come out of this too, and how he would make himself indispensable as a real source of manly strength for my mother as soon as he thought he had a foot in the door.

It resulted in a new clash between my mother and me, but I was living in Brussels then and had decided for my part to avoid Grouhy. Not a month passed before the whole Grouhy household came to my hotel in Brussels. My mother was restless and complained about her heart a lot, but there was a certain mysteriousness to her unexpected arrival. However, the next morning she said she couldn't hide it from me any longer and asked me to read some letters. They were from Hubert and were pure blackmail. My mother had fixed him up with Sylvia, he wrote, and now thought she could separate them, but she didn't realize who she was dealing with; he would come back and resort to murder, if necessary, and so on.

The story got even better. My mother had a new friend staying at Grouhy, a clairvoyant this time, a portly woman in her late forties, whose cheerfulness crackled through the whole house. She had strange light eyes and a round, supposedly Hindu face, so that everybody said she had such weird eyes. Her name was Dorine Felsen; as she practiced the common occult mixture of Buddha-Sufi-Grail mysticism, she could "see" and "withdraw" into a trance and was of course ready at any moment of the day to "help." Moreover, she was really goodness personified. She magnetized and massaged my mother and had the most fascinating encounters all day long. In her existence not a single event was commonplace. She met the spirit of my father, too. She stated that I would soon divorce Suzanne, that Suzanne had syphilis, and that my mother's new Austrian maid was a German spy. She had seen immediately that Hubert must have murdered somebody; she had told him so, and he had laughed and told her that in fact he had killed his wife's lover. Shortly thereafter a 1,000 franc note was missing from my mother's purse; nobody but Hubert had been around. He felt she suspected him and asked her if she wanted to search him. The next day he went back to Amsterdam. He had started a new business—in lace, I think—for which my mother had given him the money. But by this time she had lost her faith in him, and Sylvia began to act uncomfortable. Dorine Felsen took her aside one evening and looked her in the eyes, whereupon she admitted sobbingly that Hubert had urged her to take money from my mother's purse. "It's only an advance on your dowry; she won't notice it and it will help me," he had said.

But Sylvia hadn't sunk that low yet, so she broke down in front of Dorine, particularly after Dorine looked into her soul. A short counsel was held with my mother, and the "engagement" with Hubert was broken off by return mail. But everyone in Grouhy was so scared of Hubert that my mother came to the hotel, and I had to be told.

Whether all this was exactly true or not, I didn't much care, but I was terribly annoyed. Our last clash had been over Hubert, but now I was forced outside my own world to be my mother's bodyguard in the hotel. She started every time the door opened. I had to move into the room next to her and warn the police and write Hubert to tell him I knew all about it. Using the logic of any common blackmailer he had counted on my mother's not daring to tell me anything. So I set him straight, informed him I had taken measures, and advised him to keep quiet. After writing this little note, whose style was adapted to the subject matter, I carried a revolver until the first uneasiness was past. The craziest thing was that I was so angry that I'm still almost certain I would have shot him the moment he had shown up. And my mother's heart was taxed even more by this whole episode.

Losing Hubert didn't turn out to be as tragic for Sylvia as one might have expected. He was the man who would have "made a woman out of her," perhaps, but aside from that she may have thought he was too old or too dishonest, who knows. Her love life reached greater heights when my mother spent the winter in Brussels again, in order to be close to a good doctor. She had a number of rendezvous in the street; this time it was the concierge who warned my mother that Sylvia was having an affair with a sergeant but that his wife had already noticed and a scene could be expected to take place on the front doorstep at any moment. And just as at Grouhy, it was an intercepted letter that supplied the evidence. I've held on to this letter carefully. I've read it many times, and now I look at it again with great pleasure. I would never have thought that a sergeant could be so lyrical, could use such striking images, and could be so persuasive, calling on God as the only authority:

To you, my flower of the Orient, my little darling, you who are the center of my thoughts night and day. It makes me so hapy to be able to tell you that I'm almost beter and that Monday night we can meet at the place I told you about in my last. I re-red your letter and I cryed for joy that you are calling me and that I canot come out to console you. You asked if your still worthy of my love, if you could accept this love which belongs to the one I married and of which you could have a part of. My angel darling, God will judge us on the deeds we did not cary out, but since he prefers to have a sinner return to him, we can do what love dictates because you no that it all is done out of love. And let me say that I'm very good in love and let me ask to drink the blood of the woman I love so as to mix it with mine. I hope that soon you will allow me a visit long enough to settle our love which is eternal in my heart and which, some day, when I will be in your arms forever, will make you the happiest woman in the world. My dear, sweet Sylvia, I think that you understand what I mean in this letter and I hope that one day our dream will come true, just as God made true the dream of this great and glorious world.

I am all yours for life, my heart, body, mind, soul and actions which are really totally, totally yours. Yours, who bears for you the most wonderful name in the world,

Eugène

This letter caused a serious outburst, most of all because my mother thought Sylvia had neglected her heartlessly the last few days. Sylvia was resentful. When I came to see them I found my mother in bed deathly pale, gasping that Sylvia had killed her and she never wanted to see her again. Frieda, the Austrian, came into the room, bringing a few things, and she told me what had happened. My mother chimed in, "That child has never been so rude to me."

The same day I sent Sylvia to friends, but she couldn't stay there for long and after a week wanted a room of her own, where the sergeant undoubtedly lost no time "to settle their love." Meanwhile, my mother really was dying. What I would not experience later I went through this time. Two specialists showed up to tell me with solemn faces they had given up. But she lived, and even returned to Grouhy.

A month later Sylvia was allowed to visit her again. She sat down by her bed, said little, and before leaving went into the kitchen to put on her gaudy makeup. She felt like a real Brussels woman now, so she painted her lips crimson, her eyelids blue, and her cheeks orange. Frieda watched with amusement and couldn't resist telling my mother.

"That child must go back to the Indies," my mother said, "because here she'll turn into a streetwalker."

I didn't delude myself that it would be any different in the Indies, but with her so-called European upbringing and her few words of French she would have a couple more trump cards there. Here it seemed clear that she would end up as an authentic Japanese or Maori in an Antwerp brothel. I told Sylvia about our decision and my mother wrote to Holland for a boat reservation because, aside from worrying about the brothel, she was afraid that Sylvia's lonely room might cause her to get pregnant. In two weeks everything was arranged and I took Sylvia to Rotterdam, where I put her on the boat. Wijdenes went along with us and couldn't conceal his surprise that anyone would desire such a creature at all. At about the same time my mother wrote to the Indies, asking Aunt Hélène to find Sylvia a job, until then she would send her a monthly check.

Back in Grouhy, my mother's return to life was checked daily by the old village doctor. It was here that the reaction came in the form of a letter to me, which Aunt Hélène must have written when she was furious. This document too sounds so authentic that it should speak for itself.

Dear Arthur,

Sylvia told me that you were the one who convinced her mother to send her to the Indies. Where did you get such a crazy idea of presenting us with a *fait accompli*? You acted like a chicken with its head cut off. Who do you think you are, asking us to solve the problems that have become too much for you. If you wanted to be firm with your mother, why didn't you persuade her to let Sylvia get married? That at least would have been the fitting end to her work, that adopted child, the child of fortune, her mascot!!! But no, Sylvia's happiness was sacrificed, and your mother, who has such an intensely difficult personality, could find no other candidate, and now that Sylvia's beginning to cause problems, you think we're good enough to receive this little present. Thanks a lot for the great honor.

Jobs are really not for the asking here, what with the Depression. People are being laid off in large numbers. You can be sure that, if we don't succeed in finding her a job, Sylvia will be put right back on the boat again. Why don't you take her in with you; then you'll see for yourself how nice it is to receive such a present. We're all deeply indignant about the way you acted. I think your dealings with Sylvia are criminal and wicked. For shame! I'll ask you not to show this letter to your mother because if she faints again, she'll blame me and overlook the real cause. If you show her the letter, it's at your own risk. You are such horrible egoists. I will end now. I'm afraid my anger will make me write more than I should.

Aunt Hélène

After my mother's death I went to visit Dorine Felsen in Paris. I had to tell her what had happened, and I also wanted to feel the Grouhy atmosphere again, which I had almost completely put out of my mind in Meudon. I felt it with the first words.

"I always knew," she said, " that it would end like this. I clearly saw that they would steal terribly from your mother when she died, and I told her so. I said, 'My darling, my heart is heavy, but I can't tell you everything.' And that Austrian, who left just before she died, she knows a lot about where everything went. There's a mean woman for you, and a German spy."

I recognized, along with her crackling voice, her words: terrible, wonderful, incredible. How could I have forgotten her for so long? This time I took notes.

First of all, there was her early morning care of all her physically and morally sick friends. For that she had to get up at three o'clock in the morning and work till five. She was completely used to it by now. She would lie half naked by the open window, sometimes when it was fifteen degrees. If it weren't for the trance, she would have gotten sick a long time ago. She showed me the movements she did with her head, shoulders, and arms to get into it—that is the trance—after which she would give thanks by kneeling on the floor, and turning and bowing her head three times in all directions. This was the Hindu way her guru had taught her. Did I remember how she had met her guru, during the war, in Nice? She was walking around, obsessed, when suddenly she stood in a strange house in front of his room. She had knocked: "Come in."[3] He just looked at her. He had known for a long time that she would come. He said: "Your soul has nothing to do with your envelope; your soul is *ours*." Her soul happens to be oriental, just like mine. I am also "incredibly psychic," I now learned. Our oriental souls are related to each other; only our Western minds are different. She's now a guru herself. I am too. We are really colleagues.

As for Jesus—well, she simply can't think of that as just another story. It goes much deeper and is much more beautiful. But in the Oxford group she doesn't say that, because they need to hear about "Christ." You can't talk about deeper things with simple people. She once told a minister: "Now that we're good friends, tell me, where did Jesus live? Some people say one place, others another. You don't know either? That's because he never really existed. Buddha existed; we know the palace where he was a prince and so forth." The minister just laughed; he couldn't give away the secret after all. But later a colonel's wife had told her that in *her* opinion the Buddha story was just an oriental version of the Jesus legend. (All these people have their own ideas, and they compete with each other in their profundity.)

The symbolism is much more profound and therefore much more beautiful than the story. Everything is childishly simple if you understand it: John the Evangelist and Mary, the sister of Martha, stand for the head; Joseph and Mary are the heart; John the Baptist and Mary Magdalen are the sex organs. She put her hands on all the appropriate spots as she talked.

"Why was John the Baptist so sexual?" I asked, but I got no explanation, only an interpretation: "Yes, he represents the male sex."

When she was nineteen, she made a drawing of two triangles superimposed with a point in the middle: God in the center of the male and female triangles. The male triangle was red, the female green. Her mother was such a materialist that she said: "Don't show that to anyone, my child, because they'll think you're mad."

I listened without comment. She laughed wildly and I smiled back uncomfortably, embarrassed by her total abandon, which at the same time was so good-natured. The Hindu had told her her work would change once she was married, which meant when she had a "male fluidum" next to her, which would help her. Not if her husband were a weakling, of course; then he would only draw from her.

She gave an example. A friend of hers refused to have anything physical to do with her husband, so he was forced to be naughty. She had said to him: "Willie, have you ever been naughty?" He looked at her mischievously and said: "Let's go for a walk." And when he died nobody knew why, but it was, she whispered, sy-phi-lis!... Then she gave details about the wife, who was very sensual herself, because she was tubercular. I didn't understand why she had denied her husband her favors, but it's not worth asking such questions. Perhaps it was as a penance, or a spiritual exercise, according to one way of thinking, which Dorine Felsen disapproved of, and was never intended by the gurus.

Talking about that same friend to Rijckloff, she had said, "At nine o'clock every morning she takes incense into the kitchen to drive out all the bad fluidums of the servants, their anger and quarrels and so forth. And then she stays there till eleven."

"And what does she do there?" Rijckloff asked.

"She makes delicious croquettes."

It startled Rijckloff how close the two worlds seemed to be.

I turned the conversation to him. Yes, she remembered him very well. He would come to a bad end. He was a straight-faced hypocrite who had sent many a woman home with child. I said he couldn't be such a hypocrite, because he had quite a reputation as a lover. Yes, but in Grouhy she had caught him with that Austrian. He had kissed her on the mouth just as she was coming down the stairs. She looked sly again, and I remembered how she looked sitting at our dinner table, always sparkling and vivacious, and yet totally defenseless to Rijckloff's teasing.

"You know, of course," he said with his solemn voice once, "that séances can be extraordinarily dangerous."

She nodded vigorously: "Terribly."

"Quite recently, I don't know if you read about it, somebody at a séance raped the materialization. It was a materialized girl, and ten months later—one month is added for spirits, of course—during another séance, the child was born. It was a grayish balloon and had a little string for an umbilical cord, like children's balloons...."

She stared at him at first, her mouth open and her eyes wide, and only then did it occur to her that he might be joking.

For her, life is full of fascinating mysteries, not full of jokes. A few days before, she had visited a house where an aged maid opened the door, and she felt compelled to say: "Let me look at your face for a second! My God, is it possible there still are such pure faces on the earth! That's wonderful!" The maid had been embarrassed and must have thought she was crazy, but she had to say it. And no, she was grateful to God that he had given her a sound mind in a sound body, she said, as she slapped her upper arm with her hand. "Look, I have the arm of a girl of eighteen, and the rest is just the same."

Finally, since this was what I had come for, she got to the most fascinating revelations, those about Grouhy. She could tell me, now that I was married. My mother had done everything she could to push her into my arms. My mother was such an egoist. She had thought, "In so doing, Guy would get a good mother, my son a good wife, and I a good friend." My mother had used magic; she had felt it the entire time she was in Grouhy. She had seen a *hadji* woman materialize at my mother's bed; she had later recognized this woman in a picture on the wall. My mother sent incredible sums to the Indies for magic. She had two helpers, an old *hadji* and this woman, who was terribly strong. She, Dorine, had had to summon all her strength, because she felt the resistance when she would work in Grouhy in the early morning; that had been my mother's will, trying to push her into my arms.

I looked at her, well meaning. I could really be thankful for getting so much more than I had hoped. "Your mother," she said, "could look terribly mischievous. She could look at me from her bed laughing, but Dorine wasn't born yesterday either. 'No darling,' I would say then, 'your son and I aren't meant for each other. He's so terribly sensual, he would be done with me in three weeks, whereas I would only be beginning, because once my subliminal self is set aflame....'"

And again it was the oriental souls that clicked but the Western minds that didn't. She had known it from the first time she saw me. "And you never wanted to come to Grouhy, when I was there. Your opinion of me was: 'What a hysterical woman!' "—At this point I raised a question to divert her without contradicting her.

"Let's have a *rijsttafel* here soon, and bring your wife," she said when I left. "I make a *rijsttafel* in Paris just as elaborate as in The Hague, if only you give me a little warning. And if Dorine can do something for you, you know that I help everybody, and gladly."

Women like her, who are just a little better educated, more well read and less well meaning, write memoirs about the famous men they have known, saved, devoured, and made over.

It's as if I'm writing a satire, yet that's not exactly true. I'm not just satirical about the madhouse of Grouhy, and I would be hypocritical if

I painted myself as completely innocent. I started this chapter in bad weather; I'm finishing it during a moonlit night. A little while ago I sat for a long time on a slope, the grass against my back, softly whistling "Sourire d'Avril" while I watched the moon paint a milky way on the ocean's surface.

If I may praise myself in this sad story, it's for not withdrawing from the madhouse, because I never could decide for sure that I was the only one who was suffering, or who lost the most, since I was "worth so much more." This point of view may be vanity, but I never was so vain as to think I was more important than the rest. And then, of course, there are also the intangible factors that destroy all reasoning. I loved my mother; that was a fact. I was fond of Suzanne and felt I had to take care of her; that was another. If my mother gave me the cheapest furniture for my Brussels apartment, deep down I understood why: "He mustn't be too comfortable there, that way he'll come back soon to the comfort of Grouhy." But I owed it to both her and myself to ignore all this and, moreover, it wasn't hard to be indifferent to these tactics. Perhaps somewhere I had the dark feeling myself that I had to pay for my part in the confusion. In any case I can honestly say that I was rarely out to save my own skin at the expense of others. But hindsight is more meaningless than anything else. If you could prove that my actions were based on the most hypocritical mixture of spinelessness and character, of pride and masochism, then I would still believe that it would take other circumstances to force me to act any differently.

29 Back in Paris

December. After some difficulty we got the money for Grouhy before we left Brittany. After deducting the mortgage and the interest due, the money Jane's family had loaned us, and a fairly large sum put in escrow for Suzanne, there was exactly five hundred guilders left for me. We were still waiting for the money from the auction, so we went back to Paris, full of restraint and with a carefully calculated budget. Within three days Jane found a room with a Russian family in Auteuil. The neighborhood is new to us, but Balzac lived there and the Count of Monte Cristo, I think, had his country house there. This is no longer the country, but an outlying neighborhood of Paris. Its proximity to the Bois de Boulogne is the greatest attraction. Here and there it looks like nothing more than a prosperous village.

We still have to get used to it. The first days were completely taken up with new assignments for the paper. Nonetheless, there's little to report about Paris itself: all attention has been diverted to the so-called arsonists of the Reichstag, and Dimitrov commands the fascination of both friend and foe.

Our room is medium sized and divided by an enormous armoire with a mirror. We have made arrangements to cook in the house, which wasn't hard because the kitchen is on the other side of the dark hall. The constant feeling that we have to make do, as if we were staying with friends, is not really conducive to work, and the first week it was so miserably cold that the little stove was inadequate for our room. The old Russians—a former senator and supreme court prosecutor, now seventy, and his wife who is ten years younger and has all the charm of a sweet little old lady from one of Couperus's The Hague novels[1]—knock on the door all the time to ask if we need anything. The very first morning the little old lady came and sat on our bed to elaborate on the immediate liking she took to Jane. (I was a disappointment to her: she had expected a tall, middle-aged man with a beard.) She now comes in four times a day to apologize for the cold weather, so exceptional for Paris, and for the inadequate wood stove, which otherwise is so good for your health. She brings us a coverlet or a coat to put on the bed, since she doesn't have any more blankets, unfortunately. We tell each other: "It can't go on like this!"—but when she is there, and tells us stories about "typical Russian emigrants" like themselves, we ask her to sit down, and we listen and smile. She has a pleasant face, charming manners, and a sense of humor, although her voice is like that of a constantly whining child.

The old man with his narrow brown face and white goatee looks more like an Arab than a Russian and he doesn't make any noise when he walks, because although he limps he's very thin and small. He has invited us into their living room to talk a couple of times, but now that we still haven't done so after a week, we just pass each other in the hall. He answers our "Comment allez-vous?" every time with the admonition, "Ah! tout à fait français!"[2] Our greeting reminds him of his gout, which he doesn't want to be reminded of, and he always demonstrates to us the Russian greeting, which is so much more tactful. The old lady asked in a lowered voice about Couperus's picture, which is hanging on the wall and which she looks at over and over again, convinced that such a serious, middle-aged gentleman must be Jane's father. "My husband used to be a great orator. Do you know what it meant to be a high Russian official in the judiciary?" I said I had read *The Death of Ivan Illich* but that was all. From that moment on, she decided I was incredibly well versed in Russian literature.

She saved her husband from the hands of the Bolsheviks, and indeed seemed to have shown no fear. But he had such a good reputation that even a People's commissar had said he was the only honest man among all his colleagues. "Who was that again?" she asked him and he answered, nodding his head and smiling at us from beneath his wrinkles, "Uh huh"—a puff of air escapes from his thick lower lip when he smiles and talks at the same time— "It really doesn't matter, some bandit or other."

Because of the cold and the continuous visits we can't get used to our room. We look for a café for the hour we have to leave while our room is being cleaned, and we finally find one that suits us, at the intersection of two boulevards, kitty-corner from the race track, bordering on a huge open area from where you can see the first trees of the Bois de Boulogne. But the streets still seem empty and somber to us.

As soon as we were caught up with our column for the newspaper, we spent an evening with the Vialas. Nothing is new with them: he is doing the same proofreading with a couple of little unexpected jobs and Manou still is hoping to win the lottery. When we think of our one room, we comfort ourselves that at least it is light in comparison to the dark rooms they live in. Our Russian neighbors have visitors all the time, and the walls are so thin that I have to write with a constant din of voices around me, but I blame my sensitivity on myself and think of Multatuli, who wrote *Max Havelaar*[3] in that horrible Rue de la Montagne in Brussels, in weather that was twice as cold. And he managed to finish it in a month. His is all the more crushing an example because, compared to him, my social tragedy is mere child's play....

Today, our tenth day in Paris, we went to see the Héverlés. They have been back from their polar expedition for a long time; all the wonderful stories about polar bears have already been forgotten. Héverlé shakes my hand as if we had seen each other yesterday and hands me a newspaper clipping he has just received. There is a repulsive picture of him in which he looks like a *jeune premier* getting fat and a hateful commentary which plays off Héverlé against his talent. It accuses him of dressing too well, speaking too easily and in banalities, and as if his opinion of others is, "Poor creatures, you don't know that the only thing that matters is to be Héverlé."

I stop, excited about what I've read so far, and tell him I'm jealous of this article.

"You're not easily satisfied," he says with a laugh. "He insinuates that I'm a crook, a fool, and a homosexual, and the strangest thing is I've never even seen the man. All right, let's go on to more serious matters."

The most important thing is that now he has chosen Communism for real. Dimitrov's trial has forced him to speak out publicly and he will continue to do so. He doesn't have the slightest urge to leave Paris now. On the contrary, he thinks that something may happen here soon and, in any case, there is all this new activity. Meeting halls with thousands of people, loudspeakers which echo your previous sentence while you're speaking the next. (I say, "Which must prevent you from listening to yourself.") His voice changes. He has the same precise, nervous speed, without the slightest trace of false pathos, and a great seriousness behind it all. It's not at all a conversion, he explains, even though I may be a little surprised. It's all quite self-evident, as if everything had to lead to this logically, in spite of his individualism, which he has never denied.

"I've got something for my next speech," he says. "Let Dimitrov's executioners be careful that the axe they hold above his head does not mirror to the world the face of a hero!"[4]

"They'll applaud," I say, "even if they only understand the last word. But what do you feel when you say such a thing?"

"It's less complicated than you think. When you speak in public you project yourself, so it goes according to unavoidable laws. I'm using this to express, in the most effective way I can, what I really mean. Besides, there is a certain poetry to the image."

I don't respond. His intensity, the suspense which connects every word, his face which is pale and burning at the same time, the chaos I notice when he talks about politics, about the conflict between ideology and action, the temporizing—it's like a car without a steering wheel or brakes but which you drive as if you had everything under control—it makes me wonder what he's trying to escape when he involves himself in all this, not what society but what he is escaping in himself.

"To hang on to individualism," he says, "is still a possibility, of course. I am only afraid that soon it won't be a viable one and then you lose anyhow. That way, at least, they can't accuse you of opportunism, if that's any consolation. You say something like, 'To die on your own account,' but I don't believe that means anything. In this manner you'll soon die because of yourself."

And he comes back to his great theme, to die for what has the deepest meaning for this age, for what will replace Christianity in the end for all mankind. Is this just exchanging one lie for another? No, this can never be as much of a lie—even if you assume that everything is interpretation—because of the rationality of this interpretation. And moreover, assuming that everything is relative, that means that you automatically seek refuge in the moment you're living in. Communism offers the deepest potential now available to man. Do I want to call it a political movement and nothing else? That seems rather limited to him.

"It is perhaps a truth," I say, "just like Christianity was the Truth for Christians, but as long as that's not the case for me, I can wait until grace touches me."

"I have no quarrel with taking Communism in a religious sense, if that's what you want, not as a faith, though, but as a religion. After all, you don't have to believe in a Holy Trinity when you become a Communist! But how can you live without a feeling like that? Do you believe in art, in love? Your individuality is condemned beforehand if all you think is that it's different from the rest. It may work wonderfully in your search for your own truth, but this truth, do you think it is any better than the other ones because it's the only one that works for your individuality? What a positive concept for someone who sees everything in terms of relativity, but all right, I accept it. What is your truth then? Love? But that's another religion! Love, moreover...."

Bella comes in from the other room and asks us to join her. She has slimmed down again and looks so much younger that she reminds me of the woman who opened the door for me eight years ago, and who I took to be Héverlé's cousin. Everything is Persian in the other room, the mantlepiece, the long table, the pillows, and the painted tapestries on the doors, everything except for one thin Kuanyin statue from the T'ang period, almost male-looking, with no breasts and a protruding belly.

Bella points proudly to the couch. There is the child. It wiggles on its back between Jane and Bella, but it also can sit up by itself and then it looks around with enormous eyes. What might be funny in the rest of its little face is already canceled out by this great potential for melancholy.

"She already has an admirer," Bella says, "the son of one of Luc's communist friends. He says, 'She's very sweet and not only that, her father and mine belong to the same party. I would like to give her a ring, but wouldn't she swallow it?'"

Héverlé, who has been laughing along with us for a second, asks if "the object" can be taken away now.

"Yes," says Bella, "but she behaves admirably in this room. She likes it here best and I think it's great that these are her first impressions."

I stand by one of the tapestries on a door and nod understandingly. The scene on the tapestry is four or five naked women dancing with flopping breasts.

"I wish I had grown up in such a room," I say. And to Héverlé, "You were saying, 'Love, moreover. . . .'"

"O yes, we must continue with our delineation of what is true and what isn't. Love, moreover, is quite limited too. There's nothing so foolish as the everlasting immutability that people try to ascribe to it.

You are fooled just as much if you believe that there is only total love and only one mode for it, the absolute. Love always changes. If it changes over the years, even if it becomes deeper, then it is no longer itself. The need for eternity...."

"I don't believe all that much in an eternity which ends so irrevocably in death."

"Life is sometimes long enough. You don't choose somebody to die with but to live with, I'm sorry to say."

"And I'm sorry to say, the women who 'give themselves,'" says Bella, "give themselves only to those they have to live with, you know."

"So, to get back to your subject," Héverlé continues, "your conception of the problem of loyalty is badly stated. So Jane has no inclination to deceive you, all right; if she does get such an inclination, what has happened? Does she love you less? Perhaps not even that! I don't want to defend the idea of biological determinism because I'm not a biologist, but still the importance of things like hormones deserves some consideration. If it's true that someone who goes to bed with one person all his life is the same as somebody who lives as a celibate.... Take someone, husband or wife, who says, 'My spouse is unfaithful to me.' 'Why?' 'Because he loves me less.' 'Isn't that terrible?' 'No, because he has simply reached the next stage of his metabolism.' I don't say this would make infidelity pleasant, but it would completely alter the nature of the pain. It just so happens that there are lots of things that are difficult and unpleasant when you live with someone, but sexual infidelity is suddenly no longer a betrayal of love, but almost the opposite."

"Arthur doesn't look very convinced," Bella says. "Try to think, Arthur, that your wife wants to go to bed with another man just as she might want to buy a goldfish. What would you think about that?"

"Nothing much, I guess. It's just somewhat hard to accept if her goldfish becomes an indigestible whale. Or the ghost of a whale, maybe, but just as hard to stomach. So I stick to my idea that I'd rather leave than surrender to these stomach problems."

"You don't have the right to leave somebody who needs you and loves you."

"Bravo! And who would tyrannize me in the cruelest way by hiding behind the slogan of 'To each his freedom'? But perhaps I will convert after I have studied the complete list of determined biological changes and if that list is guaranteed to be true."

"I don't dare guarantee its truth, I again am sorry to say," says Héverlé.

"Until that time, I'll take the liberty to consider the little goldfish less innocent than Bella has suggested. You betray each other's love perhaps when you enjoy a cup of coffee too, but you can do that in the other's presence. As long as your goldfish can't be enjoyed in the other's presence...."

"What he's saying is not so dumb," Héverlé's voice sounds from far away.

"The person who leaves is always the least honest," says Bella with a certain fierceness. "If you left, you would...."

"What does he care about honesty, for God's sake," interrupts Héverlé in my place. "If he had to go on living with the other while hating her, he would be perfectly right in leaving. But perhaps he won't have that feeling; that's another possibility. He can't know what he'll feel before it comes to that. So *she* (he glances at Jane) would have to sacrifice herself first to give the necessary proof."

"I'm still not at all in a sacrificing mood," says Jane.

"And she says it with pain. What does witness Ducroo say?"

"That he can't say anything, if the others believe it won't happen anyway."

"But assuming it would," says Bella, "would you really leave and make the other suffer?"

"Oh, with the greatest pleasure. You have no idea with how much pleasure. I earnestly hope that not a speck of generosity would be left in me. If this were the only recourse for revenge, I would do my best to make the most of it. But it would probably be hard to stay away. So I would try to latch on to something else as soon as possible, something I couldn't betray right away. Communism for example. What an opportunity for politics!"

Bella and Héverlé exchange glances.

"The madness of idealizing can really be great," he begins.

"Terrible," Bella interrupts forcefully. "All evil comes from that. I would hate to be idealized as a woman. I don't need somebody to tell me how valuable I am and what I owe to that value. I'm not all that bad, at least in my own eyes, really! There was a man, Arthur, who loved a woman and so he impressed upon her twice a week that she wasn't as worthwhile as she could have been, and mind you—this is the best part—she didn't cheat on him at all. She had had two lovers before him; that was all. But imagine, two. He should have considered himself lucky; she wasn't one-eyed after all and had passed sixteen a long time ago. She met him and began to love him, but he developed a hatred for her past, as if she had placed a new lover in his lap every day. He'd say to her: 'I suffer unspeakably every day because I can't ever forget those two creeps who were able to touch you however they wanted.' Now, tell me honestly what your opinion of that is."

I shrug my shoulders. "I'd have to know all the gentlemen first. Did this man have the right to consider his two predecessors creeps?"

"If he had the right to hate them," says Héverlé. "And he had that right if they prevented him from idealizing the woman. So you see, everything is utterly logical."

"Arthur," says Bella, "it's much more serious than you think. For almost every woman her first man is a mistake. I was perhaps not as clever as you might think when I chose the gentleman over there. He could just as well have been somebody else. The first one is usually just the first idiot who presents himself. Even if she loves him; after all, it's not only she who's available, but her love too, mostly. The second is more serious, at least if she learned anything from her first experience."

Héverlé makes a gesture as if he's trying to erase it all.

"Not at all, that's an extremely optimistic scenario. There are also a number of women who go from the first to the forty-fifth glissando to the garbage heap. And in this context, the gentleman you just described has the right to ask himself, 'If those two people could touch her, who am I then?'"

All four of us begin to laugh. At the same time the child on the couch bursts out screaming, attracting everyone's attention. I don't remember which point of view each of us really defended, but this unmistakable explosion of anger takes on the character of deepest mystery. Bella lifts the child to her shoulder and with three steps she is out of the room, the slight waving of the naked dancers indicating which way.

Héverlé takes a puff of his cigarette, reflectively. "Sexuality seems more serious to me, though. In a future civilization, they will be inclined perhaps to laugh about Freud's complexes as we laugh about Woronov's monkey glands. It's all right with me. You can also imagine some tribe or other, where these torments are explained as the work of demons. Complexes, glands, secretions, hormones, demons: my preference is for the most concrete. But demons are sometimes very concrete for me. I didn't fill endless sheets of paper with them for nothing."

I own a sheet of those scribbles with a saw devil as the principal demon; it is elongated with thin legs and a trunklike protrusion on its cat's head and the toothed back of a camel-chameleon.

"I'm also very much for it," I say, "and language will take us where we want to go. Saw devils and prickle ghosts, spirit of salt and salt demons, hormodemony, hormonomania, in a word. Héverlé, when people begin laughing again about this Pantheon of the medicine men, they still won't have eliminated the demon of the crime passionnel."

"But there has always been a lot of good in the medicine men, so why not now too? You're the one who always denies evolution, and here you're wrong in thinking in such an evolutionary manner! Take a woman who can't get pregnant by one man, who takes another man and bears a child for the first one. Or take a woman who has no temperament; her husband suffers from it, the medicine man gives her four shots, and she starts bothering everybody."

"That's an ideal cure for the Dutch novel," says Jane. "For forty years they've been writing novels in Holland about cool women and passionate men and vice versa. Perhaps this will finally revive our literature."

"Arthur," says Bella, "my grandfather was fond of my grandmother, an unusually pretty woman he had eloped with. They lived happily together until late in life, in absolute fidelity, as was necessary in their time. Then my grandmother died and my grandfather cried terribly. And then he... discovered the happiness of being alone again. That upset him, but he couldn't deny it. Not until three years later did he suddenly begin to speak about 'his poor Lisa' again, and my mother said: 'Just wait, he's not going to make it much longer.' And a few days later he was dead."

"And the moral of the story is: 'Even the greatest love can look different from what you think.' Jealousy too," says Héverlé. "There are even people who think they have become jealous because of love, who, if you look a little closer, would be much less deprived without love than without jealousy. It's a grim way of sacrificing yourself to the eternal madness."

"Why," adds Bella, "is jealousy a result of the physical side of infidelity? Why is everything localized in the body? I used to be painfully jealous of Luc's friends sometimes when I thought he discussed things with them he thought he couldn't discuss with me. And if a man knew how a woman can feel for her child, he might very well be jealous of the child, more than anything else. A child is a third person in a relationship of two! Can you imagine, Arthur, how foolish a man is not to be jealous of his child?"

"I can only imagine what can be put in terms of hormodemony."

"A woman," says Jane, "can sometimes feel she betrays her husband by giving up her own personality. The more she identifies with her husband, the more she attaches herself to him, and the more he gives her, the more she may even lose of what she likes in herself. A woman gives herself quite differently from what a man usually imagines. But the worst part is when she realizes that the woman she wants to give and the woman she is, are no longer one and the same. You may laugh, but it's a fearful inadequacy. If she's loyal, she thinks it's not only inadequate for herself but for her husband too, and he perhaps hasn't even noticed it. Why isn't he jealous of the lost part of her?"

"Because he has swallowed it himself," I say. "But in this case all things go wrong for the woman, because she just can't win. You can't choose someone you admire for his stronger personality as a comrade in arms and then clash with him all the time, because his personality is too strong."

"Sexually," says Héverlé, "it's all much simpler. How many men find a new woman at home after they've just been with other secretions? If you knew a certain Parisian world better, you would talk about this much more seriously. All a husband's jealousy evaporates when he understands that according to this logic he always defeats the lover. In the first place, it's just plain wrong to think the lover always wins. On the contrary, the lover always loses, except when there is an obsolete bourgeois prejudice that prevails. The lover simply introduces the necessary alien materials. The husband is only defeated when his wife decides to leave him to follow her lover. Until that point the lover is defeated on both fronts, spiritually and sexually. Only a husband with Christian prejudices suffers any loss. So you have the free choice to win or lose, Ducroo; will you admit that?"

"No, because I never felt so fierce a Christian as with this saving word."

Why did we talk about this for so long, when we could have talked about politics and Communism? How fascinating can these skirmishes still be for Héverlé, and why do I remember almost every single word and yet have this aftertaste of irritating futility?

"You impose a law," said Héverlé, "and then you're always strong. If a law can really be broken in love and everything collapses with that...."

Of all dialectics (you can prove everything), this sounds like the only important thing. That law is the same as truth for me; to deny the sexual claim in love is suicide.

Or is it, taking everything into consideration, the man from the Indies in me who protests—against Europe, against Paris? Perhaps twice over now, after the concessions I made in my acting days? Oh well, these statements serve no purpose. The protest comes from deep within me, the rest is only intellectual analysis.

I find Guraev by himself, in a cold studio, his head totally shaven. He does that once a year. It's not so much a habit from his cadet or sailor days, he says, but because he gets bored being a pretty boy so long. He is also wearing a coarse suit and sandals like a vegetarian. He looks at me from the couch, his arms folded across his chest, nodding his head and smiling, and repeats as if surprised, "Hm! It's nice to see you again; it's really nice." Without hair, his head is rounder and his face looks both older and more cheerful. "Business is going badly at the moment," he says. "It's cold here and both women have gone out to try to find a job. Why don't we go out too?" He dons a worker's cap, takes the felt hat I admired so much from the same hat rack, and offers it to me because he remembers how well it suited me.

In the street he asks if I have heard Héverlé speak yet. "You must. He's a fantastic speaker and it makes him look young and rosy cheeked. They say that if there's a fascist revolution he will be the first to be eliminated. That's quite flattering! He explained to me the other day how he would stand behind his front door with a revolver if they came to get him, and I didn't want to tell him that they might have an arsenal with them which could pierce the door like cardboard. Well, at least he dares take a risk. That's different from you and me; we're nothing but ridiculous bourgeois."

He uses this by way of preamble to get to talk about when he wasn't a bourgeois. "You know, I fought against the Reds and can't go back to the Soviet Union. I don't care all that much, but the fact is ridiculous. I was still a child when I wore a cadet's uniform, and it wasn't because of any sense of calling. I told you that we left Constantinople when my father died. The strange thing is that as children we never believed he really had died. We weren't there when he died, and so we concluded among ourselves that he was on a dangerous mission that had to be kept secret. One day when I was about eleven, I found my mother crying. She wouldn't tell me why, and I thought this indicated that my father had now died. When I was fourteen I learned that she had rejected a marriage proposal that day because she wanted to stay with us. I decided that, as far as I was concerned, I would do whatever I could for her. I tried to figure out something and decided nothing could make her happier than my becoming a cadet. The fact that I didn't like the idea myself was proof enough I had made a good choice."

He continues. His adventures during the Russian Revolution come back to him gradually and with no seeming order: scenery, place names, later a gun boat in Vladivostok when he volunteered as a sailor. He wandered endlessly at sea, making aimless trips from one harbor to another. He vacillated between the political convictions of the commander and those of the crew. Finally he landed in London, where he quit, tired of everything and convinced that you couldn't be more aimless or alone on land.

"What do I remember really from all that?" He counts on his fingers: "One: singing at 30° C below zero when we went from Orenburg to Troitsk. I had angina then. My mouth was so swollen I couldn't put anything in it, my teeth were red, and we came to a snow-covered forest where I fell, happy, and yet certain that the wolves would come and finish me off. It was an incomparably deep happiness, Ducroo! Two: the train from Troitsk to Omsk. We struggled continuously with a cadet who was an epileptic and kept trying to throw himself out of the train. I had been constipated for two weeks and had to take care of it by hanging out of the train. Childbirth is nothing compared to that; it was a matter of life and death. Such a situation is in no way ridiculous. Three: the stop in Omsk, where I visited the military commander. Suddenly I was in a drawing room again with ladies and girls. I was sitting in a chair when I saw something white on my pants and thought it was a little hole, but it was a louse, one of the many white lice we had picked up from the peasants' houses. I was afraid I would leave it in that beautiful drawing room. Four: the first execution I witnessed in Vladivostok; it was an American prisoner—was it really an American? —who had shot at us. He tried to say, 'Let me live,' but instead he yelled, 'Mine will live,' and the others said 'No, yours shall not live.' And they shot him in the belly, three, four shots, one right after another just like in the word "precipitation." I was standing next to him, and I still know how he looked and how he fell. He was still alive when they kicked him into the water. And I thought, what if his mother saw how he died. The rest is totally different: an intense monotony filled with adventures in which I was only a spectator. At sea, in port, back to battle or not, it's all one big blur. A lot of liquor, no women. I was nine-teen and didn't want to go to the brothels, so I drank, not because I en-joyed it but to punish myself. I was pure when I disembarked in London. Pure, Ducroo, oh how pure I was!"

"And you still had the feeling that you gained something from living that way?"

"Gained something? Damn little. Not a bit, as a matter of fact. I was sick and tired of it. And then in London I saw the Russian ballet for the first time. I met a painter who worked on the sets. He took me back-stage; it was all a magic world: talent, wealth—things I'd never seen in such quantity before. And the amazing thing was that everybody was interested in me; I was Kostya Guraev, a young man of good family, former cadet, sailor-by-accident, and still so young, so modest, so artistic. The painter taught me how to work on the sets. I learned so easily that they would pat me on the shoulder in front of him and say, 'You're better than he is.' But he was the only one I admired: his ease, his impertinence to men and women alike, his disdain for all women, since he was, of course, gay. Everybody seemed to be gay, and when they admired me he would say, 'If anybody is going to go to bed with Kostya it will be me.' I didn't dare contradict him. Besides, if he had really wanted to, God only knows if I'd have dared refuse. Everything in that world overwhelmed me, and this was so much a part of it. From London I followed the ballet to Paris."

We're in a café now and he is talking loudly. An old couple behind him turns around uncomfortably all the time. He looks at me as if I'm much further away from him than I really am. There are wrinkles around his eyes, and he holds onto the edge of the table as if he were massaging it.

"And when I was in Paris I was suddenly fed up with all of that, all the gays and the directors and the rest. During this time I met Shura, who was just starting her stage career, but she barely interested me. She had a friend, also an immigrant, who had a widowed mother and was down to her last rouble. That girl, Ducroo, was so beautiful, not in a Russian way but in an Italian way. But of course she had that cursed Russian soul. Her name was Tanya, Tatyana, just like the girl in Push-kin. Watch out, if you meet a Russian woman, that you don't talk to her about mysticism or delight in her soul. They all have so incredibly much soul, far too much soul. If you compare them to French women in this, you're lost. It's as if you compared the mysticism of a cat to a pekinese. And if I say I'm bourgeois now... well, no."

He shakes his head. I think he wants to say, "I'm still Russian. You must try sometime to live with two women, as I'm doing now. I'm not saying that it's all that great, but a Frenchman couldn't pull it off."

"Ducroo," he continues with his hand on my shoulder, "if you want to know the innermost feelings of a friend, ask him to tell you what his first love was like."

This is the same surprising directness which he used when he asked me whether I felt I was a boy or a man. I often thought about writing a story in which two friends—and I would make them quite old—would mirror each other as characters in their first love affairs. I tell him about it.

"Right. I've told you before that you're so Russian. Because when I said a friend, I really meant a Russian. A Russian man has too much soul too, but it's not at all the same as with a Russian woman. A Russian man's soul makes him dumb, a Russian woman's, false. Not mean, although that's true too, but it's a by-product in the true sense of the word. But I was going to tell you. When I barely knew Tanya I asked Shura to deliver long letters to her. I got long letters in return. My letters, you understand, had so much soul in them, they were utterly ridiculous. Hers were no less ridiculous, but intentionally so. Shura told me all this later. At that time the letters delighted me. We wrote to each other, not declarations of love but hundreds of other things, mostly mysticism. When I went to see her, her mother was always there, or Shura, or one of my three rivals—all Russians about my age. Tanya and Shura were fond of dolls; they bought them and also made them; the room was full of them. Her mother was a charming woman, a little plump but still young and, in contrast to her daughter, very pale with reddish hair. She came to life when all of us were there, and she definitely liked us. One evening a strange thing happened. One of my three rivals said something insulting to Tanya, and she looked at him and paled but didn't answer. Everybody noticed it and I thought that as a former cadet, I was obliged to duel with him. But when we left that night he suddenly grabbed my arm. 'Kostya,' he said, 'I could tell that you got mad about what I said to Tanya, but you're wrong. From now on I won't see her anymore. I'll prove to myself I'm a Russian but not dumb. You'll find out I'm right about her, but I won't stand in your way.' I was so touched by those words, the 'I'm Russian but not dumb,' that my anger disappeared and I shook his hand cordially. When I was by myself I thought I wanted not to be dumb either. Meanwhile Tanya showed all my letters and hers too to Shura, and they enjoyed themselves immensely. Maybe to show I wasn't dumb, I said to Shura one day, 'Tanya doesn't know it, but she loves me.' 'Do you think so?' said Shura. 'I'm positive.' A couple of days later I was going up the stairs with Tanya when suddenly she grabbed my hand. 'You told Shura that I am in love with you,' she said, 'you're wrong, it's not true.' I was so embarrassed that I almost fell down the stairs. I didn't know what to say and spent the rest of the evening sitting somberly next to her mother. The next morning I went to Shura and reproached her bitterly. I said that I had thought she was my friend too, and I slammed the door. When I got home I realized that I was all alone in the world, and that nobody cared about me. I shared a room with a friend in a miserable hotel, and without saying anything to him I decided to end my life. But all I had was a razor blade. I took great pains to prepare myself, which is to say that I put on clean underwear and my best pajamas. Then I lay down on my bed to think about death until the moment I had decided on, five o'clock in the morning. That night was so lonely and lugubrious, even though I could hear my friend breathing in the dark. I can't describe it. But when the clock struck five I was so exhausted I couldn't go through with it. My hands trembled. I put the razor blade under my bed and fell asleep immediately. A couple of days later I tried again, but differently. I came home at one o'clock, lay down on the bed, and cut my throat, here. You can still see the scar; it's not long, but the cut was rather deep. I must have moaned when I did this. My friend woke up and turned on the light, saw me in bed with a razor blade and my shirt all bloody. All he said was, 'Oh you jerk, I'm going to get the manager.' I had half-fainted but this brought me to. 'Don't go,' I said, 'don't go.' He then helped me to wash and dress the wound and went to get a doctor. We didn't tell anyone what I had done.

"Then Ducroo,... then I felt I was Russian and incredibly dumb. But I wasn't completely better when Shura sent me a doll as a sign of peace—you'll think it's crazy, but I was elated. I went to see her right away in order to thank her. Our reconciliation was so complete that it marked the beginning of our life together, although I may still have been in love with Tanya. I moved in with Shura and didn't see Tanya anymore. I was happy because now there was somebody who cared for me. Shortly after that Tanya left Paris anyway. She had consumption and had to go abroad to a sanatorium. When she came back a year later she came to see us as if nothing had happened. But things had gone bad for her. Her mother's money was gone, and without money she couldn't get well. One day her mother went to Monte Carlo after she had studied roulette systems for months. It was the only way she could make some money for her daughter. She won ten thousand francs and wanted to take the train back immediately, but the next one didn't leave until 5 o'clock in the morning. She was dead tired but wouldn't spend money on a hotel, so she sat down in the park and fell asleep. When she woke up her purse and the money were gone.

"One evening Tanya visited us, looking thin and pale. She said she was going to the Riviera with her mother, that they were going to live in a small house there, and she wouldn't see us for a long time. She stayed until late. I walked her to the hotel door, and while we were waiting in the dark for the concierge she said, 'Kiss me.' She stood absolutely straight and didn't move. I pulled her to me and noticed that her face was covered with tears. I asked her what was the matter, but she wouldn't tell me. The door opened and she was gone.

"I never saw her again. She died on the Riviera. What I'm about to tell you is what I heard later. Once an actor talked to me about her and said she was a strange girl. He had met her in the Black Forest and had tried to seduce her. He had gone into her room and locked the door, but she had threatened to jump off the balcony. 'It was odd,' he said, 'because there was no way to be sure what she would do, and yet I was convinced she would go through with it.' Later I met one of my three old rivals, the least significant one, a Finn with straw-blond hair and black teeth. He was an epileptic, or at least he looked like one. Shura always thought it was just a gimmick to try to seduce women, for lack of anything better. One afternoon I went out while he was over, and when I came home Shura said that he had really made a fool of himself. He had had a seizure and had to lie down on the bed. With his eyes rolling and his mouth contorted, he had murmured: 'It's a seizure but it will pass. On the Riviera Tanya's mother was always so nice to me when this happened. She'd go to bed with me then.'

" 'Very sweet of her,' Shura had said. 'What do you want from me? An aspirin?' He had left, embarrassed. I told Shura she could go on seeing him but to spare me.

"Still later Shura told me that he had confided in her. He had been to the Riviera often, and Tanya had asked him to give her a child. She wanted a child before she died, and he of course had obliged. The child had been taken to Poland and lived with people he didn't know, but he had shown her a picture, she said, and it really looked like Tanya. Shura thought the story might well be true, since it was completely in Tanya's nature to choose the most impersonal father for her child. But she died very shortly after giving birth. It might even have shortened her life.

"The craziest part was that we found out she had never been honest with us, that she was in love with an older man we didn't know. Shura had seen him once or twice, and I met him much later. He was a vulgar little wimp with the face of a rat. I began to talk about Tanya, and he responded immediately. He liked to tease her, he said, because she needed it so much. He had done everything with her except 'the ultimate.' Oh,... I've talked so long and I still don't understand it. Sometimes I think my imagination has run away with me, but all this is beyond my grasp. What do you think, Ducroo? Please tell me honestly what you think. It's so nice to be able to tell each other everything honestly."

"I'm most concerned about the child. Just imagine being thrown into the world like that by the whim of a fool."

"Hmm.... Of a fool, you say. Yes, I agree, of a fool. It's terrible for the child. Yes. But... sometimes I wonder whether what I'm trying to hold onto in Shura is maybe a little bit of Tanya, or does this question come from a dumb Russian soul too? Well, there are Russians who would rather be known as bastards than just Russian and dumb. You ought to be able to understand them, Ducroo, but I've had trouble doing that. Tell me, did you read that incomparable story in the newspaper about the custom in some areas of the Balkans? When somebody dies there the youngest relative must ram some sort of a pole through the body before it's buried, a pole made of aspen wood, you know, Ducroo, the tree whose leaves always tremble ever since Judas hanged himself from one. Well, a couple of days ago an old woman died, the grandmother of the family. She was more than eighty years old, and the youngest relative—the age is not mentioned, but I imagine about eight—arrives. The old woman is in the coffin. With both hands the child bravely lifts up that enormous pole which has been sharpened to a point on one end and plants it in her navel. And guess what happens? The old grandmother comes to. She wasn't really dead, only in a coma. But, the newspaper reports laconically, she died shortly thereafter in terrible pain. Don't you think that's a wonderful story? Do you think it's sad? I can't help it, I know it's sad, but I can imagine the scene: Grandma and the youngest child. And I can laugh myself silly if I give in to my feelings. Don't you think it's poetic too, Ducroo?" he continues when I only vaguely smile and don't answer.

"Sure,... to some extent."

"No, I can see you don't have a real feel for it. Perhaps you have too much respect for old age. God knows why. But what about this; the oldest man in the world is a Turk who is one hundred and thirty, you know.... And suddenly they tell him that there's a Chinese who's five years older than he is. When they told him he got so angry that he couldn't speak for a whole minute. But then he burst out with a flood of curses, saying that the Chinese was a cheater because everybody knew he was the oldest man in the world. Ha, ha, ha! The joke, Ducroo, is that one was a Turk and the other was only a Chinese. If you don't see that, the joke is wasted on you."

He suddenly looks around quickly at the old people behind him who are just staring blankly, then back at me, and he bursts out laughing again. And then he stops. It's like an alarm clock that rings and then just trails off.

If I had told Guraev my own story he would have thought it wasn't very Russian, I'm afraid, although I was equally immature. Teresa wouldn't have appeared very colorful as a young girl in comparison to Tanya, and she would have had far too little soul, which is probably what I would have thought if she hadn't been my first important encounter in Europe. I had been in Brussels less than three months. Aunt Tina had introduced me to some artists she knew, because artists were the only people I wanted to meet. So I met a painter, and his wife who had wanted to be an actress when she was young. They both thought it was a shame I wanted to let myself slip into the life of a Parisian bohemian, which after all had nothing to do with real Art. They were certainly right, but I didn't agree with them at the time, and they decided to have me fall in love instead of nagging me any further. It would be a pity, they had decided, if I became sick instead of becoming an artist. If I fell in love and got married, I probably would escape the danger. So they took me to meet an artistic, wealthy family with two girls. The older one was very artistic but engaged. The younger one was so "sweet"—they always talked about her as if in passing, but it struck me when I visited them that she was never far away from me. Her father even liked me, although I didn't notice. I said I thought the girl was very sweet too, and I joked indifferently with her. The painter's wife had introduced me to everyone as the nephew of my well-to-do aunt, the son of no less well-to-do parents, with a fortune recently brought over from the Indies. After a litle while, however, the visits were stopped because they realized this worldly environment was not conducive to my falling in love. So in the winter they had a party at their own home, and Teresa, just back from Italy, came into the room behind her fat mama. I forgot all the artistic trivia I was discussing and this time fell in love immediately. The painter brought us together with the help of a funny story. I talked alone to her all evening, and my naïveté must have amused her. Right away she felt much older and wiser. She invited me over to complete my art education.

Even before I got there—Teresa told me later—the painter's wife had actually almost asked her mother for her hand on my behalf. I told Aunt Tina the next morning that I was madly in love with that Italian girl. I said it facetiously and laughed, but she didn't doubt it for a second. The painter's wife wasted no time; she went to see them immediately. Teresa herself received her.

"I'm afraid you'll have to wait awhile because Mama is taking a bath."

"What nonsense; we're old friends."

She went into the bathroom and sat down by the tub.

"Imagine, Arthur," Teresa said to me, "Mama, fat as she is, sitting in the hot water, which was almost running over, and her friend Loulou, dignified as ever on a chair, wearing her old-fashioned hat, its feathers trembling. And in all seriousness she asked for my hand in your name, saying you were such a wealthy young man with such fondness for the arts. Mama called me in when it was all over to talk about you. She wasn't happy at all that I had already asked you over, and Loulou's visit had startled her. But I already liked you too much to give you up."

I was very confused when I heard this, and from then on I didn't visit my aunt's artists anymore, but by then the relationship between Teresa and me was already in another stage. I had seen her in Paris and after that in Italy with friends I found intolerable, and who found me equally intolerable because I was madly in love and therefore undignified. One afternoon she let me know her heart wasn't free. When I was with her in Paris, I had met a young man with a pince-nez who walked right up to her and kissed her wrist. I remember the overwhelming sensation I had of not belonging; I felt I had to get it through my head that I was too late, moreover, that Teresa belonged to another world, that we would never understand each other, and so on. This made me very unhappy. I didn't think for a moment that the contrast itself might attract Teresa, which it certainly did during this early stage. I went away feeling defeated, tried to believe in a vicarious friendship, and wrote long letters to her from Brussels, full of nonsense, of course, but full of conviction. She wrote me back in a hurried, worldly-wise tone. It was anything but satisfying, but then the correspondence took a turn which suddenly drove me back to Italy. Without warning her I took the train, and after a thirty-hour trip I stood in front of the wall around her villa, early in the morning, dead tired, but feeling like a conqueror. I climbed on the little wall and looked over the vegetable garden which was still covered with morning haze. Finally I climbed down, walked across the lawn, and knocked at the door which was ajar. Getting no answer, I pushed the door open further. I came into a hall with a high ceiling, dark, empty, coldly disdainful. I sighed deeply and then called Teresa's name twice up the stairs. I heard stumbling behind a little door on the first floor (the kitchen door, I learned later), and Mama herself appeared, wearing an apron, her hair a mess and her face showing unpleasant surprise. "Mr. Ducroo?" she said, "I had no idea you were coming. Goodness gracious! What an early visit! Teresa is still asleep."

I announced that I would wait in the garden, and at first even there I didn't know how to make myself small enough. Finally I saw Teresa come outside; she walked slowly, her eyes down, but when she came close to me, she looked up with a sarcastic smile but friendly eyes.

"Did you think you had to surprise me like this?"

"Yes, I came to ask you if you were still in love with... that other fellow."

"Oh no," she said with the same smile, "that's more or less a thing of the past."

I said I wanted it to be completely a thing of the past, because I had come to ask for her hand. She walked alongside me, slowly, not saying anything right away; finally she said, thoughtfully, "I've been wondering for some time now, Arthur, if marriage would be good for you at this point."

I didn't let my emotions show, but it was as if I could only despise myself from then on. It didn't occur to me that Teresa might repeat her mother's words. I thought to myself, "Is this consideration worthy of either her or me? She drives me into the arms of the whores."

In the meantime she had quietly changed the subject. Her mother had decided to go back to Brussels, she said; the house was almost empty, but a few bedrooms were still kept up, and since I was there, I might as well stay. I hesitated, but she took me to her mother, who had gotten dressed in the meantime and now began to display her boisterous friendliness.

Teresa repeated her invitation and added, "You scared him, Mama."

"C'est ridicule! Ah, quel gosse!"[1] Mama yelled, chucking me under my chin. "Of course he can stay. He'll sleep badly, that's all."

I got my first kiss by the window of that villa after even I—and Teresa's mother too—had begun to think of myself as completely harmless. She had been so pleasantly condescending to me in front of Teresa, had been so cheerfully boisterous about my age, because she had discounted me as a possible husband.

"Teresa's father always said that a man had to be at least thirty before he considered marrying, Mr. Ducroo," she used to say. And now she said, shrieking, "Ah cet Arthur, il me fait rire," and "Quel gosse![2] He has to get over his romantic hatred of the world."

But one evening while I stood by the window in the third-story living room I thought I could see all of Tuscany. Teresa was next to me, dressed in a brightly colored housedress. Her mama had left her needlework for a moment, but we heard her walk in the adjacent room.

"Teresa," I said, "come close to me."

"No."

"Why not?"

"Because I'd rather not be tempted."

I took her hand, and she moved so close to me that her hair touched my cheek.

"What temptation?"

She shook her head. "Let's not talk about it."

"Or let's say that you love me just a little?"

"A little too much, perhaps."

I ventured putting my arm around her shoulder very gently and pulled her toward me. Her body gave in so willingly that it seemed to me that she was making a fool of me again, but she smiled at me over her shoulder. I found her mouth, but not for long, and the worst part was that we couldn't make a sound. She pushed me away when she heard her mother coming back, who picked up her needlework again, and I said good night because I couldn't have stayed a moment longer. I went downstairs in the dark to the floor my room was on. Mama came to the landing and asked if I had any matches and could I find the door. I said I would be fine, but Teresa followed me down the stairs with a lit match in one hand, and the box of matches in the other. When she gave me the box, the match went out. Mama was still standing on the landing above us and said something to me again. While I was answering, I felt Teresa press herself against me and as soon as I had finished, her mouth found mine in the dark. When she withdrew, it was my turn to strike a match.

"Good night," Mama yelled, jubilantly.

"Good night," I said. "Thank you, Teresa."

I heard her laugh softly as she went back up the stairs.

The next day all sorts of people came by, but I still managed to be alone with Teresa for a moment. I didn't think I had won any rights to her, of course, but she came to me, and for three days I glowed with happiness. Everywhere I went, in the garden, in the street, in cafés, in a museum, either accompanied by Teresa or alone, I thought I was the only really happy man, even in this privileged country. I helped Mama clear out a room—and broke a mirror—I pumped water for the kitchen, and I carried Teresa up the stairs to the top floor without anyone's seeing us. After that everyone left the villa. We traveled back to Brussels, and as soon as we were in the train my paradise was lost. I returned immediately to the behavior in front of other people that had been a source of annoyance for Teresa before: I was a young bear who couldn't even apologize when he stepped over people's knees. She became upset and told me frankly I was uncivilized. In response I used what I thought were delicately sarcastic jokes. By the time we got to Brussels, Teresa had been pouting for hours—later I thought a certain physical condition might be the simple explanation for her bad mood. Her mama, however, remained protective, pleasant, and cheerful.

In Brussels our conflict continued. Teresa now criticized my opinions, which she thought were ridiculous. Everyone knows that, after all, people need other people in life, and she for one would never be able to live without a lot of people around her. As soon as I realized that the good manners required of me had a social significance, I began to resist fiercely. I decided to choose Teresa's friends myself. I was pleasant to an unmarried aunt I liked, but almost rude to a married one, who had been a famous beauty and who had bleached hair and bluish-pink cheeks. When her acquaintances annoyed me I would ignore everyone but her dog, a little French bull terrier whose name was Pia. One winter evening I went out with her and her friend, who thought that she should point out the poor condition of my overcoat. She thought that it was an insult to Teresa because, since I was not poor, I did not have to wear such an overcoat when I took her out. I took the coat off, then and there, despite all the protests of both Teresa and her friend. They were afraid I'd get sick, so we went inside as soon as possible, but when we were back outside, the protests started up again; I only smiled and said I didn't want to insult Teresa. I held no grudge against her friend, but I did toward Teresa for having talked to her about me, and as a result we quarreled for several days. My behavior made it impossible for her to introduce me as a husband in her circles. She blamed me for it, I wouldn't do anything for her, and so on. I told her that she would have to give up everything for me, that I would have to be enough for her. She couldn't do that, she had never imagined such a marriage, she said. Now she realized that I was too young and needed a lot more experience. Her mother's belittling was beginning to have its effect.

I was too young. I kissed her, and held her in my arms till our faces glowed, till she walked out of the room and then came back on condition I wouldn't start all over again. But I didn't think of pushing any further. We would either have to get married or break it off completely. I slipped my hand around her bare shoulder and ran it down her arm till the back of my hand just touched her breast. It would have scared me to think she might want me to take even a little more liberty. I was not in the least a Don Juan, which perhaps disappointed her. She might have expected something different from my "oriental origin," without daring to admit it. I even wondered later if she were a virgin. At that time the opposite would have been so normal. She was about twenty-two when I met her, two months older than I was. Perhaps the Parisian gentleman with the pince-nez who had kissed her wrist so boldly had been as proper as I was, according to the modern code.

But it was over with him. My brief glory had interfered. Only it had turned out that I was not a suitable husband, and meeting my parents must have dashed Teresa's last hopes. My father would have liked this marriage, particularly since he had heard that Teresa's family had the right to the title of marquis. Like my mother, he always dressed very well, and they had done their best, but what hopelessly uneducated people they seemed to Teresa, and later to Teresa's mama! I didn't understand this right away either. It only dawned on me later, when Teresa said she could feel how much I must want to run away from tout ce radotage.[3] After she had spent a little time in Paris again, she announced to me one day that she was going to be engaged to the son of a well-known Left Bank sculptor, after which Mama (to soothe my hurt feelings?) commented that it was "ce milieu si fin, si cultivé"[4] which had attracted Teresa most of all. I was terribly unhappy, and I noticed that she really didn't care all that much for him. Was it just to get away from me that she had chosen him? He sometimes came to Brussels for a short visit and would go to the theater with Teresa and her mother. One evening he brought them home in a taxi and left them standing in front of their house while he drove away with their key in his pocket. They had to follow him to his hotel in another taxi just to get into their own house. If it had happened to me, Teresa's mama would have crucified me. The night of the engagement party he wasn't there; he was too busy in Paris. I was there and kissed Teresa a hundred times in his place. And I said out of the innocence of my own heart: "I believe you love me more than you know yourself."

"I even believe I know it," she said, "and what's more, I'm proving it to you, don't you think?"

She broke the engagement when she was in Italy and wrote me asking if I wanted to visit the country house. There was even a sentence in that letter like "Devenez donc le gentleman rêvé."[5] I went, but I had gotten over most of my pain. I was determined to play the game differently. I brought a Swiss friend with me, and they understood that this put me in a position of strength. Teresa was not friendly when I arrived, mostly because once again I had arrived so quickly and unexpectedly. There was a huge group of guests who knew all about the

broken engagement and also something about me. I went to Pisa with
my friend until I would be more welcome. We ran into one of Teresa's
Italian admirers, who wrote Mama that my friend was a parasite. I had
met him the year before, and had played tennis with him. He was
about six years older than I. He had seen some action during the war
and said that he was old, pointing to his two or three gray hairs over
and over again. His name was Mazetta, but I called him Mazetti, quite
innocently. (The name of an Italian male has to end in *i*, I probably
thought.) He corrected me again and again in a very friendly fashion
and invited me to dinner. I accepted immediately, much to Teresa's
displeasure, who wondered when I would learn to avoid such simple
European traps. I had a very pleasant dinner with the fellow, and
when he was back home, he wrote letters asking about me as questo
bravo giovane.[6] I had taken him to the station, and because he had
a stiff shoulder from a war injury, I had carried his suitcase. He must
have had a good impression of me.

In Pisa I discussed with my friend what options were still open to
me. He was afraid I didn't insist enough and rationalized too much,
and with women he felt that this ruined everything. Even before he
finished I was convinced he was right, and that the next time I saw
Teresa again, I would be able to say good-bye right away. But this fore-
taste of defeat was coupled with the strangest fantasies. Since she
would never be mine, I wanted to suggest to her that she let me see her
naked at least once. And in my imagination the spot I had chosen for
this was a second-story terrace where I knew she sometimes sun-
bathed. But it would have to take place at night by moonlight. She
would have to hide on the terrace, and when I had caught sight of her
(and worshipped her, as was fitting) I would slide to the ground from
the terrace, even taking the risk of breaking my legs. I seriously thought
of suggesting this to her, but because it wouldn't sound all that good in
person, I decided to write her. And then I thought that it wasn't proper
to write such things to a girl and I should suggest it to her in person.
Now I can laugh when I think what Teresa's reaction would have been
and how little she would have "understood" of this typical adolescent
dream, its subverted sexuality, and its poetry. But at that moment
I could not doubt the validity of the innumerable reasons why I had to
ask her exactly that.

I came back from Pisa to Teresa's with my friend and when we were
alone she called him my "beau ténébreux,"[7] and she said her mother

didn't think much of him either (perhaps they thought he was a homosexual). We had started to kiss again, but my feelings had changed. I had expected her to have forgotten her demands, while she thought I would do my best to be sociable from now on. When she expressed her disapproval of my friend, I suddenly attacked, and I mercilessly passed judgment on all her friends. I pointed out to her how insincere she and her mother were with regard to those people, how they began to gossip about them as soon as they had walked out the gate. There was a woman who had just come from Algiers, whom they referred to as "cette petite bonne femme."[8] I had other examples too. I gave Teresa a brief character sketch of herself, as I had perhaps analyzed it once with my beau ténébreux. She listened meekly, sitting straight in her chair in the dark, cool room while I paced up and down, speaking softly.

"Maybe you're right," she said. "I'm a product of my environment, a submissive daughter."

The rest of the evening she was very sweet to me, but we didn't kiss again. The next day I left with my friend after declining an invitation from Mama to go on an excursion to Assisi with her and Teresa.

When Teresa got engaged a second time it was to a man she had refused three times before. The fourth time he "conquered" her. He was thirteen years older than she was. I had met him a number of times. I used to be really touched by his loyalty sometimes, and he always treated me politely and honestly, although he must have cursed me in his heart. But when she spoke to me of his pride—I don't remember anymore on what occasion—I laughed scornfully. I thought that with my twenty-two years I had shown much more pride than he had, and I told her so, also that I still loved her, even if I had scratched myself off her list. Her mama went to Paris alone in those days, to get away from the domestic quarrels. She thought this son-in-law was too old and the least desirable of them all. She began to feel, I think, that even I would be a better choice. When I looked her up in Paris, she said I had matured so much in one year and that I certainly would get the woman I loved, that I had a great influence on Teresa and perhaps could keep her from taking this foolish step. I was the one who took the foolish step. I went to Teresa and implored her not to marry this man whom she really couldn't love. She said she thought she could and that she couldn't break off a second engagement. It escaped me how much of a struggle there had been between Mama and her.

Whether Mama had only wanted to use me or really hoped I would win, I still can't say. I tried to embrace Teresa again, but she pushed me away. So I gave her my best wishes for her marriage and said good-bye. She asked me not to be foolish and to come back soon, but I didn't see her again, except by accident, when she already had a one-year-old child.

On her wedding day I thought about going to city hall or the church, to steel myself, or to torment myself, or perhaps to enjoy her surprise if she should see me. It would have been wonderful, just as in the depressing song, "Je serai là, Nina cruelle, dans l'église où tu te marieras."[9] For a long time I comforted myself with fantasies, of kidnapping her with a car, chloroforming her, and taking her to a remote house in the country. I was visiting her mother one day when she dropped by with her child. I helped her bring in the perambulator and remarked that the child was so dark. "Oh, you don't know what you're talking about," she said. "It's because she's still so small." Later I met her and her husband at an exhibit. She came up and talked to me as if we were still good friends. I was in my cynical period then, so I made appropriately cynical remarks. Her husband stood silently on the other side. When I left I shook her hand but only nodded at him, because I thought it was foolish to shake hands with him, and because it would have been hard for me to do so.

And yet, about that time, I got over her. In the beginning I had thought Teresa was interesting; even when I thought I saw through her, when I told her "the truth," I was very disappointed. It was stiff medicine to cure my last hopes. Later, when I could see her in all her banality, my judgment softened. I tried to separate what was real and what had once existed between us from everything else. A few images, a few words—a small harvest, but perhaps a pure one. Can there be any relationship between two people without some trace of purity?

In the streetcar once on the way to the cemetery to visit her father's grave, she suddenly asked, "So, you love me?" in a tone of happy disbelief. And she would also say sometimes: "I dreamed of you," and glance at me meaningfully.

I asked her once, "How was I dressed in your dream?" (alluding to the "gentleman rêvé"), and she answered quickly, "Oh, there weren't many clothes, I don't think."

What else? Her hands on my hair, shyly but lovingly, a gesture which was both spontaneous and reticent, one afternoon in the villa, perhaps two days before I dared kiss her. I felt she was just being protective, and that's probably why I didn't respond. Another afternoon, after a long kiss, she asked me with her arms still around me, "What are you thinking about?" She looked at me searchingly and spoke almost in a whisper. I only dared say, "You," and turned my head.

One evening after she had gotten rid of an unexpected visitor she came back with outstretched arms into the dark room where I was waiting. I can still see her clearly, a silhouette in the doorway.

And once in her own room, where she had dragged me quickly to escape another visitor—her mother's visitor, really, whose daughter she had recently decided not to have anything to do with—listening to the voices from below, she suddenly took my face in her hands, brought it very close to hers, and sighed: "How can you get so attached to somebody!" That was shortly before the end.

And then she gradually became a woman I didn't know anymore, although she was living in the same city. After my father's suicide I got a letter from her: life had separated us, she wrote, but she would always be concerned about me. I wasn't over my cynical period yet. I wrote back a short, clear report about the event, without responding to her sympathy. She was completely right in not wanting to marry me, and not just from a social standpoint, because, no matter what, we would have soon made each other very unhappy. It was outside the realm of possibilities for me to conquer her the way her husband had, but I apparently was equally incapable of sweeping her off her feet in any other manner. Perhaps she would never have allowed me to, perhaps I was too young for that too, and it was all my fault. Several times I thought to myself that she had the soul of an old maid, totally lacking in spontaneity, always afraid of losing something. But on the other hand, sometimes I think that view is too one sided. Graaflant met her once, years later. She knew he was a friend of mine and asked about me immediately. When he took the opportunity to say good things about me, she responded really kindly. "I loved him very much, but he was so impossible at the time. In the end, it was just too painful for me."

I asked Graaflant how she looked.

"A pretty woman," he said, "but you can tell she's had three children. There's something matronly about her already. I saw her at the theater the other day, and during intermission she went over to a few old ladies and babbled with them. Her husband is quite gray now."

I can imagine her with those old ladies. That was part of the life she could never give up. How horrible, but it confirmed what I must have feared subconsciously. And yet, what continued to intrigue me was the attitude I might have if I ever had her alone and talked to her seriously again. "Would I have the same impression of her as I undoubtedly would, if it were for the first time?"

The last time I thought of her with any fondness was soon after we had moved to Meudon, while I was sitting across from Jane in the little commuter train we later came to know so well. It was dark outside; Jane looked tired and her eyes were closed. I had the feeling I was taking a long trip and yet was comfortable because of my happiness. I scribbled in my pocket book:

"Need to write Teresa to tell her I'm happier now than I ever could have been with her, that I lied when I said I would always be at her disposal after what we had had together, that I was taking that promise back now, as it were. But this is all nonsense, all this, and the picture I gave her too, with 'Remember Arthur'[10] written at the bottom, never meant anything to her. I never thought about it in this way, but if I had, and given my outlook then, I would have never assumed that, once she had accepted the man who is now her husband, she might simply be loyal to him. At that time it was not only comforting for me but imperative to believe that revenge would always be possible: the young bourgeois always thinks of himself as a conqueror."

Now I see her mama almost more clearly than Teresa, perhaps because her personality was stronger. Strange, how great my grief was then. How can you suffer so much from something that later becomes so vague? But as a child you went through it; you remember that the pain goes away, and even when you're still hurt, you know that the later vagueness is possible. So you fight against your feelings tooth and nail, against the comfort and the idea of it. You dig in, hold on to what is already lost. I have never been so painfully close to suicide as after Teresa's first engagement, not even during my depression after my father's death, which lasted perhaps two years. It's the feeling that everything is slipping away from you, that everything has turned its back on you, that you're sure that the one person you found has sent you away, and that it's senseless to try to find anyone else ever again. My sadness at her wedding (after she was engaged the second time) was much different. I had gotten used to the idea then, because even when I was in Italy, I never really felt things would work out for us. But the strangest thing of all is that the grief remains, isolated from its cause, and you sometimes feel it later with all its immediacy. During the period Jane and I had to wait to get married, when only a few material concerns were keeping us apart, I experienced three or four times that same sense of rejection just as bitterly and just as completely, sometimes no more than an hour or so after I had left her. In such moments you can probably renounce happiness for good, just out of fear of losing it later as totally as you feel you have lost it at that very moment. You know that the moment itself is nonsense, but all you sense is that fear, and there is no nonsense in it. You also know that it would take very little to turn that fear into an everyday reality. You suddenly feel very strongly how precarious it is that the sense of happiness has chased away the other, or that it replaces the emptiness which in "normal" circumstances you welcome as a substitute.

31   Pursuit of the One and Only

My feeling for Teresa made it easy for me to stay away from other women. Of course, as soon as it turned out she was not the One and Only, cynicism set in. A brothel, several return trips, and what I then called smilingly my first "mistress" (using the word of a young provincial)—that is to say, the first European woman who didn't want any money for it. In those days I had my own place in Brussels, a converted garage with its own entrance, separated by a courtyard from my parents' house; in short, everything I needed for my new life as a "libertine." But I had decided that I would never again get mixed up with a woman of the world, which is how I had classified bourgeois Teresa, and most important, I would never make any effort again. I was free now; that was the important thing. And I decided that I would never let my heart enter into it, because that apparently didn't work in Europe. Moreover, I made this rule: "Since the one who asks is always the weaker, I will never put myself in that position again."

When suddenly Josette from Luxemburg appeared on the scene, what tempted me most of all was the ease with which everything fell into place, and during our second meeting I thought I could see my whole future. The mood was: "So this is it. I have to listen to this vulgar dame a little. But she's nice. She must think that she's my mistress now and that she has some right to this room."

I smiled while I listened to the lies she came up with: I was the second (the first wouldn't really be believable), so the second after a very idyllic first love. It had been a thwarted love affair; her parents didn't like him, and the boy had succumbed out of grief in the Congo. Later we got along better, after I finally said to her, "All this is fine, but why don't you tell me how it really was. Try to tell the truth just as it was, for a change."

She looked at me slyly, laughed, and then told a much more believable story. He had been a dentist, and she had been only thirteen or fourteen when she had actually done it.

"And between him and me?"

"Three."

"Come on."

"Thirteen."

And suddenly she burst out laughing because the cat jumped out of the window.

"Look, just as that cat can't keep from jumping outside, I can't keep from lying."

I went to Paris; when I came back she had a marriage offer from the son of a devout Catholic woman. She showed me his letters when we were in bed, and I felt like Valmont[1] as we discussed them. "My mother says you couldn't be a decent girl. Swear to me you are and that you're pure, because I pray every night that sin will not come between us before our marriage."

She admitted that she thought he was handsome and would have liked to go to bed with him, but he was the one who had wanted it this way, from the very first. So she had written him that she was a virgin, since it meant so much to him. Later, when the young man had to capitulate to his mother after she had uncovered the most irrefutable information and had even gone to her home town, Differdange, it turned out that her greatest crime was that she had given him a crucifix and a prayer book. "I'll keep it," he wrote, "as a souvenir, but even more so as not to forget how base a woman can be."

Laughing cynically about those letters was the most interesting thing I got out of my relationship with Josette. Next to that, there was the time when I was able to listen without getting mad one evening when she let loose all the profanity she knew. I wondered vaguely, "In my place, would my father have hit her?" But I discovered the joy of being strong by being passive. While she paced the floor furiously, throwing her head back to swear better, I sank more deeply into my chair to watch better. With Teresa I had learned not to be so mild mannered in a conflict with the other sex.

Maybe this marks the beginning of my conviction that I had eliminated the human element in my contacts with certain kinds of women. "And yet," Héverlé said, and rightly so, "there's always some human contact. What did those girls think of you? What did they feel for you, perhaps, in spite of everything? The fact that you felt nothing for them doesn't count."

Maybe they thought I was "gentil" because I was a rich young bourgeois, and never did anything like hit them. Instinctively I had made one decision: I was never going to lose as I had lost with Teresa. The same simulated seriousness which gave me the upper hand in many casual relationships could make me act shamefully toward more refined women. I thought I had become very strong, but in fact I was fooled by my role-playing. This role-playing made it impossible for me to do what I really wanted, although I thought I could clearly tell what I wanted from what was only appearance. In reality I was waiting for the One and Only, but in the first years after Teresa I came to admire my role so much that I was dominated by it. I wrote a number of short stories in which I unmasked the young bourgeois and at the same time put him in the limelight as some sort of hero. It was a satirical hero-worship which seemed to apologize for the fact that life couldn't come up with any better hero.

The Swiss friend Teresa called a "beau ténébreux" had a sister, who had attracted my attention even before I went to Italy to see Teresa for the last time. She was two years older than I and lived with her husband and a child of about four, in a small house in Ouchy. When I was about to take another trip I decided to look them up. Her husband was a teacher, half Swiss, half British. He was tall and thin and had a long bony face; he was balding but had beautiful blue eyes. I liked him, but my friend had told me the details of his marriage. He had remained "innocent" until he was twenty-seven. And not only that; he used to talk to prostitutes in the streets to try to save them. When he married Denise he asked her in the very first week to be "all women" to him. This put her off for good. "The day after the wedding," she told me later, "you stand in front of the mirror, combing your hair, and you realize that it's all much sadder than you ever imagined." She had married him out of love, going against her parents' will. But after her child was born, she asked him not to force her to do what had become impossible. It turned into the usual drama; he stayed as much in love as ever, and stayed longingly at her side. She yielded occasionally, and even gave it a new try, but with more and more disappointing results. When I came back to Ouchy they had settled into being just good friends. Her brother had told me this; he also told me about Denise's disappointment over my having left so soon. I was so clearly her husband's opposite that that alone would have attracted her. Once her husband was also on the verge of confiding in me, but I managed to keep him from doing so.

From the very first moment it was clear to me that Denise was much more worthwhile than Teresa. Why then shouldn't I "conquer" her? I wouldn't even have to worry about intruding on "their marriage." Anything would be better for her than her present situation. One afternoon, when we were with some other people, I began to draw her portrait. I gave her the drawing and said that she alone could be the judge of it. Below her face I had written the words, "Where can I meet you alone?" The next morning I went to visit them again, not yet having met her alone. Her husband talked about an article he had published in a journal on psychology. He had made a serious study of psychology—not just in passing, he said, but professionally. He expanded on this, and while I was listening to him, Denise came to sit next to me on the couch. The journal was very large and was spread over her hand. Looking at her husband and thinking how large and penetrating his eyes were—so fitting for a psychologist—I took her hand under the journal and held it for at least five minutes while I sat and talked to him. In front of him that afternoon, she asked me to go to the lake with her when he would be teaching. Once we were alone, she said she was willing, but she didn't want to cheat on him in their own house. A few days later I left, taking many pictures of her with me; in the sleeping berth on the train I looked at them by a dim blue light, amazed that I could be fascinated like this so soon after Teresa.

We really hadn't cheated on her husband, because she felt that would happen soon enough, and because I wanted to prove to her—and just to her!—that I had not showed up only to seduce her. During the vacation her husband went to England, and I saw her again in Kandersteg, but we didn't cheat on him there either. She thought I had come in all guilelessness. She had written her husband that she wanted a divorce. Now that I was there, it was impossible to go on living with him, she told me, but to him she gave a different reason. He wrote back touching letters that had no effect on her. As for me, particularly in light of the divorce, I felt I shouldn't stay more than a few days this time. In that village pressed between the mountains, everybody knew her and her parents, with whom she spent her vacation in a chalet. I was staying in the hotel, but the hotel owner had known her for years too. So all we did was take long walks uphill along a mountain stream to a little lake where we went rowing, to look at the alpenglow from a certain spot. In the evening we went into the dark of the forest—something her husband never dared do, she said—far from the village, under the darkest trees. It was cold, but if we absolutely insisted on sealing our bond physically, we could have done it there, perhaps. While we were standing pressed against each other on a railroad bridge with water roaring far below, a stray cat suddenly jumped in front of us. I picked the animal up. It had a terrible cold. She begged me to let it go, but it stayed close by, keeping us company in that lonely darkness, never further than a few steps away from us, miaowing and sneezing. Like an otherworldly creature, said Denise, who then began to talk with ironic resignation about her fundamental pantheism. On one of these evening trips I gave her a ring which Teresa had given me as a remembrance. "I understand the gravity of this heirloom," she said, and laughed.

Before I left I made her cry. She had been telling me about her marriage, particularly the first year and how even then she could never say "tu" to her husband. When I responded I used the "tu" form to her. She asked me why I did that. I said it was obvious we would use it from now on. She didn't agree. I continued, and at a given moment, when we sat down on a bench, I realized she was crying. I stared at her as if paralyzed. I couldn't even take her hand. She got up abruptly and said, "I'm an incorrigible little bourgeoise."

After I had left she wrote me long letters, a little on the literary side but in good taste, incomparably better than Teresa's. In this at least she wasn't worried about compromising herself. I had always resented that Teresa never wrote "Je vous aime," but always, "Je vous aime bien" (I'm fond of you), or something like that; never "mon amour" but "mon affection." Denise wrote with great naturalness, "Arthur que j'aime" (Arthur, my love). She kept me informed about her divorce, which her husband had finally agreed to. At the same time she was studying for an exam and did very well. This was all done with an eye to the future, and I let her do exactly as she wanted, not telling her that I had enough money. When I saw her in Lausanne, just before her divorce, she mentioned marriage again, mostly for her child's sake, she said. She would have custody of the child, but if she wanted, she could leave it with her parents, though she would have to be married; otherwise they would have nothing to do with her. It was clear that her parents knew what was going on, because my friend, her brother, went out of the room to leave us alone, and her parents withdrew immediately after dinner. That bothered me a little. She was lying on the couch as she talked to me about this, and I passed up the opportunity to kiss her right away.

"Come closer to me and just tell me what you think of the idea. You don't like it, do you?"

"To the contrary, let's get married."

She kept saying she could tell I didn't want to, and I kept insisting that that wasn't true, that I had absolutely nothing against it. And I didn't. I was going through the same paralysis I had had when I saw her cry in Kandersteg. "Votre goguenarde visite,"[2] she wrote me later, in reference to that evening.

I left again to wait until her divorce was final. In her eyes as well as mine, I played the role of le monsieur qui repart[3] very well. We had never said I shouldn't see other women. During my two years with Teresa I had easily remained faithful, but this was completely un-European, I had decided, and as far as Denise was concerned, I should be more of a "man." So between my trips to her there was Suzanne. It amused me that during the same period my mother had a dear guest who would have loved to be her daughter-in-law and who spent whole afternoons with her on the loggia gossiping about me. This gossiping was essential to prove they understood each other and loved me. My mother explained I had been such a sweet boy and that it was only since we had come to Europe that I had become impossible. One thing I always appreciated about her was that despite how much she leaned on me, she never lapsed into the sickening admiration some mothers have for their sons. I would have found it absolutely insufferable.

Denise's divorce just about coincided with Guy's birth. I told her about it, as if that were the obvious thing to do, and drew a picture of Guy in his diapers: I held him in my arms and showed myself as having a round, proud face with the corners of my mouth turned up. She answered that she considered marriage out of the question now. She sent her condolences to the child's mother and said that I didn't take life seriously. Her brother thought this was no reason to break off our friendship, but said I was thoroughly amoral. This word was a revelation to me. I hadn't wanted to be bitter after my disappointment with Teresa, but I had decided the right thing to do was be amoral. I was so naïve as to think I would never be a father, simply by thinking the idea was ridiculous. At the same time I thought I could make a present of the child to my rich mother (she always said she wanted to see my children before she died). Fool that I was, I thought such a thing could easily be arranged—and here I was, already twenty-five years old. Suzanne was, as Wijdenes later described her, perfect for my indolence. She was willing, she didn't talk much—nothing of her later rich vocabulary, perfected in the "madhouse," and nothing of the distrust either, which came from her vulnerability. My mother said to me: "You love her more than you think. This woman has such a hold over you." But she was grossly mistaken, because she herself was responsible for Suzanne's "hold." Even in my most capricious period I couldn't turn Suzanne over to her unprotected. Only gradually did I feel responsible for other things too, and my affection for Suzanne increased along with my pity, yet I never felt for a moment that I had given up on the "One and Only," that I had resigned myself to never finding her.

If Denise had reacted differently, if she had written to me to come to her immediately, I would certainly have done so; what's more, I would have married her, just as we had agreed. But within a year she married a German and went to Berlin with him. It was as if she was born for trouble: the man turned out to have married her for her parents' savings. "He was very, very lazy," her brother told me later, "and he wanted to make a whole lot of money without a lot of effort."

Denise divorced him too and went back to Lausanne. Her son often asked about his father. Finally she remarried her first husband. He had been transferred to an impossible little town close to the French border, which had been one of the reasons she had divorced him. As if to underline her fate she now had to go to that place to pick up where she had left off. Did she perhaps turn it into something? Or was she maybe really an incorrigible little bourgeoise? If you look at it closely, the role I played in this drama is too insignificant to really incriminate me. "Vous vous contentez de si peu,"[4] she wrote me in her last letter, somewhat sarcastically. But in Kandersteg she had said that, although she wasn't sure of my feelings, she was sure that I would always remember her fondly. She had a long brown face and rather thick lips with a faint mustache above them, a high forehead which she hid under a mass of jet black hair, and deep-set, thoughtfully distrustful eyes. Her body was lithe and always a little bit bent over.

Years went by. I was part of the "madhouse," there was no sign of the breathlessly awaited One and Only, and the flattering myth, which our friends sometimes build around us, had to come to my rescue. I became the planter's son who hated "intellectual women." Those who were even remotely intellectual I could only talk to, and most of the time not even that. As a matter of fact, each time I had to deal with a woman who clearly had something more to offer than a body, things turned out badly. Nonetheless I was proud of myself for having recognized as wrong what seemed to have been invoked by my desire. I seemed to have directed my life in a practical vein, having consistently rejected what only was a deception on a higher level. But I didn't even have the aspiration to pretend that this state of affairs satisfied me or to disclaim the myth of the planter's son. As for my "European" attitude, I had consciously renounced it long before. I laughed at the man who explained to me with such considerate cynicism that my new demands would only bring about another phase of growing pains. I knew that I had been cured of this kind of cynicism and that his wisdom would have been silly to me more than anything else. I even noticed afterwards that there had been more method to my planter's myth than I had realized.

Then came the unsuccessful British adventure. One day in Grouhy I received a letter from a student in Oxford who had translated one of my short stories which had appeared in a Brussels magazine. She wanted to know if she could publish the translation in an Oxford student magazine and if I knew of any other Brussels authors. I answered willingly, although with the necessary irony, and her letters became longer. Gradually I got to know about her. She was twenty-two, on an international fellowship, a student of French literature, and for the moment absorbed in seventeenth-century drama. She was not really English, but Irish, from Belfast, and her name was Eveline. She believed in youthful courageousness; she also believed in humanity, in doing something for others. She hated the cheap skepticism of recent times. I soon answered with equally long letters. It became an inexhaustible exchange of thoughts between us, and she adapted herself very tactfully when I corrected her opinions. After a few months we agreed on just about everything, except love. My ideal was that we love each other exclusively three months of the year, spending that time wherever we chose, and then lead our own lives again the other nine months. The only essential thing in this was money, of course, and also that each one have his own life to lead. She thought it was ridiculous. She had been engaged eight times and had broken off each engagement because it had seemed impossible, but a solution such as mine was really far too arbitrary. Although she would always want to "exist" for other men, deep down she wanted to be fascinated by the man she would finally choose. Therefore she cherished the hope of fascinating him just as much and not, *dear sir*,[5] just for three months out of the year! What she stood for was very attractive, and the description of herself was attractive too. Finally, of course, I had to come over. She wanted to show me Oxford, England, everything. She sent me volumes of poetry written by *Oxford men*, to be discussed later. And whatever the case may be, a trip to England was necessary because, after all, she couldn't fall in love with my letters.

I wrote back that I would come, but that I didn't want to be her ninth fiancé. If everything went all right—and we certainly would be able to tell—we would become lovers. If not, we would visit Oxford as good friends. She thought this was a marvelous idea. Until my arrival we wrote each other daily. I began to believe strongly in the existence of the One and Only and wrote more and more seriously, which probably means that my letters became rather foolish.

One evening on the way back from Brussels, we were driving through the Soignes Woods. The road was pitch black; on both sides I saw how the tree trunks, lit by the headlights, leapt away very quickly. The chauffeur was in a big hurry to get home, and I suddenly thought, "It's crazy but if we would crash against one of these rows of trees, my last thought would be of Eveline...." And yet I knew that when I met her I might feel nothing, and it would be all over. But I didn't want to sabotage our meeting. I even worried about my clothes, and I noticed that for months I had been walking around in some sort of gardener's outfit. I bought a brand new suit in Brussels and—to everybody's amusement—was inspected by the Graaflants before I risked the British expedition. She had written that she never meant *French amour*, but *love, British love*.

I crossed the English Channel in the company of an old Scottish minister who offered me peppermints to keep me from getting seasick. The sea was very quiet, we didn't get sick, and he told me sad stories about his family. He was going back to his only sister. He had been a widower for years and had just lost his little son, who had drowned. At least that is what they had assumed bacause his body was never found, only his cap and the dog he had taken in his rowboat. It was not surprising, really, because the boy had become very strange after his mother's death.... By the time we got to Dover he definitely seemed attached to me and waited anxiously while I went through immigration. On the train to London he treated me to British tea, assured that I must have heard of its worldwide reputation. I got to show my appreciation in London by taking him from one station to another in a taxi. This is my one memory of London: a marvelously organized chaos with the leitmotif of buses that were much too tall. In the train to Oxford I was alone again, that is to say, with three women who all looked unmarried. I was certain that Eveline wouldn't look like anyone of those three, but the sight of them gave me a great sense of calm.

In Oxford I took a cab to the hotel she had recommended. There was a letter waiting for me, full of jubilation and asking me to take a sitting room, since otherwise she couldn't visit me. I chose an expensive, enormous room with a delightful British fireplace. After that I quickly put on my new suit and went out. It seemed to me I had just enough time to walk to her address. Asking for directions and walking through the freezing weather made me feel calmer and calmer. None of the glow caused by her letter was left when I rang the bell at her door. Someone was playing the piano, a French friend it turned out, and it had been Ravel's pavane, but from then on we called it Arthur's pavane, in honor of that moment. The door opened, and she stopped for a minute on the steps before coming down. With the light of the hallway behind her I saw that she wore a light coat. We walked side by side. She had borrowed a sitting room from a friend, she said, because she couldn't receive me here. According to Oxford customs she would have to be home at eleven, a quarter past in a pinch. And how could I be so extraordinarily calm? I told her about my train trip with the three women and the effect it had had.

The borrowed sitting room was on the ground floor. It was a rather bare room with old furniture and many knickknacks on the walls. I sat down in a chair, and she stood in front of the fireplace. She was small, with a dark, eager face and pretty black eyes. The rest was not bad but not striking either, and altogether she was prettier than I had expected. Nonetheless, although a subconscious courtesy restrained me from saying it to myself, I knew right away she could never be the One and Only. She even radiated a certain hostility. She remarked that I wasn't saying anything, that the room was ugly, that she had never been here before, and didn't I want to turn off the light so as not to have to see how ugly it was? I said something nice about the room and turned off the light. Now the only light was the red square glow of the fireplace. She slid down on the rug in front of the fire, and I understood I was supposed to move to the couch she was leaning against. I did so and even took her hand. She rested her shoulder pleasantly against my leg. It seemed fitting to entertain one another with stories of our lives. She told me about her eight engagements, and I told her I was married to an authentic live-in maid. She looked very intently into the fireplace and then began to repeat what she had said in her letter about French amour and British love. I got the impression she saw the inevitable Belgian or French sex maniac in me. I looked at my watch, saw it was almost eleven, and told her she had to go home. We both got up and she looked startled. So I gave her a kiss somewhere on her forehead. On the way home she told me she was a virgin. I said it was always important to know such things. But, she said, I shouldn't think she was totally inexperienced. At her door she gave me a letter to hold me for the rest of the night.

The letter looked like all the others, and I slept quite well, in spite of the big day that was to follow. She had asked me to meet her at a bridge at ten o'clock. Her French friend came with her; she was a rather ugly girl but not ugly enough to be her ugly girl friend, a girl who had a pleasant voice, moreover, and a soulful look. I talked to her while Eveline dragged us to innumerable buildings, derided the Oxford "aesthetes," and jumped ahead of us all the time, doing things on her own, which perhaps was to demonstrate her youthful courageousness. It became clear that the friend knew all about me and perhaps had read all my letters, but I didn't care. I could have passed the rest of the day with her as well as with Eveline. But around twelve o'clock she withdrew modestly, at the door of a student restaurant with a medieval motif, where we were going to have lunch.

As soon as we were alone Eveline began to talk again. Why had I treated her like a father, why had I not kissed her on the mouth, what did I think of her? Couldn't I tell she was British through and through, although of course Irish and not English. I told her very tersely that I personally didn't tell everybody I was a Javanese prince and that I had come to find a human being, not a representative of a race. Her sentences crowded each other out more and more hurriedly. Her face became more and more tense, and she had a distant look while she ate. What she wanted most of all to explain to me was my view of her.

"But don't go to so much trouble," I said. "When I feel I have to analyze what I think of you, I'll tell you, and perhaps I can do that better than you can."

"Oh, even if I had married a waiter, I probably wouldn't understand you," she said, thinking she had cut me deeply. (If she had been somebody else, she might have succeeded.) And would I come pick her up at five? And would I kiss her on the mouth this time?

"I sort of think not," I said. "Is it absolutely necessary? Perhaps it would be better to go look at the city."

When she left she gave me another letter which was very long and which she must have spent the whole night writing.

I went back to my hotel and my enormous sitting room to read the letter in front of the fire. She had felt terribly humiliated because I had confused innocence with virginity. She gave me all sorts of details to open my eyes, among which was a really well-written description of an encounter with her last fiancé, whom she had manipulated, to his great surprise.... "*And there he was, looking in utter astonishment at my wet hand.*"[6]

Maybe it's strange, but suddenly I got mad. I went out to tell her exactly what I thought of these games. But she wasn't there, or at least that's what I was told. The maid said she'd left a little note for me. Surprised that there was yet another letter, I went back outside. It said that I would have to leave because otherwise she would fail her exam. That was fine with me, but I wrote her that she could come to my place that evening, if only to see the beautiful sitting room she had insisted upon, and that I would wait for her until nine o'clock. She didn't come, so I had every opportunity to enjoy the room and all the tea with cookies I had ordered. At breakfast the next morning there was another envelope; she had come home late, too late to come to my place, otherwise she certainly would have, it was undoubtedly fate, and so on. I had the groom take her a letter saying my train left at two o'clock and did she want to have lunch with me. The answer was written by the French friend, saying I shouldn't torture Eveline so, she was really studying for her exam. I wrote back to the friend that I had a pleasant memory of the walk with her, and I advised Eveline to read *Lady Chatterly's Lover*, paying special attention to the passages on British women—only after she had taken the exam, of course. I mailed this letter from the station. A few hours later I was walking through London; in the evening I took a boat, and when we entered Antwerp the next morning I had the feeling a very funny incident was completely behind me.

Perhaps it was just the advantage of being eight years older. For her it now became really fascinating. She sent me a volume of Chinese translations with the inscription that this was the first stone of a huge building to be built in the future. After that, long letters arrived again. I wrote back very tersely to scold her; that was all. Now she really turned loose, furious, and asked if I didn't understand that she loved me, that I shouldn't have left, that she really cared for me since my scolding. "*While reading that, I said to myself, he is a fine man.*"[7] There seemed only one thing to do, to keep the joke going. I wrote back quite seriously that I would never be the right man for her but that we might meet again some time, and I advised her to do something about her virginity as soon as possible. After some time I got a letter from France, "*My dear Arthur, I took your advice and—bled.*" She was now traveling with her lover. By the way, he wasn't British, but Polish or Czech, and she told me his name. While I never really thought of her, every now and then I received a long letter from her with a report of what she had been doing and what she wanted, full of questions. "How many times are you supposed to have sexual intercourse in twenty-four hours?" I maintained my seriousness and answered that for a trip like hers it could vary between two and six times, but I thought I should tell her that it was usually closer to two. She thanked me with equal serious-ness and called me her "*Minister of Affairs.*" After a few months she was through with the Pole, "*because his wife chose to hurl herself into his bed,*" which she couldn't prevent, but which for her meant the end. Now she regretted having started the whole story. "*So this is what people call: to be somebody's mistress!*"

Some time later she left Oxford because she had been forced to take a teaching position. She thought she had become a lesbian and was madly in love with one of her students, a blond eighteen-year-old girl called Gay. Oh, if only she had money! She was ready to marry a rich old man if only she could keep Gay and—did I know anybody? This time I was bored by it, and I didn't answer right away. A week later I re-ceived an outburst. "*Of all the mean things I've ever heard,*" this letter began, "*this is the meanest! Getting a woman to tell you all her secrets, and then, when it comes to the point—blast! No one there!*"

I wrote that I had been very busy and that I had looked for a rich husband, although in vain, and advised her to be sure not to miss any opportunity with Gay. A couple of weeks later the story had changed. She had gone back to Belfast on vacation and had fallen in love with a policeman who was a friend of her brother-in-law. At this point I stopped the correspondence.

She was planning to write a novel. I sent back all her letters, saying that this was material for the novel she was going to write. But years later I received another message, which I showed to Jane and which revealed her once again. There were only a few lines:

"How do you do? I want to find you. The world is full of possibilities! I made an effort to find you, a little richer in years, wisdom, and money. A word, my dear sir. Remember I loved you and que voulez-vous?—one forgets not. And after all—I never knew you. Will you give me another chance? I intend to find you. Yours ever, E."

32 Newspapers

January 1934. This exercise in honesty is rather disappointing to me now that I reread it all. I was not able to escape the puzzling principle which turns every "I" into a character as soon as it is used in a story. Moreover, my surroundings and the present times form a strong counterforce. My individual understanding of life, which I acquired so clumsily, is overwhelmed by the continual turmoil in Paris of the last two weeks. There is the restlessness of the Stavisky[1] scandal: the newspaper has become a detective novel or does everything it can to imitate one, and for the first time in my life I feel unable to pull myself away from it.

For a while I tried to finish off my quest for the One and Only a little better. It's a jump from obscurity to lucidity, and when you think you're particularly lucid, boredom causes you to lose track and new obscurity sets in. After years of so-called worldly wisdom I was still green enough to indulge in a naïve experiment. I was waiting for Héverlé at the Napolitain in Paris when a young woman came in, looked around, as if she were either late or early for a rendezvous, and then sat down at the table next to me. She wore a pince-nez and a simple brown dress suit which might lead you to believe she was a student....

At this point, the old man, after loud knocking, enters cautiously.

"I'm not bothering you, I hope.... Oh, excuse me. I only wanted to ask, such a small shop like the bank in Bayonne... which hands out 200 millions worth of bonds, voy-i-ons[2]... I wanted to ask you, Monsieur, could Stavisky have done such a thing on his own? I am old and a former magistrate, etc. I tell you, it's not possible. The parliamentary system (at this point he become secretive)... the whole system is rotten to the core, I tell you,... voy-i-ons."

My opinion? I don't think about it much and I'm not an ex-magistrate, but I feel the same way.

He is certain there will be a revolution now. He knows what a revolution is like, and he dares predict that this time... he pulls on my sleeve and shuffles back to the door.

I say, "You mean, of course, a revolution from the Right."

Immediately he becomes careful again, "Well umm,... from the Right, from the Left, who's to say? But there will be one. This can't go on, voy-i-ons. Yes, probably from the Right."

...but it turned out to be an ordinary prostitute, and we made a date for that evening. Héverlé came in just when I had made the date, and asked about her as she was leaving. When I told him he looked at her attentively.

"La poule au lorgnon,"[3] he said. "She must be part of a new genre, specializing in shy foreigners."

"Maybe they're nicer," I said.

"It's not a question of nice or not nice," Héverlé said. "You'll never be anything more than a customer for her, no matter what."

I decided that evening to treat the "poule au lorgnon" in an unusual way. I took her to a good restaurant and treated her like a lady. I used a tone of complete respect and talked to her about what interested her—the French army, the political situation, the good opportunities for French prostitutes to make money in Java and, somewhat carelessly perhaps, about the Düsseldorf vampire who had not yet been caught. She was sure that that vampire had been made up for entirely political reasons, just what the French press used to say about Landru, and I assured her that the man was real and perhaps very decent looking.

"It's the decent looking people I'd be most careful of," she said, winking at me. And she quickly added a story about a very smart looking gentleman she had gone to Chantilly with, who had stolen her wristwatch. When we were through with dinner I took her to my hotel. She brought up the price while we were in the taxi. I gave her money for the whole night, and since I had a single room and worried about a complication with the hotel rules, I gave her some more to get her own room. I waited for her at the elevator. She registered, and we went into the elevator at the same time. I went with her to her room, which seemed more comfortable than mine. I threw my overcoat on a chair and asked her to wait while I went to get my pajamas from my room. In the hall, I turned back instinctively to get my coat: my wallet was in it.

I wasn't gone for more than five minutes, and I thought to myself, "If she runs away now, Héverlé is right. If she doesn't run away I'm not necessarily right, because she might just be acting out of professional honesty, having already been paid." But when I came back her door was wide open and the lights were on. A woman was knitting in the hall; I asked her if she had seen anybody.

"Oh yes, you had hardly left when a lady ran out of that room."

I turned off the lights and locked the door. "This room doesn't have to be made up tomorrow," I said.

Back in bed in my own room I suddenly felt sorry for myself. I thought I had paid too much for Héverlé's being right, and I kept telling myself that I would have spent the night more pleasantly if I had stuck to the established truth. I dreamed up a revenge of spending a whole week waiting for her at the Napolitain to tell her I hadn't thought she'd be a thief. Finally—and this is where my real naïveté began—I tried to figure out a special reason for her flight: either she had seen some kind of Düsseldorf vampire in me and had thought such a polite customer might have left to get his scalpel—the fact she had been asked to get her own room would fit in completely with that—or she thought I was a nice young man and had run away because she didn't want to leave a painful physical souvenir, preferring to teach me a moral lesson... The next morning I was over it, but I didn't tell Héverlé about it right away because I knew he'd laugh at me. The funny thing was that he brought it up himself in talking about my situation with Suzanne. "For me, it's no longer a question of whether you will pull yourself loose from her or not, but whether someone like 'la poule au lorgnon' will turn out to be the one to do it without any real reason...."

The old lady comes in, sits down on the bed to emphasize the temporary nature of her visit, and says with surprise, "He is working again," as if she couldn't understand that such a thing might be necessary. She wants to know how long we're planning to stay, because when we leave they will probably leave too, and they'll be forced to live with their married daughter in Serbia, which doesn't appeal to her at all because, she says, she knows the Serbs. "They are great warriors, that one has to admit. But they're really fools."

She gives an example:

"At a great ball in Belgrade an officer asked a girl to dance and she refused. The officer was so incensed that he slapped her in the face, right there in the ballroom. Naturally, a big uproar ensued and the generals and colonels who were present had to intervene. They withdrew to discuss the matter and concluded that... that the army, in the person of the officer, had been so insulted by the girl that she should be removed from the party. And she was! But that wasn't all, because the girl had a brother who was an officer too. And this brother... when he heard what had happened and what a scandal his sister had caused... this brother, imagine, beat her up so badly that the poor girl had to stay in bed for three weeks...."

Nodding her head, she smiles and then jumps up suddenly, excusing herself for disturbing us again.

Without a real reason, I thought, I wouldn't have left. ("I'll have to tell Héverlé that I'm 'la poule au lorgnon'," Jane said later.) I knew I would be able to free myself if I had that "reason" and yet it seomtimes seemed it would be very difficult. However, it turned out to be as simple as could be and came as no surprise to anybody when it actually happened.... If I'm disturbed again now, what a good reason to change the subject. Something has changed. I can't write about myself anymore, and not just because I'm too close to the present, but because the newspapers crowd out my diary. If I weren't living in Paris, it would probably be different. But here it's as if for the first time public life has forced me to give it all my attention.

Who am I to society, compared to a Stavisky? It may be absurd to make such a comparison, but in my present situation it seems normal to me. This Stavisky was a genius of an embezzler, people say, who brilliantly used the formulas of aggressiveness. For me he is one of the notaries, a brilliant notary who was caught in the act. That's why there is a crisis among the notaries and a crisis in almost all of France. According to the Communists, there's not a single bourgeois who deep down doesn't admire this man; only his end scares them. Everywhere you see the picture of his corpse on the floor mat, with blood running out of his nose along his upper lip like a mustache, and one or two holes in his temple. Even two bullets would not prove conclusively that this former police informer had been killed by his accomplices. It's possible he himself put the two bullets in his head, according to a proponent of the suicide theory. It's possible, but not probable. My old senator is one who does not like to consider the possibility that the police murdered him. I tell him that it's obvious, which is what I think.

"A cowardly scoundrel," somebody else says. "Is this the end of a superior person? But as far as the 200 million are concerned and the embezzlement, il était un peu là."[4]

Everybody turns out to be tainted by his money and denies it. People might as well take out ads in the newspaper saying they've never even met him. Then there is the aggressive journalist who states emphatically that they were friends and that he is not ashamed of it even now (either you've got character or you don't). That he often had dinner with him and that he always enjoyed his great charm and his special smile. The moral? He, of course, accepted money from him too, but he paid it all back. The smile must have been irresistible. This brilliant financier never asked waiters for change for a 1,000 franc bill: they were even more charmed by him than the ministers. Finally, to make him as enviable as possible, you are shown pictures of his beautiful wife, Arlette, the former model. Not only is this woman beautiful, she now mourns for him. They had two children, and she was totally devoted to him. (No doubt the official notaries will make her suffer for what they couldn't make her husband suffer for.) This man—whom I had not wanted to know, whom I loathe and even despise—Balzac could have turned into the main character of a great novel.

At the first demonstration of the concerned citizens—championed in the traditional Parisian puppet show by the Camelots du Roi,[5] although there are other taxpayers who want to air their dissatisfaction too—we went out for our newspaper. In a huge square around the Chambre des Députés[6] we find that all the streets are blocked off by the police. The metro exit is closed. No matter where we try to get closer, men in uniform bark at us to turn either to the left or to the right. At a street corner there is a café of the kind we usually carefully avoid. There are a few free chairs outside. We sit down. The place has a choice name, the Café de la Légion d'Honneur. We are there for hardly five minutes when huge police cars enter the neighborhood where there was fighting. The waiters get nervous and keep shouting at us to sit down; otherwise the police might take exception to our café.

Two patriotic ladies join us, one small, thin, and dark, like a neglected goat, the other chubby and boisterous, with a feline face. "What kind of beer do you have," she asks the waiter, "German dark, French light? The light then, please—French!" A troop of dragoons pass. She jumps up. "Look how handsome they are and what dirty work they make them do," she says, hoping to be heard by the troops. The waiter insists she sit down again, but she waves him away with her hand. He begins to collect all the empty chairs which are outside, hers included. The thin brown one joins her friend; she too loses her chair. The first one yells, "You don't know how to do your job, and you're not a patriot. We want to see!" A man joins in and demands the chairs. The lady says to him, "Oh, don't worry; if I want my chair back, it will take more than human strength to prevent me."

Every now and then demonstrators are arrested by the police. Some have radiant faces, their hats shoved back on their heads. The ones wearing caps look more defeated between the smart-looking kepis of the policemen. The paddywagons are filled. The little old lady suddenly bursts out: "Oh look! They're twisting his wrists. What animals!" The policeman yells back: "If you want to sit there, O.K., but keep out of this and don't call our men animals." The old lady, a litle less exuberant: "But you are." The waiter runs up to them again, scared to death. "Did you understand this time?" The chubby lady answers passionately: "Yes, we want to go to prison; only honest people are there."

Between the cars in the street the chief of police, Chiappe, arrives, small and elegant with a Napoleonic calm, as if he took a field marshal's position at this intersection. The same chubby lady sighs: "There's Chiappe; he must be tired. He just came in from Florence." He has a delicate actor's face and wears a derby hat and a silver-white shawl. The patriotic lady suddenly ventures into the street and comes back on the arm of a bearded gentleman with the Legion of Honor rosette on his lapel. They leave immediately, but before they go we get to hear her say: "People don't know that you have the right to sit outside a café without paying." Next time she will certainly do so.

How strikingly French this lady was! And how deserving of the attention of those Dutchmen who love to stereotype! When the number of arrests dwindled, we left.

When the second demonstration occurred, I waited till the next day to go take a look. It was good for a description of the Boulevard St. Germain in the morning light, the holes in the iron screens around the trees, and here and there a turned-over bench and a broken-off street lantern. In the Deux Magots, where there had been fighting, they barely talk about it. The newspapers carry pictures of injured journalists in the hospital. There is one of a fat colleague with a split lip and a dressing over one eye, which only looks like yet another variation on the ubiquitous picture of Stavisky, lying on the floor with blood running along his lip.

When the third demonstration was announced, I called up Héverlé to find out whether it would turn into a real revolution this time. "Vous n'y pensez pas?"[7] The next day there were reports in the newspaper that the rain had ruined it. The *Action Française* is priceless for reporting the drama in this way. It seems that Chiappe was waiting in his car in front of the Palais Bourbon for the battle to begin when Maurice Pujo, the leader of the royalist army, went up to him to say, "Monsieur le Préfet, it's raining. You know that this isn't something that will weaken our zeal and tenacity, but...." And after yelling, "Down with the thieves. Long live France," he withdrew so that the police wouldn't have to get wet either.

"They slaughtered that countryman of yours in Germany," Guraev says to me, in reference to Van der Lubbe. "I feel bad about it because I particularly liked the way in which he jumped around naked among the flames when he was caught. As far as the Bulgarian is concerned (Dimitrov), he has been acquitted. He has stated to the press, by the way, that it wouldn't surprise him if they still murdered him. I don't think it's fair that that Bulgarian was the one to get such a beautiful part and that your countryman was so drugged he could only wheeze. If they had drugged Dimitrov like him, he might have acted the same way."

Guraev walks through Auteuil with me, but he doesn't want to go to my room, for fear of the other Russians. "White Russians do nothing but whine, using the language of 1917, which has lost all contact with present-day Russian. I don't want to talk to them because they suppose I am one of them, and if they are so old...."

It's still freezing outside, but now the neighborhood doesn't look so empty anymore. All the trees make you think you're out of the city, but every day you're stopped by the unemployed who come here to panhandle from those who are still rich. I've never seen so many street-singers. What have I really enjoyed since we have been back in Paris, I asked myself yesterday. And my first thought was: *Stenka Razin*, sung under our window. But it's as if the putrifaction emanates from everywhere, pervading everything.

I leave Guraev, but I don't escape my old senator. He calls me gravely into his living room, gives me tea and candy, and tells me he has wanted to ask me for a long time what my opinion—as a journalist—is of "all this." I tell him exactly how I see my journalistic function and answer his questions truthfully, each of which he asks as if startled. When I'm through, he scratches the back of his head and laughs at me, grinning with complicity.

"Umm.... May I say something insulting? You're... umm, a terrible pessimist. A Bakunin, sir. And please let me tell you that I am Bakunin's nephew—my grandmother was his sister—but the principle of Good is still at work in this world, although perhaps in the most mysterious way, sir..."

A week has passed. Every morning the old lady brings us *Le Matin* and tells us whether or not there's been another demonstration. The people who dined with Stavisky continue to be assembled in the Bayonne prison, which is named poetically "Villa Chagrin." There is a marvelous detail for a dime-store novel: the mayor of Bayonne, who had always refused to heat the prison, is now sick from the cold and has begged for a small heater (which, unfortunately, they gave him). The people who come from Paris first have their picture taken at the station, all smiles. In a cartoon a woman says to her husband: "Don't grin like that, they might think you're one of the accused." The newspapers report a new bank collapse, also to the tune of 200 million francs.

During the last demonstration the streetcars were stopped, and there was fighting until midnight. They threw hot water on the police from houses and emptied seltzer bottles on them from the cafés. The old lady doesn't like the fact that I'm not always on the scene. But it's true, she says, some journalists have been wounded again. One of them reports the surprise of the police at being hit back. We all know about their sadism, but this detail is funny. Unfortunately, not many policemen were wounded. Only very few had skull fractures when they were hit with iron poles torn from the fences around the trees. A police commissioner by the name of Meyer lent an almost artistic balance to the scene. The first night he got a bloody nose, the second night he got a bucket of water thrown on his coat, later he stumbled over a pile of fences and injured his leg. He was present at the last demonstration, though. This time they arrested 811 people and announced that those taken into custody wouldn't be discharged until they were interrogated and prosecuted for defacing or attempting to deface public property.

There were scuffles in the Chambre des Députés. At the Palais de Justice one lawyer said to another: "How do you dare show up here?" and they began to rip each other's robes to shreds; now the seconds are trying to decide whether they will duel or not.

The investigation of Stavisky's suicide has been entrusted to the Sûreté Générale, whose agents were probably the ones responsible for his death. The people who are in Villa Chagrin will be able to say, even if they are convicted, that there was no due process of law, because already 1,200 documents have disappeared from the dossier. I tear out a picture from the newspaper of a judge in charge of unraveling the case in Bayonne. I show it to the old man, who is playing solitaire next to the tea tray.

He looks up for a second. "A picture like this doesn't mean a thing to me."

The old lady comes in and looks. "A Jew, right?" she asks, and leaves.

The old man continues to talk about his experience. "Six hundred names have been mentioned in this case. I saw that number somewhere. Sir, a judge's means are very limited... Even if he wants to be fair at all times, he is physically incapable of it. You have to cut up a case like this. That man is probably doing what he can, but umm... his means are very limited, sir." He looks at the picture again: "I can't really tell much from such a picture."

The old lady comes back and says: "No, I don't trust him. He looks like a Jew."

"There you have it. Simplistic, simplistic through and through," says the old man in his soft voice, engrossed in his solitaire again.

The old lady says: "Cher ami, from the beginning of our marriage you've tried to educate me." And to me, "He's ten years older than I am."

"Nine, between eight and nine."

"And so far he hasn't given up. I ask him sometimes, aren't you sick of trying to teach me over and over again. There's really nothing that you can do with me. Or perhaps you don't have the talent for it."

She confessed to Jane that if she were young again she would live differently, very unchaste, totally unlike the way she has done.

The two lawyers have had their duel with four witnesses, two doctors, and a referee. They were all in black with turned-up collars and derby hats. (The top hat has been abolished by the honor code.) Both men were duly examined to see whether they were wearing bullet-proof vests. They then fired twice, missed both times, as everybody had hoped, and went away without any reconciliation. In the picture the location looked like a tennis court, and the gentlemen stood at a great distance from one another (I'd guess at least a hundred feet), and their posture was such that you'd swear they had their eyes closed. I looked at the picture for a long time. In the Indies I used to think that to be a true European, or at least a true Parisian, you had to duel. Guraev and Héverlé had similar ideas when they were about twenty. The real romantic duels, like the ones in Lermontov where the duelists stand on rocks so that even a slight wound would be enough to make them fall off into the abyss, always seemed too perfect to me. But I didn't think that the duels of Dumas père and those connected to the Dreyfus affair were totally ridiculous. But it seems that during that period they missed most of the time because the seconds purposely loaded the pistols with bullets that were too small.

During the Teresa period it looked as if I might get involved in a duel. When I was in Brussels and she was in her Italian country house, she wrote that my letters were sometimes delivered to her opened. She was very unhappy about that, but her complaints were fruitless because the man who ran the village post office was an unpleasant sort and seemed to have something against her and her mother, and she suspected that he opened those letters. The blood rushed to my face while I was reading, and right away I wrote the postmaster. But since I wasn't completely certain, I crossed out the address and added: "au monsieur trop important qui ouvre les lettres d'autrui."[8] After that I thought I had a free hand: I summarized in two lines what I thought about my personal letters to "a lady" being read, and I used the words "scoundrel" and "rascal" for the person who had done such a thing. I received an Italian letter by return mail, signed "Rag. Tullio Crivelli," in which I in turn was called "il peggio dei vigliacchi e un mascalzone."[9] I asked a pharmacist across the street who knew Italian for the correct translation of these terms. The postmaster demanded satisfaction, as is required in such cases. I wrote back that if he was admitting by this that he had opened my letters, I would not take back what I had said, and I would give him satisfaction as soon as I was in Italy. I worked on the means of providing him his satisfaction as best I could. I used to fence and do some target shooting in the Indies, but since I thought Italians were good at fencing I decided it would be smart to practice. I looked for a fencing master and on the Place Stéphanie found a certain Lamour, a former officer and international foil champion. He was a young man with the worldly manners of a dance master, which as a matter of fact he was. He had one room for fencing and another for dancing, with two different phonographs. I told him my story and emphasized the importance of practical lessons. "I can't teach you any secret thrusts," he said, "because they only exist in novels. But if it's an Italian he'll probably attack you screaming. You must remember then that a scream is not a thrust." I promised, and we fenced not with foils but swords, which are much heavier. It went all right as soon as I got used to this weapon. After five or six lessons he declared I was ready to stand up to my Italian, and he then tried to enroll me as a dance student. The ladies who came to his classes were a very decent sort. I had only to look at him to believe it, and so I refused, barely hiding my horror at the idea of meeting Teresa's friends here too. That would have been the limit. When he assured me that I had to give my Italian a nice little stab, "une belle petite boutonnière,"[10] he said elegantly, "to calm him down, for example, here in the arm," I responded that I wouldn't just stab him if I had the opportunity to do more.

"Comment?" he said reprimanding me. "Vous ne voulez pas le tuer?"[11]

"Maybe not," I said, "but if I have to go that far to have a duel, I want to do what I can."

"Hmmm," he said elegantly again, "vous êtes un original!"[12]

In the meantime the Italian postmaster found out who my lady was. He wrote to Teresa, and she showed up in his office, concerned. He swore to her that he had not opened her letters, and he showed her my letter. I got an indignant message from her, saying her assumption had been wrong and she had taken care of everything, that she thought my behavior was crazy and I wasn't her fiancé, that she could take care of herself, and what would people think about this? The postmaster was a middle-aged man. He was still strong and quick, but the idea of dueling him was as ridiculous as it was crazy. He seemed to think so too. At least, I got a new message from him on green paper this time, which confirmed that the intervention of the "signorina cosi amabile e graziosa"[13] had cleared up everything. He also said he understood how I felt and would like to make the acquaintance of the "uomo d'onore come siete e come vi credo,"[14] if I came to Italy. The funny side of the whole thing made up for the heroic aspect I had been deprived of. The story ended on a completely different note. Six months later perhaps Teresa sent me a clipping from an Italian newspaper. She had written on it, "This is the man you wanted to duel." Mr. Rag. Tullio Crivelli was arrested after one of his daughters had killed herself. Her fiancé had sued because she had explained her action in a suicide note: she felt she could no longer escape being molested by her father, which he had threatened for months and which neither of her older sisters had escaped. I wrote back that I didn't know I had been up against an Italian of the old Cenci sort.

The cabinet resigned, and immediately there was an enormous demonstration on the boulevard. At six o'clock two huge groups started to run into each other, one coming from the Boulevard de la Madeleine and the other from the Boulevard des Italiens. The police left them alone. Demonstrators yelled at them: "Dear policemen, don't you want to get the thieves too?" Suddenly there was five minutes of fierce commotion at the Café de la Paix: windows were broken, tables smashed, a newsstand turned over, and the customers on the terrace got into a fight. The police kept their distance. A bus was stopped, the passengers forced to get out, and the bus placed diagonally across the street to stop the traffic. Gas lanterns were bent; flames came out of a newsstand. Finally the police moved in, but carefully. There were more than five thousand demonstrators this time, and their number was growing. A number of policemen were roughed up; a fire engine that happened to be passing by and was suspected of going to hose down the crowd was damaged. The hoses were cut up, and the water sprayed out of the holes. Pickpockets worked diligently during the demonstration. The police arrested about three hundred people in all. It's as if this time they wanted the demonstrators to run themselves out. At 8:15 Commissioner Meyer was pulled down by the demonstrators and severely bruised. But gradually their milling about calmed down; they vandalized a bit more and then left. It's hard to imagine, this dangerous swollen crowd of individuals, each of whom sinks back into his own little hole. A new cabinet is formed; somebody who has done it before is always available. The strong men are now Daladier and Frot, the latter a very young minister with a beard à la Balbo.[15]

"Sir," the old senator says, "the most truth-loving man I ever met was a thief and a murderer, sir, a thief and a murderer. A Georgian who was the leader of a band of robbers.... And, umm... everything they asked him he answered with total honesty. Now you must understand that he was accused of thirteen robberies involving murder, but one of them was the work of a lieutenant of his. Now, there was nothing that could be done about it, twelve or thirteen doesn't make a big difference, does it?... But when the day of the verdict came and he was told again he was guilty on thirteen counts, he got up, sir, and with tears in his eyes began to scream, 'Twelve! Twelve! Not thirteen! Why don't you believe me when I tell you that the last one was done by somebody else!...' He was like a child, sir, a charming robber; I'm always moved when I think of him... umm..., the most truth-loving man I ever met."

"And you convicted him?"

"And I convicted him."

He shakes his head and again looks a lot like an old sheik. Has this man necessarily been dishonest because he was a member of the judiciary? Was he perhaps corrupt, biased, and did he abuse his power? How facile, how cheap. He makes me realize it's possible for a judge to be honest (assuming it's morally acceptable to be a judge), but he also pulls me into a Russian novel far away from the Stavisky affair.

The Bayonne investigation is fruitless. Each suspect appears with two or three clever lawyers and completely justifies himself to the court. One after the other is temporarily released. The press notes that what had been announced as a big week turns out to be very minor. It was only the people of Bayonne who put the fear of God into one of the released crooks, a member of Parliament. When he left the judge's office he walked down the street between his lawyers with his broad, fat, arrogant face held high. Jeering women, children, and men wearing berets walked behind him, not touching him but yelling "En prison! En prison!" He walked faster and faster, and so did the crowd. He wasn't familiar with Bayonne and got lost. The crowd behind him grew from two hundred to two thousand. He was asthmatic and had a heart condition, and suddenly he was faced with climbing a steep, narrow street. He fell down, his attorneys carried him into a little store and then into a room on the second floor because he was still scared to death. The crowd stayed in the street, yelling, "En prison! En prison!" Finally the police came to his rescue. He changed hotels immediately. When he came back to Paris he got off the train a station early, afraid a similar reception might await him in the capital, where pictures of the crowd on his heels had been in all the newspapers. These pictures are really marvelous.

"My pessimism," I say to the old man, "takes a real childish pleasure in this. There's still a lot of good in the French, at least in those people from Bayonne."

"Of course, sir, of course," he says, "but human justice needs a little more than that, voy-i-ons. Good economic order alone... "

At the Héverlés' I bring the conversation around to the big financiers, and Jane says:

"I would like to hear a lot about this... reality, about people 'in real life' who make the decisions that affect the lives of others. I torture myself with the idea that people like us—I mean Arthur and me—are living 'in error,' that we have construed our own imaginary world, outside of which we couldn't live, perhaps, but which makes it all the worse for that. A life that changes nothing and that 'real life' doesn't bother about at all... "

"You're wrong. It's just as necessary," says Héverlé, "because all of culture consists of just that. You're not the only ones who think so; mankind has been thinking that way for more than two thousand years. To eliminate that kind of life you would have to stop thinking. Your mistake is in assuming that 'the others' are happy with what you call their reality. They aren't in the least!"

"And yet we feel these days that our values don't count."

"They always count. The important banker or the important statesman or even the great conqueror always needs to be justified by the thinker. You think that Deterding is more powerful than Nietzsche, but... "

"No," I say, "but as far as we're concerned there's cowardice in religion, in the story of a better life hereafter. If you leave out all the Deterdings and Nietzsches, doesn't the fictitious world that people like us create around ourselves really boil down to a similar cowardice? What you call culture—poetry, religion—isn't that in some sense what Jane calls 'living in error'?"

"Or madness," says Jane.

"The truth is," says Héverlé, "that this is typical intellectual masochism. It's always the same. You would like to blow up Deterding, but you can't, and so you think, why not myself?"

"I'm not thinking about Deterding," says Jane.

"I am," I say. "Héverlé is right. If I could get away with shooting someone like him and have nothing to worry about except my own moral inhibitions, I believe I would do it with the greatest calm. At least in times like these... "

"Bella thinks that she lives 'in error'," says Héverlé, "since she has had the child she always wanted. In her case the error is that she has no guarantee against all the threats to the child, to me, and to herself."

"Yes, if you were killed tomorrow," says Bella, "why wouldn't I have the right to turn on the gas and kill both the child and myself? The child wouldn't know. I'm almost sure nobody will take care of her as well as we would. How can somebody tell me this is egoism and that I don't have that right?"

"Did you have the right to carry a child for a whole year just for your own pleasure? But this conversation is ideologically absurd!"

"I want to see somebody," says Bella, "who really acts according to an ideology or has acted according to one."

It's impossible to steer the conversation away from this absurdity. On the way home Jane says: "Why are we always so crazy to contradict people who say things like Bella did a while ago? She is completely right, after all."

I try to figure out why people continue to resist, but I can't grasp it. What Héverlé said about intellectual masochism concerns me more. When we get home, there is a letter from the Brussels notary: the estate is finally settled, and he has transferred my share to my account. I received a little over three thousand guilders in all, hardly enough to put in a savings account for Jane and me. Why do I complain? There are people who have toiled all their lives and saved only three hundred guilders for their old age.

33   For Pessimists

February 1934. It's as if everything is falling hurriedly into place: my sister-in-law writes from the Indies that she's almost sure she can pay for Guy's education, but Otto's estate hasn't been settled yet. "If times were different, I would promise it now." Even if she can't help, few things in this sad story have done me as much good as this letter. Her tone is never forced, always sincere, and since she has gone through Otto's illness and death so recently, it shows that she is more than tactful—she has an unusually pure character.

I hope to see Guy in Brussels soon. In any case it seems better to leave him in the boarding school for the time being. I imagine how I will skillfully draw him out, ask him how he's doing there, and by talking to him be able to figure out what changes he has gone through. How I delude myself! Once I'm standing in front of him, it won't work. It may just be my resignation, but then I look at him kindly, understandingly, and compassionately. The final scene should perhaps end with a tear, but lacking that there is always the fatherly smile.

It's a little over a year since my mother's death. I have recorded the only times I thought about her with emotion. Apart from that she has been something like an old portrait for me. Once I forgot she was dead, when I saw an almost empty bottle of cajeput oil in our bathroom in Meudon: "When I go to Brussels I'll have to ask her to fill that up... oh, she's not there anymore." A light shock for having forgotten. Perhaps that was on account of my tropical reminiscences.

She wasn't able to arrange her final hours the way she wanted to. She had to die the way she did and probably was absorbed in it enough not to feel my absence *too* much... But it's perhaps a bourgeois prejudice—good for a certain time—that a deathbed must be a solemn good-bye. A year before my father's suicide (which he took care of in ten minutes) he thought he was going to die because he felt so strange and his feet were cold. He gathered us around him: my mother, Sylvia, Uncle Van Kuyck, and me. He spoke solemnly and looked at us with dignity and fear. After fifteen minutes Uncle Van Kuyck said, "Damn it, I think you're making fools of us, you know, and I'm going to bed." The next morning at coffee my father was still visibly disappointed that "that phlegmatic Uncle Van Kuyck" had been right.

Aunt Tina said my mother must have had a radiant vision. I thought about that later, without wanting to. "If it's true that your whole life flashes before you just before you die, just as supposedly it does for some people who drown (some people on the gallows too), if this were really the last gift of God, not the heavens or the angels but your own life..." This is a train of thought that I myself hardly feel responsible for. I put an end to it by whispering "Oh, how sweet!" in spite of myself. I had tears in my eyes when I said it. That was the last time.

We are looking for another place to live, now that we have this money in our savings account again. There is an organization of petty swindlers who have the slogan, "A little help for little people," and which Viala has warned us about at great length. You're lured in by something unusually attractive in a good neighborhood, which costs almost nothing. You go there, enter a dark office, and are told that the apartment has just been rented. But soon there'll be something else. They have a "benevolent association" that you can join for twenty-five francs (not one hundred francs, like those rental agency crooks charge; never pay those!), and with this organization you may move as often as you want; it's only twenty-five francs a year. The association also helps you find work, at least if you want, and finally as a bonus, there's a midwife who gives free advice in cases of pregnancy (the word abortion is not mentioned). Once you have become a member you're sent to an address which also has just been rented. After that you don't hear anything from them again. There may be one hundred members... "The swindle turns a profit of 211 francs and 75 centimes after expenses," says Viala.

February 7. Yesterday at 5:30, I was with Guraev in the Deux Magots. "There will be some fighting tonight," he said. "The veterans are going to join in at the Palais-Bourbon this time too. The Place de la Concorde is crowded with people yelling, 'Long live Chiappe!' Why?"

I shrug my shoulders.

"It seems that Daladier suddenly dismissed him after having embraced him the day before, while saying between sobs that he was his best friend. Chiappe seems to have answered by telephone: 'Then I'll be on the street tonight,' and the other one understood: 'I'm going to hit the streets,' which in these heroic days means just about, 'Then I'll play the eighteenth of Brumaire[1] at the head of my police force.' So Parliament is scared to death. You really don't know anything, Ducroo, if you're not up with these historic events."

"I'm not saying I don't know; I don't think anybody knows what's really going on."

"Well, yes, this much is certain: Frot is against Chiappe. Frot has been pulled out of obscurity, but he realizes now that he has the soul of a Bonaparte, and maybe tonight he will have his own coup d'état. But Chiappe is now the one the masses like—the martyr. They think it's scandalous and alarming that he has been replaced by somebody else. Did you look at the face of his replacement, by the way? Really something rather peculiar, along the lines of your notaries. But who yells, 'Long live Chiappe'? First of all, all those empty-headed camelots who can't stand to lose their playmate. It was so refreshing and French, all those riots with the compliments they gave one another afterwards."

"Tonight you'll be able to hear the soul of France sing even more seriously; those veterans—there's the blackmail that was missing."

"Do you think I want to go and look, Ducroo? No, I want to go straight home. I prefer to despise all these doings quietly, as a foreigner. But if you want to go to the Place de la Concorde... "

He gets up angrily.

"If they only knew, for even a moment, how stupid they are to be exploited by the newspapers and by big business behind the newspapers; how with their stupid reputation of 'once a hero, always a hero' they must save the face of France... If they could see this, perhaps I'd feel some sympathy for those veterans. I suggest that we do anything rather than join the cattle. For no reason, for what we owe to ourselves, Ducroo."

"To ourselves as what, as foreigners?"

"First of all, as noncattle, and then as whatever you want. As 'intellectual proletarians,' for all I care. I suggest that we spend the evening together and that we talk about anything but politics."

When I come home at eleven, the old gentleman is worried and grabs me by the sleeve.

"Is there a revolution? Is it true they were shooting at the veterans?"

I tell him how much I enjoyed spending the evening somewhere else. He shakes his head in sympathy while he limps along the hall, steadying himself by holding on to the wall.

"I heard that the veterans will go into the streets tomorrow, armed this time. Tonight they were not armed. It was a calm and dignified demonstration, sir, but if they had been shot at... umm, what will the French people say about that? You haven't been near the Place de la Concorde?"

"Sure, I even passed underneath, but in the metro. There were no veterans."

He puts his hand on my shoulder, as if he wants to pat me. "Voy-i-ons, they were shot at, sir. Maybe thirty disabled veterans have been killed. Would you like it better if there had been three hundred?"

I would like to say something reassuring now, but I stand with my hand on the doorknob of our own room. So I smile in a friendly way, and that is enough for him to go away, still shaking his head.

Today the report of what happened: fifty dead and more than a thousand wounded, it says. One charge after another. From six o'clock on, the Place de la Concorde was filled with people. Parliament met in the Palais Bourbon in terror, while outside the crowd screamed: "Resign! Throw the thieves in the Seine!" Around seven they had destroyed fences and benches again; a bus was stopped, well-dressed young men tried to turn it over, broke the windows and set it on fire. The police charged, also the gardes mobiles on foot, behind them a few on horseback, all without much result. The crowd bombarded the police with cobblestones, all the time screaming, "Long live Chiappe!" At eight the veterans began to march from the Grand Palais, carrying banners and signs that declared they were independent of any party, and singing the Marseillaise, of course. Close to the bridges of the Palais Bourbon the crowd pressed so hard that the police barricades collapsed. They laughed at the police with their drawn sabres and the horses turning around. Then suddenly a shot rang out.

They say that the disabled veterans were placed in front, pushed forward as a shield against the garde mobile. The police didn't want to shoot. It was the garde mobile. Cries of indignation went up everywhere. From that moment on the police kept charging, the whole square was wiped clean, the Concorde bridge was dripping with blood. The people fled under the trees where the horses couldn't follow them, but by then the police were back into the act and they were madder than ever. Demonstrators who fell were trampled and their skulls "smashed," according to the newspapers. As for the other side, the demonstrators pulled policemen from their horses, stabbed their horses with knives and paralyzed them; they even shot back at the police with revolvers. After being hit and shoved, only the veterans restored their procession to some sort of order, to show their calm and dignity. With blood on their faces they kept their banners high. The newspapers couldn't praise enough their singing of the Marseillaise and their noble faces which were so different from those of the menacing bands that also milled around and yelled, "Les Soviets!" or responded to the singing with the International. The rage of the police is also understandable. Hadn't they lost their beloved chief, the only one who could have maintained order? The papers had nothing but insults for his successor and for Frot's shameful order to shoot from the darkened Palais Bourbon. The representatives only dared go home by the back door under police escort. The Parisians bled, but they are now getting ready to take their revenge on the murderers. All the neighborhood pharmacies were full of injured people. The Weber café looked like one big hospital. The pictures speak for themselves: what a pathetic group, those in uniform and those not. A burning bus lends a festive light, but everywhere you see people with distressed faces, instinctive distrust, and fear. The pose some groups take, however, is striking.

I talked to people in the street and in the cafés. A young man with a strong southern accent told me how he was *almost* afraid once because of the horses, and he had to jump into a fountain. In the meantime everything on the Place de la Concorde has been cleaned up very quickly. There's still some broken glass, a slight blot on the large square—last night the pavement must have glittered like a skating rink, but there is no more blood. The obelisk looks distant and just as foreign as ever. On the pedestals of the statues representing the various cities there are bullet holes circled with red chalk with sentences written next to them like, "The murderers Daladier and Frot made the police shoot French people with French bullets." The first person killed was a chambermaid on a balcony, a curious little flower above the ocean.

February 8. The ministry resigned at three o'clock. Frot has dropped out of sight, but in the Palais de Justice his colleagues burn his robe. At four there's a new demonstration on the Place de la Concorde: "Frot et Daladier au poteau!"[2] Yet everything stays relatively quiet. At night, however, the huge department stores near the Opera and the Madeleine, on the Champs Elysées and in other well-to-do neighborhoods, are plundered with complete impunity. "Troublesome elements" profit from the police being occupied elsewhere. In the bourgeois press there is a nauseating eagerness to identify these hoods with the Communists, and the noble veterans who have already been frequently contrasted to the "scum" on the "big night" are again being cited repeatedly.

Two catch phrases become more and more frequent, the "calm and dignity" of all true Frenchmen, in contrast to those who went down in "blood and mire." Former President Doumergue is brought out of retirement; he arrived in Paris this morning to enthusiastic greetings. All the newspapers seem to agree that this smiling old man is the only person who can prevent a civil war.

February 9. On the Boulevard Saint-Germain this afternoon I saw the first wall posters giving the names of Doumergue's new cabinet. "They're all there," Viala said standing next to me, "the same jokers, only grouped a little differently. The French are crazy about their old stars. They haven't seen Doumergue for four years, so they're all excited. It is the Cécile Sorel[3] cabinet. When tonight's communist demonstration has been put down by the police clubs and Doumergue's smile has worked as a miraculous balm, we may forget again for a moment that a few veterans were trampled on. The press is upset because there were no more corpses during their great night. First there were fifty, then forty, then thirty, finally only ten. If tonight fifty Communists are killed, it'll take two weeks before the number will be established."

I ask him if he's thinking of going there.

"No," he says, "I'm going to ask Héverlé about it, but I don't expect too much to happen tonight. Let's go to the demonstration of the united front at the Place de la Nation on the twelfth. If there's going to be any serious fighting there, it'll be really serious."

I leave him after this. At home the old gentleman introduces me to a young Russian prince with a large bandage around his head. He was knocked down by a police stick on the big night, but it didn't hurt his storytelling powers, so I was called in to hear about it. He was out taking a walk—he just loves to hear the profound remarks of the Parisian people—when he heard the first shots near the Concorde. A man had climbed on a bench and said, "Tomorrow let's kill individually each of the bastards who ordered the police to shoot at the people of Paris. We'll look them up in the directory and we'll kill them. C'est promis?" And the audience said, "C'est promis! C'est promis!"[4] Then he walked on to the Place de la Concorde itself. He had walked by there only an hour before, but it was as if a century had passed. There was glass everywhere, puddles of blood and vomit from people who had been hit in the stomach... While he was watching, everybody ran away. So did he. He heard steps behind him and was hit twice with a night stick. He rushed into the Tuileries between two ladies in mink coats; he felt no pain and noticed only the mink, but he knows now that the ladies had also been clubbed and that they had bloody faces. In the Tuileries everything was dark, and suddenly the gate was closed. Somebody yelled: "They're going to kill us here." At that moment he noticed he had blood on his hands. First he thought that it came from somebody else he had touched, but a voice said: "you're wounded." And then he saw that his coat was soaked with blood. He remembers being taken to a pharmacy by two Camelots du Roi, where it was so full of wounded people that they couldn't help him. He was then driven to a hospital, along with somebody whose nose had almost been cut off. In the morning a doctor who was very generous came in and said: "I might have been a demonstrator myself. You don't have to pay me anything. You must eat a lot of spinach to make up for the loss of blood."

After that he rested for forty-eight hours and then went into the streets with his bandaged head. Within half an hour he had three different reactions. The first was somebody who yelled at him: "The next time it's going to be your head." Then he went to a newsstand to buy a paper, and the woman said: "Demonstrators don't get any newspapers until you pay for our burned newsstands." He began to regret that he wasn't wearing a hat and decided to go home by bus, and everybody yelled: "Let him go first; make room for somebody who was hit by the bastards." Inside everybody stood up, and a number of people shook his hand.

"Let me point out to you that the story is very well told," the old man whispers to me. Indeed, it was well polished. The only thing was his lisping, which was so bad that I later asked the old lady if it was a result of his wound.

"Poor prince," she said. "Let me tell you. His father was a true aristocrat but his mother less so. When she had spent all her money in the emigration and had sold all her jewels, she became impossible. Every day she and her husband had violent scenes. And one day there was such a violent scene that the young prince couldn't bear it any longer: he jumped out of the window from the sixth floor. Fortunately his fall was broken by a balcony on the second floor, and that's what saved him. But oh, he had one broken leg, a triple chin fracture, and all his teeth were gone. His lisping comes from his dentures. And he used to be such a handsome boy! You can still tell."

It's strange that anyone who went through something so dramatic would bother to tell a story about getting hit on the head twice. But the best part is that this young prince is one of the very few White Russians who don't support the Grand Duke Cyril as pretender, because they think that the czar is still alive. He must have become an optimist after living through all these accidents.

February 10. Fiercely attacked, the Communists resisted just as fiercely, but there were only six or seven thousand. The entrance to the Place de la République where the demonstration was to take place had been blocked, but there was fighting in the whole neighborhood. The police pursued the fugitives furiously, even into the metro. Out of the houses they hurled everything at the police, even stoves. They supposedly stormed some of the houses from which shots were fired. The Gare de l'Est was in the hands of the workers for a short while. The result is that the newspapers now breathe fire, and even in the smallest shops in our neighborhood the people suddenly sigh sympathetically about the injured policemen. Six Communists were killed; this time it's in the open: no more, unfortunately. This blood is worthless and cannot be compared to the "noblest blood of the land," which was spilled on the sixth. "Those communist animals had revolvers."

"While those courageous policemen had nothing but loaves of gingerbread," said Héverlé, when I visited him in the afternoon.

Contrary to what Viala had told me, they did go where the fighting was. Both with their wives. Bella is proud that they made it to the heart of the Place de la République, past three police checkpoints. Manou went along without a trace of fear, talking to Bella about a ball given by left-wing people which wouldn't take place now. Héverlé didn't wear a hat and was searched at the first roadblock. Viala had on the typical cap of the "troublesome element," but he was walking between the two women and was only searched at the third roadblock. The policeman who searched him suddenly found a suspicious object in his pocket and revealed a large bottle of aspirin. During the charges what had struck Héverlé the most were all the faces crowded together in the windows, and how they all dropped just as in a puppet show, as soon as the uniforms appeared in the street.

February 13. Here is the sober report of what happened yesterday. Even today I don't know what feelings to add to it, because I went through all this almost without any feelings. At about 2:30 we were at the Place de la Nation: Manou, Viala, Jane, and I. The last metro stop had been sealed off, so we got off at the one before it and went on foot among a growing crowd. A few yards from the huge square with the statue of Marianne in the middle we are cut off by an orderly procession coming out of a side street. The first line is made up of respectable-looking men with beards, with faces from the time of Jules Guesde,[5] next to workers who had their arms around each other's shoulders. In the lead is a sturdy old man with a gray mustache and a cap, a proletarian père noble type, holding a flag. Behind them many women are yelling, louder than the men: "Venez avec nous, camarades!"[6] The first impression is exhilarating. People are hanging from all the windows in the street. On the sidewalks they laugh and talk sympathetically with the people in the crowd, but few join. I buy a card of solidarity with the striking taxi drivers and a revolutionary newssheet: *Merci, camarade.* The implied solidarity certainly doesn't go beyond a certain level, but so far it is quite real.

Slowly—it is about three o'clock now—the square fills up. Crowds of people meet other crowds; they scream with excitement. A big portrait of Dimitrov hangs from a branch of a tree: they salute it with clenched fists like Communists, but many also take their caps off. The socialists, whom the Communists usually call bourgeois and social-fascists, have come to honor the courage of this Communist. The Communists feel strengthened and inclined to admire the larger crowds and the discipline of the socialists. This demonstration has to be carried out with "dignity and calm."

At four o'clock the square is chock full. There are people draped around the statue of Marianne like bunches of grapes on the vine, also around the secondary statues. Around them, and in a bandstand as well, are speakers you can't hear. There are red flags everywhere: on telephone poles, in the branches of a tall, bare tree, on a still taller scaffolding of a house under construction. Somebody climbs on the shoulders of Marianne and in a rather childish way waves a red flag above her bonnet and finally places it like a pen over her ear. All this takes place in a gray light, and the enemy doesn't interfere. What do such symbols matter? The slogans screamed by the speakers are those you can read in any newspaper. Here you can see their gestures, but fortunately the texts don't need to be long: "Down with the bourgeoisie which furthers fascism! Get the crooks out of Parliament! Punish all the guilty!" The crowd mostly screams, "Les Soviets partout!"[7] and after that they just walk around, chanting, "Uni-té d'ac-tion, uni-té d'ac-tion!"[8]

Among the signs there is one cynical one: "On ne suicide pas la République comme on a suicidé Stavisky."[9] The others are regular slogans: "Contre la politique du moindre mal,"[10] "Les fascistes ne passeront pas,"[11] "La mort plutôt que le fascisme."[12] We stop here and there, pick up a few words, and walk on. After an hour we realize we are getting tired. It looks more like we are walking in a circle, and what we see around us all looks the same. What makes them happiest is that there is such a big crowd, that they seem to have great strength, that the proletariat shows up from all over, and not just the proletariat. "How many people are here? One hundred thousand or more? The others will say it really doesn't mean anything."

Only if you pass by the streets that fan off around the square, like spokes, would you immediately sense the difference. Each street is blocked off no more than three hundred feet away by policemen and by gardes mobiles on foot and on horseback. There are copper helmets everywhere. And the hate you can imagine on their faces is the most despicable there is, the callous hate of mercenaries. An ordinary policeman would probably say: "If only we could kill all those Communists, then we'd be rid of our troubles for good." At each street there is jeering and whistling from this side and scornful silence from the other, but you can feel the tension in their watchfulness. Their uniforms are gray in the misty light behind them; only their helmets are shining. We imagine what would happen if they suddenly charged from all those streets, like wedges driven into this merry-go-round. What damage would result! When some demonstrators—still excited about the ninth, or were they agitators?—try to go into the streets, discipline is enforced; marshals slide in between and push the reckless quietly back into the circular movement, "Back, comrades! Ne provoquez pas, laissez-les, enfin... gentiment, quoi!"[13] At a street full of gardes on horseback the jeering doubles. "Aux chiottes,"[14] they drawl out evenly, and everywhere they yell, "Chiappe en prison,"[15] the dominant slogan.

Suddenly in front of us limps a dumpy little man with a white beard, a beggar wearing a Tyrolean hat with pictures of Lenin, Dimitrov, and Romain Roland pinned on it. On his chest and on his back he has signs which he had drawn in red and black letters: his name is Coeur-Joli, he is seventy-two, has had eight work-related accidents, and finally the words: "If I die today, my death will have served the cause of the proletariat."

A show of strength, with calm and dignity. "Abject intellectuals" seem to think that such a large crowd didn't show enough muscle. But since it is a show of strength, you can't help but think of the weapons they might carry and of those which they certainly don't have. You ask yourself what a revolution can accomplish, even with 150,000 enthusiastic fighters, if the other side can send in a couple of planes to bomb them. If it comes down to war, what modern weapons does this side have?

By 4:30 we have walked around in circles for more than two hours. The crowd isn't making its circles anymore. Huge groups drift away along the Cours de Vincennes. We enter a café bursting with people. In all the telephone booths are journalists reporting on the events. I overhear one who says, "Riot in Ménilmontant." Manou wants to go take a look, and she gets us going. "Let's go in the metro and find out which exits are blocked. That's where something will have happened."

We find a long list of closed stops written in chalk, all along the Avenue Voltaire. So again we go to the closest metro stop. Nothing: empty boulevards, police patrols everywhere. The Place de la Bastille was full of gardes mobiles in short leather coats with short rifles. There are cars at the street corners with machine guns under canvas. It is cold and damp in the streets. It feels like a state of siege, despite the official reports. Finally we get hungry and go some place to eat. The waiter tells us proudly that at least nothing has happened there.

When we are walking to the main boulevard and crossing a square, a tinkling noise suddenly startles us. A small thin fellow with a cap knocks a fatter one in shirt sleeves against a window, and glass falls everywhere. Viala and I go up to see the man in shirt sleeves stagger after a few blows, put his hand on his bloodied face, take a step backwards across the threshold of a half-open door to a courtyard, and disappear into the dark. A woman appears from the same doorway, crosses her arms on her chest, and shrieks. The man in the street screams past her at the man who disappears, "Aren't you ashamed?"

"It's over the woman," Viala says.

A couple of passers-by stay to watch, but a group of gardes mobiles a little further on decide this is not part of their battle.

On the boulevards, the movie theaters and cafés are open as usual. A woman who insults a policeman is almost taken to the station; the bystanders think she was in the wrong. At nine o'clock the metro suddenly appears to be shut down. Without either taxis or the metro Jane and I are forced to walk home. From the Place de la Nation to the Porte d'Auteuil we cross the entire width of Paris from east to west. Bravely we begin. Everything is abandoned but well lit. Our steps sound hollow and yet cheerful. Everything is so sedate, so far from the general turbulence. It is impressive sometimes with the huge buildings, and suddenly we realize how strange it is to live as foreigners in this "eternal Paris." When we get home, we tell the old Russians the demonstration was very exciting.

February 14. There's a fifty-fifty chance that everything will stay calm now, according to Héverlé. But he talks enthusiastically about the demonstration of the Popular Front. He even uses the word "grandiose" in reference to the attendance, the assembled strength. And a crowd is not the same as the sum of all the individuals, he explains. You must have spoken to a crowd to realize that. The crowd understands as a group what individuals would not understand separately. He develops the idea, and I wonder in the meantime how I would have had to delude myself to see the spectacle of two days ago as grandiose.

"It seems as if no one nowadays is interested in politics," I say. "I will never be able to admit that. I've been thinking about this for two months, and the day before yesterday I could check very accurately how little it means to me existentially. Somebody who loves exists. A great brotherly feeling for the masses would perhaps give me this existence, and intense hatred for the enemy too. But I'm not up to any of these feelings, since I'm nothing but an abject intellectual or whatever you want to call it. I've felt myself unquestionably overwhelmed these days, but not part of the crowds."

"But why are you still looking for something else then? Because you and your whole existence are threatened. You'll have to join the party that is the least objectionable to you, because there you could be useful, just as it could be useful to you to have these comrades. Once you have that rapport... You think of what would be intolerable if this side wins and takes over the government. But that's not your problem yet, whereas the government of the others, the generals and the fascists is."

"Possibly, but I think it's cheap to let that kind of pressure push me into offering my services. I want to put all my courage into staying outside of this, as long as I can, admitting that I'm only an intellectual, if I must, but that is all I can be. I can't do anything but what I can really do."

"But why are you searching?" he repeats emphatically. "Why don't you resign yourself to that, then?"

"Because I too have a feeling for the Marxist notion that you are never really an outsider. Because I can't be happy either, living with the idea that I'm a little good-for-nothing petty bourgeois. And yet, if that happens to be the case... I could publish my autobiography under a title like The Little Bourgeois Son."

"No good. Your title comes after the fact and wouldn't prove a thing. It isn't that simple. Be careful not to pay too much attention to Marx's popularizers. There is no reason for you to listen to the lesser minds in this field, since you ignore them in every other. No, the important part of all this is that, indeed, you probably won't be able to live outside these conflicts. You might think that you are part of a dying civilization, and you want to sit back quietly and watch this happen. Try it. I told you that there's a good chance for a renewed peace. In France you're not in such a bad position. Perhaps you'll have three years' reprieve now."

"And then?"

"The revolution from the left or from the right, or war—whatever. Those who know predict that there will be a war within the next three years. I would say, go to Persia, there you would find a fascinating civilization, but the war would catch up with you there too."

"As a matter of fact, we could almost forget that. But at this point nothing seems so cheap to me as committing yourself to a part of humanity, called a party, which wants to conquer some place or other, having no time for nuances, sacrificing everything to the idea of 'getting there,' which then turns out every time to be just a temporary step, not being human anymore except as a Communist, for example, no longer able to define yourself as a human being except through Marx. And if you don't want that, then you lower yourself to resentment, like those who feel they can never win anyway, and who remain so powerless that the only compensation they have is their intellectual contempt."

"To each his own defense mechanism. But there are two things you may be confusing now: the idea, or the myth, and the people. You can overlook the people, if the myth inspires you enough."

"I don't think I'll ever be able to. Perhaps I'm not intellectual enough. If it comes down to a war, then all I can do is take part in it wholeheartedly alongside my friends."

"I'm afraid that the war won't be declared on them."

"Too bad. Any other war I'd like to have the courage to decline."

On the way home I met a group of young men in the quiet of Auteuil. As I was passing a voice said emphatically: "But I'm telling you, you're wrong. He's against the socialists." I felt like I'd been hit in the stomach; something made me nauseous for a second.

February 15. Jane comes in to tell me she's eyeing a studio which might be within our means. She looked out of the windows to check whether there were any trees to be seen. There was also a larger place for the same price, but it looks out on a white, Caligari-like courtyard, and from a window she heard the hollow sound of a radio. This was smaller, but you could indeed see one tree, and the room was clean and near this neighborhood.

"If only for the bourgeois aspect," I say, "take it, by all means, please. I'm already used to my café, and until they come to get us, let's choose this little spot of a world now past."

I notice I say this with conviction, with a stubbornness such as I haven't felt in a long time. If Jane would like to have a child, just like Bella, I would not stand in the way: why not defy the future when it looks so bleak? Why not raise a family, now that the whole world can be blown to bits at any moment; with my experience, there is little cause for illusions.

"The bourgeois make family life impossible for one another," Viala said once, "because they've got nothing better to do. It's often the same with the proletarians, but that's because they are miserable and worked to death."

How true something like that sounds at first; how little of it is, when you take a closer look. There must be many proletarians who are completely bourgeois in their desire to have a family, and perhaps they're even the best at it. But on the other hand, if they had all the comfort they wanted and rightly deserve, they would really make life impossible for one another, "because they've got nothing better to do."

February 18. Wijdenes writes that he thinks they took care of everything so pleasantly and democratically here. What a difference between Doumergue and Hitler! I will send him these pages. Perhaps it's nothing more than bad journalism, but so much the better; even if this seemed to be the main topic of our daily meditations, it's all the better for me not to have been able to render it more intimately. Furthermore, I stopped, although the real drama hasn't yet ended. The cheap detective novel which all the newspapers have turned into with ever-increasing zeal is more exciting and more confusing than before; even the stupidest reader doesn't believe them anymore. Reading the newspaper every day has had its effect on the readers. Everyone's fundamental dishonesty has now become clear to everyone. But everyone also thinks: "Did I use to be so stupid to believe it wasn't so?"

February 20. On second thought, I'm sending everything to Wijdenes. I'm asking him to tell me what he thinks about the product of one year:

"...When I started it, I had the vague notion that it would all come down to love, but I was wrong. I told you once why I thought so. I might be able to formulate it better for myself, but it doesn't matter.

Even if equipped with all the virtues of cynicism, we don't write what we want, but only what comes out at a given moment. After all, we cannot give a true picture of ourselves. We resign ourselves to the notion that at best we only create our own double. Mine seems to be an individualist. That word has been tossed about lately in an intriguing fashion. Having rediscovered with relief that he is allowed his individuality again, the individual spits on obsolete individualism all the more eagerly. That doesn't matter either. It doesn't even matter if the individual emphasizes either his differences or his similarities with other individuals. I have never tried to tighten the bond between my own 'I' and the ever-present 'we,' nor have I consciously underlined how different I was.

"But what's the lesson in all this—this past year? I would like to oppose the scum, but all things considered, I'm not much different from the crowd on the Place de la Concorde. I've also become incredibly moralistic these days, and if that coincides with the loss of my money and my personal contact with the 'notaries,' too bad. But as soon as you look for the means, then the differences immediately show up, all by themselves. Recognizing my fate more clearly than you do, I am in the final analysis more of a 'hopeless intellectual' than you are.

"If I had to look for my milieu, I would find it among the intellectuals, among those who have not yet gone over to politics, under no matter what pretext. I've questioned myself quite diligently why I don't belong to one political party or another, and have come up with two reasons: a refusal to accept compromise and an aversion to deadening authority. 'That's fine,' says the expert, 'but everybody belongs to a party: you have been fooled by another dirty trick and another compromise, if you really think that you don't belong to a party.' I would seriously like to believe that that is precisely my case; but if so, then, according to political definitions, I'm a bourgeois. What the hell! You can't always like what you are.

"What a strange fate, though: not to escape the bourgeoisie and yet not to belong to it; not to be hostile toward what is not bourgeois, and to have no sympathy for what is; no longer to cultivate anything—*anything*, that is the problem—that has to do with a nonbourgeois attitude, which people think is so interesting. To be already now, I sometimes think, what I'll be to Guy in my best moments, later on.

"When I had just arrived in Europe, someone cautiously suggested to me that my parents must have stolen their money in the colonies, because otherwise they couldn't be so wealthy. Then I was so naïve that I was sure this was not the case. But I'm now forced to admit that for more than thirty years I have lived quite happily on money that was tainted. And yet I absolutely deny that the first revolutionary who comes around would have the right to call me bourgeois, as if this were the final word that explains the difference between him and me. He could be bursting with the most bourgeois resentments and desires, and in his own way be just as narrow-minded as the worst bourgeois, and, consciously or not, he may have been bought three times over.

"While I'm writing to you, I'm trying to recall the route I had to take to get to all of this: how short it was, and yet how definitive. There are thousands of people who would know exactly what to call this: the Depression. Six months ago you sat with me in the Feuilleraie. Jane and I have just been back there. The management has changed, and it is now run by a woman who looks sprightly but is faded. She said to us, 'This is the first time I have been in business, but this is a family pension, not a hotel. I would never have wanted a hotel, but a family pension, after all, ce sont des gens du monde qui reçoivent d'autres gens du monde.'[16] She said this to us before we had been there five minutes, and she will undoubtedly say the same thing to all her other guests. She also has to define her position these days! In the very same place where you were wondering what you, an intellectual who writes in Dutch, could do if it came to the point that you would have to emigrate....

"If you can only support yourself with your writing, or some related activity, then you are also just a hopeless intellectual. Since last year I have been in the same situation, and I ask myself how I got here. Because I lost my money, the money my parents knew how to hang on to for so long, with the tenacity of the true bourgeois. Why is it gone now? Because of the Depression. If I could content myself with this answer, I would be no individualist. I want to look more closely now, to go back further. I have lost my money because my father left everything in my mother's name. Why? Because he had declared bankruptcy after he went to debtors' jail. Is that all? No. Because quite unexpectedly my mother turned out to have other heirs; because she had a son from a previous marriage; because she had loved a man with a large mustache before she knew my father. Because.... No, the line breaks off. It's better to ask why my father had money. Because his grandfather,

Colonel Lami, had married a rich widow from the Indies. This colonel with his excellent business sense (see chap. 3) was the source of my social position and of my 'class,' until my mother's role in the family put a stop to what had lasted three and a half generations. Historical materialism becomes much more colorful when you investigate an individual case.

"If I were a true pessimist, I would still try to figure out why all my writing has not changed anything and won't be able to change anything, why in my thirty-fourth year I am a dead weight in the social struggle, why I am capable of this kind of honesty but not of any other. I will spare you as well as myself. If I were certain that you are enough of a sentimentalist (I write this word with pleasure) to think that nothing of what I'm sending you equals my childhood recollections, I would send you some more. I forgot to mention, for example, the enormous *palang pintu* in Gedong Lami: the iron bar that was put behind the big door at night, just behind the dome. Yung or Isnan would struggle mightily with the thing, and in the morning there it would stand behind the door, twice as tall as I was. I was ordered never to touch it, because if it fell down on me, I would be dead. When I was scared about thieves, this iron bar calmed me down. The house could easily be broken into anywhere, but I couldn't be sure that the thieves wouldn't try to force open the only door in the house—it wasn't there for nothing, after all—even though they would never be able to open it! And I forgot to tell about the *angin barat* in Balekambang, the great wind that came from the sea, and Isnan running around the house with his head cloth fluttering, yelling, 'Barat! Barat!' as he secured the rattan blinds against the windows.

"All these 'dreams' finally—and now what? Will I ever become wise in the ways of the world? Uncle Van Kuyck, with his protruding little eyes, used to point this out to me, saying, 'You must learn to be practical, young man!' You have an advantage over me in this respect. From your childhood on, life has made you different from me: you knew how much depended on 'earning a living.' You were aware much earlier than I, that is, according to the somewhat stale logic that explains man only through his circumstances. I must admit that I'm indulging my sentimentality again; I still want to believe in a different truth. I am completely indifferent to the theory that explains everything historically—everything—even my own little niche in history. The thought that our civilization is declining, just like ancient Rome, and that we look with heroic resignation on this decline and on the (no less heroic) emergence of the new barbarians; that our relativistic civilization is being swept away by a new dogmatic civilization—what a privilege to realize all of this! And then to realize that we once envisioned our lives as personal adventures, that anyone who was not born a slave (what a bad aftertaste of class struggle this classic metaphor leaves us with today) must have wanted it this way, and as a result has not been able to resign himself to his destiny of an anonymous animal among other animals.

"And we also used to think that we had great times ahead of us, and our heroism too, if only something would happen! What would we have wanted to do? Wage war? Fight—like children throwing stones at one another, only on a larger scale? Now we ask ourselves how stupid we must be to bury our heads in the sand, so we can still glory in 'the great thrill of war.' Peace for us, also in the sense of being left in peace. Or should we also bless the circumstances that will force us to bring out the best and the worst in us? In the face of such words I have an empty heart and an empty mind. To show character, greatness... It's such sad knowledge that the strongest character can be destroyed in a concentration camp. And the drama in all this: greatness with drama, or without it? Great times, with great deeds: if you're no longer a child, you can smell the theatrics. I know that the theatrics for which you suffer become your own, that you can make certain theatrics real. But from this point it's only one step further to say: no greatness without theatrics. And yet the greatest is without it, or should be.

"The last Romans and the new barbarians satisfy me precious little, and the protruding eyes of Uncle Van Kuyck come back to me again; they look over a volume of Streckfuss: 'A human life, my boy? That used to be simply nothing!' We now have the honor of living intensely through something like that. In a time when the masses must achieve greatness, you learn to feel a bitter pride in being thrown onto the garbage heap by the others, while remaining true to yourself. It may be better than having to experience a slow betrayal—through decline or through circumstances—of your delicate and endlessly variable self.

"But let's keep other possibilities open. I'm not writing a funeral oration, after all; I'd rather have you do anything than agree with this part of my reflections. Pay attention to all the optimistic notes: the curiosity that saves us, even if we accept ourselves as we are, even if tomorrow will put us in the wrong and we have to pay with our blood, because we refuse to make a commitment to any one party.

"How will I fill the coming year? If you aren't curious to know, I at least am. Even for pessimists, a horizon means that there is still hope. Is this vague? To express it more concretely, I mean that you and I are too good to come to an end under the heels of whatever social beast with boots. Nobody escapes his destiny—mostly because you can always say this in hindsight—but before that day comes you can at least comfort yourself with a few ideas and thoughts. I can imagine returning to the country of origin, not just to be liquidated by the 'krisses of liberation.' I can also abjure that past and think that I'll never leave here again, but that I'll go on, slipping past the dangers with what has become my strongest support in life.

"You spoke recently about a possible bombing of Paris. It's indeed a strange notion that in less than an hour the German air force may appear above this city and shower destruction on it. One may keep in mind that being gassed or burned is not really so much different from dying from leukemia or angina pectoris. After all the soul-searching I have found one piece of wisdom: as long as one is alive, one should live according to his own nature and as if one still had a whole world before him, with all the curiosity and hope one still has, but also with a sufficient dose of pessimism to be instantly reconciled with the end of everything that made our lives possible, possible in every sense of the word. The wisdom is old, but the notion is new. I don't know if you've found something that could be called more real, more practical, since you realized there might be a war, but if you have, let me know right away what it is that you have to offer."

Notes

Chapter 1   An Evening with Guraev

1   Corneliu Codreanu (1899 – 1938) was a Rumanian anti-Semite and anti-Communist, and the leader of the Iron Guard. He was jailed and shot during an escape attempt.

2   Achin was an area in North Sumatra, Indonesia, where between 1870 and 1942 the Dutch attempted to establish their colonial authority, which led to bloody guerrilla warfare.

3   This is the same murder (committed by Christine and Léa Papin) that became the subject of Jean Genêt's *The Maids*.

4   "Life there is aimless and full of pleasure, and death comes easy." From André Gide, *Amyntas*.

Chapter 2   All Roads...

1   *Wild Blaze*

2   In English in the original.

Chapter 3   Family Album

1   "Azure a chevron argent with three towers argent"

2   Action Française was a French right-wing monarchist and proto-fascist organization which existed from 1899 to the beginning of World War II. Their storm troopers were known as the Camelots du Roi.

3   Dirk van Hogendorp (1761 – 1822) was a Dutch colonial administrator who later fought with Napoleon in Russia and ended his life in Brazil.

4   The Batavian Republic was the name of the Netherlands during the Napoleonic era, from 1795 to 1806.

5   The Batavians have, as far as I know, three names for a Frenchman: *Prasman* (from Dutch *Fransman*), *Prantjis* (from *Français*), and *didong* (from French "dis, donc," "tell me") [author's note].

6   Dipo Negoro led the central Java uprising against the Dutch (the "Java War," 1825 – 1830). He was finally taken prisoner, although the Dutch had given him a safe-conduct.

7   The Military Order of William, Militaire Willemsorde, can be compared to the Congressional Medal of Honor.

8   "Live and let live"

Chapter 5   *The History of My Parents*

1   Fr. *barboteur*, pilferer

2   "Kill him, he's a Prussian."

3   The Council of the Indies was the highest advisory council of the governor-general.

4   *Mandiën*, to bathe

5   "Don't be afraid time will ever erase the friendship that I feel for you."

6   "All but the memory"

7   "Like a typical French asshole"

8   Susuhunan, prince of Surakarta, was the highest ranking Javanese ruler. The title is sometimes translated as "emperor."

9   *Pajung*, cermonial umbrella

10 *Gros-mari*, Big Daddy

11 "All I will have seen of the Indies are Madeline's eyes."

12 "Daniel is just *beginning* to love his wife a little."

13 Louis Couperus (1863 – 1923) was a major Dutch fin-de-siècle novelist. His popular novel *Eline Vere* (1889) was translated into English in 1892.

14 Under the pen name of Multatuli, Eduard Douwes Dekker (1820 – 1887) wrote *Max Havelaar*, an autobiographical account of his problems as an assistant commissioner in West Java. This landmark of Dutch literature in the nineteenth century subsequently greatly influenced colonial attitudes toward the Javanese.

15 Private-*sadja*, a person who is "merely" a landowner, not a government official or an army officer

16 *Batavia Times*

Chapter 6   *Mostly Viala*

1   *La Vie de Henri Brulard* is Stendhal's early autobiography, written in 1835 – 36. It served as a model for Du Perron when he wrote *Country of Origin*.

2   "Basically, Viala is generous."

Chapter 7   *The Child Ducroo*

1   H. W. Daendels (1762 – 1818) was a Dutch revolutionary politician and governor-general of the Indies from 1807 to 1811. He took the initiative of building the famous Post Road traversing Java from west to east.

2   "Swinging in a tall coconut tree," one of the best-known Krontjong melodies

3   "Say 'table' (in Dutch)" "Oh no, oh! 'table' (in Indonesian)."

4   Cornelis Speelman (1628 – 1684) was governor-general from 1681 to his death. *Prikkebeen* was a nineteenth-century humorous poem by J. J. A. Goeverneur.

Chapter 8   Gedong Lami

1   Old Dutch lullaby: "Sleep, little child, sleep."
2   "I threw away my face" is a literal translation of *buang muka* [author's note].
3   "It doesn't touch me, my heart is not moved by it," an Italian pseudo-quotation. (Du Perron noted in the margin: "Stendhal could have written it.")
4   Old Surehand refers to a hero in Karl May's novels about American Indians. May, a German who never visited America, remains one of the most popular writers for boys in the Netherlands.

Chapter 9   Bella on the Couch

1   L'amour-goût, affection
2   ". . . your loving, suffering smile, so pure"

Chapter 10   Balekambang, Sand Bay

1   Dèn: abbreviation of Raden, a title of nobility [author's note].
2   Marie Corelli (1855 – 1924) was a popular British author and pianist. Justus van Maurik (1846 – 1904) was a Dutch short-story writer and playwright.
3   The poem is by Maurice Roelants (1895 – 1966), from his volume *Het verzaken* (Maastricht, 1930).

Chapter 11   Conversation with Héverlé

1   This scene takes place in Malraux's *Man's Fate*, between Kyo and May.
2   The Pit is a satirical version of the Amsterdam artists' center, De kring (The Circle).

Chapter 12   The Precocious Child of the Indies

1   *Buah*, fruit
2   *Paal*, old Indian measurement of nine-tenths of a mile

Chapter 13   Sukabumi

1   HBS stands for Hogere Burger School, the name for a Dutch secondary school, which was university preparatory but without Latin and Greek. There were only three or four of these schools in the Indies, mainly for the children of the Dutch colonial establishment.

2   With a defiant expression
3   Pieter Erberveld was a Eurasian who led a revolt against the Dutch authorities in the early eighteenth century.
4   This is a variety of terrier.

Chapter 14   *Dreams and Notaries*

1   Sir Henry Deterding was president (1900 – 1936) of Royal Dutch Shell Oil. Sir Basil Zaharoff (1849 – 1936) was an international arms merchant.

Chapter 15   *Pelabuhan Ratu*

1   Abraham van Riebeeck (1653 – 1713) was the son of the founder of the Cape Colony, governor-general from 1709 to his death, and, reportedly, the first European to visit Wijnkoops Bay.

Chapter 16   *The Last Years in Balekambang*

1   F. W. Farrar (1831 – 1903) was the author of immensely popular books on school life in England.
2   "My Javanese friend, who gives away islands." Compare André Malraux, *Anti-memoirs* (Bantam Book, 1970), p. 400.
3   *Peter Simple* is a book by Frederick Marryat (1792 – 1848).

Chapter 18   *The School and Baur*

1   *Procureur-bambu*, "barefoot attorney"
2   Chr. Snouck Hurgronje (1857 – 1936) was a specialist of Arab culture and Moslem law and an adviser of the Dutch East Indies government. His book on *The Achinese* was translated into English in 1906.
3   Old Shatterhand is a hero in Karl May's works (see chap. 8, n. 4).
4   "Fervent spiritualist"
5   *The spirits*, and *outburst* and *on the bottom of the sea* (below) are all in English in the original.
6   "The spirits"
7   "As if this weren't enough"

Chapter 19   *The Child Continues to Mature*

1   Klikspaan is the pen name of J. Kneppelhout (1814 – 1885), who published his satirical sketches of student life at Leyden around 1840.

2 In English in the original.

3 "Don't make a fool of yourself."

Chapter 20 Joies de Meudon

1 "Well, to tell the truth, I don't have any. Your friend seems nice enough, but he's asleep."

2 "All pleasure strives for eternity," from Nietzsche's *Thus Spoke Zarathustra*.

3 Emotional stocktaking

Chapter 21 A Young Man in the Indies

1 *De Telegraaf* is the most popular Dutch tabloid.

Chapter 22 The Real World

1 J. B. van Heutz (1851 – 1924) "pacified" Achin and became governor-general (1904 – 1909). He was an exponent of military expansionism in the Dutch East Indies.

2 *Les cinq sous de Lavarède* by Paul d'Ivoi

3 Aneta was a press agency in the Dutch East Indies.

4 In English in the original.

5 In 1919, when there were serious food shortages, a certain Hadji Hassan organized resistance against government rice requisitions. Four people were killed in the town of Tjimareme, West Java.

6 Abdul Muïs, one of the leaders of Sarekat Islam, was held responsible for this assassination which took place in 1919.

7 Dr. Tjipto Mangkunkusomo was one of the early Indonesian nationalists.

8 The National Council, an elected advisory body, was created in 1918 to channel some of the political aspirations of awakening nationalism.

Chapter 23 Farewell to the Indies

1 The Borobudur is an ancient Buddhist sanctuary in central Java.

2 *Kawi* is the language in which the ancient literature of Java and Bali is written.

3 See chap. 5, n. 3.

4 "Is this where Miss Hortense and Miss Zize live?" "Yes, here."

5 "Good-bye, chaste, pure resting place" (from Gounod's *Faust*). "You have the whole night to be chaste and pure."

Chapter 24 Wijdenes Comes to Visit

1 *Der Anti-Christ* is a short treatise by Nietzsche (1888). *Braunbuch* is a report on the

Reichstag fire, largely based on fantasy and concocted by a propaganda official of the Communist party, who branded Van der Lubbe as an accomplice of the Nazis.

2   "Pretty Adolf, Superman"; "super-rabble"

3   "As I am in my deepest instincts, alien to all things German, to the point that the presence of a single German slows down my digestion."

4   Supersergeant

5   Goropius Becanus, a Renaissance linguist from Antwerp, maintained that Dutch was the language spoken in paradise.

6   "Above the battle." This is the title of a pacifist book by Romain Rolland (1915).

7   The salute given to the wounded commander

8   A French soldier of World War I

9   Sarekat Islam was an early nationalist movement founded in 1911.

10 Digul is the name of a concentration camp in New Guinea that was built in the thirties by the Dutch for the internment of Indonesian nationalists.

Chapter 25   Double Portrait of Arthur Hille

1   Francis X. Bushman, Sr. (born 1885) appeared in 417 movies.

2   In English in the original.

3   First line of "The Horseman's Morning Song," by Wilhelm Hauff. This famous German lied deals with duty and dying for one's country.

4   Peutjut is the military cemetery at Kutaradja (Achin).

5   Maréchaussée was the name of an elite counterinsurgence corps, created in 1890 and consisting mainly of Indonesians, operating chiefly in Achin.

6   "Impossibly sordid, absolutely deplorable"

Chapter 26   The Torment

1   Charles Webster Leadbeater (1847 – 1934) was a British theosophist and occultist.

2   "Denise takes care of Marcel, Monique takes care of Paul, Eliane takes care of Jules, Gaby takes care of Guy."

Chapter 27   Contact with the Law

1   In reality, Pierre MacOrlan (1882 – 1970), the author of *Quai des brumes*, had written a slightly pornographic text, *Mlle. de Mustelle et ses amies*.

2   "But I don't know her, neither her nor her cousins."

3   "Your mother should ask King Albert for a public apology."

4   "What do you expect? We had to surprise you."

5   This poem was written by Pascal Pia, with only the last line slightly altered.

6   André Tardieu (1876 – 1945) was a conservative French politician and a hard liner against Germany.

Chapter 28   The Madhouse

1   "But she's just a crazy old lady"; and "I hope your mother still keeps some crazy ladies on her estate?"
2   "At least, that's what they say. As for what they think—does one ever know?"
3   "Come in," "ours," and "Christ" (below) are in English in the original.

Chapter 29   Back in Paris

1   See chap. 5, n. 13. The sister of Du Perron's mother was married to one of Couperus's brothers.
2   "How are you?" "How French."
3   See chap. 5, n. 14.
4   In *Le Temps du mépris*, André Malraux has used a sentence that is rhetorically somewhat similar to this one.

Chapter 30   Tanya-Teresa

1   "That's ridiculous! That boy!"
2   "Oh, that Arthur makes me laugh!" and "That boy!"
3   "All this drivel "
4   "This refined, cultivated milieu "
5   "Be the gentleman of my dreams, then."
6   "That nice young man "
7   "Handsome melancholy friend"
8   "That nice little lady"
9   "I'll be in the church, cold-hearted Nina, when you get married" (the quotation is slightly incorrect).
10 In English in the original.

Chapter 31   Pursuit of the One and Only

1   Valmont was the conspiring character in *Les Liaisons dangereuses* (1782) by Choderlos de Laclos.
2   "The time you were so sarcastic "
3   "The gentleman who keeps going away "
4   "You're so easily satisfied."
5   This phrase and *Oxford men* and *love, British love* (below) are in English in the original.
6   In English in the original.
7   This phrase and the other italicized phrases from here until the end of the chapter are in English in the original.

Chapter 32   Newspapers

1   Stavisky was involved in a big corruption scandal in France early in 1934. The cause of his death, officially a suicide, was never satisfactorily determined. Since cabinet ministers were implicated, the Stavisky affair rocked the government of the French Republic.

2   "Let's see-e-e...."

3   "The chick with the pince-nez"

4   "Smart fellow"

5   Camelots du Roi were right-wing storm troopers; see chap. 3, n. 2.

6   Chambre des Députés is the House of Representatives.

7   "God forbid!"

8   "To the self-important gentleman who opens other people's letters"

9   "The worst of the poltroons and a rat"

10   "A nice little buttonhole"

11   "What? You don't mean to kill him?"

12   "What a character you are!"

13   "The amiable and gracious lady"

14   "Man of honor, which I believe you to be"

15   Balbo (1896 – 1940) was an Italian fascist leader, pilot, marshal, and minister.

Chapter 33   For Pessimists

1   The eighteenth of Brumaire is the date of Napoleon's coup d'état against the Directory (November 9, 1799).

2   "Frot and Daladier to the gallows!"

3   Cécile Sorel was a popular French actress (born in 1872) who made a comeback on the stage in 1933.

4   "Is it a promise?" "Yes, it's a promise!"

5   Jules Guesde (1845 – 1922) was the leader of French left-wing socialism.

6   "Join us, comrades!"

7   "Soviets everywhere!"

8   "United action!"

9   "You can't make the Republic commit suicide as you did Stavisky."

10   "Down with the politics of lesser evil."

11   "Fascists will not get by."

12   "Death rather than fascism."

13   "Don't start anything.... Leave them alone."

14   "To the shithouse"

15   "Chiappe in prison"

16   "It's just a matter of taking in our kind of people."

Glossary

In this glossary as well as in the text, the archaic colonial spelling of Indonesian words has been retained, with the exception of *oe* which has been replaced by *u*, to be pronounced as English *oo*. The spelling *dj* approximates the English *j*, *nj* is the sound in English *canyon*, *sj* approximates English *sh*.

alang-alang, tall grass

alun-alun, large town square

ampun, mercy

andjing basah, wet dog

angin barat, west wind

artja, statue

babu, housemaid

bahmi, Chinese noodles

bandjir, river flood

banteng, wild buffalo

Bapa Rusni parantos sumping?, Has Father Rusni arrived yet?

bedak, powder

bendoro, title of nobility

Berani sumpah, we dare swear it

bintang Surabaja, Star of Surabaya

bintaro, poisonous tree

Bismilah, in the name of Allah

Blanda, Dutchman

Blanda-hitam, litt. Black Dutchman: Ambonese

brandal, rascal

buaja, crocodile

bukan, no

buka puasa, the breaking of the Moslem fasting period

bung, brother

bungur, tree with pink and purple blossoms

demang, district police chief

desa, native village

djahat, wicked

djajèng sekar, native soldiers

djarak, castor oil plant

djin, evil spirit

djongos, houseboy

djuragan, overseer, master

djuragan anom, young master

gamelan, Javanese musical instrument

gang, alley

gudang, barn, storehouse

guru, teacher

hadji, someone who has made the pilgrimage to Mecca

kabaya, Indonesian blouse

kali, river

Kali Besar, street in Batavia

kamar pandjang, long room

kampong, native district or neighborhood

kassian, it's a pity

kebon, garden

kembang sepatu, hibiscus

kidung buaja, crocodile hole

klambu, mosquito netting

kléwang, short sword used first by Achinese, later standard equipment in the Dutch army

koki, cook

kolong, open space under house

kondor, enlarged scrotum

kongsi, commercial association

krés, blinds

krontjong, popular Dutch-Indonesian music

krupuk, shrimp-meal cookies

kuntianak, spirit of a woman who died in childbirth

kutjiah, professional actor

loh!, gosh!

lurah, village chief

lurah préman, retired village chief

Ma Lima sudah tua, Ma Lima is already old

mandur, overseer

medja, table

melati, jasmine

mesigit, mosque

mitra nu tani, friend of the peasants

momok, bogeyman

nèng, polite form of address

njai, native concubine

njonja, form of address to a European lady

nona, miss

noni, little girl

obat, medicine

paal, Javanese mile

pagar, fence (also spelled pagger)

pala, nutmeg

palang pintu, door bolt

pantjuran, water jet

pasar, market

patih, regent, native ruler

pentjak, Indonesian martial art

perkutut, turtledove

persèn, percent, tip, money

pondok, cottage

Raden, title of nobility

rangga, ruler, chief

ratu, queen

regent, Dutch term for patih, native ruler

rèntjong, Achinese kris

resident, commissioner, Dutchman cooperating with the regent

rijsttafel, Dutch word meaning rice table, an Indonesian dinner with many courses

ronggèng, dancing girl

sadja, just plain

sado, small two-wheeled carriage

sambalan, condiments

sapu lidi, broom made of palm-leaf ribs

sarong, skirtlike wrap

saté, skewered meat

saté kambing, skewered goat meat

sedekah, religious meal

sètan, evil spirit

sial, misfortune

sinjo, European or Eurasian boy

slendang, sling

soto, soup

stroop susu, mixture of syrup and evaporated milk

surak manisé, long live the Maréchaussée

tafel, table (Dutch)

tahi kotok, droppings

tandak, to dance

tempajan, water jar or barrel

tètèk, breast

tjaplok, to snap at

tji, river

tjies, tjies, come off it (Eurasian Dutch)

tjintjang, to chop to bits

tjintjao, syrup, lemonade

tjitjak, house lizard

tjokèk, dance party

tjulik, kidnapper

toko, store

tòtòk, nonadjusted European

tuan, sir

tuku bangsat, scoundrel

wajang, Javanese puppet show

warong, small store

wedana, district chief